THE FOREIGN POLICY RESEARCH INSTITUTE

UNIVERSITY OF PENNSYLVANIA

COMMUNISM IN GUATEMALA

1944 • 1954

By RONALD M. SCHNEIDER

with a foreword by
ARTHUR P. WHITAKER

OCTAGON BOOKS

A DIVISION OF FARRAR, STRAUS AND GIROUX

New York   1979

This study was published by Frederick A. Praeger, Publishers, under the auspices of the Foreign Policy Research Institute at the University of Pennsylvania, established under a grant of the Richardson Foundation, Greensboro, North Carolina. This study was subjected to the extensive and critical discussion of the Associates of the Foreign Policy Research Institute. However, the views expressed in COMMUNISM IN GUATEMALA: 1944-1954 are those of the author.

Reprinted 1979
by special arrangement with Holt, Rinehart & Winston

OCTAGON BOOKS
A DIVISION OF FARRAR, STRAUS & GIROUX, INC.
19 Union Square West
New York, N.Y. 10003

Library of Congress Cataloging in Publication Data

Schneider, Ronald M
    Communism in Guatemala, 1944-1954.

    Reprint of the ed. published by Praeger, New York, which was issued as no. 7 of the Foreign Policy Research Institute series and as no. 80 of Praeger publications in Russian history and world communism.
    At head of title: The Foreign Policy Research Institute, University of Pennsylvania.
    Bibliography: p.
    1. Communism—Guatemala. 2. Guatemala—Politics and government—1945- I. Pennsylvania. University. Foreign Policy Research Institute. II. Title. III. Series: The Foreign Policy Research Institute series; no. 7.
[HX128.5.S35   1979]   335.43'097281   78-20874
ISBN 0-374-97130-7

Manufactured by Braun-Brumfield, Inc.
Ann Arbor, Michigan
Printed in the United States of America

FOREWORD

Ronald M. Schneider's book deals with an earlier but still quite recent aspect of a problem which has just been sensationally illustrated by the results of Vice President Richard C. Nixon's good-will tour of South America. The problem is Communist exploitation of Latin American discontents.

In April 1958, Vice President Nixon set out from Washington on a highly publicized good-will tour of eight South American countries—all the independent states of that continent except Brazil and Chile. The immediate occasion of the tour was the inauguration of Argentina's first constitutionally elected President since the overthrow of dictator Juan Perón.

Mr. Nixon represented the United States at this ceremony, which marked the restoration of democratic government in Argentina. The rest of his itinerary included three other countries (Peru, Colombia, and Venezuela) in which democratic regimes had recently supplanted dictatorships. It also included Uruguay, one of the most steadfastly democratic of all the twenty Latin American countries, and Bolivia, to which the United States had given substantial aid for several years past in an effort to strengthen its democratic regime against the threat of Communism.

Since the United States was the generally acknowledged leader of the free world, cne might have expected that such an itinerary would have assured its representative of a sympathetic, and perhaps even an enthusiastic, welcome in at least these six of the eight countries he was to visit. Instead, beginning with his very first stop, at Montevideo, Uruguay, he ran a gauntlet of verbal and physical abuse which increased in violence until at his last stop, in Caracas, Venezuela, the threat to his personal safety became so great that he had no choice but to cut short his visit and return to Washington, as he did on May 15.

Many people in the United States attributed this outcome to Communist machinations in South America, and doubtless these were a factor. Nevertheless, they were very far from being the only factor; indeed, it seems most likely that in this case the South American Communists did little more than exploit a situation arising out of the convergence of other factors which they did not create and which would almost certainly have come into being even if Communism had never been invented. They included widespread social unrest among the Latin American masses, a fervent nationalism among all classes, and a resentment against the United States, on many grounds, which has had a steady growth since the end of World War II. Any informed observer of the Latin American scene could add to this list.

Many of these factors have now become so firmly woven into the fabric of Latin American life that they will have to continue to be reckoned with for a long time to come, whatever the outcome of the cold war may be. But since that outcome is not in sight, it is highly important to remember that there are Communists on hand to exploit Latin American discontents and that they have already given proof of their skill in doing so.

The outcome of the Nixon good-will tour may prove a boon in disguise, as a warning to the public (the experts did not need it, but who listened to the experts?) that Communist agents may help to turn the long-quiescent Latin American front into one of the most active fronts of the cold war. If that happens, it will be cold comfort for our side to point out that the Communists merely took advantage of a situation which was largely not of their making. It would be the part of prudence, and less inglorious in the end, to do some hard thinking about this problem now, and follow it quickly with appropriate action.

Two of the many questions that need to be answered are: What are the elements in the Latin American situation that play into the Communists' hands? And how do the Communists go about exploiting the possibilities of this situation? Let no one shrug these and the other questions off with the observation that the Communists are numerically so weak in Latin America that they need not be taken seriously. They are indeed weak in this sense, for at the present time they probably number not more than half a million in a total population of more than 170 million; but surely at this late date no informed person needs to be told that numbers mean little in this connection.

For anyone who does still need to be told this, Dr. Schneider's book should be made required reading, for the story he tells is one of the virtual take-over of the government of a country with a population of approximately three million by a Communist party which at its height numbered not more than about four thousand members. Moreover, this was a country in which the Communists had no previous record of achievement to give glamor to their cause.

The country in question was, of course, Guatemala, and the period of the Communists' greatest success there coincided with the administration of President Jacobo Arbenz Guzmán, which began in 1951 and was overthrown at the end of June 1954 under circumstances of international as well as domestic crisis that will doubtless be remembered by most readers. The international aspects of this story are treated only incidentally in the following pages, except as they involve international Communism. With this exception, Dr. Schneider focuses his attention on the Guatemalan scene and on the rise of a handful of Communists to power in that country under Arbenz. At the time of the latter's overthrow, many people in other countries questioned the charge that his regime was in effect controlled by the Communists, for their control was camouflaged. Dr. Schneider has documented the charge. In order to give his story greater depth, he takes as the starting-point of his detailed narrative the overthrow of Guatemalan dictator Jorge Ubico in 1944 and buttresses this with a description of the Guatemalan people, their society and their government in the decade covered.

Guatemala is only one of twenty Latin American countries, which differ widely from one another in many respects, and Guatemala differs greatly from most of the rest in that an exceptionally large part of its population—more than half—consists of Indians who have not been assimilated to the dominant Spanish-creole type of culture. For this and other reasons, one must be very cautious in generalizing about the rest of Latin America from the single case of Guatemala.

Yet, there are many things in the following pages that have a larger significance. These include the account of the glaring inequalities of wealth and poverty; of the failure of the democratic political leaders to solve old problems or even to cooperate effectively with one another in meeting the new Communist menace; of the success of the handful of Communists not only in penetrating labor unions, mass media, and the government itself, and in making themselves indispensable to a powerful chief executive, President Arbenz, but also, and above all, in identifying their cause in the minds of great numbers of non-Communist Guatemalans with the social aspirations of the masses, with the national aspirations of the people at large, and indeed with the whole "revolutionary program" of the revolution of 1944 which had overthrown dictator Ubico—with little help, it may be added, from the Communists.

In short, in the Arbenz period the Communists filled a political vacuum. The manner in which they did so supports the thesis of Robert J. Alexander, a leading authority on Communism in Latin America, that a strong Democratic Left provides the best protection against the spread of Communism in that area by "trying in a democratic way to bring about the social revolution which is so necessary to the future of Latin America." Conversely, the lack of such a Democratic Left, as in the Guatemala of the period covered, opens the way to Communist penetration; and dictatorships, such as Ubico's, are at best a stop-gap which is counter-productive in the long run.

In preparing this study for the Foreign Policy Research Institute of the University of Pennsylvania, Dr. Schneider made extensive use of a large collection of copies (mostly photographic) of Guatemalan materials which the Institute was able to place at his disposal. This collection has now been deposited in the Library of Congress, Washington, D.C., where it can be consulted by anyone who wishes to follow further the story so patiently and painstakingly unfolded in the following pages.

This study was prepared under my supervision, with the important aid of counsel from the late Miron Burgin in the early stages and from James S. Cunningham at various stages. Our special thanks are due also to Robert J. Alexander, mentioned above, who read the manuscript and made suggestions for its improvement. Of course, none of the persons just mentioned is responsible for any statements of fact or opinion in this book.

Foreign Policy Research Institute   ARTHUR P. WHITAKER
University of Pennsylvania

PREFACE

The years since the Revolution of 1944 in Guatemala present a number of challenging questions to the student of politics. None is more fascinating than the study of why and how a handful of relatively inexperienced Communists were able to seize the leadership of a national social revolution. In addition, the study of Communism in Guatemala provides a unique opportunity to gain important insights into the appeals, techniques, and program of Communism in Latin America.

The Guatemalan experience is particularly significant since it casts doubt upon the validity of certain widely-held generalizations concerning the relatively low vulnerability of Latin American society to Communist penetration. It has been frequently argued that the low level of industrialization, the strength of Catholicism, the decisive political importance of the army, the stubborn individualism of the Latin Americans, and the existence of a large Indian population clinging to their traditional way of life, particularly when backed up by the proximity of the United States, would serve as an effective bar to the growth of Communist influence in this vital area. This should have been especially true in the case of a small "banana republic" such as Guatemala, which was economically dependent upon the United States.

The question of why the Communists attained as much success in Guatemala as they did, and conversely, why they did not achieve more, forms the heart of this study. This in turn requires a discussion of the conditions which afforded the Communists an opportunity to gain a hearing, an examination of the political process through which they attained a position of influence, and a study of the way in which they exploited these opportunities.

Research for this book began in October 1956 under the auspices of the Foreign Policy Research Institute of the University of Pennsylvania. In the late Spring of 1957 my wife and I travelled to Guatemala and Mexico City for the purpose of gathering additional material and interviewing participants and first-hand observers of the events of 1944-1954. Credit for the success of this phase of the work must go largely to my wife, Panamanian by birth and Latin Americanist by training, facts which aided immeasurably in breaking down the antipathy toward myself, an inquisitive *gringo,* which threatened to inhibit meaningful communication with those Guatemalans whose sympathies lay with the deposed Arbenz regime. Her material collaboration as secretary and critic as well as unflagging moral support made possible the completion of this study within a relatively short period of time.

I wish to express my heartfelt appreciation to the Foreign Policy Research Institute of the University of Pennsylvania, which initiated this project and engaged me to carry it out under appropriate supervision. For the generous financial assistance which enabled me to devote a year's full-time effort to this study I am grateful to Dr. Robert Strausz-Hupé, Director of the F.P.R.I. Mr. Erasmus H. Kloman, Jr., Assistant to the Director, proved ever helpful in facilitating administrative matters which might otherwise have disturbed the author's peace of mind. I am particularly grateful for the guidance and encouragement provided by Professor Arthur P. Whitaker, an Associate of the F.P.R.I., who supervised the project. His many suggestions based upon long and careful study of Latin American affairs and deep understanding of the forces at work in modern Latin America were of great help to me in my initial effort in this field. Among the many others who read this study in manuscript form and offered advice and encouragement I would like to single out Professors Dana G. Munro,

Gabriel A. Almond, and John B. Whitton of Princeton University. While all these individuals should receive credit for the merits of this study, the author assumes sole responsibility for the facts and interpretations which it contains.

RONALD M. SCHNEIDER

GLOSSARY

Political Parties and Organizations:

FDE   — Frente Democrático Electoral (Democratic Electoral Front)

FDN   — Frente Democrático Nacional (National Democratic Front)

FPL   — Frente Popular Libertador (Popular Liberating Front)

PAR   — Partido Acción Revolucionaria (Party of Revolutionary Action)

PGT   — Partido Guatemalteco del Trabajo (Guatemalan Labor Party)

PRG   — Partido de la Revolución Guatemalteca (Party of the Guatemalan Revolution)

PROG   — Partido Revolucionario Obrero de Guatemala (Revolutionary Workers' Party of Guatemala)

PS   — Partido Socialista (Socialist Party)

PUA   — Partido Unificación Anticomunista (Party of Anti-Communist Unification)

RN   — Partido de la Renovación Nacional (Party of National Renovation)

Front Organizations:

AFG   — Alianza Femenina Guatemalteca (Guatemalan Women's Alliance)

AJDG	— Alianza de la Juventud Democrática de Guatemala (Alliance of Democratic Youth of Guatemala)
CNP	— Comité Nacional de la Paz (National Peace Committee)
FUD	— Frente Universitario Democrático (Democratic University Front)

Labor Organizations:

CTG	— Confederación de Trabajadores de Guatemala (Confederation of Workers of Guatemala)
CGTG	— Confederación General de Trabajadores de Guatemala (General Confederation of Guatemalan Workers)
CNCG	— Confederación Nacional Campesina de Guatemala (National Peasant Confederation of Guatemala)
CNUS	— Comité Nacional de Unidad Sindical (National Committee of Trade Union Unity)
CPNT	— Comité Político Nacional de los Trabajadores (National Workers' Political Committee)
CTAL	— Confederación de Trabajadores de América Latina (Confederation of Latin American Workers)
FSG	— Federación Sindical de Guatemala (Guatemalan Trade Union Federation)
SAMF	— Sindicato de Acción y Mejoramiento de los Ferrocarrileros (Railwaymen's Action and Improvement Union)
STEG	— Sindicato de Trabajadores en Educación de Guatemala (Guatemalan Union of Educational Workers)
WFTU	— World Federation of Trade Unions

Government Agencies:

DAN	— Departamento Agrario Nacional (National Agrarian Department)
IGSS	— Instituto Guatemalteco de Seguridad Social (Guatemalan Institute of Social Security)
INFOP	— Instituto de Fomento de la Producción (Production Development Institute)

Business Concerns:

IRCA   — International Railways of Central America
UFCO — United Fruit Company

International Organizations:

OAS   — Organization of American States
ODECA — Organización de los Estados Centro Americanos (Organization of Central American States)

Spanish Terms:

Campesino — Peasant, literally "countryman"
Caudillo   — Leader, generally connoting dictatorial tendencies
Finquero — Owner of a "finca" or large farm
Ladino   — The non-Indian segment of the population, including all those who have adopted Western ways

CONTENTS

1

THE GUATEMALAN REVOLUTION

On July 1, 1944, General Jorge Ubico was forced to resign as President of Guatemala after thirteen years of orderly but sterile government. Ten years later, on June 27, 1954, the much shorter, but far more tumultuous and dynamic regime of Colonel Jacobo Arbenz Guzmán came to its end in the midst of domestic disorder and international controversy. Within the short space of a single turbulent decade, Communism in Guatemala was born and grew until it exerted greater influence than in any country outside of the Iron Curtain. Whereas in 1944 there were no Communists in Guatemala except for a small group who had been rotting in prison for a dozen years, less than ten years later there were perhaps 4,000 card-carrying party members and several times that number of sympathizers. By the end of 1953, the Communists held commanding positions in the labor movement, the coalition of political forces upon which the government rested, and even in the government itself. This small country which had been either unknown or simply written off as another sleepy "banana republic" suddenly became the center of a raging international controversy and a battlefield in the cold war.

This study is an attempt to answer the significant questions concerning why and how these developments took place and to put them into proper perspective. As the first step it is necessary to analyze the nature of Guatemalan society and of the revolution which shook the traditional order in 1944. Only when viewed against this background can the developments of the revolutionary decade be understood and their significance assessed.[1]

THE SETTING: THE TRADITIONAL ORDER

The Republic of Guatemala, often and quite accurately described as the "land of eternal spring," covers an area of some 42,000 square miles located just south of Mexico. In many respects it is a poor and backward country; in 1944 it was even poorer and much more backward economically, socially and politically. Primarily an agricultural country, the bulk of its population was composed of subsistence farmers, most of whom lived in essentially Indian communities cut off from the mainstream of national life. Indeed, Guatemala was run by and largely for a small group of large landowners allied with the officer corps of

---

[1] The best study available on this subject is Daniel James' *Red Design for the Americas: Guatemalan Prelude,* New York, 1954; also published in Spanish under the title *Tácticas Rojas en las Américas, Preludio Guatemalteco,* Mexico, 1955. Unfortunately this book was written before the full story became known and was based upon somewhat sketchy sources and materials. The most useful volume on Guatemalan government and politics is K. H. Silvert's *A Study in Government: Guatemala, Part I, National and Local Government Since 1944,* Tulane University, 1954. Among the better studies by Guatemalan observers are Mario Efraín Najera Farfán's *Los Estafadores de la Democracia (Hombres y hechos en Guatemala),* Buenos Aires, 1956; Jorge del Valle Matheu's *La verdad sobre el caso de Guatemala,* Guatemala, 1956; and Carlos Samayoa Chinchilla's *El Quetzal no es Rojo,* Guatemala, 1956. The first of these dwells largely upon the Arévalo administration, the second was edited from an incomplete posthumous manuscript and the last is largely descriptive and lacks sufficient analytical depth. Among those studies written by exiles and members of the Arbenz government, Luis Cardoza y Aragón's *La Revolución Guatemalteca,* Mexico, 1955, is the most useful, although written from a thoroughly Marxist point of view. Manuel Galich's *Por Qué Lucha Guatemala,* Buenos Aires, 1956, is more useful and less biased than Guillermo Toriello's *La Batalla de Guatemala,* Mexico, 1955, or Raúl Osegueda's *Operación Guatemala $$ OK $$,* Mexico, 1955.

the army and backed by the representatives of foreign corporations and the hierarchy of the Catholic Church. A small but growing middle class composed of businessmen, professional people and office employees had little influence, while the embryonic urban proletariat was almost a political cipher.[2]

The heart of Guatemala is formed by the temperate highlands which cover the central half of the country. In this region of fertile valleys enclosed by mountains lived most of the nearly two-and-one-half million persons who inhabited Guatemala in 1944. (The population of Guatemala rose to an estimated 3,200,000 by 1954 and has now passed the three-and-one-half million mark.) Along the narrow coastal lowlands on the Pacific side and in the Motagua river valley on the Atlantic side, the banana industry flourished in a subtropical climate. To the north of the highlands lies the large undeveloped jungle of El Petén, Guatemala's Amazonia.

More than three-fourths of the Guatemalan people gained their livelihood from the approximately ten per cent of the country which was under cultivation. By far the greater number of these people lived upon the three-fifths of the country's cropland which was devoted to subsistence farming and had little connection to the national economy. While these persons were poor by the standards of the industrial countries, it was not an abysmal or grinding poverty and they, for the most part, accepted their lot. Another twenty per cent of the cultivated area was given over to the production of coffee, chiefly on large "fincas." Bananas were raised on only five per cent of the cropland with the bulk of the production centered on the United Fruit Company holdings at Tiquisate on the Pacific coast and Bananera on the Atlantic. Together coffee and bananas accounted for nearly ninety per cent of the value of exports with coffee nearly five times as important as bananas. Political and economic power was largely concentrated in the hands of the producers of these two export crops. This ruling elite which constituted slightly over two per cent of the total number of landowners held title to more than sixty per cent of the cultivated area of Guatemala while two-thirds of all landowners together held only ten per cent of the farmland. Since industrial development was

---

[2] For the best treatment of Guatemala in the period before 1940 see Chester Lloyd Jones' *Guatemala, Past and Present,* Minneapolis, 1940.

relatively insignificant, it was this small but powerful group of large *terratenientes* who monopolized the top of the social structure and ran the country in alliance with the military *caudillos*.[3]

Guatemalan society was, and essentially is, composed of two major groups which have coexisted within the boundaries of the country without forming an integrated society. Over sixty per cent of the population are descendants of the indigenous peoples who inhabited the area before the coming of the Spaniards in the sixteenth century. The other forty per cent lay claim to some European ancestry, although their Spanish blood may have been considerably diluted over the years. The distinctions upon which this sharp division of society is based are not entirely racial, since cultural and economic factors enter into the total pattern—that of a way of life.[4]

The Indians, who form a majority of the country's population, early in the colonial era closed their minds to the ideas and way of life introduced by the Europeans and retreated up the mountainside as the more desirable valleys were taken over by the *Conquistadores*. In

[3] On the Guatemalan economy see John H. Adler, Eugene R. Schlesinger and Ernest C. Olson's *Public Finance and Economic Development in Guatemala*, Stanford, 1952; International Bank for Reconstruction and Development's *The Economic Development of Guatemala*, Washington, 1951; and J. A. Palacio's *Ingreso Nacional de Guatemala*, Guatemala, 1951. Also useful is the *Primer Censo Industrial de Guatemala, Año de 1946*, Guatemala, Dirección General de Estadística, 1951.

[4] On Guatemalan society and on the Indian groups in particular there is an extensive and varied body of writings. Robert H. Ewald's *Bibliografía Comentada Sobre Antropología Social, 1900-1955*, Guatemala, 1956, contains a seventy-page discussion of work in these fields along with a bibliography of 292 items by 132 scholars and serves as a useful tool for the researcher. Several publications of the Seminario de Integración Social Guatemalteca are extremely helpful. *Cultura Indígena de Guatemala*, Guatemala, 1956, is a collection of essays by 11 leading scholars. *Integración Social en Guatemala*, Guatemala, 1956, contains papers and comments from a conference held in June, 1956. Richard N. Adams' *Encuesta Sobre la Cultura de Los Ladinos en Guatemala*, Guatemala, 1956, is another product of this series which also contains Spanish translations of several outstanding studies published in English. Future volumes in this series include *Economía de Guatemala, Relaciones Indígeno-ladinas en Guatemala*, and *Integración Social en Guatemala, Volúmen II*. For the nature of the relations between ladino and Indian society see Melvin Tumin's *Class and Caste in a Peasant Society*, Princeton, 1952, and John Gillin's *The Culture of Security in San Carlos*, Tulane University, 1951. Classic studies on Guatemalan communities include Charles Wagley's *Santiago Chimaltenango*, Guatemala, 1957, and Sol Tax's *Penny Capitalism: A Guatemalan Indian Economy*, Washington, D.C., 1953.

general the history of relations between the two groups is one of slow acculturation on the part of the Indians. Even on the village level the contact between the two groups was kept within certain accepted limits and relations between the two groups generally bordered upon indifference.[5] At the time of the revolution, the bulk of the Guatemalan people were Indians living in defensive isolation in their relatively self-contained highland communities. Ignorant of and largely unconcerned with affairs beyond the bounds of their immediate area, they played a negligible role in national life and politics. The Indians formed not a nation within a nation, but rather a number of separate communal groups who viewed the government with suspicion if not hostility. If one could properly speak of a Guatemalan nation, it was the exclusive concern of the ladino minority.

The political history of Guatemala was not unlike that of the other Central American republics. Soon after independence was gained from Spain a conservative dictatorship was set up under General Rafael Carrera, who occupied the presidency from 1839 through 1865. In 1871 Guatemala experienced the closest thing to a real social revolution previous to 1944. Under the leadership of General Justo Rufino Barrios the Catholic Church was stripped of its privileges and much of its political influence. In addition to the establishment, on paper at least, of a system of secular education, the "Liberal" revolution introduced coffee as the chief money crop in place of indigo and cochineal. Along with the introduction of this new crop, which was to serve as the economic basis of a new ruling class, Barrios instituted changes in the system of landholding and labor. The communal holdings of the villages were abolished with the end result that the best land soon ended up in the hands of the large coffee planters or *finqueros*.

To furnish the necessary labor for the fincas, particularly in the harvest season, some way had to be found to induce the Indians to leave their highland villages and come to the fincas.[6] A wage contract

---

[5] The nature and extent of the changes brought about during the decade after the Revolution of 1944 are discussed in John Gillin and K. H. Silvert's "Ambiguities in Guatemala," *Foreign Affairs*, Vol. XXXIV, No. 3 (April, 1956), pp. 469-82. A fuller treatment is contained in Richard N. Adams (ed.), *Political Changes in Guatemalan Indian Communities: A Symposium*, Tulane University, 1957.

[6] The most complete treatment of this subject can be found in Jones, *op. cit.*, pp. 149-67.

system evolved and was successful in providing cheap labor for the production of export crops. The majority of those who left the village to work came from the families which had, through misfortune or indolence, sold their share of the old communal holdings. In most cases only dire necessity would induce the Indian to give up his way of life and become an unwilling part of the money economy.

In 1934 Ubico abolished the wage contract system and replaced it with a series of vagrancy laws which compelled Indians who cultivated less than a required amount of land to hire out as laborers for at least 150 days each year. While this served to give the Indian a greater degree of choice between competing employers, the labor card which each Indian had to carry became a hated symbol of the Ubico dictatorship and the system was abolished after the Revolution of 1944.

Perhaps the most significant fact of Guatemalan political history is that the country never experienced a violent social revolution. From the victory of the "Liberals" in 1871 until 1944 there was little effective interplay of ideas and social forces with the inevitable result that the political as well as the social and economic development of Guatemala fell behind that of the western world as a whole. In general, long periods of personalistic dictatorships alternated with much shorter periods of political instability. The Liberal revolution of 1871 brought General Justo Rufino Barrios to power from 1873 through 1885. 1898 saw the inception of the twenty-two year dictatorship of Manuel Estrada Cabrera. After a short period of relatively freer and more progressive government during the 1920's, Jorge Ubico began his thirteen years of orderly but stagnant government in 1931. In the 105 years preceding the Revolution of 1944, four men had occupied the presidency for a total of seventy-three years.

The resulting political immaturity of the Guatemalan people and lack of preparation for running their own affairs was a crucial factor in the course of events after the Revolution of 1944. Guatemala has paid and is still paying dearly for the years of dictatorship.

Ubico: Last of the Dictators. The thirteen years during which Jorge Ubico occupied the presidency of Guatemala set the stage for the Revolution of 1944 and much of what followed. In its fundamentals, his program was that of his "Liberal" predecessors, policies which by the 1930's were essentially conservative. His methods were even more outdated than his program, and both were rapidly becoming obsolete and inadequate in a period during which great world changes were making themselves felt even in isolated Guatemala.

Since the first steps of the revolution and the government which followed were greatly influenced by the reaction to *Ubiquismo* and Don Jorge became evil incarnate in the demonology of the revolution, it is necessary to look at the man as well as his government.[7]

Jorge Ubico y Castañeda was born on November 10, 1878, as the only son of an upper-class lawyer who was *jefe político* (governor) of Antigua. After the sheltered boyhood typical of a member of the privileged class, young Jorge entered the *Escuela Politécnica,* Guatemala's West Point, in 1894. Having left the academy before graduation for a life which promised less rigorous discipline, he took an abortive fling at bank work and the life of a gentleman farmer. His ambition soon led him back into the army where, with advancement opened to him by his father's influence, Ubico rose to the rank of Lieutenant Colonel by the time he was twenty-five. The ambitious young officer who took Napoleon and Justo Rufino Barrios as his models spent several years as a staff officer in the border conflicts with Honduras. Under the dictator Estrada Cabrera, Ubico became *jefe político* for the Department of Alta Verapaz, and four years later assumed the same post in Retalhuleu, a richer and more productive area. In this post and as Chief of Sanitation for the Pacific Coast, Ubico gained valuable experience and built up a reputation as a vigorous administrator.

Ever ambitious, Ubico moved into national politics as a supporter of the official Liberal Party. Promoted to the rank of General, he became Minister of War at the end of 1921 and soon after was named First Designate, the nearest equivalent to a Vice President under the Guatemalan Constitution. His presidential ambitions received a setback when he lost the 1922 elections to General Orellana and again

---

[7] The most nearly objective study of Ubico is Carlos Samayoa Chinchilla's *El Dictador y Yo: Verdadero Relato Sobre la Vida del General Ubico,* Guatemala, 1950. For the most detailed and impassioned attack on Ubiquismo see Efraín de los Ríos' *Ombres contra Hombres: Drama de la vida real,* Guatemala, 1948. A less substantial indictment can be found in J. Humberto Aguilar P.'s *Vida y muerte de una dictadura: El drama político de Guatemala,* Mexico, 1944. In support of Ubico see F. Hernández de León's *Viajes Presidenciales,* Guatemala, 1940.

in 1926 when General Chacón became president. These defeats and his subsequent retirement to private life as a prosperous *finquero* proved a boon to Ubico as he was not associated with the government when Guatemala was caught up in the world economic disaster in 1930. As the candidate of the *Partido Liberal Progresista,* Ubico emerged the victor in the 1931 election. Although his party ostensibly stood for "no reelection," Ubico practiced the Central American custom of *continuismo* and maintained himself in office for thirteen years, until overthrown by a civic protest movement in 1944.

The picture which emerges of Ubico as president is that of an impulsive, arbitrary, stubborn, opinionated, dominating, energetic and inflexible individual who was a policeman at heart. Remarkably self-centered, Ubico would brook no opposition. His attitudes were shown in such statements as "I have no friends, only domesticated enemies," and "Be careful, I am a tiger and you are monkeys."[8] Writers, Communists and thieves were said to be his three phobias, and in the category of Communists Ubico was apt to include anyone whose social, economic and political thought was more advanced or progressive than his own.

Government under Ubico was intensely personalistic, with the secret police and its network of informers receiving his closest attention. He was fond of saying that "my justice is that of God," and his servile officials knew better than to disagree. In general the policies of the government were the reflection of Ubico's personal thoughts. Although he was very active as an administrator, Ubico tended to become immersed in the details and was unable to generalize, preferring to take each matter separately and often letting his whimsy enter into the final disposition.[9] A conservative militarist, Ubico was deeply suspicious of the modern currents of thought which were becoming prevalent in the Western world and attempted to isolate Guatemala from these influences. In the material realm, order and some progress characterized at least his first term, but the price was high. The inmates of his prisons and the victims of his firing squads in 1934 bore mute evidence of Ubico's determination to run Guatemala as he saw fit.

Ubico was the last in a long line of Guatemalan strongmen. Within the limits imposed by his own self-seeking, Ubico may well have gov-

---

[8] Samayoa Chinchilla, *El Dictador . . .,* pp. 62 and 107.
[9] *Ibid.,* p. 78.

erned Guatemala as he thought best for the country. In the end, however, his policies were bound to be self-defeating and to pave the way for what he dreaded most, violent and drastic change. As late as five days before his fall, Ubico summed up the basic tenet of his government: "While I am President, I will not grant liberty of press nor of association, because the people of Guatemala are not prepared for democracy and need a strong hand."[10] His inability to see that times were changing and failure to take constructive steps to assure that the impact upon Guatemala would be moderate and gradual contributed materially to the conditions which the Communists would soon exploit. The legacy which he left Guatemala consisted of a combination of political immaturity, an archaic social structure and economic backwardness.

THE REVOLUTIONS OF 1944

The Guatemalan Revolution of 1944, which ushered in a new era, was a complex phenomenon which unfolded in several stages. Once the people of Guatemala City decided to lay claim to their civic rights, the task of bringing down Ubico was much easier than anyone had expected. The defeat of the system and forces which he had represented proved a much more formidable undertaking. The search for a constructive solution and workable alternative severely tested the capabilities of the new leadership. In the final evaluation, the last half of 1944 remains a period of which the Guatemalans can justifiably be proud.

Guatemala on the Eve of the Revolution. As the 1940's opened in Guatemala, the obsolescence of the Ubico regime became increasingly apparent. In a world which was talking of the four freedoms and the triumph of democracy, the personalistic dictatorship of Ubico with the alternatives of the grave, prison or exile for those who opposed the dictator's whims or dared to question his policies, seemed outdated. The students and young professional men were most affected by the democratic propaganda of the allies which served to awaken their sense of civic consciousness.

The expropriation of the large German-owned coffee fincas, a war-

---

[10] *Ibid.*, p. 176.

time measure taken in 1942, had cost Ubico the support of a group which had once been among his closest backers. The decree issued late in 1943 which allowed landowners to dispense summary justice and even kill poachers and trespassers caught in the act seemed to many Guatemalans to be carrying the sanctity of private property too far and holding human life too cheap. Ubico's deflationary economic policies kept salaries low and credit scarce while prices were rising under the impact of wartime inflation. His refusal to allow the United States to pay more than 50¢ a day for laborers constructing an air base alienated the workers while his personal interference and multiple restrictions irritated the business community. Ubico's known intention to seek yet another term through the machinations of his hand-picked Congress added to the growing feeling that his regime was outdated. Throughout the spring of 1944 this dissatisfaction was increasing, but largely inarticulate. The necessary spark was still lacking.

The First Phase: The Overthrow of Ubico. During the early months of 1944 the more active and informed groups in Guatemala City began to overcome their fear of Ubico and to give guarded expression to their dissatisfaction. Inspired by the example of the general strike which overthrew dictator Hernández Martínez in neighboring El Salvador in April, 1944, the university students sparked a movement to reclaim their civic rights from the increasingly hesitant Ubico. This reached its climax during the last week of June when the business and professional men shed their fears and followed the students into the streets to demonstrate against the President. Unable to cope with the almost universal feeling that it was time for a change, Ubico resigned.[11]

---

[11] The details of these developments can be followed in Manuel Galich's *Del Pánico al Ataque,* Guatemala, 1949, which traces the story of the university generation which sparked the movement. From the fear and spinelessness of the 1930's through the first feeble sparks of initiative in the early 1940's to the final burst of bravery and bravado in June, 1944, Galich pictures the development of the generation from which many of the leaders of the Arévalo and Arbenz regimes were drawn. Arcadio Ruiz Franco's *Hambre y Miseria,* Guatemala, 1950, dwells largely on the later stages of the revolution and shows that the politically backward workers played only a secondary role in the revolution. Not as reliable or useful is Medardo Mejía's *El Movimiento Obrero en la Revolución de Octubre,* Guatemala, 1949, which purports to cover the period from June, 1941 to March, 1948 but is of little value after 1944. The revolution is also treated in Najera Farfán, *op. cit.,* pp. 25-75. All of these books show that the over-use and mis-use of the word Communist by the Ubico government predisposed many young students and workers to look favorably upon Communism and to afford it a full hearing.

Late in May, forty-five lawyers dared to petition the President for the removal of a judge who had presided over most of the trials of political opponents of the regime. Shortly thereafter, the schoolteachers began to press their demands for increased wages. As one of the few organized groups in Guatemala, the university students, and particularly those law students grouped in the association *El Derecho,* formed the vanguard and backbone of the anti-Ubico movement. Early in June the university students made a series of demands for the replacement of school officials who were not acceptable to the student bodies of the various faculties.

When the government showed a conciliatory attitude, the students seized upon it as a manifestation of weakness and demanded a sweeping program of university reform, presenting the government with a 24-hour ultimatum. This final challenge was handed to the President on June 22; seeing that his unwonted conciliatory attitude had only succeeded in making the students bolder, Ubico chose to return to his old and familiar policy of repression. By suspending constitutional guarantees, the government turned the affair into a major political crisis. The most active of the student leaders sought asylum in the Mexican Embassy, but the young lawyers and professional men came to the support of the students and on the 24th presented the famous *Memorial de los 311* to the government. This document, signed by 311 of the leading citizens of the capital, explained the reasons behind the unrest and asked for the effective reestablishment of constitutional guarantees.[12] The final paragraph of the memorial stated that:

> Guatemala cannot remove itself from the democratic impera-
> tives of the era. It is impossible to frustrate with coercive means
> the uncontainable impulses of that generous ideology which is
> being reaffirmed in the world's conscience by means of the blood-
> iest of struggles between oppression and liberty.

With both sides taking an intransigent position, matters soon came to a head.

At noon on June 24 the students organized the first *huelga de brazos caídos* or peaceful demonstration of protest. From six to eight in the evening of the same day a second demonstration, at which Guillermo Toriello read from the Atlantic Charter, saw the leaders raise the first demands that Ubico resign. Clashes between persons shouting anti-

---

[12] For the text of the memorial see Ruiz Franco, *op. cit.,* pp. 47-8; Medardo Mejía, *op. cit.,* pp. 54-59; Galich, *op. cit.,* pp. 334-336.

Ubico slogans and the dictator's strong arm squads led to considerable property destruction and some injuries during the night. The following day, while Ubico and his ministers were meeting with a courageous committee of students and young lawyers, a protest march by the middle class women of Guatemala City was fired upon by the government troops. The death of a young schoolteacher, María Chinchilla, who was shot in this clash, gave the revolution a badly needed martyr and symbol. Talks between the representatives of the people and the government were immediately broken off by the enraged citizens.

On Monday the 26th, Guatemala City was in the silent grasp of a general strike. When the businessmen and workers joined in the movement of quiet protest, the government found itself powerless to cope with the situation. As the strike went on, petitions requesting Ubico to resign flooded the National Palace. The army, which could have broken up mass demonstrations and crushed an armed revolt, found no organized group to attack. On July 1, Jorge Ubico handed over the reins of government to a military triumvirate composed of Generals Federico Ponce Vaides, Eduardo Villagrán Ariza and Buenaventura Piñeda. Far from being over, however, the revolution was merely approaching its second stage; the crucial "hundred days" of political organization had begun.

The Second Phase: Political Organization. The fall of Ubico did not automatically entail any great political, social or economic changes, but it did open the door to immediate and unaccustomed political ferment. Unfortunately there was no organized leadership and few individuals agreed on what was to be done next. On July 3 the holdover Ubico Congress voted to accept the president's resignation. General Ponce quickly responded by sending troops to close the meeting of Congress. On the following day a cowed and thoroughly intimidated Congress named Ponce as provisional president. The new government bowed at least temporarily to public sentiment and permitted the organization of parties and unions. On July 10, the leaders of the mushrooming new parties met with Ponce and sought to extort a promise that he would not be a candidate, but had to settle for his promise to call elections in the late fall.

As soon as Ubico resigned, embryonic labor and political organizations sprang up throughout the capital to fill the vacuum. Exiles began to stream back into Guatemala from Mexico, Chile, Europe and other places of refuge. On the very day Ubico resigned a small group of intellectuals and professionals organized the National Renovation Party (*Renovación Nacional—RN*). The students and young professionals soon gathered in the Popular Liberating Front (*Frente Popular Libertador—FPL*). The RN chose as its candidate Juan José Arévalo, a Guatemalan educator who was living in Argentina as a university professor, and on August 3 the FPL accepted him as their standard bearer. Other parties and candidates representing all political hues sprang up, but the most ominous sign was the announcement that Ponce, the provisional president, would run as the candidate of the old Liberal Party.

During the latter part of July and throughout the month of August, Ponce began to crack down upon those who stood in the way of his desire to become another Ubico. On August 15 a large number of young lawyers were arrested and two days later the leaders of the FPL were rounded up by the police. On September 3 Arévalo arrived in Guatemala and was enthusiastically received by the people of the capital. This evidence of popularity goaded Ponce into stepping up his campaign of repression and many leaders of the Arévalo forces sought refuge in the Mexican Embassy while their less fortunate colleagues were apprehended by the police.

Phase Three: The October Revolution. When the political strength of Arévalo became evident, Ponce Vaides saw that he would have to take drastic action to retain the presidency. Terror had been used against his political opponents and particularly the supporters of Arévalo, but this did not seem to be enough to insure his election. On October 1 Alejandro Córdova, the publisher of the influential newspaper *El Imparcial,* who had opposed Ponce's attempt to have the legislature amend the constitution so that he could continue in power without an election, was murdered by agents of the police. In the wave of terror and violence which followed, Arévalo and his supporters had to go into hiding or seek asylum. On October 16 the *Frente Unido de Partidos Políticos y Asociaciones Cívicas* issued a manifesto drawn up by Arévalo, Jorge García Granados and Roberto Arzu in which they declared a political strike. It was obvious that these parties could not continue their campaigns in the face of overwhelming government repression. Two days later the university students went on strike once again.

By this time, however, it was apparent that an armed revolt would be necessary to put an end to the dictatorship. Jacobo Arbenz Guzmán, an army captain who had resigned in protest against the actions of Ponce, and Jorge Toriello, an influential businessman and older brother of the young lawyer Guillermo Toriello, had been plotting a revolt for some time. At the beginning of October they were joined by Major Francisco Javier Arana, a tank commander who brought to the cause the military power necessary for its success. In order to minimize the chance of failure as well as to avoid prolonged bloodshed, Arana planned a sudden, swift stroke. Shortly after midnight on the 20th of October a small group of revolutionaries took over control of the fort *Guardia de Honor* and began arming student and worker volunteers. The military leadership of Arana and Arbenz, coupled with a lucky shot on the magazine of the main government held fort, led to a rapid victory for the revolutionary forces. By five that afternoon the *Junta Revolucionaria del Gobierno,* composed of Arbenz, Arana and Jorge Toriello was installed in the National Palace as the government of Guatemala. This day came to symbolize the beginning of the "new Guatemala," as the revolution then passed on to its constructive stage.

CONSOLIDATION OF THE REVOLUTION

The lack of an organized opposition during the Ubico regime meant that there was no alternative government ready to step in after his fall. Even after the threat of Ponce had been beaten down by the October 20 revolution, months of consolidation were necessary before the transition to a popularly elected government could be completed. Some form of caretaker government was necessary while the Presidential elections were being held and a modern democratic constitution written.

The Revolutionary Junta. Arana, Arbenz and Jorge Toriello formed the Revolutionary Junta which governed Guatemala from October 20, 1944, until the inauguration of Arévalo on March 15, 1945. This provisional government was based upon an uneasy alliance between the leaders of the *Arevalista* parties and the army chiefs. The FPL leaders were particularly suspicious of the military and eager for a quick transition to constitutional government. On October 25 the junta issued its first decree, dissolving the Ubico Assembly and calling elections for a new National Assembly, which were held on November 3, 4 and 5.

The junta, dominated by Arana, refused to call the new Assembly into session and demanded that they, rather than a provisional president, should govern until the inauguration of an elected president. According to the junta, Toriello was to be Vice President and Arana installed as actual head of the armed forces under a new law which would give the army considerable autonomy and independence from the president. Eventually a compromise was worked out and on November 28 the Legislative Assembly was convoked in order to summon a Constituent Assembly which was to write a new constitution.

Decree No. 17, issued on November 27 set forth the political principles of the junta, which included the provision that none of its members or its cabinet would be a candidate for the presidency.[13] Presidential elections were called for December 17, 18 and 19, and those for the Constituent Assembly were to be held on December 28, 29 and 30. Thus in less than two months the voters of Guatemala went to the polls three times for what were probably the freest elections in the history of the country.

The Presidential Campaign. The youth who had played such a key role in the overthrow of Ubico and Ponce were unwilling to let the older politicians who had been in exile or had remained quiet under Ubico take over the leadership of the revolution. Many of the older generation of revolutionaries had gathered in the Social Democratic Party behind the candidacy of Guillermo Flores Avendaño and in the National Democratic Front which had Adrián Recinos as its standard-bearer. Among a flock of lesser parties, the most radical was the National Vanguard led by Ernesto Capuano, Alfonso Solórzano and Enrique Muñoz Meany. This Marxist group attempted to connect itself with the Arévalo forces and played a minor role in the United Front of Arevalista Parties (FUPA).

In the elections which were held on December 17, 18 and 19,

---

[13] See Silvert, *op. cit.,* p. 10.

Arévalo was the overwhelming choice of the Guatemalan people as he polled 255,000 of the 295,000 votes cast by the literate male population, the only ones who were entitled to vote.

Juan José Arévalo Bermejo was born of middle class parentage in the village of Taxisco, Santa Rosa, on September 10, 1904.[14] His father was Mariano Arévalo, a small farmer and cattle rancher, and his mother was a schoolteacher, Elena Bermejo. As a youth Juan was sent to the best schools in the capital, and with his thesis at the Central Normal School for Boys won a scholarship from the Argentine government for study in that country. In 1934 he acquired his doctorate in philosophy from the University of La Plata. During the next two years he worked in the Guatemalan Ministry of Education. Feeling that his talents were not being fully utilized or appreciated in Guatemala, he traveled briefly in Europe and then returned to Argentina where he taught at several universities. There he married an Argentine schoolteacher, Elisa Martínez, and through his writings gained a considerable reputation as an educator. Arévalo was teaching at the University of Tucumán when summoned back to Guatemala as the presidential candidate of the FPL and RN in August of 1944.

Taking into account the attitudes of the groups which made the revolution, Arévalo was a logical choice for President. From the point of view of the students and young professional groups a military man or a member of the old ruling class was unacceptable. Arévalo appealed to them as an educator, as a man who had risen from a middle class background, and as a person not associated with the Ubico dictatorship. His age—40 at the time of his election—seemed to them to offer a combination of an understanding of the aspirations of youth with the requisite degree of experience and maturity. If nothing else, Arévalo looked every inch the president. Six feet tall and weighing narly 200 pounds, Arévalo furnished the young revolutionaries with a leader they could look up to, both literally and figuratively.

Arévalo's political ideas, as expounded during his campaign, cen-

---

[14] Two biographies of Arévalo are in existence, but neither is very reliable and both were in the form of official biographies paid for with government funds. Pedro Alvarez Elizondo's *El Presidente Arévalo y el retorno a Bolívar,* Mexico, 1947, and Medardo Mejía's *Juan José Arévalo o El Humanismo en la Presidencia,* Guatemala, 1951, are about equally laudatory and uncritical. The Ministry of Public Education put out a collection of items praising Arévalo under the title *Arévalo Visto por América,* Guatemala, 1951.

tered around a concept which he called spiritual socialism.[15] In his political writings and speeches, all of which were completed before he had any political experience or attempted to apply his ideas in practice, Arévalo declared his faith that "individuals work principally for spiritual motivations."[16] Under Guatemalan conditions, socialism for Arévalo consisted in "softening" feudalism with "discreet measures," designed to improve the lot of the masses and to restore their "dignity."[17] In Arévalo's eyes,

> We are socialists because we live in the twentieth century. But we are not materialist socialists. We do not believe that man is primarily stomach. We believe that man is above all a will for dignity. . . . Our socialism does not, therefore, aim at an ingenuous distribution of material goods, or the stupid economic equalization of men who are economically different. Our socialism aims at liberating men psychologically, granting to all the psychological and spiritual integrity denied by conservatism and liberalism.[18]
>
> We shall initiate the era of sympathy for laborers of the fields, workshops, barracks, commercial establishments. We shall equate man with man . . . Let us add justice and happiness to order, . . . and revalue civically and legally all the inhabitants of the Republic.[19]

Governing a people was "a task comparable to the function of teaching."[20] While his speeches sounded appealing and highminded to the Guatemalan public, the ideas which he expressed were to prove a wholly inadequate basis for his government and never attained any

---

[15] For the political thought of Arévalo see his *Escritos Políticos,* Guatemala, 1945, and his *Discursos en la Presidencia,* Guatemala, 1948. These are also available in a single volume, *Escritos Políticos y Discursos,* Havana, 1953. His writings since leaving the presidency include two very polemic books, *Guatemala, La Democracia y el Imperio,* Santiago de Chile, 1954, and *Fábula del Tiburón y las Sardinas, América Latina Estrangulada,* Santiago de Chile, 1956. Neither of these books would seem to justify the reputation which he still enjoys as a "pensador." An unpublished thesis on "The Social and Political Ideas of Juan José Arévalo and their Relationship to Contemporary Trends of Latin American Thought" by Marie-Berthe Dion, The American University, Washington, D.C., 1956, attempts to appraise his political thought without relating it to his actions or its application in Guatemala and overrates him as a political theorist.

[16] Arévalo, *Escritos Políticos,* p. 187.

[17] *Ibid.,* pp. 187-8.

[18] *Ibid.,* pp. 146-7.

[19] *Ibid.,* p. 199.

[20] *Ibid.,* p. 140.

significant acceptance as the philosophy of the Guatemalan social revolution. Spiritual socialism soon disappeared and was followed by the more practical approach to politics known as *Arevalismo.*

The Constitution of 1945. The Constitution of 1945 was drawn up rapidly and under pressure by a group of relatively inexperienced lawyers and students whose chief aim was to prevent the recurrence of a dictatorship of the Ubico type. The Constituent Assembly was elected on December 28, 29 and 30, 1944, and met early in January of the following year. As Decree No. 17 of the revolutionary junta provided that the constitution should go into force on March 15, the day of the inauguration of the new president, the Assembly had to work under extreme pressure. The situation was complicated by the fear of many civilian politicians that the junta was seeking an excuse to prolong its life by delaying the inauguration of Arévalo in case the drafting of the new constitution was not completed on time.[21] The Assembly contained a wide variety of viewpoints, and was in general more conservative than the governments which were to attempt to govern under the Constitution which it produced. Among the influences at work in its drafting, in addition to past Guatemalan practice and the desire to curb the influence of the executive, were the United States Constitution, the 1917 Mexican "revolutionary" Constitution, the 1935 Constitution of the USSR, and the experiences of the various delegates while in exile in Mexico, the United States, France or other Central American countries.[22]

The actual drafting of the constitution was in the hands of a fifteen-member committee headed by the President of the Assembly, Jorge García Granados. Under his effective leadership the basic agreement of the delegates upon a democratic document, modern social guarantees and the strengthening of the Congress vis-à-vis the Executive was translated into specific provisions. The fourteen lawyers and students and the one physician who made up the drafting commission ranged from the moderate right to the moderate left, but García Granados and three companions who represented democratic socialist

---

[21] See Silvert, *op. cit.,* p. 10 for a detailed discussion of this point.

[22] For an excellent discussion of the drafting of the constitution and interpretative analysis of its provisions see Silvert, *op. cit.,* pp. 13-18. The proceedings of the Assembly were published by the Tipografía Nacional in 1951 under the title *Diario de Sesiones de la Asamblea Constituyente de 1945.*

thought were able to shape the constitution along their lines. The resulting document has been described as establishing a "libertarian, unitary, semi-parliamentary government designed to carry out neo-Socialist economic policies."[23]

One provision, the ban on parties of "a foreign or international character" contained in Article 32, was to lead to serious controversy in later years. While Arévalo held this to apply to organized Communism, under Arbenz it was a dead letter. Although the political realities in Guatemala doomed the attempt to institutionalize the principle of Congressional supremacy, and the separation of powers did not stand up in practice as well as on paper, the new constitution proved generally adequate.

The race against time was barely won as the Constitutional Assembly adopted it on March 11 and approval by the junta came two days later. In keeping with the spirit of the new constitution, a new president and a new generation of politicians set out to build a new Guatemala.

---

[23] Silvert, *op. cit.*, p. 13.

2

THE REVOLUTION UNDER AREVALO:
FROM NOBLE EXPERIMENT TO POLITICAL FAILURE

On March 15, 1945, Juan José Arévalo received the reins of government from the hands of the junta. It appeared to many observers that Arévalo, backed by the overwhelming sympathy of the Guatemalan people, had immense powers to build a new Guatemala. Yet, if the opportunities of the new government were great, the tasks which faced it were still greater. Had Arévalo been able to transform the favorable attitude of the masses into effective support for a well-planned and realistic program, these obstacles would have been formidable but not insurmountable. As it turned out, the enthusiasm of the young revolutionaries could not offset their total lack of experience and the first years of the new government were characterized by improvisation. The unrealistic masses who had hoped for miracles from the schoolteacher president were disappointed by the slowness of progress during these difficult years of adjustment. Even the young idealists upon whom the revolution depended for motive power became disillusioned by the disparity between promise and fulfillment.

In this atmosphere of frustrated hopes, opportunism began to creep into the revolution while the opponents of social and economic reform became increasingly intransigent. As the government resorted to sheer expediency in the face of continual threats to its existence and the lack of political and administrative experience made itself felt, *Arevalismo* grew shabbier and lost much of its appeal. The generation which led the revolution and undertook to build a "new Guatemala" showed little capacity for effective political action and were unable to satisfy the demands which the revolution unleashed.

In short, after the destruction of the old regime there was no organized group to inherit power, furnish leadership and put forth a practical program suited to the needs and capabilities of the Guatemalan nation. Owing largely to the political, social and economic backwardness of Guatemala, no homogeneous force evolved to back the revolution. Lacking experience and having to fight against an intransigent and often conspiratorial opposition, the revolution under Arévalo never fulfilled its early promise.

GENERAL CONSIDERATIONS

Arévalo's leftist orientation soon alienated the traditional economic, social and political elite.[1] As a result he was driven to rely more and more upon the government bureaucracy and the labor unions as the two groups whose future was inextricably linked with that of his administration. In addition he was forced to seek the support of the young Army officers, since the threat of a successful military coup was always in the background.[2]

As time went on, new forces slowly developed to challenge the old power structure of the landowners, conservative military officers, Guatemala City businessmen and, to a lesser extent, the church. Organized labor, young professional and middle class groups linked to the revolutionary parties, and the young officers "of the school" fur-

---

[1] It is mute testimony to the stagnation and backwardness of Guatemala under Ubico that as essentially moderate a program as that supported by Arévalo should be thought of as radical or even "Communistic" by the Guatemalan employers.

[2] More than two dozen abortive attempts to overthrow the government occurred in the first four years of his term, as well as several more serious ones in 1949-1950.

nished the backbone of the Arévalo regime. The leaders of these groups followed ideologies ranging from welfare capitalism through a variety of socialist beliefs to Communism. This confusion of rival ideologies was encouraged by Arévalo's concept of democracy as the unrestrained interplay of competing ideas. Although the president might talk of the coexistence of all men and ideas within the revolution and express the view that all problems had a political solution, he found it difficult to carry this into practice. Unfortunately the ideas of the various revolutionary leaders had never been put to the stern test of practical application. At its lowest point the Arévalo regime appeared as a somewhat uneasy coalition of groups competing for the spoils of office while watching apprehensively over their shoulders for a military coup which would put an end to it.

Arévalo proved to be a fairly shrewd practitioner of political expediency who was able to survive thirty-odd plots and serve out his full six-year term, no mean accomplishment in itself. In view of the intransigence of the opposition and the lack of experienced political leaders who could add maturity to the youthful revolutionary government, Arévalo was faced with a difficult situation in which to govern successfully. Nevertheless his political juggling was not conducive to progress in the political sphere and we must judge that Arévalo fell short of being an effective political leader, statesman and administrator. While his policy of dropping the barriers to freedom of thought and political expression led to greater democracy than Guatemala had ever known, it did not contribute greatly to the orderly and systematic solution of the country's pressing problems.

AREVALO AND COMMUNISM

The official position of Arévalo as president toward Communism was based upon toleration of Communists as individuals but opposition to the formation of an organized Communist party. In practice his government followed a policy of expediency which, while not directly encouraging the spread of Communism, did not hinder it and indirectly facilitated the growth and influence of the Communist movement. In general, Arévalo's policy toward the Communists swung back and forth with the dictates of the domestic political situation. While in some of his earliest speeches he professed disagreement with the principles of Communism, he accepted the help of the Communists on the ground that he needed all possible support.[3] The sum of his public statements was that Communism as a doctrine was innocuous, but the Communists as a political power were a danger, although less so than the falangists. While Soviet imperialism was a potential threat, according to Arévalo that posed by the United States was immediate.

The task of ascertaining Arévalo's true attitude toward Communism is complicated not only by his government's fluctuating and ambiguous policy, but also the fact that until his assassination on July 18, 1949, Chief of the Armed Forces Francisco J. Arana was sufficiently powerful to prevent the government from taking any action which openly favored the Communists. In addition during the years before the Communists came out into the open it was difficult to ascertain just who were Communists, and even Arévalo may have been unaware that many of his young protégés had fully embraced Communism. Nevertheless there is irrefutable proof that Arévalo numbered some of the Communist leaders among his close friends and political collaborators and appointed them to responsible and influential positions in his government. It would appear that Arévalo viewed them as a home-grown variety of Communists, felt they were useful to him and that he could control them, and was more interested in avoiding trouble than in having a showdown with the Communists. While their influence in his own administration never became dominant, the end result of Arévalo's tolerance toward the Communists was that they were in a position to strike a more advantageous bargain with his successor.

Arévalo opened the doors of Guatemala to Communists and pro-Communist exiles and employed many of them in technical posts in his government while looking with favor upon their efforts to organize the workers. Nevertheless, on January 25, 1946, under pressure from Colonel Arana, he ordered the closing of the *Escuela Claridad,* a Communist-run indoctrination center and training school for labor leaders, whose activities had led to a split in the nascent labor movement. Again in October, 1947, fifteen foreign Communists, including the Cuenca brothers, Miguel Mármol and Virgilio Guerra, were ex-

[3] For Arévalo's early statements on Communism see his *Discursos,* pp. 223-4, 238 and 243-8.

pelled from the country in response to growing anti-Communist sentiment. Yet within a few months many of these exiles were back in Guatemala, "doing business at their old stands." At the same time Arévalo was welcoming to Guatemala and to his payroll such prominent Chilean Communists as Virginia Bravo Letelier, César Godoy and Manuel Eduardo Hubner.

In these early years a small group of young Guatemalan Communists rose to positions of influence within the Revolutionary Action Party (*Partido Acción Revolucionaria*—PAR) and in the labor movement. In their guise as members of the official party and union officials, Arévalo worked with them and elevated some to high government positions.

Most of the future leaders of the Communist Party were active in the Arévalo government. José Manuel Fortuny, Guatemala's number one Communist, twice became Secretary General of the chief administration party, the PAR, and was a leader in Congress. In these positions he was often consulted by Arévalo and in 1950 became one of the three members of the influential National Election Board (JNE). Alfredo Guerra Borges, later the Communists' top propagandist, was appointed the first Inspector General of Labor, served as editor of the official paper, and for a time headed the government's propaganda office. Mario Silva Jonama served as Under-Secretary of Education in 1948, resigned to run unsuccessfully for Congress, and returned to a job in Arévalo's publicity office. Arévalo appointed Víctor Manuel Gutiérrez, the leading Communist in the labor movement, to several positions in the Ministry of Education's Travelling Missions of Initial Culture and on the board of directors of the Social Security Institute (*Instituto Guatemalteco de Seguridad Social*—IGSS). Bernardo Alvarado Monzón served in the Ministry of Economy, Huberto Alvarado in the Publicity Office of the Presidency, Carlos René Valle in the Ministry of Education and National Petroleum Institute, and Virgilio Guerra, one of those exiled in October, 1947, was employed by the Social Security Institute in 1948. Even the Communist firebrand Carlos Manuel Pellecer, whom Arévalo had kept out of the country as Secretary and Chargé in Paris, was appointed head of the Travelling Missions of the Ministry of Education when he returned to Guatemala in 1949.

This use of Communists in his government should not be taken, as it has often been in the past, as irrefutable evidence that Arévalo was a Communist or actively favored Communism. In the same period, during the era of good feelings which followed the allied victory in World War II and preceded the outbreak of the Cold War, several other Central and South American presidents went as far as Arévalo in tolerating the Communists and striking a bargain with them. At this time the Communists in Guatemala were a small, select group of able young politicians and labor leaders whose only organization was in the form of study groups and clandestine cells within the revolutionary organizations. Facing a shortage of trained and experienced manpower, Arévalo saw no reason not to utilize them. In brief, Arévalo tolerated the Communists, although he was not one himself. The extent to which he may have favored them over the other revolutionary political forces in Guatemala is a point upon which debate is likely to continue for years.

THE COURSE OF GUATEMALAN POLITICS UNDER AREVALO

The full story of the political maneuvering, intrigues and ceaseless plotting of the early years of the Arévalo administration is too complex to be told here. The emphasis of the junta had been upon organizational and administrative matters rather than on basic policy issues. This carried over at least partially into the early months of the constitutional government. When Arévalo entered the presidency he was partially a captive of the triumvirate which had composed the provisional government. Jorge Toriello was Minister of Finance, Arbenz the Minister of National Defense and Arana the semi-autonomous and very powerful Chief of the Armed Forces. In addition, such leaders as Jorge García Granados had built up substantial followings within the Congress. Arévalo soon got García Granados out of the country to the United Nations and undermined Toriello until the latter resigned from the Cabinet in January, 1946. Arana posed a constant threat to Arévalo's position and supported the government only because he saw no workable alternative. As late as 1949, Arévalo was reported to have stated concerning Arana that "In Guatemala there are two presidents and one of them has a machine gun with which he is constantly threatening the other." Knowing that Arana was always willing to listen to plans to overthrow his government,

Arévalo had little sense of security and was forced to give him a tacit veto power over major actions of the government. In addition he reportedly had to promise Arana the presidency in 1951 to prevent him from seeking it sooner by a coup.

During the course of 1945 the old government employees were gradually replaced by new faces drawn from the ranks of the revolutionary parties. To make up for lack of experience, Arévalo utilized a number of left-wing exiles who had previous experience in government and administration. Individuals representing a wide variety of political views mingled under the umbrella of *Arevalismo,* which became merely a generalized political orientation based upon the lowest common denominator of the competing revolutionary ideologies. No well-defined indigenous revolutionary philosophy developed to serve as the basis for a consistent program of government and rallying point for the revolutionary forces. In this climate a number of young politicians turned to the doctrines of Marx, Engels and Lenin as a means of establishing order out of the ideological chaos.

At the end of 1945, the two government parties, National Renovation (RN) and Popular Liberating Front (FPL) merged to form the Revolutionary Action Party (PAR). This extremely heterogeneous party held together through the enactment of the Labor Code in April of 1947. It then broke up and the reconstituted FPL, which was the most moderate of the revolutionary parties, became the dominant force in Congress and in the administration during 1947 and 1948. The PAR was left in the position of a minority party closely linked to organized labor. Within it a small clique of Communists and their allies strove to convert the party into a front for Communist activities and nearly succeeded during 1948. During the first half of the Arévalo administration, three fundamental pieces of legislation were enacted. The Social Security law in October of 1946, the Labor Code in April of 1947 and the Institute for the Development of Production (INFOP) in August of 1948 were the only pieces of basic legislation upon which agreement could be reached before the forces of the revolution divided over its future course and direction.

The Political Crisis of 1948. By the middle of 1948 it was apparent that the revolution was entering a critical period. The Arévalo regime's lack of an effective myth or of a systematic plan for meeting the country's needs had led to increasing disunity within the ranks of its supporters and a growing stream of criticism from all quarters. All the independent newspapers were openly critical of the government and the majority of the people in the capital supported the opposition parties. The revolutionary parties were weakened by internal disunity and competition among themselves for the spoils of office. Serious labor conflict between the United Fruit Company and the unions plagued the country from June 1948 to March 1949. In addition a wave of plots against the government were discovered as the Congressional elections approached.[4] On August 6, 1948, the leaders of organized labor announced the discovery of a subversive plot and petitioned the government for arms, but were turned down by Col. Arana. On November 31, a large shipment of arms was discovered in railroad cars in Puerto Barrios, the Atlantic terminal of the railroad. As a result of these attempted coups, a state of national emergency was declared. Early in 1949 another conspiracy broke out in the form of an invasion by a small band of exiles from across the Mexican border.[5] The weakness of the Arévalo government posed a constant temptation to the strongman of the army, Col. Arana, to oust Arévalo as President. The announced determination of the workers to declare a general strike and take up arms should the government fall and the fact that a significant group of the younger officers were loyal to Lt. Col. Arbenz, Arévalo's Minister of Defense, were among the factors deterring Arana, who had high hopes of succeeding Arévalo through constitutional means in the 1950 elections.

The elections for the Congress which would take office in March, 1949, held great significance for the revolutionary forces in Guatemala. With presidential succession on the political horizon, disagreement over the future course of the revolution came to threaten the unity of the revolutionary forces. The moderate revolutionary leaders who controlled the Popular Liberating Front (FPL) and the extremists who led the Revolutionary Action Party (PAR) disagreed over who was to be the ultimate beneficiary of the revolution. To the young

---

[4] For conditions in Guatemala in the summer of 1948 see Leo A. Suslow's *Aspects of Social Reforms in Guatemala, 1944-1949,* Colgate University Bookstore, 1949, pp. 123-4. The labor disputes are treated in Archer C. Bush's *Organized Labor in Guatemala, 1944-1949,* Colgate University Bookstore, 1950, Part Two, pp. 25-28.

[5] See Bush, *op. cit.,* Part Four, pp. 10-11.

professionals who led the FPL, the PAR-Guatemalan Confederation of Labor (CTG) alliance, which contained an influential Communist faction, was attempting to go too far too fast. In the eyes of the *Paristas,* the FPL leaders had their own essentially middle class interests at heart and were neglecting the problems of the workers and peasants which called for a fundamental transformation of Guatemalan society.

In the spring of 1948 the moderates of the FPL seemed to enjoy the favor of the President who was preparing to remove PAR leader Augusto Charnaud MacDonald from the Ministry of Economy and Labor. The PAR, the smaller National Renovation Party (RN) and the leaders of organized labor banded together to curb the expansion of the FPL's influence.[6] In the elections the opposition took advantage of this division of the revolutionary forces and won a dozen seats in the new Congress. Knowing that an unfriendly president could literally destroy the budding labor movement, its leaders swore that they would not allow anyone unfriendly to labor to become president. The elimination of Col. Arana as a presidential contender was given high priority by these revolutionary leaders; for the Communists, upon whose influence Arana had been an effective check, his removal was essential.

The Death of Arana. Almost from the mid-point of the Arévalo administration, politics began to focus around the question of who would be the next president. At the time of Arévalo's serious injury in an auto accident in December, 1945 the revolutionary parties signed the so-called "pact of the ravine" which provided that, if Arévalo died or was unable to resume his duties, Arana would be their choice as president.[7] By the latter part of 1948 it became apparent that the revolutionary parties no longer desired to back the candidacy of Arana. As the first avowed candidate for the presidency, the Chief of the Armed Forces was in an exposed position; his every word, move and action were carefully watched and weighed. While Arana was popular with conservative and moderate politicians and respected by the people as a whole, he was feared by the leftist politicians and labor

---

[6] See 8021:297-319 for documents on inter-party relations in the 1948 campaign.

[7] See Najera Farfán, *op. cit.,* pp. 105-6.

leaders who saw in him a threat to their plans for a radical transformation of the Guatemalan social, economic and political order.
Labor leaders were alienated by his background as a soldier "of the
line" and his apparent disapproval of the growing influence of
organized labor.[8] For the PAR and RN leaders he was too conservative and linked too tightly to the established order, while the bulk of
the younger FPL leaders were committed to the idea of a civilian
president. Arévalo saw in Arana a rival for power and influence who
might not be willing to wait until the election and who was not
inclined toward carrying on the policies of his administration. These
forces began to gather around the only other figure who could attract
the support of the politically important officer corps, Minister of
Defense Jacobo Arbenz.[9]

With what was probably poor timing, Arana sought in 1948 the
support of the *Frente Popular Libertador,* at that time the most important of the revolutionary parties. When the FPL split over this
question, Arana ran his own candidates in the Congressional elections
under the banner of the Social Revolutionary Party, a move which
backfired by costing him his last chance of support from the President
or the government parties. Under the Constitution of 1945, Arana
would have to resign as Chief of the Armed Forces once he was an
open and avowed candidate for the presidency. For this reason the
elections to renew half the membership of the Supreme Council of
Defense were particularly important, since it was this body which
would choose his successor as the head of the army. Lacking a majority
on this important body, Arana would have found himself without a
power base. He made every effort to assure himself of victory, but
the results of the first balloting were annulled and a new vote
scheduled for the latter part of July.[10]

---

[8] On several occasions Arana expressed concern over the growing power of
the labor unions and dissatisfaction with the political orientation of their
leaders.

[9] For a discussion of Arana's candidacy see Silvert, *op. cit.,* pp. 11-12;
Najera Farfán, *op. cit.,* 106-8; Galich, *op. cit.,* pp. 201-2. The first author
takes an entirely objective view; the second is a partisan of Arana and the
third an avowed opponent of Arana.

[10] See Najera Farfán, *op. cit.,* pp. 108-9. Interviews with several leading
Guatemalan political figures substantiate this portion of the story. From this
point through the death of Arana on the 18th, there is considerable disagreement over who was making the decisions and giving the orders.

Stories were by this time circulating that Arana was planning to take over control of the country and remove Arévalo from the presidency. There seems no doubt that the conservative interests were encouraging Arana to take such a step, claiming that it was necessary for the national welfare for Arana to put a stop to the "communization" of the country and to end the prolonged political crisis and stating that he could not afford to wait until the elections. Certainly Arana was endeavoring to reestablish the army's monopoly over military weapons which could be used by organized labor to make a revolution or defend the government from a coup. On June 20 there had been an attempt, sponsored by Arévalo, to launch an attack upon the Dominican Republic by the so-called Caribbean Legion. When this failed, Arana demanded that the arms be turned over to the army, which was under his control. On July 16, Arévalo complained to Arana that he was not leaving the President with enough weapons for his security or the police with enough to do their job. Arana replied sarcastically that by Arévalo's criteria, even the boy scouts needed arms. Apparently each had just about decided that the other would have to be eliminated. Feeling that Arévalo and the parties had broken their word by not backing his candidacy, Arana was probably receptive to suggestions that he take over the government.

With either the active participation or tacit consent of the President, the leaders of the Arbenz forces laid plans to seize Arana, take him before a special session of Congress, have him removed as Chief of the Armed Forces for engaging in politics in violation of his oath of office, and immediately exile him from the country. Whether it was planned in advance or occurred on the spur of the moment, the indisputable fact is that Col. Arana was ambushed and shot to death on July 18, 1949, by a group of armed men as he returned from a trip to Amatitlán to inspect a cache of weapons which had been reported discovered there. According to the best available evidence, the group who killed Arana included the chauffeur of Sra. de Arbenz, who later became a Deputy in the Arbenz Congress, and was headed by Lt. Alfonso Martínez Estévez, a close friend of Col. Arbenz who afterwards served as Private Secretary of the President and Chief of the National Agrarian Department. The masterminds of the plot reportedly included Augusto Charnaud MacDonald and the Communist firebrand, Carlos Manuel Pellecer. While we cannot be sure who made the decision to kill Arana, it was done in the interest of Arbenz, and Arévalo cannot be considered blameless, since the government failed to conduct any inquiry into the matter.[11]

The death of Arana and the successful defense of the government against the military revolt which broke out immediately afterwards led to a situation in which Col. Jacobo Arbenz was in effect the real power in Guatemala. No matter which thesis we accept, the majority view that Arbenz was the choice and favorite of President Arévalo or the minority view that Arévalo more or less reluctantly had to accept Arbenz as his successor, the fact remains that the Minister of Defense was all but certain to be the next president of Guatemala. Although the fate of the government was in doubt for several days, the combined strength of the military forces loyal to Arbenz and to the Arévalo government, with the aid of organized labor, put down the revolt by Arana's friends and assured the success of the bold gamble which had removed the number one contender for the presidency.[12] A new force was coming into control of Guatemala, an alliance of the young "school" officers of the army with the extremist leaders of organized labor. This alliance was to be forged during the presidential election and eventually led to the partnership of Arbenz and the Communists which shaped the course of Guatemala in 1953-1954.

The Minute of Silence. On the first anniversary of the death of Col. Arana the opposition organized a demonstration against the Arévalo government aimed at obtaining the President's resignation. Led by an old conservative, Manuel Cobos Batres, several hundred university students and a few business and professional men gathered in front of the National Palace at 6 p.m. on the 19th of July to observe a "minute of silence."[13] When the demonstration was repeated the following day, forces from the Communist-controlled labor unions

---

[11] For a detailed story of an eye-witness see the Guatemala City *Mundo Libre,* July 23, 1954. For other treatments see Samayoa Chinchilla, *El Quetzal No es Rojo,* pp. 125-132 and Najera Farfán, *op. cit.,* pp. 109-112. The author has also taken into account views expressed by the individuals whom he interviewed in Guatemala and Mexico City.

[12] For the course of the battle see Samayoa Chinchilla, *El Quetzal No es Rojo,* pp. 132-4 and Bush, *op. cit.,* Part Four, pp. 11-14.

[13] In addition to the daily press of Guatemala, see Theodore Draper, "The Minutemen of Guatemala" in *The Reporter,* Vol. III, No. 9 (October 24, 1950), pp. 32-5.

were on hand and a serious clash occurred; before the police finally moved in and broke it up, three persons were dead and scores injured. Since the government took no action against those responsible for the death of medical student Edgar Lempke, the students called a strike and demanded the resignation of the officials in charge of maintaining public order. The National Political Committee of the Workers organized a counter-demonstration in support of the regime and the business and professional men closed their offices in support of the striking students. The Arévalo government, fearing for its continued existence, suspended constitutional guarantees on July 25 and announced the resignation of Interior Minister César Solís. In an effort to crush the strike heavy fines were levied against businessmen who refused to open their offices.

On the 26th President Arévalo felt it necessary to hand the powers of his office over to the Chief of the Armed Forces, Major Carlos Paz Tejada, and install Lt. Col. Elfego T. Monzón as Minister of Interior. The army proved that it was still a key factor in the political game by quickly reestablishing order. Although the leaders of the opposition may have felt that the resignation of Arévalo was implied in their understanding with Paz Tejada to end the strike, the government was handed back to Arévalo as soon as normality returned.[14]

After this affair there could be little doubt that Arévalo was no longer in control of the situation. Arbenz, with the backing of the army and organized labor, was the master of Guatemala.

The Election Campaign. While Arbenz did not publicly announce his candidacy until early in 1950, the extremist political and labor leaders had decided to back his candidacy by the end of 1948.[15] Late in 1949

---

[14] For the official line of the Arévalo government on this incident see *"Los pueblos de la República contra la conspiración No. 27: indignación nacional contra la minoría de la sexta avenida. Las grandes mayorías organizadas en partidos y sindicatos y las municipalidades revolucionarias expresan su repudio. La Revolución de Octubre, el Gobierno Constitucional, el ejército y el Presidente Arévalo tienen en su favor a las masas de todo el país",* Guatemala, 1950.

[15] This decision was kept secret until after the death of Arana, but was volunteered by several of the political leaders of the period in interviews with the author. Documentary evidence shows that the leaders of the railroad workers' union met with Arbenz and endorsed his candidacy in April of 1949, and Charnaud MacDonald and Fortuny had pledged their support considerably earlier. See 8031:2347-8, eighteen SAMF leaders to Arbenz, November 13, 1950.

the unions began to organize a network of political committees to work toward his candidacy and the National Workers' Political Committee officially came out for Arbenz on February 24, 1950, a few days after the RN and PAR made their support public.

The FPL, the only revolutionary party not to back Arbenz, was split badly in the election. One group broke off to support Jorge García Granados, a distinguished statesman and "father" of the Constitution of 1945, who founded the moderate People's Party. Víctor Giordani, Arévalo's Minister of Health was named the official FPL candidate, but Manuel Galich also ran, splitting the party hopelessly. On the first day of the three-day elections, Galich withdrew in favor of Arbenz, receiving as his reward the choice position of Foreign Minister. General Miguel Ydígoras Fuentes, Director General of Roads under Ubico and Arévalo's Minister in London, carried the banner of the conservative elements.

The election was never very much in doubt. Arévalo did not publicly endorse Arbenz, but the latter's election propaganda was built around the theme of carrying on the work begun by the Arévalo government and the use of posters bearing the pictures of Arbenz and Arévalo. The electoral machinery of the government bureaucracy and the subsidized parties was put at the disposal of the Arbenz forces.[16] Under conditions such as have traditionally prevailed in Guatemala, the election would largely depend upon who could control the votes of the rural masses. The well-planned and organized campaign of the Arbenz forces with the support of the military, the government and the labor unions was bound to triumph over the relatively unorganized opposition.

The government used the July "minute of silence" riots and an attempted coup on November 5 by Col. Carlos Castillo Armas as pretexts for taking action against the leaders of the opposition and disorganizing their parties shortly before the elections. Ydígoras was forced to leave the country in July, while both he and García Granados spent much of November in hiding within the country. Although Arbenz was probably the choice of more voters than were any of the opposition candidates, nothing was left to chance. The trucks of the government were used to bring the workers of the national fincas to the polls, in many cases more than once. After the three days of voting

---

[16] See Najera Farfán, *op. cit.*, pp. 134-6; Samayoa Chinchilla, *El Quetzal No es Rojo*, pp. 138-145.

—November 10, 11 and 12—Arbenz was declared the winner with approximately 267,000 votes, followed by the conservative Ydígoras Fuentes with 74,000 and García Granados with nearly 29,000.[17] Arbenz received 86% of the illiterate vote as compared to 56% of the vote on secret ballots.[18] In the capital, where the voting was quite honest because of the large number of foreign observers, Arbenz received only 25,000 of the 58,000 ballots cast.[19] It appeared that the new president would enter office with less popular backing than Arévalo had enjoyed at the beginning of his term, but with greater support than Arévalo could command in the last years of his term. In spite of the long campaign and owing to the personalistic and often demagogic nature of Guatemalan politics, few persons knew precisely what Arbenz stood for or could accurately judge the course which his administration would follow.

---

[17] The exact figures are not reliable and differ slightly. These were taken from *El Imparcial*, December 6, 1950. Seven minor candidates shared another 40,000 votes.

[18] Silvert, *op. cit.*, p. 60.

[19] *El Imparcial*, November 14, 1950.

3

THE REVOLUTION UNDER ARBENZ:
TOWARD A NEW PATTERN OF POLITICS

On March 15, 1951, Jacobo Arbenz Guzmán became President of Guatemala.[1] Many observers expected the new government to swing away from the "radicalism" of the Arévalo period, particularly since Arbenz was both an army officer and a substantial landowner. Instead the next three years saw the emergence of a new pattern of politics, one in which the Communists played a dynamic and, in many respects, decisive role.

In addition to depicting the nature of the Arbenz regime and sketching the major developments of this crucial period, this chapter attempts to pull together the factors contributing to the success of the Communists. We shall endeavor to raise and place in proper perspective the major questions which will be explored in greater detail in the chapters which follow.

---

[1] Arévalo soon left the domestic political scene with an assignment as roving ambassador, a post with which were associated few duties and a comfortable expense allowance.

THE ARBENZ REGIME

When the new government took office, its policies and orientation were not yet clear. Publicly at least, Arbenz's attitude toward the Communists was undefined. Their work in his campaign had earned them at least official tolerance, and Fortuny, Gutiérrez and Guerra Borges were numbered among the President's inner circle of friends, advisors and confidants. Nevertheless the Communists' position was still far from secure and depended largely upon the continued good will of the President. In the next three years Communism rapidly came of age in Guatemala.

During Arbenz's first year as President, the Communists succeeded in gaining control of a unified labor movement and healing the split within their ranks which had existed since the end of 1949. Using their control of the labor movement, the Communists were able to go far towards neutralizing a series of anti-Communist demonstrations directed against the government during March of 1952, and by so doing worked themselves further into the favor of the President. The leading role which Arbenz accorded the Communists at this time in his efforts to unify the pro-government forces alienated some of the more moderate elements among the revolutionary parties, which in turn left the government even more in the hands of the extremists.

By the summer of 1952 Arbenz had decided to push ahead with agrarian reform as the keystone of his program. In this he had the backing of the Communists and those revolutionaries who had lost faith in more gradual measures and felt that it was necessary to bring about a fundamental transformation of the country's economic structure. Agrarian reform, they believed, would open the door for economic liberation, industrialization and a higher standard of living.[2]

The Communists took advantage of the hesitation of the middle class politicians to appear as the President's most reliable backers and as the champions of the peasant masses. While the "progressive" land owners who had formed the right wing of Arbenz's support had to be bludgeoned into line to give the legislation their reluctant support, the Communists furnished in Gutiérrez the leading Congressional exponent

---

[2] For the thinking of the non-Communist backers of Arbenz's program see Galich, *Por Qué Lucha Guatemala*, pp. 274-5.

of agrarian reform and could truthfully say that they had been working on the problem for almost five years. Fortuny, who was not even a member of Congress, acted as one of the floor managers for the President's agrarian bill. As many of the deputies of the revolutionary parties proved somewhat hesitant in their support, the stock of the Communists rose in Arbenz's eyes. Through their control of the labor movement they held out to him an efficient arm for the implementation of agrarian reform and mobilization of campesino support. The Communists were accepted by the President as the spokesman of the working class and peasant masses and given control of the administration of the agrarian reform program.

As a reward for their services and an acknowledgement of their strength in certain areas, the Communist leaders Fortuny and Pellecer were included on the government's coalition ticket for the January 1953 congressional elections. In protest against this sign of increased Communist influence, a number of liberals broke with the government and tried to form a "third force" in the elections. Caught between the official parties and the intransigent opposition, this new movement was stillborn. The government showed the extent of its acceptance of the Communists by granting their party full legal status just before the end of 1952.

By the beginning of 1953 the political structure of the Arbenz regime was becoming apparent. The Communists were now a full partner in the official coalition and in a position to aim at establishing their hegemony over the other parties. During the third year of Arbenz's presidency the Communist party grew rapidly in size and influence. In the government they were able to bring about Guatemalan withdrawal from the Organization of Central American States in April of 1953 and were instrumental in shaping the ultra-nationalistic policy which resulted in a defense of Communism by the Guatemalan delegation at the Caracas Conference in March 1954. In the countryside they exploited agrarian reform and the rivalry of the major government parties to become the most dynamic factor in Guatemalan politics. By the time the Arbenz regime was three years old, the Communists, through their relationship with the President, control of the labor movement, penetration of the bureaucracy and influence over the other revolutionary parties, were in a position to shape government policies and determine the course of national affairs to an extent greater than that of any Communist Party outside of the Soviet orbit.

The outstanding characteristic of Guatemalan life during 1953 was the high level of agitation centering around agrarian reform. Not only was there friction between the landowners and the campesinos with the local officials often caught in the middle, but rival groups of campesinos often met in bloody clashes over land. The activities of the parties came to center on the rural areas as each sought to build a mass base and its own campesino organizations. Politicians rushed through the countryside in their government-owned jeeps while the National Confederation of Campesinos (CNCG) headed by Leonardo Castillo Flores became the largest organization Guatemala had ever seen. The long-neglected rural population was being drawn into politics and slowly brought into the mainstream of national life.

In this upheaval the Communists were able to reap proportionately greater benefits than any of the other parties. The increasing dissension within the official parties and the bitter rivalry between the two largest (the PAR and the PRG) played into the hands of the Communists, who achieved a strategic balance of power position within the Arbenz coalition. As well as benefiting through the receipt of an increasing share of the President's trust and confidence, the Communists were able to make inroads into the new generation which was beginning to enter political life. To many of the young left-wing nationalists, the Communists seemed preferable to the eternally quarrelling, thoroughly opportunistic and often corrupt leaders of the other revolutionary parties. Even the PRG, which like the Communists was a young party on the upgrade, was torn by internal dissension in late 1953. Only the Communists escaped without a single public scandal.

As 1954 opened, the Communists were extending their influence in the countryside through exploitation of agrarian reform and had gained virtual control of the rich agricultural Department of Escuintla. There Communist Deputy Pellecer was aided by Manuel Sánchez as head of the labor organizations and Gabriel Camey as Mayor of Escuintla. In addition, the labor inspectors, agrarian inspectors, and campesino organizations in that Department were all controlled by the Communists. Even as powerful a person as the Chief of the National Agrarian Department (DAN), Major Alfonso Martínez, found it virtually impossible to curb the illegal seizures of land which were being encouraged by Pellecer as part of the Communist campaign to foment class struggle and to appear to the peasants as their champion and defender. In other Departments such as Chimaltenango and Chiquimula the Communists were also building up considerable strength, but they had not yet had an opportunity to reach the more remote Departments with an intensive propaganda, recruitment and organizational drive.

Most indications point to the fact that the Communists were counting upon three more years under the protection and sponsorship of Arbenz in order to build a mass base throughout the country. Their chief concern would be to find a successor who would be as favorably disposed towards Communism as Arbenz and at least as dependent upon their aid and support. Their strategy and tactics in 1956 and after would have necessarily depended upon the prospects of presidential succession. In the meantime they concentrated upon exploiting their favorable situation.

THE PATTERN OF POLITICS UNDER ARBENZ

The leadership of the Arbenz regime was drawn chiefly from the ranks of organized labor, the revolutionary parties, and the young army officers who had gathered around Arbenz during his years as Arévalo's Minister of Defense. During 1953 and 1954 the leaders of the labor and peasant organizations came to have increasing influence, primarily at the expense of the military and the moderate politicians. That youth was the outstanding characteristic of the political leadership of the Arbenz regime is apparent from the fact that the median age of the 1953 Congress was only 35.

The mushrooming bureaucracy, drawn exclusively from the official parties, joined organized labor and the army as the three main props of the regime. In opposition were the landowners, the business community, most of the urban middle class and the Catholic Church. The government was making considerable progress in winning the support of the rural masses, who had previously voted for the candidates favored by their employers or landlords. The General Confederation of Workers (CGTG) and the National Campesino Confederation (CNCG), rather than the parties, proved to be the most efficient instruments for bringing the rural masses into the national life and developing them into an effective political force. The first of these was completely controlled by the Communists; the second was subject to increasing Communist influence.

The Communist Party, the CGTG and the CNCG were three of the five groups which made up the government coalition in 1954. (This is discounting the *Partido Renovación Nacional* which was clearly on its last legs and without significant support.) The others were Revolutionary Action Party (PAR), a large amorphous entity, weakened by dissension and opportunism, and the Party of the Guatemalan Revolution (PRG), smaller but growing and less subject than the PAR to the ravages of internal strife. Compared to Communists, both of these parties suffered from the lack of a definite program or ideological underpinning, a shortage of effective leadership, weak discipline, and the absence of internal cohesion. Above all they dissipated their energies in a struggle over the spoils of political victory. The PAR was increasingly subject to Communist influence, while the PRG contained an influential group of Communists and sympathizers who prevented it from developing into a rival of the Communist party. In the next few pages we will take a closer look at the extremely advantageous position which the Communists held within the Arbenz regime.

Labor. Under Arévalo the labor unions had become an important political force and constituted a major source of organized support for the government. During the Arbenz regime organized labor became far more important politically than in the preceding administration. In the first place the labor movement was considerably stronger and more united than it had been in the earlier period. At its peak in 1954 the CGTG claimed over 100,000 members, while its agrarian counterpart, the CNCG, boasted of a membership more than twice as large. These allied organizations contained at least one-fourth of the adult male population of the country, and their cooperation was essential for the success of the government's economic policies.

In addition, both the personal inclinations of the President and the political situation dictated a larger role for labor in the political pattern of the new regime. As the moderate elements wavered in their support for the government and the opposition gathered strength, the labor and campesino organizations became its chief support. Since the Communists controlled the labor movement, they necessarily became increasingly prominent in the government and ranked high among the President's advisors.

Through the unions the Communists won the confidence of the workers, first on labor and economic matters, then in politics. Through their control of organized labor the Communists were able to exert influence over the government and the revolutionary parties. In short, control of the labor movement gave the Communists a lever in the political process and put them in a position to offer Arbenz readily mobilized popular support. When the President faltered and hesitated to take a step favored by the Communists, they would initiate a stream of messages or organize demonstrations which would make it appear that the masses supported the move and were behind the President. In addition to gratifying Arbenz, these manifestations of support helped convince him that the Communist leaders were the most reliable barometers of popular sentiment. Once accepted by the President as the spokesman for the working class, the Communists strove to make themselves appear indispensable in his eyes.

The President. Perhaps the most distinctive characteristic of the Arbenz regime was the close relationship between the Communists and the President. The favor of the Presidency gave the Communists access to the seat of political power, control of certain key agencies and programs, a chance to shape government policies and a free field for their propaganda. In addition it kept the other parties from attempting to isolate the Communists. Lacking presidential approval, no effort to freeze out the Communists had any real chance of success. This was particularly obvious in the summer of 1951 when a number of Guatemalan politicians led by Augusto Charnaud MacDonald felt that Arbenz would back a revolutionary party free from Communist control. By October it was apparent that the President did not approve of this move, and the Socialist Party fell into line with the other official parties. At the same time the entire weight of the government was placed on the side of the pro-Communist wing of the National Renovation Party, which was engaged in a dispute with the non-Communist forces within the party. A similar situation developed within the important railroad union (SAMF). The knowledge that Arbenz favored the pro-Communist groups made some doubtful workers vote for them. The fear that Arbenz would not allow anti-Communists to take power in the union if elected, had a similar effect. Through his financial subsidization of the government parties, Arbenz was able to exert considerable control over their policies. In general, once the Communists could sell Arbenz on a policy, they could be confident that the other parties would fall into line.

Revolutionary Parties. During the Arévalo administration the official parties had become increasingly interested in patronage and the spoils of political victory. As they lost their first bloom of revolutionary fervor, opportunism quickly invaded the ranks of the young revolutionaries. The scarcity of economic opportunities for the middle class in an underdeveloped country such as Guatemala caused the professional and salaried classes to put a premium upon political office and the opportunity to exploit positions in the government.[Since there were few jobs which offered comparable prestige, status and opportunity for economic betterment, once in office the bureaucrats and politicians concentrated upon the task of perpetuating themselves in power.] Under the Arbenz regime this situation became more acute than ever and was combined with increasing graft and official corruption.

The concentration of the revolutionary politicians upon the spoils of office and outward trappings of political power afforded the Communists several opportunities which they were not slow in exploiting. In the first place, they appeared less self-seeking than the other politicians and were entrusted with the administration of such critical programs as agrarian reform and control of the government propaganda machinery. The internal dissension which was endemic in the PAR and RN and beginning to make itself felt in the PRG caused the disciplined Communist Party to appear in a relatively favorable light as an alternative for the generation just entering Guatemalan politics. The bitter rivalry between the PAR and the PRG enabled the Communists to assume a balance of power position within the government coalition. The large but increasingly decrepit PAR came to lean heavily upon the Communists for support against the pretentions of the younger and more dynamic PRG and had to pay the Communists' price for this aid. As a counter-measure the PRG leadership in 1954 attempted to woo the Communists away from their tacit alliance with the PAR by offering them a potentially more advantageous relationship.

The Army. The makers of the Constitution of 1945 had hoped to convert the army into an "apolitical, essentially professional, obedient and non-deliberative" body. The Arévalo government had attempted to democratize the army by drawing the officers from the lower middle class and had weeded out the supporters of Arana after the 1949 revolt. The rank and file of the army was drawn from the rural Indian population and "educated" by the government towards "continually closer identification with popular causes and the patriotic objectives of the October Revolution."[3]

During the Arbenz regime these measures were supplemented by a policy of favors designed to buy or insure the loyalty of the officer corps. Increased pay, tax exempt imported goods, easy credit and many other benefits were designed to keep the bulk of the officers happy and unreceptive to proposals to overthrow the regime. Those officers whose political views were most "progressive" were rewarded with good government jobs. In 1954 the President of Congress and seven other deputies, the Chief of the National Agrarian Department (DAN), the Director General of Highways and all the twenty-two Departmental Governors were army officers. Lt. Col. Carlos Aldana Sandoval served as Minister of Communications and Public Works in Arbenz's cabinet, and Major Carlos Paz Tejada held various high government posts. Even as staunch a non-Communist as Col. Elfego Monzón was kept by Arbenz as Minister without Portfolio to satisfy the more conservative officers that this was no radical government.

As will be shown in the epilogue, even these measures were not enough to guarantee to complete loyalty to the officer corps in the final crisis. Nevertheless the Arbenz regime throughout most of its existence could count upon an army which was at worst neutral and in most cases favorably disposed toward the government. The attitude of the army was typified by Col. Carlos Enrique Díaz, who as Chief of the Armed Forces held the same position with respect to Arbenz as Arana had with Arévalo. While Arana had constantly posed a threat to the President and had been almost his equal in power, Díaz was apparently willing to leave politics to the President and to assume a role as a loyal subordinate.

THE PATTERN OF COMMUNIST OPERATIONS

The outstanding characteristic of the Guatemalan experience was the ability of a handful of Communists within the span of a single decade to gain a position of influence and control in the political

---

[3] Silvert, *op. cit.*, p. 30, taken from Arbenz's March 1953 report to the Congress.

process of the country and to imbed themselves in the fabric of Guatemalan national life. During the four years from May 1950 to May 1954 alone the Communist Party in Guatemala grew from a small clandestine nucleus of a few dozen labor leaders and intellectuals to a well-organized national party which could boast of nearly 4000 members

The Guatemalan experience raises doubts as to the universal validity of certain widely-circulated generalizations concerning the lack of receptivity to Communism on the part of Latin Americans and the relatively low vulnerability of Latin American society to Communist penetration. It has been argued, in the not too distant past, that the low level of industrialization, the strength of Catholicism, the stubborn individualism of the Latin American, and the existence of a large Indian population clinging to their traditional way of life, particularly when backed up by the proximity of the United States, would serve as an effective bar to the growth of Communist influence. This should have been particularly true in the case of a small "banana republic" such as Guatemala. Why then did the Communists become so influential in Guatemala during the early 1950's? In the pages which follow we shall attempt to discuss the conditions which afforded them an opportunity to gain a hearing. A close examination of the anatomy of the political process through which the Communists attained a position of influence and the details of Communist operations will be left for later chapters.

The why of Communist success is closely linked to the question of who were susceptible to the appeals of Communism and what these appeals were.[4] In general Communism in Guatemala thrived upon "new" groups which were misfits in the traditional order. Among these groups, which included the lower-middle class intellectuals, the urban proletariat and the "mobile" rural workers, the demand for a better way of life took on increasing strength. The Communists rode with this

---

[4] On this subject see United States Department of State, External Research Paper No. 116, *A Study of Receptivity to Communism in Rural Guatemala* by Stokes Newbold (pseudonym); Gabriel Almond's *Appeals of Communism,* Princeton, 1954; and Lucian W. Pye, *Guerrilla Communism in Malaya,* Princeton, 1956. A slightly refined version of Newbold's study can be found in "Receptivity to Communist Fomented Agitation in Rural Guatemala," *Economic Development and Cultural Change,* Vol. V, No. 4 (July, 1957), pp. 338-61.

demand for change and gave it direction, enjoying greater success than those who tried to stem the tide. One of the secrets of their success was the fact that Communism offered different things to different people.

The first progress made by the Communists in Guatemala was among the young lower-middle class intellectuals, perhaps the sector of society most frustrated by the traditional social order. These ex-students who eked out a living through part-time teaching, journalism, and office work were a marginal group in Guatemalan society. In addition to finding in Communism a key for understanding the perplexities of society and a blueprint for social change, these young intellectuals found some degree of security and recognition in the party. Educated far above their social status, they had previously felt thwarted by the established order. The party offered them a chance to gain recognition commensurate with their own estimates of their abilities.

The more mobile ladino urban workers were the second area of Communist strength. The working class in Guatemala was relatively unsophisticated and free from previous political commitments. While attempting to raise Communists to positions of leadership in the labor movement, the Communists also sought to identify and win over those workers with leadership potential. The Communists made use of the prestige of Gutiérrez in recruiting workers to the party and were quite successful with their claims that Communism was *the* political expression for the working class throughout the world. Among the working class the greatest susceptibility to Communism was shown by the so-called "uprooted." These individuals had often, in leaving their native villages to work on the fincas or in the factories, given up a whole way of life in return for an elusive promise of material betterment. The new life was not usually as satisfying as the old, since there was a large element of uncertainty which was often compounded with an inability to understand the new factors with which they were involved.

The "mobile" ladinos and ladinoized Indians in the rural areas were the third major social group to prove susceptible to the appeals of Communism. These individuals, who were found in the greatest numbers on the Pacific slope and south coast (particularly the departments of Escuintla, Retalhuleu, and Santa Rosa), were free of long-standing social relationships and traditional responsibilities. Working largely for wages on the coffee fincas or banana plantations, they constituted the rural proletariat of Guatemala.[5] For them as for the urban workers, capitalism was represented by their reactionary employers or foreign enterprises such as the United Fruit Company (UFCO) or International Railways of Central America (IRCA), corporations which appeared to them as huge voracious monopolies.[6]

These mobile wage laborers were only a relatively small minority of the total rural population. Many other ladinos could be reached by the Communists through the opportunities which the party afforded them for political activity and advancement. Such individuals often furnished the local leadership for the PGT in rural communities.

The bulk of the Indian population who clung to their traditional way of life and lived in their self-contained communities were relatively difficult for the Communists to contact and impervious to their appeals. Nevertheless many Indians were being affected, however slightly, by the social and economic programs of the government and could be reached through the promise of land. Even the draft served as a means of acculturation by plucking the Indian youth from their traditional way of life and teaching them at least to read, write, and wear shoes. After this taste of ladino life, these individuals found it difficult if not impossible to fit back into the traditional way of life of their village and were at least somewhat receptive to the appeals and propaganda of the Communists. Under the Arbenz regime their susceptibility was increased by the "civic instruction" which they received while in the army and which consisted of indoctrination in the aspirations of the Revolution.

The Communists were able to use their control over the machinery of agrarian reform to win recruits in the rural areas.[7] Many of these were Indians who were drawn to the party only by the promise of land

---

[5] See Richard F. Behrendt's "The Uprooted: A Guatemalan Sketch," *New Mexican Quarterly Review*, Vol. XIX, No. 1, (Spring, 1949), pp. 25-31. Reprinted in Olen E. Leonard and Charles P. Loomis (eds.), *Readings in Latin American Social Organizations and Institutions*, Michigan State College Press, 1953, pp. 281-3.

[6] Guatemala had no large-scale manufacturing enterprises and most Guatemalans could not conceive of modern capitalism as practiced in the United States or Western Europe.

[7] On Communist exploitation of land reform see Nathan L. Whetten's "Land Reform in a Modern World," *Rural Sociology*, Vol. XIX, No. 4 (December, 1954), pp. 329-34.

of their own. Nevertheless the Communists felt that in time they could be sufficiently indoctrinated and satisfactorily assimilated into the party. In the meantime they were essential to the PGT's plans to become a mass party and to expand Communist influence through electoral channels in so far as possible. (Since discontent over agrarian problems was the root of the vulnerability of the rural society to Communism, it is necessary for us to take a closer look at the agrarian problem in Guatemala. This will be done in Chapter VII.)

The workers and campesinos were not informed on international affairs nor were they particularly interested in the working of international Communism or the realities of life behind the Iron Curtain. What they were concerned with was improving their day-to-day life. In this respect they saw that the Communists showed great interest in their problems and offered what seemed a reasonable program for solving them. It was useless to tell these people that they would lose their freedom and basic liberties under Communism, since they felt they had none to lose. Nor could they be reached by the argument that their standard of living would suffer, since it was already extremely depressed. They were not concerned with Communism in the abstract nearly as much as with the individual Communists who professed to be their champions and protectors. The endorsement which the Communists received from prominent intellectuals and political leaders made it even more difficult for many Guatemalans to regard the PGT as part of an international conspiracy.

A sore spot in the Guatemalan situation which was exploited by the Communists and helped pave the way for their success was "Yankee imperialism" as personified by the United Fruit Company. Resentment toward *la Frutera* and other United States companies operating in Guatemala contributed towards making the extreme nationalists susceptible to Communist propaganda. Under the "cold war" situation which prevailed on the international scene, hostility towards the United States was perhaps more important to the Communist cause than the development of pro-Soviet sentiment. By fanning the latent hostility into flames, the Communists created a mental and emotional climate in which their Leninist explanation of imperialism would be accepted by many nationalists. In addition to creating anti-Yankee and anti-capitalist sentiment, the Communists used this as a basis for their "peace" campaign which pictured the "imperialist" United States as economically driven to plunge the world into war. The Communists were able to convince many Guatemalan nationalists that the "national liberation" of Guatemala demanded a reorientation of their trade away from the United States and toward the Soviet bloc.

For many Guatemalans the United Fruit Company was the United States. Together with International Railways of Central America, in which it was the major stockholder, *la Frutera* appeared in the eyes of the Guatemalan nationalists to have a stranglehold on the nation's economy.[8] While many things can and have been said in defense of UFCO's actions, what is important to an understanding of events in Guatemala is not necessarily the truth, but how the Guatemalans viewed it. For it was upon their often biased perception that the Guatemalans based their actions. With the help of extreme nationalist and Communist agitators, the Guatemalan workers and many intellectuals remembered the numerous items on the debit side of the ledger. In the past, UFCO and its sister companies had bribed politicians, pressured governments and intimidated opponents to gain extremely favorable concessions. To the Guatemalans it appeared that their country was being mercilessly exploited by foreign interests which took out huge profits without making any significant contribution to the nation's welfare. In the eyes of many Guatemalans, the foreign corporations had to pay for their past crimes and for the years in which they had operated hand-in-hand with the Estrada Cabrera and Ubico dictatorships to exploit the Guatemalan people.

The psychological factor must be taken into account. UFCO controlled hundreds of square miles in their Bananera and Tiquisate holdings and had virtually acted as the government on these lands. Perhaps 40,000 Guatemalans were directly or indirectly dependent upon the company for their sustenance. The "great white fleet" of the UFCO virtually monopolized the shipping of Guatemala. United Fruit

---

[8] For the Guatemalan point of view on United States corporations in Guatemala see Alfonso Bauer Paíz's *Cómo Opera el Capital Yanqui en Centroamérica (El Caso de Guatemala)*, Mexico, 1956; Oscar de León Aragón's *Los contratos de la United Fruit Company y las Compañías Muelleras en Guatemala,* Guatemala, 1950; or any of the works by Guatemalan exiles previously cited. In English see Charles D. Kepner Jr.'s *Social Aspects of the Banana Industry,* New York, Columbia University Press, Studies in History, Economics and Public Law, No. 414, 1936. See also Charles D. Kepner, Jr. and J. H. Soothill's *El imperio del banano,* Mexico, 1949.

and the railroad company which was its subsidiary not only monopolized the railroad system of the country, but also controlled and administered the port facilities. A subsidiary of *la Frutera* controlled much of the telegraphic communications within the country and with the outside. It is not difficult to see how Guatemalan nationalists could accept the Communists' claim that their country was economically a captive of the United States corporations. From anti-imperialism it was but a short step to anti-Yankee and anti-capitalist sentiments.

Even the actions and attitudes of their opponents played into the hands of the Communists. Organized anti-Communism was essentially negative, too closely linked to retrograde forces to be effective, and often self-defeating. By calling social security, the labor code, and agrarian reform Communist-inspired, the anti-Communists actually enhanced the prestige of the Communists among the workers and facilitated their effort to identify themselves as the champions of popular demands. As the anti-Communist movement was dominated by the opponents of social reform, it could not make common cause with the moderate and centrist elements who supported the revolution, but were opposed to the growth of Communist influence. As a result Guatemala never developed any opposition party which was willing to face up to the facts of political and economic life, accept change and reform as legitimate, and devote its efforts to providing more satisfactory solutions to the nation's pressing problems than those offered by the Communists and their allies.[9]

The inadequacy of anti-Communism from the right and center was only part of the picture. No native revolutionary movement or ideological force capable of rivaling Communism developed, nor was there any effective opposition from an advanced left-wing party. To a considerable extent the Communists were able to play upon the political ignorance, inexperience and preoccupation of the other revolutionary parties. For a number of reasons the majority of the leaders of the Arévalo and Arbenz regimes were relatively naive regarding international affairs and unconcerned with, if not unaware of, the basic differences between international Communism and the indigenous national revolutionary movements. No major political leaders realized

---

[9] See Najera Farfán, *op. cit.*, p. 93, for a trenchant criticism by an anti-Communist liberal of the organized opposition to the Arbenz regime. Silvert, *op. cit.*, p. 55 is useful for a similar criticism by an objective scholar.

the necessity of keeping the revolution to a purely Guatemalan course. Those groups which wished to curb Communist influence within the regime, but had no desire to overthrow the elected government, were caught on the horns of a dilemma. Loyal to the principles and aims, however vague and nebulous, of the Revolution of 1944, these moderates could not join hands with the self-styled anti-Communists who insisted upon denouncing everyone and everything concerning the government or organized labor as Communist. Nor could they find sufficient support within the government, organized labor, and the revolutionary parties to effectively contain Communist growth. Many resolved their ambivalent feelings by rationalizing that the regime needed Communist support to avoid overthrow by the intransigent opposition and the subsequent destruction of all the gains made since 1944. Others followed the negative policy of dissociating themselves from the regime and withdrawing to the margin of the political arena.

The very smallness of Guatemala and of its politically active population was an advantage for the Communists. In many cases they were related to or closely connected with leading political and governmental figures. The Communists and other revolutionary politicians had often been classmates through secondary school, the University and even law school. In addition they had worked closely together in the overthrow of Ubico and the months which followed. During the years before the Communists came into the open, their work within the revolutionary parties, the labor movement and the Arévalo government led to the development of ties which were strong enough to serve as the basis for cooperation even after the Communist Party made its public appearance.

Even the timing of events in Guatemala aided the Communists. They started out as a new movement at the time when Communist influence was at its peak throughout Latin America and while there was still considerable residual sympathy toward the U.S.S.R. carried over from its role in World War II. (By the time the cold war had dissipated this sympathy in many countries, the Guatemalan Communists had already gotten their roots down.) In the end it proved relatively easy for the Communists to gain acceptance as part of the revolutionary movement and difficult for their opponents to picture them as instruments of the international Communist movement.

In Guatemala nationalism was not a force opposed to Communism, but was instead effectively exploited by the Communists. As Guatemalan nationalism generally took the form of anti-imperialism, the Communists found a ready audience for their claim that the foreign imperialists and reactionary landowners were at the bottom of the nation's social, economic and political ills. The nationalists accepted the Communists as fellow revolutionaries and accepted the thesis that Communism must be tolerated in the name of democracy and anti-imperialism. Since the Communists disclaimed any intention to push for the immediate establishment of socialism, most of the nationalists saw no reason why they should not join forces with them in the struggle to throw off the imperialist yoke and liquidate the remnants of feudalism. The evils of imperialism they had seen at first hand, the nationalists argued, while the evils of Communism were only scare stories told by the reactionaries (who had no first-hand knowledge) and the servants of the United States.

The Communists assiduously cultivated the belief in the "coincidence" of their interests and those of the revolutionary parties and set out to appear more nationalist than the nationalists. In the meantime they worked diligently to strengthen their position in anticipation of the day the divergency of their aims and the interest of the nationalists would become apparent. The Communists hoped to be able to ride the wave of nationalism and even direct it into channels which would lead to the eventual establishment of a Communist state. To accomplish this they were working to win the workers and campesino masses away from the bourgeois parties and form them into an effective political instrument under Communist leadership.

As this would be a long process and a rupture with the bourgeois parties was to be avoided if at all possible, the Communists hoped in the meantime to exploit the anti-imperialist sentiment of the nationalists and turn it against capitalism and the United States. An intensification of the pace of revolutionary changes and emphasis upon the elements of class struggle present or latent in the Guatemalan situation was designed as the second prong of a campaign to make Marxism appear as the most adequate means for analyzing developments in Guatemala.

At a time when most of the nationalists and revolutionaries were surer of what they were against than what they were for, the Communists had the advantage of appearing to be the only ones who had a clear idea of what they wanted, where they were going and how they intended to get there. With the anti-Communists appearing as reactionaries, the moderates seemingly vacillating and opportunistic, and the other revolutionaries hesitant and confused, the Communists were the most purposeful political force. As time went on, many of the exuberant young revolutionaries became impatient with the aimlessness and bickering of the other parties and were attracted by the Communists' sense of mission. Conditions in the relatively disorganized Guatemalan society appeared tailor-made for the Communists who possessed a systematic doctrine and approach to political action which the other parties lacked. To an increasing number of Guatemalans under the Arbenz regime, the Communist boast of riding the wave of the future appeared to have some substance and considerable appeal.

Summary. The Guatemalan Communists successfully identified themselves with the aspirations and demand for change unleashed by an indigenous social revolution. In their rapid rise toward power they rode the swelling tide of nationalism and took advantage of the unrest among the urban workers and intellectuals. Once accepted as part of the national revolutionary movement, they spoke out loudly and unceasingly as the self-proclaimed champions of the masses. By dint of long hours and persistent work the Communists were able to convince large segments of classes which previously had not been politically active that the PGT program best defended their interests. At the same time the Communists strove to organize the masses so that they could play an effective role in national politics under Communist direction.

From the very beginning they sought to gain control of the labor movement and to obtain positions of influence in the fields of education, public information and social services. Once in a position to mold public opinion and to make an effective entrance into national politics, the Communists were able to exploit the opportunities afforded them by the retarded nature of Guatemalan political development. Possessing both a revolutionary theory and a program of action, as well as superior organization and discipline, the Communists were at a considerable advantage over both their rivals and opponents.

The dictatorship had left the country barren of experienced political talent and had prevented the effective organization of the various groups and interests within Guatemalan society. Hence the Communists did not have to defeat any well organized or experienced competition. The failure of a strong native social revolutionary movement to develop led many of the idealistic revolutionary youth to turn to Communism as a cause to serve and an outlet for their emotions and energies. Through superior organization and discipline the Communists made it appear difficult to oppose them successfully and politically profitable to collaborate with them.

Thus for a variety of reasons the Communists were able to seize the leadership of a national social revolution. If one factor played a more crucial role in the Communist success than any other, it was the support of the President. From Arévalo they had received toleration during the critical period when it would have been possible for the President to undermine them or crush them with ease. Under Arbenz toleration turned to something more.[10] The Communists led in supporting social and economic reform at the time when the other politicians hesitated. This, in addition to the fact that they had amassed more information on national and local problems than had anyone else, led the President to rely upon them for advice and assistance. In return, Arbenz allowed them a freedom of action which added greatly to their effectiveness. Acceptance and endorsement by the President opened many new doors to the Communists.

Thus, while the Communist position in Guatemala depended to a considerable extent upon the good will of the President and the neutrality of the armed forces, the party had risen seemingly from nowhere to a position of prominence and influence in a remarkably short space of time.

The remainder of this study is devoted to an examination of the most important facets of Communist operations in Guatemala and the analysis of the techniques employed in establishing control over certain spheres of national life. The study of the development and program of the Communist Party (Chapter IV) and of its structure and operations (Chapter V) furnishes a picture of the spinal column of the Communist movement. The story of Communist operations among the workers (Chapter VI) and the campesinos (Chapter VII), penetration of the government (Chapter VIII), relations with the other parties (Chapter IX), and use of front groups (Chapter X) rounds out the

---

[10] For a detailed discussion of the relationship between Arbenz and the Communists see the first portion of this chapter and Chapter VIII.

portrayal of the sources of Communist influence and strength. In order to place Guatemalan developments in perspective and to see the complete pattern of Communist operations, the international aspects of the problem are discussed (Chapter XI). Finally an attempt must be made to analyze the collapse of the Arbenz regime (Epilogue). It is hoped that the reader will be able to find the answers to most of the significant questions concerning Communism in Guatemala and to gain an understanding of the nature of the Arbenz regime. If in addition these pages furnish some insight into the workings of Guatemalan politics or of Communist operations in general, so much the better.

4

THE COMMUNIST PARTY IN GUATEMALA: DEVELOPMENT AND PROGRAM

Although the Communist Party was the nerve center of the Communist movement in Guatemala, it did not come into the open during the six years of Arévalo's government and enjoyed only eighteen months of full legality. From 1944 until 1950 Communism lived within the labor movement and in small study groups. Not until September 1947 was a clandestine organization formed which can be considered as the nucleus of a Communist Party. When the Communist Party held its first Congress in September 1949, it probably had fewer than forty members. Four years later, the figure was nearer four thousand. Aside from the fact that Communism predated a Communist Party in Guatemala, even after the party came out into the open it preferred to conduct many of its activities through a facade provided by the labor movement and the so-called mass organizations.[1] Only after 1950 did the active participation of the Guatemalan Communist Party in the Arbenz government push its activities into the public eye. Fortunately for us,

---

[1] See Chapters VI, VII and X.

material from the files of the party and its leaders makes it possible to recreate the picture of Communist Party operations even during its clandestine period.

THE EARLY YEARS: CLANDESTINE OPERATIONS

The shortlived Communist movement of the 1920's had little relation to the development of Communism in the years after the Revolution of 1944. After the fall of the dictator Estrada Cabrera in 1920, an embryonic trade union movement developed, and with it a Communist group known as the *Unificación Obrera Socialista*.[2] Soon after coming to power in 1932, Ubico arrested seventy-six radical leaders whom he accused of being Communists and put ten to death. A few, including Antonio Obando Sánchez, Miguel Mármol and Alfredo Pellecer, survived prison and played a secondary role in the post-1944 Communist movement.

Communism in the Early Years of the Revolution. Among the many Guatemalans who came back from exile in 1944 there were a handful who had been active in the Communist movements of the countries where they had spent their exile. The thought of most of these radicals was a mixture of nationalism and Marxism which fell short of militant Communism of the variety shown by the Fortuny group a few years later. These Marxists such as Alfonso Solórzano and Roberto Alvarado Fuentes eventually provided much of the leadership for the radical wings of the bourgeois parties. Soon after the revolution they joined with Communist exiles from the neighboring countries who sought a haven in Guatemala and a number of the more radical students and teachers to consider forming a Communist Party. However, when President Arévalo served notice that, in spite of his tolerance of Communists, he would not permit an organized Communist Party, it was decided to seek a home in the revolutionary parties and among the labor unions. The future leaders of the Communist Party gathered in Marxist study groups while they worked their way up toward positions of leadership in the parties, labor movement and the government.[3]

---

[2] For a more detailed treatment of Communism in Guatemala in these years see Robert J. Alexander's *Communism in Latin America,* Rutgers University Press, 1957, pp. 350-353.

[3] This development is closely examined in the Chapters VI, VIII, IX and X.

Meanwhile the progress of the Revolution brought about changes in the political environment which were favorable to the further development of Communism.

Vanguardia Democrática Guatemalteca (VDG). On September 28, 1947, a small group of lower middle class intellectuals and part-time labor leaders founded a clandestine Communist organization known as the Guatemalan Democratic Vanguard.[4] Those whose membership in this secret group can be established include Fortuny, Gutiérrez, Antonio Sierra González, José Luis Ramos, Bernardo Alvarado Monzón, Francisco Hernández, Pedro Fernández, Antonio Ardón, Carlos René Valle, Humberto Ortíz, Rogelio López, Carlos Manuel Pellecer, José Alberto Cardoza, Mario Silva Jonama, Alfredo Guerra Borges and Virgilio Guerra.[5] The very existence of this group was unknown to most Guatemalans until near the end of the Arévalo administration, since under the leadership of Fortuny and Gutiérrez, the VDG members remained active in the PAR and the labor movement. Aside from the fact that President Arévalo was unwilling to have an overt Communist Party operating in Guatemala, the Communists felt that conditions were not yet ripe for them to come into the open. They did not wish to make Communism an issue in Guatemalan politics until they had strengthened their position by consolidating their control over the labor movement. While striving to establish links with the masses and to create a climate of acceptance, the handful of Communist leaders made a bid to take over control of the PAR, a move which was thwarted at its March 1949 Convention.[6]

By the middle of 1949, the "labor" faction within the VDG headed by Gutiérrez was arguing that the Communists must come into the open and provide the working class with an opportunity to "act under their own banners." Convinced that the PAR was essentially a "bourgeois" party in which the interests of the workers were subordinated to

---

[4] In a press interview on July 1, 1951, José Manuel Fortuny set this as the date on which he and other Communists who were members of PAR organized a secret Communist Party. The PGT officially dates its anniversaries from the First Congress of the Guatemalan Communist Party held on September 28, 1949, the second anniversary of the founding of the VDG.

[5] 8019:376, V. M. Gutiérrez to Camaradas del Comité Central de la VDG, September 19, 1949; also Document 973: José Manuel Fortuny and ten companions to Secretary General of the Partido Acción Revolucionaria, May 20, 1950; 8019:136.

[6] See Chapter IX, pp. 225-26.

other considerations, Gutiérrez resigned from the Political Commission of that party.[7] The decision of the new PAR leadership not to send a delegate to the Continental Peace Congress in Mexico soon led Gutiérrez to sever all connections with that party.[8]

All had not been going smoothly between Gutiérrez and Fortuny. Gutiérrez's action in leaving the PAR brought the smoldering ideological and personal disagreements to a head. In addition to the sharp differences over strategy and tactics, Gutiérrez felt that several of his associates had been unfairly treated by the VDG leadership dominated by Fortuny.[9] On September 19 Gutiérrez resigned from the Central Committee of the VDG.[10] Gutiérrez now held that Matilde Elena López, Miguel Angel Valladares, Medardo Mejía and other foreign Communists had followed the correct line in refusing to join the PAR and accused Fortuny of attacking them unjustly.[11] Gutiérrez felt that the Communists had to emerge from beneath "the protective shadow of a party which cannot become exactly what we desired." The differences between Gutiérrez and the Fortuny clique stemmed chiefly from the former's insistence upon the political independence of the working class. In Gutiérrez's eyes this meant their own independent party led by "authentic workers." [12] Finally Gutiérrez and his followers felt that Fortuny was obstructing their work toward agrarian reform and that this conflicted with the Communists' duty to take the lead in implementing the aspirations of the working class. They demanded that major policy matters be discussed openly among the unions rather than settled within the closed circle of the VDG.

---

[7] 8019:367, V. M. Gutiérrez to Roberto Alvarado Fuentes, March 17, 1949.

[8] 8019:373, V. M. Gutiérrez to Roberto Alvarado Fuentes, September 1, 1949.

[9] 8019:368, V. M. Gutiérrez to Compañeros de V.D.G., November 7, 1949.

[10] 8019:376, V. M. Gutiérrez to José Manuel Fortuny, Antonio Sierra González, José Luis Ramos, Bernardo Alvarado Monzón, Francisco Hernández and Pedro Fernández, September 19, 1949.

[11] 8019:377-8, Algunas consideraciones críticas para la organización.

[12] *Ibid.* Gutiérrez's key statements were "Political alliances of democratic unity or popular fronts are always made with the working class playing its independent role without being incrusted or encysted in any middle class party. . . . I don't believe that it is too much to insist that the direction of our movement ought to be in the hands of authentic workers, without compromises with other social classes and the government, since this is the best guarantee that it will prosper and fight most consistently in favor of the interests of the working class."

Dissension within the VDG had reached a point where a showdown was necessary. In addition to Gutiérrez's mistrust of the bourgeois politicians and fear that the interests of the working class would be sacrificed to political ends, changes had occurred in the political climate which necessitated a reconsideration of goals and tactics. The Communists had received a setback at the PAR convention in March; in May Fortuny had gone to Moscow for the first of his extended stays; the assassination of Arana in July had made the election of Arbenz a probability. Against this background the First Congress of the *Partido Comunista de Guatemala* was held on September 28, 1949, with Gutiérrez delivering the opening address.[13]

In dealing with the situation of the Communist Party and the ways in which to improve its political position, Gutiérrez stressed the failure to capture the PAR and convert it into a Communist Party. Now, in addition, the VDG leadership was apparently passing up the opportunity to withdraw from the PAR and get a new start through Labor's Political Action Committee, "whose direction is completely in the hands of our comrades." Calling upon the writings of Lenin and Stalin for support, Gutiérrez argued at length for the formation of an essentially working class Communist Party.

The most serious charge brought by Gutiérrez was that, since returning from Moscow, Fortuny had followed a policy of "converting the party into a brake upon popular aspirations" by obstructing efforts in favor of agrarian reform.[14] Before Fortuny went to Russia, the party had adopted the line of the XVII Congress of the Communist Party of the USSR on agrarian reform. Thinking that they had the approval of the party, Gutiérrez, with the help of Pellecer, had published studies of agrarian reform in the Peoples' Republics, and the National Committee for Labor Unity (CNUS) had prepared a draft of a law for Guatemala. Now Fortuny returned with the dictum that agrarian reform was not an approved policy for semi-colonial countries such as Guatemala at that time. Against this, Gutiérrez's appeal to the words of Stalin's *History of the Communist Party (b) of the U.S.S.R.* was in vain.

Gutiérrez put forth a number of arguments in favor of the Communists' operating through the Political Action Committee of the labor

---

[13] 8019:135-9, A manera de palabras de inauguración.
[14] *Ibid.*

movement rather than the PAR in the presidential campaign and the 1950 elections.

> The CAP has a program of action, a declaration of principles and a regular acceptance among the workers; the CAP, without being organically linked to any party, can direct the democratic sectors, offering its fighting program and combating the errors and vices of the parties of the petty bourgeoisie, which stuff themselves in the division of official monies during the campaign and in the posts of the bureaucracy when they reach power.

He saw in the CAP the "transitory legal instrument of the party" which could later be converted into a legal Communist Party.

In his report to the Congress, Secretary General Fortuny did not attempt to meet the challenge and arguments of Gutiérrez head on. Instead he undertook an analysis of the international situation based on the speech of Zhdanov delivered at the 1947 Warsaw meeting at which the Cominform was founded.[15]

> . . . we ought to take fundamentally as point of reference the work of companion Zhdanov, not only because, as I have already said, it constitutes the most valuable political document of recent times, but also because it is of incalculable help in adapting our appreciation of the facts and conclusions of our Congress.

According to Fortuny, the fundamental tasks of the Guatemalan Communists had been set down for them by Zhdanov as the "struggle against imperialism, against war and for national sovereignty and peace." The Communist Party should put itself at the head of all the democratic and patriotic forces of the people in the "fight against the new expansionist plans of the North Americans." In the eyes of the internationalist Fortuny, the questions of tactics and organization must be subordinated to these tasks. For Gutiérrez, on the other hand, the problems and aspirations of the working class took higher priority. We can only speculate on the debate which went on within the Congress over the political line and tactics to be followed, but it appears that Fortuny's faction was clearly in the majority. The Congress formally adopted the name *Partido Comunista de Guatemala* (PCG) and drew

[15] 8019:140-151, "Sobre la situación internacional. Informe del C. José Manuel Fortuny, Secretario General del C. C. de Vanguardia Democrática Guatemalteca, en el I. Congreso del Partido," September 28, 1949.

up a set of statutes which stated that the PCG was to be "the party of the working class to which campesinos, the middle class and, in general, all democrats who faithfully serve the interests of the working class can also belong."[16] The motto finally accepted was "For the construction of Socialism, Guatemalan workers, unite." Since the discipline imposed upon the members was quite strict, these statutes must be considered another victory for the dominant Fortuny faction and a rebuff for Gutiérrez, who favored greater intra-party democracy and restricting membership to authentic workers.

In general the program laid down by Fortuny at this Congress served as an over-all guide for the policy of the PCG for the next two years. The dissension within the party was settled, but at what proved to be a considerable cost. Gutiérrez's dissatisfaction with the leadership and orientation of the PCG continued to grow, and on November 7 he resigned from the Party.[17] Stating that in the future he would dedicate himself to showing the workers the right road to follow to avoid the errors of opportunism, Gutiérrez reaffirmed his faith that:[18]

> . . . some day something worthy of our most absolute confidence will arise: a party of the working class, directed by its best sons with a good theoretical preparation and a selfless attitude which will win them the sympathy and aid of the masses of workers and campesinos.

PARTIDO REVOLUCIONARIO OBRERO DE GUATEMALA (PROG)

Within a few months after his break with the PCG, Gutiérrez began work toward the establishment of the Revolutionary Workers' Party of Guatemala. The purpose of the new party was to implement the course of action which Gutiérrez had urged upon the First Congress of the PCG. On June 1, 1950, the Organizing Committee of the PROG, composed of Gutiérrez as Secretary General, Emilio Grajeda A. as Secretary of Organization, Antonio Obando Sánchez as Secretary of Propaganda and Isaías Ruíz Robles as Secretary of Finance,

---

[16] Document 2081: "Estatutos del Partido Comunista de Guatemala: aprobados en el Primer Congreso del Partido, 1949." See also Document 1015: Proyecto de Estatutos del Partido Comunista de Guatemala.

[17] 8019:368, Gutiérrez to Compañeros de VDG, November 7, 1949.

[18] *Ibid.* See also Y-X-4:108, Gutiérrez to Rufino Alvarado, October 7, 1949.

issued a manifesto which embodied the aims and programs of the new party.[19]

The founders of PROG felt that the revolutionary parties were concerned with elections and political maneuvering rather than working to satisfy the aspirations of the working masses. For this reason the workers needed their own organization which would defend their class interests and work particularly for agrarian reform. The first step in this direction was the CAP or Political Action Committee of the working class organized in 1948 for the elections of that year. A further step had been made through the series of Political Committees which sprang up at the end of 1949 and were welded into the National Political Committee of the Workers (CPNT) in January of 1950. The CPNT was merely a transitory body which was to be replaced by an "independent and revolutionary political party of the proletariat." (See Chapter VI, pp. 132-38.)

Although this manifesto contained a thoroughly Communist analysis of the international and national scene, it differed from the declaration made by the PCG a few weeks earlier in that it placed greatest emphasis on the problems of the workers and peasants. According to the PROG leaders the chief problem was to keep the movement free from international treason on the Trotsky or Tito model, gangsterism as in the captive labor movement in the United States, or manipulation by bourgeois politicians as had previously been the case in Guatemala. All these enemies of the workers were constantly trying to prevent the working class from carrying out its immediate historical task of taking its place at the head of the revolutionary forces in Guatemala.

The progress of the revolution was endangered, they felt, by the fact that its direction was in the hands of the "most advanced sectors of the urban middle class, the intellectuals and professionals, various government functionaries and the most democratic and progressive portions of the army . . ." The working class must fight for its independence from the predominantly middle class leadership of the revolutionary parties and repudiate the petty bourgeoisie and in-

---

[19] Y-X-1:1102-1116, "Manifiesto a la clase obrera y al pueblo de Guatemala del Comité Organizador del Partido Revolucionario Obrero de Guatemala, PROG," June 1, 1950.

tellectuals who claimed to be the spokesmen of the workers.[20] Above all it was necessary for the workers to direct their own destinies. For this reason the membership of the new political party must be carefully chosen. While some of the best and most revolutionary elements of the campesinos and middle class could be admitted to the party, the overwhelming majority should be recruited from the "most loyal and best tested proletarian fighters, the most firm, honest, selfless, and capable, the best-oriented and those who have the greatest experience. . . ."

The Guatemalan revolution, according to the founders of PROG, had to enter a second era in which the economic power of the imperialists and reactionaries would be curbed. This could only be done if the working class moved to take the leadership of the revolution. As the democratic parties had lost their desire to push ahead, it was imperative for the proletariat to forge its own political instrument. The program of this party would, during the existing historical phase, be one of "national unity." Spelled out in detail this involved as its key step the formation of a single labor organization supplemented by reform of the labor code, agrarian reform, curbing of foreign capital, and civic education. Foreign trade should be diversified so that the coming crisis in the United States would not drag Guatemala to economic ruin. In the international sphere the PROG would oppose the warlike designs of the imperialists and fight for the cause of peace. On the Guatemalan political scene PROG would work for a united front of the democratic and progressive forces and strive to become the majority party, although this last was considered a long-term task.

The founders of PROG were largely CTG leaders who by taking the initiative got the jump on FSG Secretary General Pinto Usaga, who had held somewhat the upper hand in the earlier political efforts of labor. While Gutiérrez was founding PROG, Pinto and his followers were still affiliated with the PAR and were feuding with Fortuny's PCG.[21] Late in June the Organizing Committee issued a

---

[20] This last was meant as a slap in the face of Fortuny and the PCG.

[21] For the differences between Pinto and Fortuny's Communist group see the report of Corozo to the January 1950 session of the Central Committee of the PCG. Also 8019:101-102, Pinto to Gutiérrez, November 9, 1949, in which Pinto objects to Fortuny's meddling in FSG affairs.

set of statutes for PROG which embodied in concrete form the design and thinking of the Gutiérrez group.[22] Its first article set forth the basic purposes of its founders.

> *Article 1*. The creation of the Revolutionary Workers' Party of Guatemala, (PROG), obeys the historical imperative of the manual and intellectual workers, consisting in having their own independent political organ which serves as the vanguard of the proletariat in order to orient and carry out to the final consequences the postulates of the democratic, agrarian and anti-imperialist revolution initiated on the 20th of October, 1944, and at the same time to prepare the workers' and peasants' masses for the struggles for national liberation and democracy, for the day of the future or the construction of socialism in our country.

Article 2 required that members be "manual and intellectual workers . . . of proven revolutionary conduct" and Article 3 obliged them, among other things, to: "Accept and observe in a disciplined manner the instructions of the party within the popular organisms and entities to which they belong," as well as work actively within a party cell. The party was organized on Leninist lines in support of a Marxist program and its members were expected to be disciplined, militant activists. As its motto, the PROG took "For Peace, the Sovereignty of Guatemala, and Socialism" and for its emblem, a red star with the slogan "Workers of the World Unite," usually accompanied by a hammer and sickle.[23]

In spite of its rigid requirements for membership, the PROG soon built a significant following among the more militant of the urban workers, and won a major victory on March 16, 1951, when the leaders of the FSG decided to join.[24] Gutiérrez remained as Secretary General, while Pinto Usaga moved into the number two position as Secretary of Organization and Eduardo Castillo H. became Secretary

---

[22] *El Organizador, Organo del Comité Organizador del Partido Revolucionario Obrero de Guatemala (PROG)*, Año I, No. 2, 24 de Junio de 1950, Ante-Proyecto Estatutos del Partido Revolucionario Obrero de Guatemala (PROG).

[23] Y-X-2:2752.

[24] Document 2077 or Y-X-2:3235, Requisitos para ser miembro del Partido Revolucionario Obrero de Guatemala. PROG; Y-X-2:3236 or Document 256: El PROG comunica a sus organismos de base, la integración de su Comité Central, invitando a los trabajadores sin partido a que estudien nuestros materiales y consideren su ingreso a nuestra organización, March 18, 1951.

of Finance. All other officers were loyal associates of Gutiérrez.[25] A Constituent Assembly in April ratified the steps already taken and the program laid before it by the Central Committee.

The Communist orientation of the PROG becomes apparent from a study of its publications.[26] Many of its early publications were Marxist explanations of the subjects with which they dealt, but were not readily recognizable as Communist by many of their less politically sophisticated readers. However as soon as Arbenz was inaugurated as President, the PROG published Gutiérrez's *Brief Summary of the History of the Communist Party (Bolshevik) of the USSR* as a "homage to the memory of Karl Marx on the 68th anniversary of his death."[27] This pamphlet was a simplified introduction to the basic Communist text, Stalin's *History of the Communist Party (b) of the USSR,* and in its introduction Gutiérrez made it evident that the PROG was to be a Communist Party.

Only the indoctrination of the working class within the framework of Marxist-Leninist theory, that is to say, within the framework of Scientific Socialism, will show it the road to its liberation, the road for the construction of a new society, the Socialist Society, in which private ownership of the means of production no longer exists, and as a consequence of this, the division of society into antagonistic classes no longer exists.

From the development of Communism in the USSR, Gutiérrez drew six lessons which the members of PROG were to bear in mind at all times. These included the necessity of a proletarian party as the *1.* vanguard of the revolution, the possession by this class of an understanding and appreciation of Marxist-Leninist theory, the expulsion *3.* of the bourgeois parties from within the working class, the purging of *4.*

---

[25] Matilde Elena López was Secretary of Education; Antonio Obando Sánchez, Secretary of Propaganda; Isaías Ruíz Robles, Secretary of Records; Emilio Grajeda A., Secretary of Campesino Affairs.

[26] Y-X-2:3237, Comité Organizador del Partido Revolucionario Obrero de Guatemala, PROG, programas de capacitación ideológica: lecciones elementales de Marxismo; also *Las luchas de la clase trabajador para crear su organización internacional* by Gutiérrez; *Bosquejo histórico universal* by Matilde Elena López.

[27] At approximately this same time, the Social Security Institute (IGSS) published his introduction to the study of Marx' *Kapital* under the title of *Breves Resúmenes de Economía Política.* See 8019:111, Carlos H. Ruíz to Víctor Manuel Gutiérrez, April 26, 1951.

all opportunists from within the ranks of the working class and the party, humility and readiness to admit their errors, and the maintenance of close and strong links to the masses. All members were obliged to read the *History of the Communist Party (b) of the USSR* and were to pay no attention to those Communists who claimed that PROG was a deviationist movement. In their eyes Communism consisted of fighting for the defense of the independence of the working class as PROG was doing; however they were ready to collaborate with other Marxist groups to forge a united party.

The admission of the FSG leaders meant that the PROG contained all the major labor leaders with the exception of a few young CTG officials who belonged to the PCG. While relations with the PAR were strained at first, as the older party had considered labor one of its prime supports, the PAR soon adjusted to the changed situation.[28] Gutiérrez was elected to Congress in the 1950 elections with the backing of all the revolutionary parties and was chosen Chairman of the politically important Agrarian Reform Commission.

Although relations between the two Communist parties were strained at first, cooperation between them gradually increased. As early as July, 1950, Gutiérrez made it clear that he had no quarrel to pick with the PCG.[29] In January of 1951 Gutiérrez took the initiative in meeting with the PCG so that the two Communist parties could present a united front in their dealings with the FPL.[30] Previous to the 1950 elections, the PROG, the PAR and the PCG signed a secret pact which was rather more than a non-aggression pact, but considerably less than an alliance, and which was to run for 16 months.[31] However, as late as April 1951 Gutiérrez complained that the "Octubrist" or PCG fraction in the CTG, under the leadership of Pellecer, had almost succeeded in dominating the Executive Committee and freezing him out.[32]

After Lombardo Toledano and other international Communist labor leaders came to Guatemala in May 1951 in an effort to restore unity,

---

[28] 8032:2960-2 or 8032:3002-5, Plan de lucha para 1951; 8024:1148 and 8021:38.

[29] Y-X-4:152, Gutiérrez to Berto Delio Castro, July 11, 1950.

[30] Document 1082: V. Manuel Gutiérrez to José Manuel Fortuny y Compañeros de la Dirección de *Octubre*.

[31] Document 1543: Puntos para un convenio electoral.

[32] 8019:400, V. M. Gutiérrez to Lombardo Toledano, April 4, 1951.

the relations between the PROG and the PCG improved. Gutiérrez represented the PROG at the rally held by the PCG to celebrate the first anniversary of *Octubre*.[33] A few days earlier the PCG had stated that they knew that the PROG would not be involved in any "dirty maneuvering" against it. The main dispute between the two Communist parties seemed to be which had the greater right to use the hammer and sickle as its emblem. A month later the two parties joined in an attack on the reactionary motives of anti-Communism.[34] At the beginning of September they joined in support of the 80¢ minimum wage[35] and two months later PROG published in the PCG paper a statement of the effect that the best homage they could pay to the 34th anniversary of the Russian revolution would be the unity of action of the two Marxist-Leninist parties.[36]

When Gutiérrez went to Moscow in December of 1951, unity for the Communists of Guatemala was all but a foregone conclusion. From Warsaw Gutiérrez directed a letter to Fortuny and Guerra Borges in which he stated that his trip to the Popular Democracies, which had begun in East Berlin in mid-November at a meeting of the General Council of the Communist-dominated WFTU, had given him new perspective and a realization of his responsibilities.[37]

> Today more than ever we understand the urgent necessity of the organic sindical unity of the working class, as well as the organic political unity in a single party: the Communist Party of Guatemala. To this grand task we must dedicate our effort.

The formal dissolution of the PROG followed immediately upon the heels of Gutiérrez's return from the USSR. On February 2 the representatives of the local organizations ratified the decision by a vote of 25 to 6.[38] While each member was formally free to join whatever party he wished, Gutiérrez issued a blanket invitation for them to follow him into the PCG, and most of them accepted his advice. For reasons having to do with an internal power struggle within the railroad union (SAMF), Pinto Usaga and a group of thirty-seven

---

[33] *Octubre,* June 29, 1951.
[34] *Octubre,* August 2, 1951.
[35] *Octubre,* September 6, 1951.
[36] *Octubre,* November 8, 1951.
[37] Document 1056: V. Manuel Gutiérrez to José Manuel Fortuny and Alfredo Guerra Borges, December 8, 1951.
[38] *Octubre,* February 7, 1952.

workers joined the PAR rather than the Communist Party. (They did not wish to feed fuel to the fire which was burning within SAMF over the issue of Communism. Several of these individuals later joined the PGT.) The behavior of this group within the PAR, especially during the dispute over the participation of that party in the PRG in the summer of the same year, raises some question as to whether their rejoining the PAR was not also part of a renewed effort of the Communists to infiltrate that party.

That the reincorporation of the Gutiérrez group into the PCG had its effects upon the policy of that organization becomes apparent from a study of the readjustments in the line and organization of the party which took place at the fourth and fifth sessions of the Central Committee and its Second Congress. While the Fortuny group remained dominant in the party machinery, changes in policy and program in the direction of closer links with the masses and intensified support for their demands indicate that it was a compromise and not an abject surrender on the part of Gutiérrez. Yet it is apparent that the influence of the international Communist movement was used to induce Gutiérrez to submit to Communist Party discipline.

Looking back upon the split within the Guatemalan Communist movement it appears that a number of factors were probably involved. Of Gutiérrez's original reasons for leaving the PCG, two, failure to push agrarian reform and the hesitance to withdraw from the PAR and form an independent party, were removed with the passage of time and shifts in the policy of the PCG. What differences remained —personal, tactical, and to a lesser degree ideological—were not sufficient to offset the appeal of unity. The opportunities afforded to the Communists by the growing rapprochement with the President were too great to endanger by continued disunity. Their agreement as Communists on fundamental matters more than offset the friction between the labor leaders and the petty bourgeois intellectuals.

PARTIDO COMUNISTA DE GUATEMALA (PCG)

The First Plenum of the Central Committee. When the Central Committee of the PCG which was elected at the September 1949 Congress held its first formal session the following January, it found that the party's position was weak and vulnerable. Although the PCG was attempting to counter the "treason" of Pinto and the "deviation" of Gutiérrez by seeking to gain control of the Political Action Committees of the unions, little progress had been made.[39]

Juan Ruíz, in his capacity as Secretary of Education and Propaganda pointed out that the tasks of organization and education were of primary importance to the party in this early stage of its development, quoting recent Cominform resolutions to that effect.[40] With respect to the PCG, Ruíz found that "the theoretic level of the comrades is extremely low and their Communist conscience is too weak, which, naturally, is reflected in their party life." He lamented that, for the lack of cadres, the work of the parties had to "rest upon the shoulders of a small group of comrades."

The Party is moving in a delicate and complex situation which Comrade Secretary General has outlined for us already. The Party, through recommendation by the Congress, must proceed towards its independence and legalization for which certain fundamental objectives must be met. The Party must strengthen and enlarge itself, not only to become legal, but also to be able to withstand the furious offensive of the opposition and the possible blows which the police might strike against it. To struggle and reach all these objectives it is necessary that the Party prepare soon and well a promotion of cadres, the minimum number of cadres which it needs to basically fulfill such objectives. The Party does not have those cadres, therefore it has to mold them.

The Communists Come into the Open: The Break with PAR. On May 20, 1950, the PCG broke decisively with the PAR. Their formal resignation was embodied in a document designed to attract sympathy from the more radical wing of that party.[41] The high posts which the Communist leaders had held within the PAR indicated how great their influence had been and how close they had come to succeeding in their attempt to take over that party. In addition to Fortuny, the ex-Secretary General of PAR and still a member of the Political Commission, the signers included: Mario Silva Jonama, Secretary of

---

[39] Document 2078: "Informe de José Corozo al Primer Pleno del C.C.," January, 1950.

[40] Document 2079: "Informe del Camarada Juan Ruíz, Secretario de Educación y Propaganda al Primer Pleno del Comité Central del Partido Comunista Guatemalteco," January, 1950.

[41] Document 943: letter to Secretario General del Partido Acción Revolucionaria, May 20, 1950.

Training and Propaganda; Bernardo Alvarado Monzón, Secretary for Youth Affairs; Antonio Ardón, Secretary for Social Affairs; Humberto Ortíz, Secretary for Rural Affairs—all of whom were also members of the National Executive Committee—and Pedro Fernández and Alfredo Guerra Borges, ex-members of the Political Commission. The other signers were José Luis Ramos, Carlos René Valle and Rogelio López.

The Communists began their explanation with an analysis of the international scene and its significance for Guatemala and other Latin American countries. Commencing with the familiar theme of the aggression planned by the "camp of warlike imperialism" headed by the United States against the "camp of peace, socialism and democracy" guided by the USSR, the Communists pictured Guatemala as the last obstacle to the imperialists' plan to dominate Central America. Since the PAR did not recognize that the "imperialist offensive" was the fundamental problem facing Guatemala, the Communists felt that they could no longer continue within that party. Owing to the attack upon the revolution by the reactionaries and imperialists, it was important for the Guatemalan people to realize that the 1950 presidential election was not a simple contest between candidates, but rather "a decisive battle in which the unity of the people has to defeat the reaction and imperialism."

The Communists claimed that they had stayed with the PAR until its internal contradictions had come to a head and the party leadership had begun to discriminate against the Marxists. In spite of their endorsement of the principle of revolutionary unity, the Communists had reached the conclusion that they could best serve their principles, the revolution and the Guatemalan people by withdrawing from the PAR.

> The struggle for the unity of the progressive forces against reaction and imperialism is our banner. But this does not mean that such unity has to be realized within a single party. Although some parties at a certain moment bring together various classes, the natural thing is that each social class tends to rely upon its own party, and it is only in the united front of the parties which represent the progressive classes that the unity of the same against the imperialists and reactionaries is realized.

> But the conditions have changed fundamentally, calling forth a new disposition of the forces of the united front. The growth

of imperialist pressure characteristic of recent days has detained the progress of revolutionary ascent in those forces which are only progressive. Those who in the euphoria of the struggle have placed themselves farther along than the position they authentically represent, now find themselves obliged to back away. Those who being moderate leftists in their enthusiasm began to talk like Communists, now recognize their "imprudence" and retrace their steps.

Under these conditions the Communists felt it preferable to withdraw from the PAR rather than to provoke further controversy within the party. The Communists would not enter into rivalry with the democratic parties but would concentrate upon the "organization and education in Marxism-Leninism of those who best represent the interests of the working class."

> Our friends of the PAR can be sure that they are our most immediate allies and that we will not for a moment neglect the task of maintaining united the democratic forces which have to give battle to the reaction and imperialism, that we will not ever forget the imperative necessity of winning the presidential elections.

The basic motive for the break appears to have been an overwhelming feeling among the Communists that, in light of the fact that they had lost ground in their attempt to take over the PAR, the time was ripe for them to take a step in the direction of a legal, recognized party. While they had some apprehensions as to how the public would react, and perhaps as to how the government might respond, the Communists realized that their future hinged upon the outcome of the presidential elections which were by them only six months away. As a practical matter for them, Arévalo no longer counted; their future prospects were embodied in Jacobo Arbenz.

Reaction to the Appearance of the "Octubre" Communists and the PROG. At the First Congress of the PCG in September of 1949, concern had been expressed over the possible reaction of the government and the public to the emergence of an open Communist organization. Anti-Communist sentiment had been expressed by a considerable segment of the Guatemalan people, and the President had made it evident that he did not approve of the Communists entering Guatemalan politics as an organized group, but would prefer to have them participating as individuals within the various revolutionary parties and organizations. The gradual way in which the PROG and the PCG made their appearance was designed to keep this reaction to a minimum. Neither group sought recognition as a legally registered party. The PROG operated under cover of the Political Committee of the Working Class (CPNT), while the PCG expressed its views through a weekly paper *Octubre,* which it founded on June 21, 1950, and came to be known as the "Octubre" Communists.

Immediately after *Octubre* began publication, Guerra Borges, Silva Jonama and other prominent Communists were separated from their government positions. The Communists took advantage of the so-called "minute of silence" demonstrations on the anniversary of Arana's assassination (July 18) to mastermind a counter demonstration which impressed upon Arbenz their ability to mobilize the workers. After conditions returned to normal, the Communists decided to go one step further and on September 1 opened the *Jacobo Sánchez* School of Marxist indoctrination to replace the defunct *Escuela Claridad,* which had been closed down by the government in 1946.[42] However this school was immediately closed down by Col. Elfego Monzón, the Minister of Interior, who also ordered *Octubre* to cease publication. When the Communists protested to Arévalo, they received a disappointing reply.[43]

> In conformance with Article 36 of the Constitution, you have the right to express your ideas without previous censorship, as long as you do it individually and not organized in a group of international character, because then you violate Article 32 of the same Constitution. By the insignias which you have used, "Octubre" is the organ in Guatemala of an international organization.

Outwardly at least the situation did not look good for the Communists, who now felt that their future hinged entirely upon the election of Arbenz.

However Monzón's actions did not stand for long. On October 11, scarcely a month after he had ordered the closing of *Octubre* and the *Escuela Jacobo Sánchez,* Col. Monzón was called before the Congress

---

[42] Alfredo Guerra Borges was the director of the school and Gutiérrez was one of its instructors, indicating that the two groups of Communists could work together in spite of their differences.

[43] Document 1525: Juan José Arévalo to José Manuel Fortuny y Compañeros, September 20, 1950.

and subjected to a hostile interpellation. The Communists won a major victory when, after Congress declared that his actions had been illegal, Monzón resigned. As soon as the elections were over, Fortuny began signing his corespondence "for the Communists of Guatemala."[44] With the inauguration of Arbenz they became bolder, and on April 4, 1951, Fortuny signed "for the Communist Party of Guatemala."

The Fifth Plenum of the Central Committee. At the end of November 1951 the PCG published the "Fundamental Bases of the Program of the Communist Party of Guatemala," a document which was widely circulated among the labor movement and left-wing politicians.[45] Improvement of the conditions of the workers, agrarian reform, industrialization, nationalization of the public services, incorporation of the indigenous population into the national life, social and cultural development of the masses, the struggle against imperialism and for national independence, international solidarity of the working class, the struggle for peace, and finally "the abolition of the exploitation of man by man, for the classless society, for the socialist society and Communism"—these were the "fundamental bases" of the Communist program in Guatemala.

The Fifth Enlarged Session of the Central Committee of the PCG met on February 16th and 17th, 1952, with 46 leading members of the party in attendance.[46] The only working paper of the session was a report by Fortuny on "The National Political Situation, the Perspectives of the Democratic Movement and the Activity of the Party." Thirty-one members participated in the discussion of the report which outlined five immediate tasks for the Communists of Guatemala—immediate agrarian reform designed to "destroy feudalism and make way for capitalism," "improvement of the material conditions of the masses and the fight against misery and the high cost of living,"

---

[44] 8021:63, José Manuel Fortuny to Secretary General of the CNCG, January 21, 1951.

[45] *Octubre,* November 29, 1951; also Document 972 or Y-X-4:516, "Bases fundamentales del programa del Partido Comunista de Guatemala." In general this program was similar to that of the PROG as set down in its June 1950 manifesto and April 1951 call to the workers, a fact which facilitated the rapprochement with the PROG.

[46] For a summary of Fortuny's report and several other articles on this meeting, see *Octubre,* February 21, 1952.

"patriotic resistance to the pretensions of the United Fruit Company and the other monopolistic companies," the struggle for peace "which is the central task and ought to serve as guide and axis," and "the unity of action of the democratic forces upon the base of the widest possible program."

Fortuny felt that the revolution in Guatemala had definitely been in the ascendant since the inauguration of President Arbenz and listed nine actions or attitudes on the part of the government which had been favorable to the Communists. On the negative side of the ledger, the economic power of the feudalists had not been affected and hence the reaction had been able to take the offensive against the democratic government. This reactionary offensive, supported by imperialism and hiding behind a mask of anti-Communism, had been detained by the democratic forces and particularly the Communist Party. The report foresaw an alliance of all the revolutionary parties including the Communists as the only possibility for carrying out the immediate tasks of the revolution.

In the eyes of Fortuny the party had made progress since the last plenary session. It had begun to link itself to the masses and to build a solid proletarian base. It had increased its influence and authority among the working masses and had been successful in its propaganda efforts, particularly the "un-masking" of the anti-Communists and the attack against imperialism. The return of the Communists of PROG to the fold and the 371% increase in the circulation of *Octubre* were important and gratifying signs of progress, but the party was still "far from being a true Leninist organization." The major weakness and shortcoming of the party was diagnosed as a failure to link itself closely with the masses and a tendency to feel that it was easier to work from above than from below. While this tactic had its uses and was not to be disparaged, the Communists must remember that "our principal method is mass action, 'action from the mass organizations, orienting our activity toward them.'" The party was to work for the six goals of its immediate program, but the fundamental thing was to work ever more closely with the masses—only then could they call themselves true Communists.

As indicated in an editorial by Guerra Borges, the inspiration and guide for the party's newly adopted program of "going to the masses" so as to gain their confidence, was the report of Liu Shao-chi to the

Seventh Congress of the Chinese Communist Party.[47] The emphasis upon agrarian reform was natural as it was apparent that this was the one program most dear to the heart of the President. The Fifth Plenum rejected the two types of agrarian reform which had first been considered by the Communists, collectivization on the pattern of the USSR and "democratic" reform as in the Peoples' Democracies of Eastern Europe. Corresponding to the backward stage of Guatemala, the proper program was "bourgeois-campesino" agrarian reform which would divide the ownership of land as widely as possible and do away with all vestiges of feudalism.[48] It is difficult to say for certain whether this was the true feeling of the Communists on agrarian reform or whether they were accommodating themselves to the preferences of the President.

When the Executive's Agrarian Reform project went to Congress, the Communists gave it their backing. The PCG declaration on this matter is indicative of the division of its goals and objectives into long-range and immediate plans and programs. While making it clear that their ultimate end was to abolish private property completely, the Communists stated that this would not be possible until "power is in the hands of the alliance of the workers and the peasants, that is to say, the establishment of a popular-democratic regime or a Socialist regime." They made it equally clear that, as in the present stage of Guatemalan economic and political development there was no question of transferring power to the hands of the workers and peasants, they would support a program designed to do away with the remains of feudalism and set Guatemala on the path of capitalistic development. The Communists felt that the President's project, under present conditions, was both the most that could be done and the least that should be done.[49]

The Sixth Plenum of the Central Committee. On June 14 and 15 the Central Committee of the PCG met to hear Secretary General Fortuny's report on the "Agrarian Question of Guatemala."[50] According to Fortuny, the Guatemalan revolution really began on May 9

---

[47] *Octubre,* February 28, 1952.

[48] *Octubre,* March 6, 1952.

[49] Statement of the Political Commission of the PCG on May 19, 1952, in *Octubre,* May 22, 1952.

[50] See *Octubre,* June 19, 1952, pp. 3-14.

with the attack upon the agrarian problem. This move opened the way for the fundamental change in the economic relations of Guatemalan society and should be accompanied by an attack against imperialism.

The project of the President was acceptable to the Communists, who particularly approved of the large role given to the workers and campesinos in the implementation and administration of the program. In addition, the proposal to keep the agrarian reform program separate from the influence of the regular government bureaucracy and the courts was extremely gratifying to the Communists. After showing that the project of the General Association of Agricultural Producers (AGA) was entirely inadequate, Fortuny undertook a detailed analysis of the agrarian problem in Guatemala drawing on experiences of other countries and Lenin's *The Agrarian Problem of Social Democracy in the First Russian Revolution of 1905-1907*. The closest parallel he could find to Guatemalan conditions was the situation in the United States around the time of the Civil War. Other patterns were for more industrialized countries or required the establishment of "the revolutionary dictatorship of the workers and peasants" as a pre-condition. The "North American" pattern of small independent farmers would lead to the rapid development of capitalism in Guatemala and, by implication, bring nearer the day for the establishment of the dictatorship of the proletariat.

The Communists did advocate a number of reforms to bring the law more in line with Marxist-Leninist theory. The nationalization of a portion of the land and titles in usufruct rather than perpetuity were among their chief proposals. While they felt that expropriation without payment would have been more just, they were willing to abide by the provisions of the Constitution of 1945. However, they made it plain that agrarian reform of this type was only an intermediate step and that, as conditions in Guatemala changed, they would eventually press for complete nationalization of land as part of the total abolition of private property.

The Communists prepared to accompany the enactment of the agrarian reform bill with a wide-spread campaign of organization and propaganda in the countryside. Agents went out to "aid" in the formation of the local agrarian committees and special teams of agitators and propagandists were trained for work in the rural areas.

The front organizations were directed to carry their campaigns into the countryside and link them with agrarian reform in the eyes of the peasants and rural workers. In particular, agrarian reform and peace were to be linked by stressing that the pressures of the warlike imperialists threatened successful implementation of agrarian reform. The new watchword of the party was "Toward the Rural Masses! For Agrarian Reform and Peace! Beneath the Banners of the Proletariat, with the Scientific Guide of Marxist-Leninist-Stalinist Doctrine!" The resolutions passed by the Sixth Plenum endorsing Fortuny's report showed that the party intended to exploit agrarian reform to the fullest possible extent.

> The political vanguard of the working class . . . ought to take advantage of the class contradictions which will become more acute through Agrarian Reform, and the democratic-bourgeois revolution, in order to accentuate the fight against imperialism, to fight capitalism, to make its evils apparent to the working class and the most exploited and poor peasants, to strengthen the proletariat, to recruit the proletariat of the city and the field to its party and to construct the party of the working class, which in such conditions, will be able to fight better for its grand objectives, Socialism and Communism.

SECOND CONGRESS OF THE PARTIDO COMUNISTA DE GUATEMALA

On October 9, 1952, the Central Committee issued a summons for the first public congress of the Guatemalan Communist Party.[51] The chief purpose of the Congress was to prepare the party to assume a new role as the Communists had reached an agreement with the President and the revolutionary parties that they were to be accepted as a legal party with full rights under the law and as a full member of the governing coalition. In addition the Congress was designed to complete the task of bringing the Guatemalan Party fully into line with the resolutions of the XIX Congress of the Communist Party of the USSR. As Silva Jonama explained to the Congress:[52]

---

[51] See *Octubre,* October 9, 1952, or 8039:618-9, October 9, 1952.

[52] Intervención del Camarada Mario Silva Jonama en torno al Informe sobre el trabajo del Comité Central del Partido, reprinted in *Octubre,* January 9, 1953.

The discussion of the materials of the order of the day of the II Congress in all the party and the initial examination of the Report of Comrade Malenkov to the XIX Congress of the Communist Party of thè USSR, which was made in the Central Committee, are already a valuable experience, which ought to be followed immediately by the assimilation by all the comrades of the resolutions of this Congress, the study of the materials of the XIX Congress of the Communist Party of the USSR and the new work of comrade Stalin.

The purpose of the Congress was outlined in an editorial by Alfredo Guerra Borges:[53]

Marxism-Leninism requires that we interpret with complete fidelity the reality of Guatemala, the present stage of the Guatemalan Revolution, the grade of political and social development of the working masses in order to delineate objectives and adopt methods of struggle suitable for the Guatemalan people and revolution, with distinctive national peculiarities. Lenin taught that Marxism is not applied equally in Germany and in England, in France as in China, in the United States as in Guatemala.

The chief working papers of the Congress were to be a report by Fortuny on the activity of the Central Committee, a report on the proposed program by Alfredo Guerra Borges, and the draft project of new statutes by Bernardo Alvarado Monzón.[54] The Congress provided the party with an opportunity to conduct an extensive indoctrination campaign among the rank and file. For two months preceding the Congress, *Octubre* carried a series of articles by the party leaders which were to be studied by each member.[55] In addition, each cell was furnished with a copy of the program of the Communist Party of India, the Statutes of the Chinese Communist Party, a reprint of the chapter "The Party" from Stalin's *Fundamentals of Leninism,* the reformed statutes of the Communist Party of the USSR,

[53] *Octubre,* October 9, 1952.

[54] "Tésis que contendrá el Informe de C. José Manuel Fortuny, sobre el balance del trabajo del Comité Central, que presentará a la consideración del II Congreso del Partido Comunista de Guatemala"; "Proyecto de programa del Partido Comunista de Guatemala"; "Bases fundamentales de los estatutos del Partido Guatemalteco del Trabajo"; "Sobre el proyecto de los nuevos estatutos del Partido"; "Proyecto de estatutos del Partido Guatemalteco del Trabajo."

[55] *Octubre,* November 6, 1952, through December 4, 1952.

and several other pertinent documents.[56] To aid with the task, the Commission of Education sent representatives to the cells to help with the assimilation of the materials.

The Congress opened at 9:00 P.M. December 11, 1952, with 184 representatives of the elite of Guatemalan Communism sitting beneath huge portraits of Lenin, Fortuny and Stalin.[57] During the next three days the delegates listened to over 100 speakers. In spite of all this activity, they were there more to be taught than to play any real role in shaping the party line.[58] The chief document produced by the Congress was the report of Secretary General Fortuny, an expanded version of the working paper circulated to the members in advance.[59] The first portion of Fortuny's report dealt with the international situation and followed the usual line of international Communism, with the Soviet Union pictured as the peaceful champion of the oppressed masses and the United States as the warmongering nation of Fascist oppressors. This section hewed closely to the line of Stalin's *Economic Problems of Socialism in the USSR* and Malenkov's report to the XIX Congress of the Communist Party of the USSR.

On the basis of this analysis Fortuny formulated a six-point program for the party's international policy:[60] a stepping-up of the peace campaign, dissemination of the "truth" about the superiority of the way of life in the Communist countries, denunciation of all treaties or organizations which "might involve Guatemala in the North American imperialist policy of aggression," solidarity with the liberation and resistance movements in the colonial countries, the struggle against the rebirth of fascism, and the establishment of trade with the Soviet bloc.

---

[56] Copies of these documents are included in the collection upon which this book is based.

[57] See *Octubre,* December 18, 1952. As each cell was allowed two delegates, the size of the party must have been between seven and nine hundred.

[58] The story of the Congress is told in *Octubre,* particularly the issues of January 9 through February 5, 1953.

[59] See 8024:1188-1207 for the early draft. The entire report was published by the party as *Informe sobre la activadad del Comité Central del Partido Comunista de Guatemala, rendido el 11 de Diciembre de 1952 por José Manuel Fortuny, Secretario General del Partido Comunista, al II Congreso del Partido,* Guatemala, 1953.

[60] *Ibid.,* pp. 23-4; also *Octubre,* December 18, 1952.

Turning to the national situation, Fortuny stated that the Party had erred in considering the last eight years as "a true anti-feudal and anti-imperialist revolution," since the "semi-feudal and semi-colonial economic structure" had not been affected. A far-reaching program of agrarian reform was necessary in order to create a powerful force of rural workers and peasants which, under the direction of the working class and the Communist Party, would be able to drive all "imperialist" capital out of Guatemala and assure its economic and political independence. The nationalist-bourgeois government of Arbenz was already a step in this direction, but only the leadership of the Communist Party could convert it into the true anti-imperialist revolution. As Guatemala was so far from the Communist countries, so near the United States and surrounded by the "iron fist" of imperialism, it must pass through a capitalist stage. However the experience of China and the Peoples' Democracies had shown that this capitalist stage could sometimes be very short.[61]

> These historic examples also show that even the period of capitalist development through which it is necessary to pass will be less painful and shorter if the proletariat as the directing force of society heads the struggle against feudalism and imperialism, if the proletariat knows how to construct the alliance with the campesinos and on this base, the united and patriotic front of all the social forces which are opposed to feudalism and imperialism.

As Stalin had shown, the bourgeois was not sufficiently revolutionary to fulfill its historical task, hence the proletariat must play the directing role in the bourgeois-democratic revolution.

The forward progress of the revolution had enabled organization of the workers and democratic forces to move forward to a point where they were able to fight effectively for their demands. The most significant development along these lines had been the emergence of the Communist Party into the open where it could act as the guide for the working class and the masses. The process of decomposition of the bourgeois parties, according to Fortuny, should be viewed as part of the development of an increasing political consciousness on the part of the masses. As large segments of these parties were becoming increasingly discontent with their leadership, the Communists should prepare to "point out to them the just road, orient them and direct them."[62] The establishment of unity among the democratic forces was indispensable and could be brought about only by the Communists.

To cope with the problems and take advantage of the opportunities afforded by the situation, Fortuny put forth a seven-point program which came to be known as "The Guatemalan Way."[63]

1. Denounce without respite the feudal-imperialist reaction and . . . combat its plans to liquidate the democratic and revolutionary process of our country. . . .

2. . . . elevate the level of combativeness and strengthen the organizations of the workers of such foreign enterprises. . . .

3. Fight for the correct application of agrarian reform ; . . . aid the campesino leaders in the solution of the problems of their class and daily strengthen the bonds of the alliance between the workers and the campesinos.

4. Strengthen the bonds of unity among the working class . . . combat the agents of the feudal-imperialist reaction who operate within the unions. . . .

5. Augment the action of the workers for better conditions of life . . . and elevate the capacity for leadership of the labor cadres.

6. Develop the mobilization of the masses beneath the direction of the organizations of the workers, campesinos, youths, and women, and strengthen these organizations in order that they may be converted into true popular fronts. . . .

7. Develop the unity of action . . . of all the democratic and popular forces of our country toward the formation of a grand patriotic front with the prospect of completely transforming the democratic and revolutionary movement into the anti-feudal and anti-imperialist revolution of Guatemala; strengthen the various alliances already reached and those which may be reached in the future between our party and the democratic parties . . . establish more solid bonds and push the unity of action between the masses of these parties and of our party.

The final section of Fortuny's report dealt with the steps necessary to build the party into an instrument capable of carrying out this ambitious program. In spite of the impressive number of successes

---

[62] *Ibid.*, p. 46.
[63] *Ibid.*, pp. 46-8; also *Octubre*, December 18, 1952.

which the party had scored in the past year, certain shortcomings were noticeable. Among these faults which must be corrected were a superficial and sometimes mechanical application of Marxism, low ideological level, weak links with the masses, insufficient propagandizing, lack of discipline, a too prevalent bureaucratic attitude, and insufficient use of self-criticism.[64]

The program adopted by the PCG drew heavily upon that of the Indian Communist Party, which had been recommended by the Cominform as "the model of a minimum program for the struggle of colonial peoples under present conditions." The keynote was an effort to identify the party with the demands and aspirations of the masses and to picture it as the indigenous response to the need for a party which could adequately express and defend the interests of the working class. Nevertheless:[65]

> The final objective of the Communist Party of Guatemala is the classless society, or socialist society and later the Communist society, in which production, the cultural level and the well-being of the masses has developed and risen to such a grade that it is possible to run society by the principle: *"from each, according to his capacity; to each, according to his needs."*

What was to prove the fundamental point of the new program was the adoption of the tactic of a "united front of the democratic, progressive and anti-imperialist forces." Based to a large extent upon the experience of China this was to include the workers, peasants, petty bourgeoisie and the progressive elements of the national bourgeoisie —all led by the working class and its organized vanguard, the Communist Party. This united front was to be the fundamental instrument in the struggle for "national liberation."

One of the steps taken at the Congress was to change the name of the party from *Partido Comunista de Guatemala* to the *Partido Guatemalteco del Trabajo,* a purely pragmatic and opportunistic move aimed at eliminating any obstacle to the rapid growth and legal inscription of the party.[66] The leaders felt that the name Communist caused many of the peasants and Catholic workers to shy away from

---

[64] *Ibid.,* pp. 61-2 or *Octubre,* December 18, 1952.

[65] 8039:636-643, "Puntos de vista acerca de proyecto de programa del Partido."

[66] The reasons and justification for this change of name were fully spelled out in the document "Sobre el Proyecto de los Nuevos Estatutos del Partido," which was circulated to the members in advance of the Congress.

joining the party. As the fundamental task of the party at that time was rapid growth and spread to the countryside, the change of name was an entirely proper tactic and justified by its success in other countries. The party could not afford to let anything stand in the way of the opportunity which was being afforded them to reach out to the masses and bring them into the ranks of Communism; however the change in name signified no deeper change, and the members would continue calling themselves Communists.

The changes in the statutes were designed to reinforce discipline through strengthening of "democratic centralism," the organization of a Secretariat of the Central Committee and the more extensive practice of "criticism and self-criticism." Based upon the "rich teachings and experiences of our sister parties," it was decided that members of the party elected to public office would turn their salaries over to the party and receive from it "a salary which permits them to live in a dignified manner." In this way the party would avoid the evils of careerism which weakened the bourgeois parties. On the other hand, the requirements for membership were eased in order to "facilitate the entrance into the party of the best sons of the working class and the people in general."

PARTIDO GUATEMALTECO DEL TRABAJO (PGT)

Follow-up of Second Congress: Communism Spreads to the Country-side. Immediately after the inscription of the PGT as a legal party on December 18, 1952, the Communist leaders undertook to formulate a plan of action designed to take full advantage of its new position. The first step was a campaign to enlarge and strengthen the party as rapidly as possible and to entrench the party so deeply in the political process of Guatemala that it would be able to withstand any future proposals or attempts to curb its activities and influence. With its full acceptance on equal footing by the other government parties, no roadblocks remained to an all-out campaign of organization and recruitment.

The inner core of the Communist leadership, the five member Secretariat, formulated a master plan for the "construction and ideological strengthening of the party."[67] The key elements of this pro-

---

[67] Y-X-1:959-964, Algunas ideas para intensificar el trabajo de construcción y fortalecimiento ideológico y orgánico del Partido.

gram were: the widespread dissemination of the political line of the Second Congress both within the party and among the popular masses and progressive elements; the establishment of closer ties to the masses and a far greater variety and amount of contact with non-members of the party, with new emphasis on the work of the fractions within the mass organizations and front groups; intensification of propaganda and agitation among the people of Guatemala; a sustained campaign to raise the ideological level of the party's cadres; and a careful and systematic drive to recruit new members and build new organizations. Bernardo Alvarado Monzón was relieved of his duties as head of the Departmental Committee in Guatemala and made responsible for the expansion of the party into the countryside. In short, the party was adjusting to its new role as a full member of the governing coalition and taking advantage of its ability to operate in the open to build a nation-wide organization. The PGT sought to bring its membership into line with its political power and influence; the party itself was to become a larger part of the total Communist movement.

Preparatory to carrying its organizational efforts to the Departments of the interior, the PGT undertook a large-scale program of familiarizing the public with its principles and programs.[68] Five thousand copies of the PGT program, 15,000 copies of its manifesto on the political situation, 50,000 copies of its call to the campesinos and rural laborers, and hundreds of public meetings to introduce Communism to the masses marked the first stage of the campaign.[69] As a second step, each cell and intermediate organization was to formulate a program of tasks in keeping with the aims of the over-all plan.[70] The Puerto Barrios organization alone pledged 150 new members in three months, and by August the party was at least twice the size it had been at the first year and growing at an even faster rate.[71]

---

[68] 8039:661, Liceas generales de la propaganda del Partido, January, 1953.

[69] As part of this intensification of propaganda, the sale of the review *Unión Soviética* was raised to 1000 copies per edition.

[70] See Document 806: Tareas a desarrollar por los Comités de Base del Seccional Sur-Poniente, propuestas por el Comité Seccional de acuerdo con las indicaciones del Informe del Comité Central al Segundo Congreso del Partido; Document 1152: Plan de trabajo para el Comité Municipal de Puerto Barrios: tres meses a partir del 25 de Junio, 1953.

[71] While exact totals on party growth are difficult to reach, it is known that 40 joined the party on July 9, 1953; 41 campesinos in the little community of San Pedro Yepocapa joined in a group on November 7; and even

Plenum of May 16-17, 1953: "Reject the Imperialist Intervention."
Five months after the Second Congress, the Central Committee met
to consider the strategy to be followed in creating and exploiting the
fear of foreign intervention. Fortuny's report stressed the necessity to
exploit the anti-imperialist sentiment of the Guatemalan nationalists
and to strengthen the alliance between the workers and the campesinos
and reinforce the unity of "all the democratic and popular forces."[72]
Fortuny reiterated the party's charges of October 9, 1952, and April 1,
1953, that the Organization of Central American States (ODECA)
was an instrument of North American intervention in the affairs of
Guatemala and stated that the party had been remiss in not bringing
about Guatemala's withdrawal at an earlier date.[73] The threat of
intervention was to be stressed and the concept of "continental solidarity" depicted as a means of tying the Latin American countries
like puppets on a string to the "warlike" policies of the United States.
Peace propaganda should be stepped up and linked to the economic
well-being and security of Guatemala. While posing as the chief defenders of democratic liberties, the Communists urged the necessity of
curbing these rights for the "subversive" anti-Communist movement.[74]
Reaffirming the seven basic points of the program adopted at the
Second Congress, Fortuny stressed the necessity of party growth and
reminded the Communists that "at our side is the international solidarity of all the workers and peoples of the world."[75]

Plenum of October 16, 1953: "For a United Front of the Masses."
The PGT had come a long way in the five months since the last
meeting of the Central Committee. The Communists were now ready

---

old Communists such as Alfredo Pellecer, who had never bothered to join
the new party after the revolution, humbly begged to be received into its
ranks. See Document 49: Lista de solicitudes de ingreso, Guatemala, 9 de
Julio de 1953; Document 46: 41 campesinos to PGT, November 7, 1953;
Document 1042: Miguel Mármol to PGT, August 5, 1953; Document 620:
Alfredo Pellecer to Alvarado Monzón, September 30, 1953.

[72] Y-X-5:951-961, *Rechazar la Intervención Imperialista, Defender el
Régimen Democrático de Guatemala e Impulsar las Tareas del Movimiento
Democrático: Informe de J. M. Fortuny, Secretario General del Partido
Guatemalteco del Trabajo, al Pleno del C. C. celebrado los días 16 y 17 de
Mayo de 1953;* also reproduced in *Octubre,* May 21, 1953.

[73] *Ibid.,* pp. 6-8.

[74] *Ibid.,* pp. 15-16.

[75] *Ibid.,* p. 18.

to take an important step on the road to power, the establishment of a "United Front of the Masses." The alliance at the national level of the revolutionary parties, the Communists, and the labor and peasant organizations was to be strengthened and carried to the local level. This move was designed to guarantee that the alliance would never be broken by connecting these organizations in a nation-wide network of "united front committees."[76] The danger of the overthrow of the Arbenz regime was to be emphasized as a situation calling for increased unity of the "democratic, progressive and anti-imperialist forces."

Fortuny began his report with a detailed study of the nature of a united front and reached a definition based upon the writings of Dimitrov and Stalin and the experience of the Peoples' Democracies The tactic of the united front would enable them to "elevate the conscience of the masses of the allied parties and the popular masses in general to the level at which they will understand, on the basis of mutual criticism, the justice of the line of the Communists."[77] Already under the FDN, which was only a shadow of the united front, many members of the other parties and particularly the PAR had joined the PGT. The contrast between the Communists and the hesitant bourgeois parties was so apparent that the "most combative and wide-awake" members were switching to the Communists.[78] No active effort to win recruits from the other parties was necessary nor should such attempts be made. Disillusioned and deceived by their own irresponsible leadership, the "best of the fighters of the working masses and of the local leaders of the democratic parties" would seek on their own to join the ranks of the Communists. The tactic of the united front would put the PGT in contact with the politically backward local organizations of the other parties, which would have an opportunity to see the superiority of the Communists.

The FDN was only an instrument of the united front; the front itself would be based upon a network of local, regional and national committees and alliances of various kinds such as that of the CGTG and CNCG. A government of the four progressive classes would be built upon the united front. This would be considerably more than a

---

[76] *Por un Frente Unico de Masas para impulsar el movimiento revolucionario y rechazar la intervención extranjera, Informe presentado al Pleno ampliado del Comité Central del Partido Guatemalteco del Trabajo por José Manuel Fortuny, Secretario General del C.C., el 16 de Octubre de 1953.*
[77] *Ibid.,* p. 7.
[78] *Ibid.,* p. 8.

bourgeois government with Communist participation; but less than a Communist government.[79] The special conditions in Guatemala had created a unique situation which required a special type of united front.[80] Since the desperate imperialists were apt to take drastic action against the democratic government of Guatemala, it was necessary to bring the non-party and unorganized masses effectively into the struggle. Extreme flexibility and variety was to be the keynote of this campaign. In the PGT blueprint such specialized organizations as the League of Renters or general groups as the Committees of Defense of National Sovereignty all had their place.[81]

To insure Communist control of the united front, it was necessary to bring about the replacement of those campesino leaders who opposed the Communists.[82] Since the question of presidential succession was apt to divide the parties, as it already was weakening the PAR, it was necessary to forge a stronger organ of unity. Only the work of the Communists through the united front could prevent a rupture of the alliance of revolutionary forces which might result in the isolation of the Communists from the masses or even lead to an opposition victory.[83]

The leaders of the PRG, PAR, RN, CNCG, and all the Communist-oriented mass organizations hurried to express their approval of the PGT proposal. Charnaud MacDonald, González Juárez and Castillo Flores—the three most important political leaders outside of the PGT—led the parade of over a hundred leaders who expressed their approval in the pages of *Tribuna Popular*.[84] Nevertheless progress toward the establishment of united front committees did not proceed as rapidly as the Communists desired. Again it was a case of Communist influence being stronger at the top than at the local level.

The Communist Program in 1954. The PGT issued no official statement of its program after the Central Committee session of October 16, 1953. Agrarian reform, the fight against foreign monopolies, anti-

---

[79] *Ibid.*, p. 11.
[80] *Ibid.*, pp. 13-15.
[81] *Ibid.*, pp. 25-27.
[82] *Ibid.*, pp. 28-30.
[83] *Ibid.*, pp. 31-34.
[84] See *Tribuna Popular*, October 24, through November 6, 1953. Each day this Communist Party newspaper featured a column of letters and interviews endorsing the United Front of the Masses. For analytical articles dealing with the nature of the united front, see *Tribuna Popular*, October 20, 1953, November 1, 1953 and November 13, 1953.

imperialism, support for the progressive measures of the Arbenz government, improving the living conditions of the masses, unity of the working class, tightening of the alliance between the workers and peasants, rejection of foreign intervention and the construction of the united front of the masses still constituted the official Communist program. Particular emphasis was given to the anti-imperialist plank and the propaganda campaign against U.S. intervention in preparation for the Caracas Conference.

Apparently the youthful Communist leaders tended to overestimate the strength of their position and to feel that the Arbenz regime would be able to weather the storm. Their attention was focused beyond the immediate crisis to such matters as the November Congressional elections and the youth festival scheduled for December. (It is the author's impression that some of the more optimistic firebrands may even have welcomed the Castillo Armas attack as an opportunity to strengthen the party's position by arming its supporters and dealing a crushing blow to its enemies.) There is little evidence that the Communists felt that the Arbenz regime would collapse and none that this was what they desired. If there was any conscious plan to sacrifice the Guatemalan party for the propaganda benefit which could be gained from exploiting the issue of Yankee intervention, it would appear that only Fortuny could have known of it. However, in a limited sense it might be said that for the purposes of the international Communist movement, the Arbenz regime was of equal propaganda value in life or death.

5

THE COMMUNIST PARTY IN GUATEMALA: LEADERSHIP, ORGANIZATION AND OPERATIONS

In the preceding chapter we studied the development and program of the Guatemalan Communist Party from its birth until the achievement of relative maturity in the last year of the Arbenz regime. The present chapter is concerned with the instrument through which the program was put into practice, the Guatemalan Labor Party (PGT). In·this discussion of the structure and operations of the party at its highest stage of development, particular attention will be paid to the leadership of the PGT, its size and composition, functional organization, and methods of operation. Finally an effort will be made to discuss the categories of individuals who, though not known members of the PGT, contributed materially to the advancement of Communism in Guatemala.

LEADERS AND MEMBERS

With few exceptions, the leadership of the PGT came from among the young intellectuals from the lower middle class who were finishing or had recently finished school at the time of the Revolution. This group was characterized by a level of educational attainment far beyond that of most of the members of their class. Many of them were frustrated *universitarios*—individuals who had aspired to a university education, but for economic reasons had to settle for the normal school and a career of teaching. Although they had nearly as complete an education as the sons of the upper and upper middle classes, the economic and social system appeared to block the road to the professions and doom them to a life as poorly-paid teachers or employees. In short, a marked contrast between educational level and economic and social position characterized this group. The social order was, in their eyes, the root of their lack of opportunity. After the merger with the PROG in February 1952, the membership of the party took on a more proletarian cast. As the Communists exploited the issue of agrarian reform in 1953, campesinos came to form more than half of the party's rank and file. Throughout, the national leadership remained essentially lower middle class, although some authentic workers rose to secondary positions within the party hierarchy.

José Manuel Fortuny Arana. Clearly the number one Communist in Guatemala, Fortuny was Secretary General of the party from the time of its founding, and was a member of all its controlling bodies. Perhaps as much as his intellectual ability and qualities of leadership, Fortuny's preeminence and early dominance in the Communist movement stemmed from his seniority. Twenty-eight at the time of the Revolution, Fortuny was from five to ten years older than most of the young intellectuals who were attracted to Marxism. This age advantage enabled him to achieve almost immediate prominence in the politics of the Arévalo Government and to appear as the natural leader for the young Communists. In spite of his obvious talents as a writer, speaker and theoretician, Fortuny's effectiveness was hampered by his unpleasant personality and the lack of morality in his private life. While Fortuny's contributions to the Guatemalan Communist movement cannot be underestimated, he, less than any other leader, fits the image of the selfless, dedicated champion of the people.

Born in Cuilapa, Santa Rosa, on May 22, 1916, the son of a local attorney, Fortuny attended the National Institute for Boys and worked toward a law degree at the University of San Carlos. A part-time radio announcer and newscaster at the time of the Revolution, Fortuny reached political prominence as Vice President of the *El Derecho* association of law students and as leader of the radical wing of the FPL. After acting as Fourth Secretary of the Constituent Assembly, he served in Congress from 1945 to 1949. In 1950 he was named President of the National Elections Board.

One of the powers in the PAR from its founding, Fortuny soon rose to Secretary General and held that position until March 1949. In 1948 he became Secretary General of the clandestine Communist Party and remained in the top post until May 1954. Several times a visitor to the USSR, Fortuny was one of the closest advisers of President Arbenz and a good friend of Sra. de Arbenz. His third wife, María Jérez de Fortuny, was active in the party and in the AFG as well as serving in the key post of Secretary General of the National Agrarian Department.[1] His brother Alfonso was PAR Secretary of Propaganda and a member of Congress.

Bernardo Alvarado Monzón. Successor to Fortuny as Secretary General, Alvarado Monzón had made a name for himself as one of the most dedicated of the Communist leaders. Previous to his elevation to the number one position, he had been Secretary of Organization, one of the five Secretaries of the Central Committee and of course a member of the Political Commission and Central Committee. Alvarado Monzón, whose father had been Minister of Government in 1922 and Rector of the University of San Carlos, was born in Mazatenango in 1926. When he was eight, his father was arrested in connection with the 1934 conspiracy against Ubico. The Revolution of 1944 found Alvarado Monzón an eighteen-year-old student who threw himself into the revolutionary politics at the side of Fortuny. During the Arévalo administration he combined his political activities with a post in the Ministry of Economy, editing the semi-official paper and teaching history at the National Institute for Boys. In addition he found time to participate in the labor movement, rising to Secretary of Press and Propaganda in the CTG.

---

[1] Fortuny's third wife had previously served as secretary to President Arbenz. His first wife had been the sister of PAR leader Francisco Fernández Foncea and his second the half-sister of Col. Carlos Aldana Sandoval, one of the most pro-Communist of the Army officers and Arbenz's Minister of Communications.

Alvarado Monzón followed Fortuny from the FPL into the PAR and the clandestine Communist group called the VDG. Within the PAR he rose to the National Executive Committee as Secretary of Social Affairs. At the March 1949 PAR convention Alvarado Monzón was elected to the post of Secretary of Youth Affairs as an unopposed candidate on both tickets. In May 1950 he resigned from the PAR along with the rest of the Communist leadership. While he was in the PAR, he joined Fortuny and Pellecer in running the party newspaper *El Libertador* and became editor of the leftist daily *Diario de la Mañana*. In front activities he was a founder of the AJDG and the Grupo Saker-Ti, as well as a delegate to the 1949 American Continental Peace Congress. An active campaigner for Arbenz, he was later named to a post in the Social Security Institute.

Within the party Alvarado Monzón was the organizational expert and did a very effective job of directing the party's rapid expansion during 1953 and 1954. With the removal of Fortuny, he was the logical successor to the post of Secretary General. He was one of the few top leaders to stay on in Guatemala after the fall of the Arbenz regime and attempted to keep the party functioning. His wife, Irma Chávez de Alvarado, was a member of the PGT Central Committee, Secretary of Feminine Affairs, and AFG Secretary of Organization.

Alfredo Guerra Borges. The Communists' number one man in the field of propaganda, Guerra Borges was Editor of the party papers *Octubre* and *Tribuna Popular* and one of the five Secretaries of the Central Committee as well as a member of the Political Commission. Born in the capital on February 2, 1925, he was a nineteen-year-old law student at San Carlos University at the time of the revolution. Plunging into radical politics, he became editor of the FPL paper, a follower of Fortuny in the PAR, and a founder of the AJDG and Grupo Saker-Ti, as well as an active leader in the National Peace Committee. Named by Arévalo as the first Inspector General of Labor after the enactment of the Labor Code, Guerra Borges, at the time a member of the Political Commission of the PAR and an activist in the clandestine Communist movement, was transferred in 1949 to the Embassy in El Salvador. After acting as contact between the Guatemalan and Salvadorean Communists in this post, he returned to Guatemala to head the Arévalo government's publicity office and to serve as editor of the official paper, the *Diario de Centro América.*

Dismissed from these posts when the Communists broke with the PAR and came into the open, Guerra Borges became the head of the Communist training and cadre school *Jacobo Sánchez* and editor of *Octubre*. Throughout the period he had been active among the labor movement and rose to be CTG Secretary of Conflicts.

Within the party he worked closely with Silva Jonama in the Education Commission and was a champion of tightened discipline while striving constantly to raise the ideological level of the party. He and his wife, Elsa Castañeda de Guerra Borges—herself a leader of Communist women, an active worker in the peace campaign, and an official of the AFG—won several commendations and awards from the party for their complete dedication to its work.

Mario Silva Jonama. The Communist Secretary of Education and member of the key five-man Secretariat was born in 1923 and a university student and school teacher at the time of the revolution. Active in politics, government, labor and front groups, Silva Jonama started out with Gutiérrez in the STEG and rose to be its Secretary of Training and Propaganda. While serving as Sub-Secretary of Public Education under Arévalo, Silva Jonama played a key role in the Communist penetration of the educational system. As a prominent member of Fortuny's Communist faction in the PAR, he remained active in the labor movement. An official of the CTG and Secretary General of the Political Action Committee of the Federation of Workers of the Department of Guatemala (FTDG), he was Secretary of Propaganda as well as a member of the Political Commission of the PAR before resigning in May of 1950. Silva Jonama was one of the top leaders of the National Committee for Peace and rose to be Secretary General of that Communist front organization in 1953, the same year that he visited Moscow and China twice.

The chief contribution of Silva Jonama to Guatemalan Communism was in the work of indoctrination. Within the party he was responsible for raising the ideological level of the members and was an effective propagandist of Communist doctrines in the STEG and National Peace Committee. He was one of the few top Communist leaders whose wife was not prominent in the movement.

Carlos Manuel Pellecer Durán. The number one agitator and firebrand of the Guatemalan Communists, Pellecer was usually considered to be far more important than his formal post in the party hierarchy as a member of the eleven-man Political Commission might suggest. As one of the four PGT Deputies in the National Congress and Secretary of Conflicts of the CGTG, Pellecer was extremely influential. In 1952-4 he was the Communists' chief agitator and troubleshooter in the area of agrarian reform and virtual czar of the Department of Escuintla, where the Communists built up their strongest mass support. Son of a middle class family, Pellecer was born in Antigua on January 17, 1920, and spent three years in the *Escuela Politécnica*. Having switched to the Central National Institute for Boys, where he studied toward being a teacher, Pellecer was accused of participating in subversive activities against the Ubico government and fled to Mexico in 1939. There he lived as a worker, miner and teacher while gaining some experience in agrarian reform.

Returning to Guatemala in July of 1944, Pellecer was one of the founders of the FPL, a participant in the overthrow of Ponce and a member of Congress. Resigning in 1945, he went to Moscow as Secretary of the newly-opened Guatemalan Legation. Transferred to Paris, he acted as the chief contact between the Guatemalan Communist movement and the leaders of the WFTU and European Communism. In this diplomatic position Pellecer was able to help a large colony of Spanish Republican exiles settle in Guatemala. In 1948 he went to Warsaw for a Communist sponsored youth meeting and then returned to Guatemala where he was appointed Chief of the Travelling Cultural Missions. Aside from editing the paper of the PAR, Pellecer became active in the labor movement and played a key role in organizing the workers of the United Fruit Company's Tiquisate holdings. His accusations that the United States was responsible for the July 1949 revolt and his other extremist public statements embarrassed the government, and he was again sent to Paris as Secretary of Legation, but the French government refused to accept him and the British also declared that he was *persona non grata*. Upon his second return to Guatemala in 1950, he took an active role in the Communist movement and became Secretary of Conflicts of the CGTG. In the January 1953 elections Pellecer was the only successful Communist candidate and became Deputy from Escuintla.

Víctor Manuel Gutiérrez. In many respects the most valuable human asset of Communism in Guatemala was the honest, humble and soft-spoken Gutiérrez, the revered leader of the Guatemalan workers.

Through hard work and devotion to the interests of the working class, Gutiérrez built up a reputation and following among organized labor which he used in the interests of the Communist Party. A man of strong convictions, Gutiérrez once broke with the Fortuny leadership and for nearly two years headed a Marxist labor party before rejoining the Communist party of Fortuny and the other top Communist leaders. As Secretary General of the 100,000-member CGTG, Chairman of several Congressional Committees and mentor to the campesino leaders, Gutiérrez was far more important than his position as one of the eleven members of the PGT Political Commission and head of its Labor Commission indicated. Nicknamed the "Franciscan" for his ascetic manner of living, Gutiérrez was the complete opposite of Secretary General Fortuny and his chief rival within the party.

Born of ladino parents in Barbarena, Department of Santa Rosa, on January 10, 1922, Gutiérrez attended local schools for the first six years.[2] In 1935 he enrolled in the Central Normal School for Boys in Guatemala City and graduated four years later as a primary school teacher. For the next three years he taught at the National Boys' Institute in Chiquimula. After teaching in Guatemala City for a year and a half, in the middle of 1944 he was appointed sub-director of the Industrial Institute for Boys. Thus the Revolution found him a young man of 22 who had been earning his way as a poorly paid teacher for five years and who possessed first-hand contact with the problems of the working class.[3]

Gutiérrez was active in the labor movement from the first days of the revolution and rose rapidly to become the leader. A founder of the teachers' union (STEG), he soon became its Secretary General and representative to the CTG. In October of 1946 Gutiérrez was elected to the top post of the CTG and in 1951 became Secretary General of the unified labor movement. He was elected for a second term to the top office of the labor movement in 1954. The fact that by the age of twenty-four he was one of the two most important labor leaders in the country and four years later was without a serious rival is a record which indicates a recognized capacity for leadership.

Gutiérrez was elected to Congress in 1945 by the PAR. He served

---

[2] Gutiérrez himself claims that the correct date was 1923; see 8019:393-4, Gutiérrez to Civil Registrar of Barbarena, December 6, 1950. All official records give the earlier year.

[3] See 8019:191, Datos correspondientes a V. M. Gutiérrez.

on the Executive Committee and the Political Commission of that party before resigning in September of 1949 to form the PROG. When his term as Deputy expired in 1947, President Arévalo appointed him Secretary of the Travelling Missions of Initial Culture. In 1948 he returned to teaching at the Central Normal School for Girls where he taught Marxism in his political economy courses. Arévalo, who was quite fond of Gutiérrez and approved of the work which he was doing in the labor movement, appointed him to the Board of Directors of the Guatemalan Institute of Social Security, a job which left him virtually free for his work as Secretary General of the CTG. In 1950 Gutiérrez ran for Congress wtih the backing of all the revolutionary parties, and in 1954 became its First Secretary.

Other Members of the Political Commission. José Luis Ramos, the least well known of the five members of the Secretariat, was active chiefly in the labor and agrarian fields. A Communist since the days of the *Vanguardia Democrática*, Ramos held a high position in the CTG and became the Secretary General of its Political Action Committee in 1950. In October 1951 he became Vice-Secretary of Agrarian Relations of the CGTG and the following year was named Secretary of Training of the CNCG. During the 1952-1954 period he served simultaneously as the head of the PGT's Peasant Commission and the CGTG representative on the important National Agrarian Council. During October and November 1953, Ramos attended several important Communist labor meetings in Vienna and toured the USSR.

José Alberto Cardoza, one of the four PGT Deputies and a Political Commission member, was second only to Gutiérrez among the Communist labor leaders. A twenty-six year old printer at the time of the revolution, Cardoza helped found the Graphic Arts Union (SAG). As its Secretary of Propaganda, he played a key role in the Communist take-over of the Guatemalan Union Federation (FSG). An ally of Gutiérrez, Cardoza served as a leader of the PROG and First Vice-Secretary of the CGTG. When his term as Secretary General of the Graphic Arts Union expired in 1953, Cardoza moved up to the top post in the newly-created printing trade federation. In Congress he became Chairman of the strategic Special Committee on Revision of the Labor Code.

Carlos René Valle y Valle, head of the PGT Finance Commission, was a nineteen-year-old law student at the time of the revolution and came to the party through the AJDG and PAR. While an employee of the Ministry of Education and National Petroleum Institute, he was also business manager of the party paper *Octubre*.

Virgilio Guerra Méndez, born in Chalchuapa, El Salvador, in 1906 and a carpenter by trade, was the oldest of the PGT leaders and senior in terms of experience. A founder of the *Escuela Claridad* and Secretary General of the carpenters' union, Guerra was expelled from Guatemala in October 1947 by Arévalo, but returned within a few months and was employed by the Social Security Institute. After serving as advisor to the United Fruit Company workers in their 1953 contract talks, Guerra became CGTG Secretary of Organization in January 1954. In May of that year he went to Moscow to represent the Guatemalan Communists at the Soviet trade union congress.

Antonio Ardón, a Honduran by birth and a tailor by trade, was perhaps the least prominent of the Political Commission members. An early CTG leader, he was elected Secretary of Social Matters of the PAR in 1949. Within the party his chief importance was as Secretary General of the Departmental Committee for the Department of Guatemala. In 1954 he became the head of the "League of Guatemalan Renters," an important "mass organization" manipulated by the Communists.

Factions and Rivalry Within the PGT. While it would be unrealistic to believe that all was harmony and perfect accord within the PGT leadership, a close study of the development of Communism in Guatemala does not provide any conclusive proof that factionalism was a major problem. The course of events from the First Congress in 1949 to the Second Congress in 1952 would seem to indicate that the major difference was between Gutiérrez and his labor group and Fortuny and the political group, between those who had developed primarily in the CTG and those whose path to Communism was through the PAR. The basic difference seems to have been over the question of an independent working class party versus close cooperation with the bourgeois politicians and parties. That there was a divergence as late as 1950 and 1951 between the intellectual and worker elements of the Communist Party seems evident.[4] While there may also have been differences

---

[4] See Y-X-6:2175, *Puntos de vista para la unidad de los Marxistas,* a proposal for the unity of the PCG and PROG based upon 55% representation of the workers and 45% for the intellectuals.

along lines of nationalism and internationalism or over the *caudillo* instinct of Fortuny, they were decreasing by the time of the Second Congress and should not be exaggerated. Certainly factionalism and rivalries within the PGT were insignificant when contrasted to the internal bickering and rampant factionalism of the other Guatemalan parties. Several leaders such as Pellecer and Ramos were equally active in labor and political affairs, and the operation of democratic centralism was a barrier to the development of factions.

A study of the leadership of the PGT shows that the labor movement had at least 10 representatives on the 21-member Central Committee (including 7 officials of the CGTG) and at least five on the 11-member Political Commission. However only one of the five members of the important Secretariat was closely connected to labor and only two of the eight functional commissions were headed by labor leaders. Nevertheless it is entirely possible that the top Communists in the labor movement, four of whom were members of Congress in addition to their duties as high officials of the CGTG, were too busy to take on a full-time party job. The five secretaries were the only Political Commission members who had no outside responsibilities. Those who argue the supremacy of the Fortuny clique point out that Alvarado Monzón, Silva Jonama, Guerra Borges and to a lesser extent Ramos were all protégés of Fortuny from the early days in the PAR and the VDG.

LEADERSHIP OF THE PGT

Secretary
  General   — José Manuel Fortuny

Secretariat   — Fortuny
                  Mario Silva Jonama (Responsible for Education)
                  Alfredo Guerra Borges (Responsible for Propaganda)
                  Bernardo Alvarado Monzón (Responsible for Organization)
                  José Luis Ramos (Responsible for Campesino Affairs)

Political Commission	— the five members of the Secretariat plus
	Víctor Manuel Gutiérrez (Responsible for Labor; Deputy)
	Carlos Manuel Pellecer (Deputy)
	José Alberto Cardoza (Deputy)
	Virgilio Guerra
	Antonio Ardón
	Carlos René Valle (Responsible for Finance)
Central Committee	— the eleven members of the Political Commission plus
	Max Salazar
	Concepción Castro de Mencos
	Huberto Alvarado (Responsible for Youth Affairs)
	Irma de Alvarado (Responsible for Feminine Activities)
	Oscar Edmundo Palma (Responsible for Peace Campaign)
	Efraín Villatoro
	Félix Osorio Velis
	Octavio Reyes
	Pedro Fernández
	Francisco Hernández

The Replacement of Fortuny. One of the most interesting episodes in the internal life of the Guatemalan Communist Party was the replacement of Fortuny by Alvarado Monzón as Secretary General of the PGT on May 26, 1954. Outwardly the party claimed that this was only temporary and due to Fortuny's poor health. In reality much more was involved. At the October 1953 session of the Central Committee, Alvarado Monzón delivered a report on collective leadership based upon the editorial of the Cominform journal *For a Lasting*

Peace, For a Peoples' Democracy on September 4. Since the "rich experience of the Communist Party of the Soviet Union" had shown collective leadership to be the true Marxist-Leninist policy, it was to be adopted by all Communist parties.[5]

In November of 1953 Fortuny was called to Moscow, reportedly as a result of the demand of Gutiérrez who was already there.[6] He remained there for two months during a period when the rush of events would seem to have required his presence in Guatemala. If nothing else, his absence enabled the PGT to begin practicing collective leadership in earnest. After his return to Guatemala the Central Committee met on March 13 and 14 and removed one of its members, Pedro Fernández, for "apathy," replacing him with Manuel Sánchez, a campesino leader from Escuintla and assistant to Pellecer.[7] Meeting again on May 26, 1954 the Central Committee listened to a report on Fortuny's "health" and voted to elevate Alvarado Monzón to the post of Secretary General "for the time that the recovery of J. M. Fortuny takes."[8] Ramos was to take over as head of the Commission of Organization and Antonio Ardón chosen as the new member of the Secretariat.

Claims were immediately made by Guatemalan political observers that the replacement of Fortuny was the result of a sharp difference within the leadership over the strategy of the "step backwards." Fortuny was rumored to have favored the resignation of Communists in exposed Government positions so that the opponents of the Arbenz regime would have less concrete evidence of Communist penetration of the government and to have been opposed by Gutiérrez, Pellecer and others of the CGTG leadership. The formal charges brought against Fortuny appear to have been "bourgeois weakness" and "conduct unworthy of a Communist leader," involving his predilections for women and alcohol. The matter was carried over into the period of

---

[5] 8039:594-5, Algunos elementos del informe sobre la dirección colectiva y el reforzamiento de la disciplina, Guatemala, October 13, 1953.

[6] *Tribuna Popular* claimed that he had gone to participate in the November 7 celebration of the anniversary of the Soviet Revolution, but did not explain how he could leave Guatemala on the 5th, be in Mexico on the 9th and get to Moscow by the 7th.

[7] 8039:654 or *Tribuna Popular,* March 16, 1954.

[8] Document 925: Reunión del Comité Central del PGT, May 27, 1954.

exile and in Mexico in 1955 he was formally relieved of all positions of leadership.[9]

One basic reason for Fortuny's removal was his feeling that the party was trying to go too far too fast and losing touch with the realities of the Guatemalan situation. Alvarado Monzón, Silva Jonama, Guerra Borges and Pellecer accused him of timidity. The case was "tried" by Alejandro Severo Aguirre, a Cuban Communist leader. In his various autocriticisms, Fortuny mentioned repeatedly that the other leaders frequently compared the Guatemalan situation with that of Viet Nam and felt that the establishment of a peoples' democracy in Guatemala in the foreseeable future was not out of the question. In Fortuny's eyes conditions in Guatemala did not justify such hopes.

Party Membership. The exact size of the PGT is difficult to ascertain as no complete listing has ever been made public.[10] Growth during the 1953-1954 period was extremely rapid and it is probable that party membership was nearly 4000 by the time the Arbenz Regime fell. This estimate appears to be borne out by the numbering of the carnets given out in 1954, statements on rate of growth found among PGT records, and the reconstruction of party rolls from fragmentary documents.

ORGANIZATION AND OPERATIONS

The Partido Guatemalteco del Trabajo was organized along the Leninist principles which are characteristic of Communist Parties

---

[9] The story can be pieced together in part at least through a number of "auto-criticisms" written by Fortuny during 1954 and 1955. Several of these are included in Del Valle Matheu, *op. cit.*, pp. 115-130. We can be concerned here only with that part which occurred before the fall of the Arbenz government.

[10] Reel 8001 is an incomplete set of the carnets of the PGT. A list of 532 members was submitted to the Civic Registrar on December 18, 1952, but was not a complete listing as of that date. Documents which contain partial lists of membership in various subdivisions of the party include 1481: Comité Central del Partido Guatemalteco del Trabajo, December 14, 1952; 809: Nómina de los Camaradas que integran el Comité Central del Partido Guatemalteco del Trabajo; 1035: a list of Central Committee members just before the Second Congress; also 928, 654, 1153, 1782, 1783, 656, 810, 812, 18, 20, 19, 226, and 931. Also 8039:623-8; 8021:78; 8021:79; 8029:624, 625, 626, 627, 633/1, and 655.

throughout the world.[11] Its organization and discipline proved a unique asset when contrasted to the other Guatemalan parties. The National Congress, which was to meet each third year, elected the Central Committee of 21 members which "constitutes the highest authority of the party when the Congress is not in session." The Central Committee, which met three times a year, elected an eleven-man Political Commission which "directs the Party's activities when the Central Committee is not in session." The five members of the Secretariat were chosen by the Political Commission and were collectively responsible "for the daily work of the Party leadership, for organizing the execution of the resolutions of the Central Committee and Political Commission, for the assignment and training of leaders." The Secretariat and Political Commission were presided over by the Secretary General, who was elected by the Central Committee. The basic committee or cell is the fundamental unit of party organization. Above it was to be erected a network of district, sectional, municipal, departmental, and regional "intermediate" organizations. However, with the exception of the Department of Guatemala, the entire system of echelons was never completed. All these organizations were bound to carry out the resolutions of the higher party organs. "Democratic centralism" and rigid discipline insured the supremacy of the party leadership.

Comisión de Organización. The internal administration of the party was in the hands of the Organizational Commission and its able leader, Bernardo Alvarado Monzón. At the Central Committee meeting of May 26, 1954 José Luis Ramos took over this job as Alvarado Monzón was carrying the responsibilities of the Secretary General. The commission strove constantly to strengthen the organization of the party and to found new organizations in areas to which the Communists spread their operations. Its goal was a strong, unified party solidly linked to the masses, and it was in organization and discipline that the PGT outstripped the other Guatemalan parties. In December of 1951 the party launched the first of its recruitment and propaganda drives in honor of Lenin and Stalin.[12] In the first four weeks the party gained

---

[11] See *Estatutos del Partido Guatemalteco del Trabajo, Aprobados por el II Congreso del Partido,* December 11-14, 1952.

[12] *Boletín de Organización,* No. 1, November 27, 1951.

151 new members in Guatemala City alone.[13] At the end of eight weeks, 200 new members had been recruited with 186 of them living in Guatemala City and more than two-thirds coming from the ranks of labor. Sales of *Octubre* were raised by 1100 to a total of 2600 and nearly 150,000 pieces of propaganda circulated.[14] Another emulation, this time in honor of Karl Marx, led to the recruitment of 188 new members by June 21. One hundred and twenty-seven of these new members were from the capital, with Escuintla and Puerto Barrios furnishing the bulk of the others. A total of 7000 copies of the special edition of *Octubre* on agrarian reform were sold and over 210,000 items of propaganda circulated.[15]

On August 8 and 9, 1953, the PGT held a National Conference on Organization attended by the Secretaries of Organization of each local cell and the Secretaries of Organization and Secretaries General of the intermediate committees.[16] The party had doubled in size in the eight months since the Second Congress, and its social composition stood at 50% workers, 29% campesinos and 21% middle class intellectuals. Those who had entered the party during 1953 were 43% workers, 41% campesinos and 16% middle class, indicating that the party was moving into the countryside and taking advantage of agrarian reform to recruit among the campesinos. The geographical distribution of the Communists was evident from the fact that departmental committees had been established in Guatemala, Escuintla and Chimaltenango, a sectional committee in Santa Rosa and a municipal committee in Puerto Barrios. In his report on "Boosting the Growth of the Party and Strengthening its Organizations," Bernardo Alvarado Monzón undertook a probing self-criticism of the party's organizational work and developed a detailed program which included: a) A wide diffusion of its political line among the masses and a tenacious effort to apply it. b) A tighter linkage with the masses. c) The improvement of the work of all the organizations of the Party. d) Regular payment of dues. e) The strengthening of discipline and of criticism and self-criticism. f) A rapid elevation of the ideological level of all the militants

---

[13] *Boletín de Organización,* No. 2, January 4, 1952.

[14] *Octubre,* January 24, 1952.

[15] *Octubre,* July 3, 1952.

[16] See *Boletín de Organización,* No. 7, September, 1953 and *Octubre,* August 13, 1953.

and cadres of the party. g) An intense work of recruitment of new members.

The key role of the Organizational Commission can be seen from the fact that it shared in the responsibilities of the other commissions, as in the case of assigning members Antonio Ardón and Efraín Villatoro the responsibility for seeing that the fractions in the labor organizations "are not merely lists of members affiliated with the unions."[17] In 1954 the organizational plans of the party were even more ambitious than the preceding year as the Communists wished to build a strong base for the proposed "United Front of the Masses."[18]

Comisión de Educación y Propaganda. This body and its head, Mario Silva Jonama, were entrusted with the never-ending task of raising the ideological level of the members and keeping them informed of the party line. Since the PGT was growing rapidly and accepting members with little or no education, some of whom were even unable to read Spanish, the commission had a formidable job on its hands. Its second task was to supervise the propaganda work of the party and see that this material reached a wide number of persons outside the ranks of the party. The scope of the Communists' propaganda work can be seen from the fact that they distributed 200,000 copies of propaganda favoring the united front of the masses and regularly circulated from 3000 to 5000 copies of the reports of Fortuny and Alvarado Monzón to the Central Committee meetings. The size of the party can be appreciated when we realize that 8000 copies of the statutes were ordered printed as were 2500 copies of such an esoteric book as Liu Shao-chi's *How to Be a Good Communist.*[19] Important policy statements such as the Communist line on ODECA were sent to every top government official down through the governors of the 22 Departments.[20] Taking the distribution of propaganda as indicator, the Communists were most active in Guatemala, Escuintla, Izabal, Jutiapa, Chimaltenango, Suchitepequez, Santa Rosa, and Retalhuleu; somewhat

---

[17] Document 940: B. Alvarado Monzón to Antonio Ardón, May 12, 1954.

[18] See Document 1548: Elementos para la elaboración de un plan de trabajo, February, 1954.

[19] See Document 814: pamphlets published by the PGT. See also 811.

[20] Documents 744: Alfredo Guerra Borges to Leonardo Castillo Flores, October 16, 1952; 1477: Alfredo Guerra Borges to President of Congress, October 16, 1952; 1478: list of persons to whom the statement by Fortuny on ODECA was sent.

less active in Quezaltenango, San Marcos, Sololá, Chiquimula, Baja Verapaz and Alta Verapaz, and carried on a minimum of activity in the other seven departments.[21]

On the education side the commission was equally busy with its representatives frequently visiting the local organizations. In addition to publishing a bi-monthly *Boletín de Educación y Propaganda* and preparing study courses on various aspects of Communist doctrine and party work, the commission supervised the work of the Department and Sectional Committees in the education field.[22] Much of the material had to be simplified and paraphrased from the original to make it meaningful to the poorly-educated rank and file, but the national, departmental and in many cases the local leaders faithfully followed the international Communist line through the pages of *For a Lasting Peace, For a Peoples' Democracy* and pursued their study of Communism back to the writings of Marx, Engles, Lenin, Stalin and Mao Tse-tung.[23] Gutiérrez's introduction to the study of the *History of the Communist Party* (b) *of the USSR* was used by the rank and file, many of whom later attempted to cope with the original.[24]

This commission—composed of Silva Jonama, Guerra Borges, Tischler, Heberto Sosa and Paúl Castellanos—constantly sought ways to overcome the ideological backwardness of the rank and file member. A National Conference on Education and Propaganda was scheduled for June 26 and 27 of 1954 to discuss means of implementing the slogan: "For the elevation of the Communist conscience and militance of all the members of our Party and the widening of its influence in the grand masses of the people!"[25] The Conference, needless to say,

---

[21] Document 813: Plan de distribución de volantes, December 3, 1953.

[22] For a sample of the work of the commission see 8013:296-7, *Boletín de Educación y Propaganda*, No. 3, August 1-15, 1953; 8024:1439, Circular of Comisión de Educación y Propaganda del Comité Central, June 10, 1953; 8039:663-665, Comisión de Educación y Propaganda, Material de Educación No. 3, Questionario y Guía de Lecturas del 1er. cursillo: La Construcción y Organización del Partido; Y-X-1:778-781 or 8039:651-3, "Tres Problemas Importantes de Nuestra Labor Ideológica" by Mario Silva Jonama; 8024: 1380-1383, *El Camarada*, No. 12, March 6, 1954; 8024:1352-3, *Propaganda: Boletín de la Secretaría de Propaganda del Seccional Parroquia*, No. 1.

[23] See Document 1154: Proposiciones para el estudio en la Dirección del Partido: Tema inmediato: El Frente Unico en la actual etapa de nuestra Revolución.

[24] See 8039:646.

[25] Document 1389 or 8039:647, Convocatoria a la Primera Conferencia Nacional de Educación y Propaganda del PGT, May 6, 1954.

was one of the many Communist projects which were interrupted by the fall of the Arbenz regime.

The Party as the General Staff of the Revolution: Links with the Mass Organizations. As has been pointed out repeatedly, the Party constituted the spinal column of the Communist movement in Guatemala. However, as we shall see in subsequent chapters, much of the work of Communism in Guatemala was carried on using the labor unions and the other so-called "mass organizations" as a front. Each member of the party was required to work in one of these organizations. The policies of the Communist "fractions" in these organizations were determined within the Political Commission of the party and coordinated and implemented through the various specialized commissions of the Central Committee. In addition to the Commissions on Organization, Education and Propaganda, and Finance—bodies which dealt largely with the functioning of the party itself—there were the labor, youth, women, peasant and peace commissions. In those Departments in which the full array of party organizations existed, the Departmental Committee designated one member as "responsible" for each of these areas of work.

Comisión Sindical. The Commission on Labor Unions was headed by Víctor Manuel Gutiérrez, Secretary General of the CGTG and the unquestioned leader of 100,000 organized workers. As colleagues on the Central Committee of the PGT he had most of the top leaders of the trade union movement: José Alberto Cardoza, Vice-Secretary General of the CGTG and czar of the printing industry workers; Virgilio Guerra, Secretary of Organization of the CGTG; Carlos Manuel Pellecer, Secretary of Conflicts of the CGTG and leader of the workers and peasants in the rich Department of Escuintla; Max Salazar, Secretary of Campesino Relations of the CGTG; José Luis Ramos, Associate Secretary of the CGTG and a campesino leader; Concepción Castro de Mencos, Associate Secretary of the CGTG and leader of the numerous textile workers; Efraín Villatoro, leader of the workers in the Department of Guatemala; Antonio Ardón, President of the League of Renters and a leader of the tailors' union. In addition the Secretaries of Finance, Records and Conflicts of the CGTG were PGT members Rafael Solís Barrios, Antonio Obando Sánchez and

César Montenegro Paniagua. In Chapter VI it will be shown that the leaders of many of the most important constituent unions and federations which made up the CGTG were also controlled by members of the Communist Party. In every significant union there was a Communist fraction operating under the directions of the PGT's *Comisión Sindical.* For all practical purposes the Labor Commission of the PGT and the Executive Committee of the CGTG were one and the same. Not only the political line, but all major policy decisions of the labor movement were determined in the *Comisión Sindical* of the PGT.[26]

The Communist fractions within the various unions were not casual groupings, but were tightly organized and disciplined bodies working under the direction of the Labor Commission of the party. Meeting regularly, each had its own executive bureau and was subject to the control of the Organizational Commission of the party. The general task of the fraction was to insure the "correct application of the line of the party" and to recruit new members for the party. Since on the level of the individual unions a majority of the members were not Communists, the fraction played a key role in winning their support for the directives of the Communist leadership of the labor movement.[27]

Communist aims and tactics in the labor field were summarized in a document circulated to PGT fractions and leaders late in 1953. In addition to an exposition of the party's political line for labor,[28] the document formulated the relationship of the party and the "popular organizations."[29] The party was to "direct" these organizations without causing them to lose completely their individual identity. The party was to be the nucleus or spinal column around which the mass organizations were grouped. In the case of labor, the complete control

---

[26] See Documents 1774: Problemas para los Miembros de la Comisión Sindical del PGT, February 13, 1953; 930: V. Manuel Gutiérrez to members of the Secretariat of the PGT, March 11, 1954.

[27] For the tasks of the fractions see 8039:658-9, El Funcionamiento de las Fracciones; 8039:623, Florentín Sánchez to Secretary General of Departmental Committee of the Partido Guatemalteco del Trabajo, March 16, 1954; Y-X-4:492, Fracción in Obras Públicas al Camarada Responsable de la Comisión Sindical, April 9, 1952; 8027:254, 255, 256, or 257, Plan de Trabajo del Responsable Sindical del Comité del PGT, April 1954.

[28] United front of the masses, worker-peasant alliance, peace, liquidation of "reformist" tendencies, international solidarity with CTAL and WFTU affiliates, etc.

[29] 8032:2522-6, Conclusiones sobre la política sindical; Conclusiones sobre los métodos de trabajo sindical, December 1953.

of the Executive Committee of the CGTG by the Communists raised a problem, as the tendency of the Communists in the unions was to go directly to it, bypassing the Sindical Commission of the PGT. Especially in the case of criticism, labor matters should be taken to the *Comisión Sindical* of the PGT first. Very possibly Fortuny was afraid that Gutiérrez was becoming too influential through his complete ascendance over the CGTG. In any case the principle of collective leadership, which had been adopted by all Communist parties after the death of Stalin, was being violated by the practice of taking matters directly to Gutiérrez.

Comisión de la Juventud. The task of coordinating the work of the Communist fractions in the various youth groups was in the hands of Huberto Alvarado and Edelberto Torres h. As thoroughly documented in Chapter X, these two and their young Communist companions were the most active members of the various youth organizations. Other Communists who held high positions in these groups included Otto Raúl González, Armando Villaseñor, Octavio Reyes, Bernardo Lemus, Hugo Barrios Klee, Otto Peñate, Ricardo Ramírez and Carlos René Valle—leaders whose control was so effective that it appeared as if these groups would lose their identity and become mere adjuncts of the party. Since the chief purpose of the various Communist-controlled youth groups was to give the party an opportunity to come in contact with as many as possible of the new generation which would soon be taking a leading role in Guatemalan politics, this development was considered undesirable.

In the days before the emergence of an open Communist Party, the AJDG, along with the PAR and the CTG, had served as an organizational home and mouthpiece for the clandestine Communist movement. By 1951 Communism had made considerable progress and it was decided to revamp the AJDG, which was felt to be at a crossroads.[30]

> The Alliance can take two roads: either be a broad-based organization of the young masses, capable of fighting for peace, national independence, democracy and the specific demands of youth; or be a Communist Youth which would fight in addition for the destruction of capitalism and the installation of the dictatorship of the proletariat and the Socialist society.

[30] Document 2082 or 8029:688-693, Partido Comunista de Guatemala: Puntos de vista acerca de la Organización de la Juventud, April, 1951; also 8021:145-150, Sobre el Trabajo de la Juventud.

After an examination of the stage of party development and the conditions prevailing in Guatemala at the time, it was decided that the AJDG should operate as a mass organization and that the party should eventually establish its own organization of Communist youth. The time was not yet ripe for an open and public Communist Youth organization, but the party would begin building a nucleus within its ranks. The AJDG, in keeping with its role as a mass organization, was to seek to recruit working class and campesino youth rather than continue as a predominantly student organization. In addition it was to strengthen its organization, fill out its program with cultural and sporting activities so as to broaden its appeal, stress unity of action of all Guatemalan youth and bring into its work the youth of the other revolutionary parties. The Communists within the AJDG were to avoid the extreme of appearing to dominate the organization, while at the same time carrying on the task of educating the members with the "progressive" doctrines of Marxism and friendship for the Soviet Union. The party was to pay greater attention to youth activities and to look to the future.

> The young Communists should not hide their militance, but neither should they make a show of it. They can carry out the tasks of the Party, but principally the tasks of the struggle of youth, so that they will be better known by the masses as youth leaders than as activists of the party. Our daily work, and not leftist show, must be what wins influence and posts of leadership for us in the youth organizations.

Communist plans and progress in the youth field met with such success that the beginning of 1954 was set as the date for the organization of "a Marxist organization of the youth, which will come to be the vanguard of the Guatemalan youth movement and will give it force, orientation and direction." This organizational campaign was shrewdly planned to capitalize upon the work of the Festival of Friendship, whose Preparatory Committee was headed by PGT member Hugo Barrios Klee, and to tie in with the CNCG's organization of rural youth clubs. A "grand united front of the masses of youth" was to be formed incorporating the AJDG, FUD, CEPP, campesino youth clubs, the young workers organizations and the youth groups of the PAR and PRG. The young Communists were to provide the "dorsal spine" for this movement and to spread Marxist doctrines among the youth of Guatemala. For this purpose "nuclei of Communist youth" were to be organized immediately in the Boys' Normal School, National Institute for Boys, the national press, SAMF, throughout Guatemala City and Escuintla, and in the capitals of the other Departments.[31] A National Conference was to be held in September 1954 with a Constituent Congress scheduled for early in 1955. On July 1 a six-month study plan in which all young Communists were to participate was to go into effect.[32] Weekly study meetings of the Youth Commission were to examine such materials as Lenin's speech on the tasks of the Young Communist League, Stalin's writings on the subject, Dimitrov's book on the United Front, the biography of Lenin and the report of Jacques Denis to the Third Congress of World Youth. The membership of youth groups would regularly study the basic documents of the PGT. Showing an appreciation of the psychology of youth, the party leadership decreed that these study sessions should take place in attractive surroundings and recommended excursions, bull sessions and friendly gatherings in the evenings as the proper environment.

Comisión Femenina. Headed by Irma Chávez de Alvarado, one of the two women on the PGT Central Committee and wife of Bernardo Alvarado Monzón, this body supervised the work of the Communist fraction which controlled the *Alianza Femenina Guatemalteca.*[33] With her in the leadership of the AFG were such active Communists as Dora Franco y Franco, Concha Castro de Mencos, Elsa de Guerra Borges, Lilly de Alvarado, María Jérez de Fortuny, Hortensia Hernández Rojas, Laura de Piñeda, Liliam de Leiva, as well as a number of sympathizers and possible party members headed by Sra. de Arbenz.[34] The AFG was considered by the party as an important "fighting front" which had to be made into the "united front of women" and was the best tool for winning the women of Guatemala away from their traditional conservatism.[35]

---

[31] Document 47: Sobre los Núcleos de Jóvenes Comunistas.

[32] Document 927: Plan de Estudio para la Comisión Juvenil del Comité Central del Partido Guatemalteco del Trabajo y para los Núcleos de Jóvenes Comunistas.

[33] See 8013:479-485 or 486-492, Intervención especial sobre el trabajo en el frente femenino a cargo de Irma de Alvarado en el Segundo Congreso del Partido Guatemalteco del Trabajo, PGT, December, 1952.

[34] See 8039:698, Planilla que propone el Presidium para integrar el Consejo Nacional de Alianza Femenina Guatemalteca.

[35] 8039:657, B. Alvarado M. circular to all PGT committees, November 5, 1953.

In our party we ought to give every type of aid to this organization of women and to its congress. Take great care not to sectarianize the movement and to keep it from appearing as an organization of our party.

Comisión de la Paz. This group handled liaison with the National Peace Committee and directed the work of the peace campaign within the party. Since the head of the Commission, Oscar Edmundo Palma, occupied various high posts on the CNP as did Gutiérrez, Silva Jonama, Carlos Alvarado Jérez and many other Communists, the task was handled with little difficulty. One member of each Communist cell was given responsibility for this propaganda campaign which was accorded highest priority by the international Communist movement. This network of propagandists had the responsibility to constantly carry on the campaign both within the party and among the non-Communists where they lived and worked.[36]

Discipline. The Communists maintained a degree of discipline which was previously unknown to any Guatemalan political organization.[37] While other parties were constantly torn by internal dissension which resulted in numerous schisms and splinter groups, the PGT members toed the line or faced expulsion.[38] The PGT was the only cadre party in Guatemala and required much more of its members than merely voting for the party's candidate as was the case in the other parties. Rolando Calderón Banegas, a leader in the important railroad union SAMF, was expelled by his cell for leading a "licentious life outside of the high moral level which ought to be inherent in every member of the party."[39] The fundamental sin of Calderón had been to attend the Stockholm meeting of the International Confederation of Free

---

[36] 8039:714-715, circular from Oscar Edmundo Palma to Comités de Base, March 1953; see also Document 48: Informe del Responsable de la Paz del Comité Departamental del Partido Guatemalteco del Trabajo en el Departamento de Guatemala; also 8039:631, 648, 650, 713; 8013:470.

[37] See 8039:620-622, El Reforzamiento de la Disciplina.

[38] See Documents 16: Report of Efraín Villatoro Q. to the National Commission of Organization of the PGT on those expelled for "poor militance" in the Department of Guatemala, June 3, 1954; 594: list of those expelled in the Department of Guatemala, December 5, 1953; 939: Carlos Alberto Figueroa to Secretary of Organization of the Departmental Committee, February 6, 1954.

[39] Document 937: Javier Castellanos and Carlos A. della Chieza to Secretary of Organization of the Departmental Committee of the Partido Guatemalteco del Trabajo, July 28, 1953.

Trade Unions without the permission of the party. A minor youth leader, Melvin René Barahona was suspended for two months for "disorder" and Central Committee member Pedro Fernández was replaced for "apathy."[40] Two members of the Communist fraction within the Social Security Institute were suspended for six months for breaking the fraction's united front in a union election.[41] Abel Mazariegos was expelled for drinking, sleeping on the job of selling *Tribuna Popular,* as well as for following the usual bureaucratic practice of putting the "bite" on those who fell under his jurisdiction as an Inspector of Public Sanitation.[42]

A good example of Communist discipline was the case of Jesús Galeano, a rising young Communist militant who was expelled as "unworthy to be a Communist" for embezzling in excess of 63 cents from the *Tribuna Popular.* Expelled by his cell, Galeano appealed to higher organs, but they confirmed his expulsion.[43] Galeano attempted to prove himself worthy of readmittance by working long and faithfully for the Third Congress of the CNCG, the Second Congress of the CGTG, and the Organizing Committee of the Festival of Friendship. He spread Communist propaganda, worked for the AJDG, and used his job as Labor Inspector to the advantage of the party.[44] Finally he humbly sought to be readmitted to the party, but the leadership ruled that his request was "very premature" and that he would have to continue proving that he was worthy of the honor of being a Communist.[45]

Dissension within the ranks of the Communists did occur, but they generally proved able to keep their dirty linen out of the eye of the public. The classic case was the removal of Fortuny as Secretary General, which has previously been discussed. Differences which may have taken place within the ranks of the Political Commission or Cen-

---

[40] Document 926: Carlos René Valle to Secretary of Organization of the Departmental Committee of the PGT, June 2, 1954; 8039:654, press release of the Central Committee, March, 1954.

[41] Document 1039: report of the PGT fraction within the STIGGS to the Comisión Sindical del PGT, December 7, 1953.

[42] Document 303: Informe al Comité Departamental en el caso de Mazariegos, January 16, 1954.

[43] See Document 1544: collection of seven documents on the case of Galeano, September, 1953.

[44] Documents 298-302.

[45] Documents 303-310.

tral Committee never became public. An insight into the type of internal difficulties to which the party was subject is furnished by two letters discovered in the correspondence of Fortuny. A group of Spanish and Dominican exiles, who were members of the PGT, took exception in September 1953 to the failure of the Guatemalan leaders and particularly Fortuny to pay attention to their advice.[46] Although this group had been careful to couch their criticism in terms of "the spirit of comradeship," Fortuny accused them of "factionalism" and threatened punishment should the offense be repeated.[47]

PGT Grass Roots Activity: Chimaltenango, a Case Study. During 1953 and 1954 the Communist Party made notable progress in increasing its strength outside of the capital. Representative of its operations in the countryside were those in the Department of Chimaltenango, which lies in the heart of Guatemala about one hour's journey northwest from the capital. In 1950 the population of this primarily agricultural area was 122,310, of whom 77.5% were Indians and approximately the same percentage were illiterate. About one-third of these people lived in the 16 towns, the most important of which was Chimaltenango with a population just over six thousand. What little industry there was in the department was centered in this city.[48] In most respects Chimaltenango was as typical of Guatemala as any one department could be. Greater gains were made by the Communists in Escuintla, but there the impact of agrarian reform was considerably greater than in the rest of the country. On the other hand Communism made less progress in some of the more isolated departments where neither unionism nor agrarian reform had penetrated sufficiently to have altered the traditional order. In six months the PGT in Chimaltenango grew from a handful of members in the capital to a membership in excess of 140 spread throughout fifteen communities.

At the beginning of 1953 the only Communist cell in Chimaltenango

---

[46] Letter from Antonio Román Durán, Rafael de Buen y Lozano, Juan Ducoudray and five others to José Manuel Fortuny and the Political Commission of the PGT, September 24, 1953. Photostatic copy in the possession of the author.

[47] J. Manuel Fortuny to Antonio Román Durán and comrades, September 26, 1953. Photostat in possession of the author.

[48] Jorge del Valle Matheu, *Guía Sociogeográfica de Guatemala,* Guatemala, 1956, pp. 115-126.

was the Comité de Base Enrique Muñoz Meany with seven members located in the departmental capital.[49] The leading members of this cell were Pablo Morales S., Andrés Barrera C., Manuel Escobar González, Agrarian Inspector Natzul Aguirre Cook, and the schoolteacher, Elsa María Zayas. In line with the plan adopted after the Second Congress of the Communist Party of Guatemala, five new cells were established in the spring of 1953 with a total of 34 new members.[50]

In June of 1953 the six cells and 41 members of the PGT in the Department of Chimaltenango undertook an ambitious plan of expansion and consolidation.[51] This three-month plan followed the lines laid down by the Central Committee's Secretary of Organization Bernardo Alvarado Monzón. The major tasks undertaken were agitation and propaganda, elevation of the ideological level and the recruitment of new members, and strengthening of the organizations of the party. Under the first portion of this three-pronged program, the party was to carry out a great variety of meetings on every village and finca, to put out a monthly bulletin, to disseminate all the materials sent out from national headquarters and to sell at least 125 copies of Fortuny's Report to the Second Congress and 75 copies of the party statutes, and to "realize activities which call attention, such as movies, fiestas, etc. and to take advantage of them politically." With respect to the second point, study and discussion meetings were to be held at least once a week, using the materials of the Party Congress as a foundation. A

---

[49] This section is based upon original documents contained in a folder labeled "PGT: Chimaltenango."

[50] A cell was established at San Jacinto on March 11 with eight members, another at Parramos on the 13th with eight members and a third at San Andrés Itzapa on the same day with seven recruits. (Pablo Morales S. to Bernardo Alvarado Monzón, March 14, 1953). On the 17th a cell was founded at El Tejar with six members, (Pablo Morales S. to Bernardo Alvarado Monzón, March 18, 1953), and on the 9th of April the fifth new cell was organized at Ciénaga Grande with five militants. (Pablo Morales S. to Bernardo Alvarado Monzón, April 10, 1953). Another cell was organized at Santa Isabel on the 17th (Pablo Morales S. to Bernardo Alvarado Monzón, April 18, 1953), but it soon fell apart and Escobar found it necessary to direct a message to them stressing that "we the Communists" are the true friends of the campesinos and those who tried to tell them differently were enemies. (Manuel Escobar G. to Comité de Base de Aldea Santa Isabel; May 5, 1953). This cell was reconstituted on July 2 with six members. (Pablo Morales S. to Bernardo Alvarado Monzón, July 2, 1953.)

[51] See Plan de Trabajo para Chimaltenango, 3 Meses, in folder labeled "PGT: Chimaltenango."

goal of 100 new militants was set for the department. The oldest and best established cell in the department was to be dissolved and its members assigned to lead the new cells in the outlying communities so that they would have the benefit of experienced leadership. In all, nine new cells were to be established and the existing six enlarged.

On July 12 a Departmental Assembly was held for the purpose of setting up a Departmental Committee. This committee was composed largely of the veteran Communists from the *Comité de Base* "Enrique Muñoz Meany." Barrera was Secretary General, Escobar Secretary of Organization and Aguirre Cook Secretary of Education and Propaganda. These three relatively sophisticated and comparatively well-indoctrinated Communists formed the Secretariat of the Departmental Committee.[52] Aguirre Cook had been active in the labor movement since immediately following the revolution and had held several offices under Gutiérrez in the CTG, FTDG and CGTG. Barrera and Escobar followed the international scene in the Cominform journal *For a Lasting Peace, For a Peoples' Democracy* and subscribed to Communist periodicals such as *New Poland* in order to keep up with the "works of political, social and economic transformation carried out in the USSR and the Popular Democracies."[53]

The Secretaries of the fifteen cells participated in the National Conference on Organization on the 8th and 9th of August.[54] The PGT took an active part in the municipal elections of November and carried on the full array of youth, feminine and peace activities.[55] However the organization lacked some of the levels found in the Department of Guatemala as there were no district, sectional, municipal and regional committees between the base organizations and the Departmental Committee.[56] The PGT in Chimaltenango worked closely with the CGTG and the CNCG.[57]

Discipline was relatively strict among the departmental leaders.

---

[52] Manuel Escobar G. to Secretary General of each Comité de Base, July, 1953.

[53] Andrés Barrera to agent of *La Nueva Polonia* in Mexico, June 19, 1953.

[54] Manuel Escobar G. to Secretario General del Comité de Base, July 29, 1953.

[55] Andrés Barrera to Manuel Escobar G., December 11, 1953.

[56] Circular from Bernardo Alvarado Monzón to Secretario General, February 2, 1953.

[57] CGTG Secretary of Finance circular, August 17, 1953.

When Escobar seemed to be putting personal and family matters on a plane with party work, Barrera chastised him for a lack of "Communist conscience" and asserted that he knew that Escobar's "profound Communist conviction" would help him do his duty.[58] In June of 1954 Pablo Morales S., who a year earlier had been Secretary General of the *Comité de Base* "Enrique Muñoz Meany," was expelled from the party "for not accepting its discipline" and another of the seven original members, Elsa María Zayas, was removed from the position of Secretary of Feminine Affairs "for not being able to attend the meetings and thus preventing a correct functioning of collective leadership." Since Barrera had recently become an Agrarian Inspector and was required to travel, Escobar replaced him as Secretary General of the Departmental Committee and Barrera took over responsibility for the workers and campesinos front.[59]

Even before they began their expansion, the Communists were entrenched in strategic positions in Chimaltenango. Of the seven members of the original cell, Pablo Morales S. was the representative of the CGTG on the Departmental Agrarian Commission (CAD), Andrés Barrera was the governmental representative of that same body, and Manuel Escobar the Secretary.[60] In addition Natzul Aguirre Cook was Agrarian Inspector for that area. With this control of the departmental agrarian machinery by the PGT, it is easy to see why the campesinos became willing recruits for the party. Although the Communists attempted to recruit as many workers as possible, an increasing proportion of their new members were campesinos and in many cases Indians. The opportunistic nature of the attraction felt by many of these new recruits is evident from a letter written by Escobar to Gutiérrez complaining that some cattle were given to PAR campesinos instead of members of the PGT and that this made many campesinos in that area lose confidence in the party.[61] Much of the Communists' work and growth was closely linked to agrarian reform, and an increase in the tempo of agrarian reform accompanied the recruitment and organizational drive of the PGT. The progress made by the PGT was largely among the lower middle class and working class ladinos and those

[58] Andrés Barrera to Manuel Escobar, October 22, 1953.
[59] Document 932: Manuel Escobar González and Angel Julían Ochaeta to José Luis Ramos, June 15, 1954.
[60] Pablo Morales S., Andrés Barrera and Manuel Escobar G. to Alfredo Guerra Borges, March 10, 1953.
[61] Letter by M. Escobar G. to V. M. Gutiérrez, July 8, 1953.

Indian campesinos whose traditional way of life had been affected in some way by the social and economic changes being brought about, chiefly through the agrarian reform program. Many of the larger centers of traditional integrated Indian life had no Communists or at least no party organization.

The Communist Press. The Guatemalan Communists followed Lenin's maxim on the role of the press:

> The role of a newspaper is not confined solely to the spreading of ideas, to political agitation and to attracting political allies. A paper is not merely a collective propagandist and collective agitator. It is also a collective organizer.[62]

Their first paper was the weekly *Octubre* which was launched on June 21, 1950 and gave way in the middle of August 1953 to the daily *Tribuna Popular*. This change from a weekly to a daily was in keeping with the rapid growth of the party and the spread of Communist influence. *Octubre* had raised its circulation to nearly 3000 by the end of 1952 when the decision was made to convert it into a daily. In the middle of May 1953 a fund-raising campaign was undertaken by the Party and collected well in excess of $10,000.[63] While the sales and subscription list of the new paper grew rapidly, advertisements from the government helped get the daily on its feet. Six government agencies, including the Publicity Office of the President, paid in more to the Communist paper than did all its subscriptions and sales during 1953.[64] By May 1954 the Communist paper was selling over 15,000 copies daily, more than any other Guatemalan newspaper with the possible exception of *El Imparcial*.[65]

Tribuna Popular, as did its predecessor *Octubre*, gave heavy play to the Communist line on international affairs and to sympathetic articles on the Soviet Union, China and the Eastern European Peoples' Democracies. Many of these articles were taken from the Soviet Government news agency TASS as well as from the pages of *Pravda, For a*

---

[62] *What is to Be Done.*

[63] See Y-X-2:2173, circular of Comité de Iniciación de *Tribuna Popular*, May 25, 1953; Document 1403: circular from B. Alvarado M., May 4, 1953; also Documents 1427 and 1428.

[64] See Documents 1481 and 1772: financial statements of *Tribuna Popular* as of December 31, 1953.

[65] *Tribuna Popular*, April 25, 1954 and May 16, 1954.

Lasting Peace, for a Peoples' Democracy, New Times and other Communist publications. Articles depicting favorable views on Communist countries were skillfully juxtaposed with those describing terror, suffering and oppression in the Western world. In addition, however, the Communist paper contained sports, amusements and almost everything which would entirely satisfy the reader so that he would not be tempted to turn to the "bourgeois" press.

The Communists also controlled *Unidad,* the monthly "voice of the CGTG." PGT deputy Pellecer was the director and José Alberto Cardoza the administrator of this paper which was financed by means of advertising contracts with government agencies such as the National Agrarian Department, National Agrarian Bank, Social Security Institute and the Presidency.[66] Since *Unidad* seemed to be duplicating the work of the Communist daily, *Tribuna Popular,* Gutiérrez recommended that it be transformed into a review rather than a news sheet, and that every effort be made to convert it into a more effective propaganda instrument.[67] In general *Unidad* was useful to the Communists primarily as a means of reaching those workers who did not regularly read *Tribuna Popular.*

Communist books and other materials were readily available in Guatemala through the "Future" book store (*Librería Futuro*), which was owned by the party.[68] Spanish editions of Communist classics and Soviet publications put out by the Foreign Languages Publishing House in Moscow were sold at extremely low prices.[69] At these bargain prices and with Communist influence growing, business was brisk.[70]

---

[66] See Document 497 or Y-X-2:1843-8, report of *Unidad* director Guillermo Max González to the Second Congress of the CGTG, January 29, 1954; Y-X-2:2011, Julio César Ordóñez, Sub-Secretario de Gobernación to Carlos Manuel Pellecer, July 28, 1951; Y-X-2:2018-24, correspondence dealing with advertising contracts from various government agencies, September 3, 1952.

[67] Y-X-2:2007-9 or 8024:1040-2, Proyecto de resoluciones sobre el informe de: "Unidad Como Orientador y Organizador del Movimiento Obrero"; 8024:1260-1, Resoluciones aprobadas por la comisión que estudió el informe *Unidad* como organizador y orientador del movimiento obrero, March 21, 1953; also 8024:1295-6; Y-X-2:1834-5, 2040-57, 2166, 2240-1 and 1796.

[68] See Document 1950: Servicio de la Librería "Futuro" para los C. de la C. P. del C. C.

[69] 8031:1444-1445, booklist of Librería Futuro. Prices ranged from 2¢ to 75¢.

[70] See Document 808: Número de ejemplares vendidos en la Librería Futuro de los libros más importantes que han vendido. Sales of most books ran from 500 to 900 copies with the *Revista Unión Soviética* selling over 13,000.

THE VEILED COMMUNISTS

In addition to the membership of the PGT, the Communist movement in Guatemala could count upon several other groups. The first of these includes those individuals who were clearly Communists but, due to personal and tactical disagreements with Fortuny and his colleagues, never joined the PGT. On the one side of this category of "non-party Communists" were the "crypto-Communists" or secret party members who were more useful to the Communist movement as leaders of the other revolutionary parties. Farther from the party and shading over into the ranks of sympathizers and fellow travellers were the "intellectual pro-Communists," a group which had been subjected to the same influences and experience as the PGT leadership but who for one reason or another stopped short of party membership. An important fact about the Guatemalan political scene is that the leadership of the other revolutionary parties was largely drawn from these groups. (Since it is impossible to investigate each case of individuals accused by the Guatemalan government of having been secret members of the Communist Party, the author has not attempted to judge into which of these categories each individual falls.)

The most prominent of these veiled Communists were the three PRG leaders—Abel Cuenca, Alfonso Solórzano and Roberto Alvarado Fuentes—labor leader Manuel Pinto Usaga, and Jaime Díaz Rozzotto, Secretary General of the Presidency.[71] In general these individuals supported the thesis that the Communists should operate through the revolutionary parties rather than on their own. Disagreement over tactics was complicated by personal feuds and the fact that Cuenca, Solórzano, Alvarado Fuentes, and even Pinto Usaga felt that they were wiser and more experienced than the young PGT leaders. They had

---

[71] Cuenca, a Salvadorean, had been one of the younger leaders of the 1932 Communist revolution in his country. Solórzano had probably belonged to the Mexican Communist Party while a close associate of Lombardo Toledano during the late 1930's. He was attacked several times during the Arbenz regime by Pellecer, who referred to him as "another Anna Pauker" (a Roumanian Communist leader who was purged in 1952). Alvarado Fuentes worked closely with the Chilean Communist Party while a student in that country. Pinto was a Marxist labor leader who eventually accepted unification of the labor movement under Communist control. Solórzano and Alvarado Fuentes were active in many pro-Soviet efforts and were elevated to membership on the Communist-controlled World Peace Council in 1952.

felt that the break with the PAR in 1950 was premature since the Communists were forced to go through a period of at best semi-legality with all its drawbacks. In 1952 this group supported the efforts of Socialist leader Augusto Charnaud MacDonald to form a single party of the bourgeois revolutionary forces. This move was strongly criticized by Fortuny in the name of the Communist Party of Guatemala. (A detailed examination of this incident can be found in Chapter IX, pp. 238-43.)

In his reply to Fortuny's attack Cuenca defended the formation of the PRG from a Marxist-Leninist viewpoint.[72] Cuenca argued that, under the conditions prevailing in Guatemala, unity of the democratic and progressive forces of the bourgeoisie in one party was a forward step. Such unity was a prerequisite to the establishment of a "popular front built on the foundation of the united front." By provoking the withdrawal of the PAR from the new party, Fortuny had violated the premises laid down by the old Comintern leader Dimitrov. In the long run this would hurt the interests of the Communist movement and Fortuny would have to assume full responsibility for "pushing the petty bourgeoisie of Guatemala to the right," which "if not an anti-revolutionary crime, is at least a most grave tactical error." Cuenca denied that he had ever acted "against the Communist movement in general, or against the Guatemala Communist movement in particular" or that he had ever "defamed the clean and honest leaders of the C.P." Cuenca claimed to have the highest "affection, friendship, appreciation and respect" for all the Communist Party leaders except Fortuny, whose "malicious slander" had gotten Cuenca into trouble with the President.

The same incident brought a response from another non-party Communist, the labor leader Manuel Pinto Usaga.[73] Pinto, who had rejoined the PAR after the dissolution of the PROG, had recently been appointed Consul General in Mexico City. (His diplomatic appointment, along with the anti-Communist feeling in the railroad union, was the chief reason Pinto did not openly join the PCG. The author

---

[72] Document 1086: A. Cuenca to José Manuel Fortuny, August 1952. See Chapter IX, pp. 223-25 for Cuenca's contribution to the Communist Party during its clandestine period.

[73] Document 1066 or 1370: Manuel Pinto Usaga to "Chemanuel" Fortuny, July 30, 1952. For other evidence of Pinto's Communist orientation see Chapter IV, pp. 64-68 and Chapter VIII, pp. 211-13.

has seen evidence indicating that in 1953-54 he was probably a secret member of the PGT.) Pinto's views on the unity of the bourgeois revolutionary forces and the founding of the PRG were midway between those of Fortuny and those of Cuenca. Since large numbers of the less politically advanced workers and peasants belonged to the bourgeois revolutionary parties and would probably continue to do so for some time, Pinto saw the task of the Communists as one of influencing and manipulating these parties "to orient the most consistent leaders of the workers and peasants who belong to these parties and insure that they keep the masses from being used for ends contrary to their class interests and consequently to those of the Revolution." The bourgeoisie, although vacillating, unstable and unreliable, could "for a certain period play a revolutionary and anti-imperialist role." The task of the Communist Party was to retain them as allies for as long as possible. While making the original efforts at the level of the leaders, the Communists should work to convince the rank and file members of the other parties, who were mostly workers and peasants of low political development, that "what the Communists propose today is exactly the same as those masses crave." Following the experience of China, the PGT should form a united front with the bourgeois parties while concentrating upon closer ties with the masses. Pinto's advice came very close to the line which the party adopted during the last two years of the Arbenz regime, and showed a close personal identification with the Communist cause.

The crypto-Communists are not easy to identify, since it is virtually impossible to separate the secret members of the party from the pro-Communist intellectuals, sympathizers and fellow travellers. Charges have been made by the Guatemalan officials entrusted with the study of Communism during the Arbenz regime that many high government officials and political leaders were secret members of the Communist Party. Since the Communists operated as a clandestine organization from 1947 to 1950 while gaining control of the labor movement and infiltrating the political parties and mass organizations, it is reasonable to expect that they might carry this tactic into the later period. In spite of the influence of Communism in Guatemala, there were still positions whose occupancy by a recognized Communist would have created a furor among public opinion. In addition, the well-known desire of the Communists to have a "fraction" or at least an agent within each significant organization and their desire to keep in the background so as to be able to refute charges that Guatemala had a Communist government, lends support to these charges. As indirect control was a keynote of Communist operations in Guatemala, the existence of a crypto-Communist group seems almost a certainty.

The many allies and sympathizers whom the Communist Party had in strategic positions among the government parties, labor unions and mass organizations were far more important to the Communist cause than were the hundreds of campesinos who joined the party ranks in 1953 and 1954.

6

CONTROL OF LABOR:
THE KEY TO COMMUNIST SUCCESS

Organized labor played a crucial role in the rise of Communism in Guatemala. Without control of the labor movement the Communists could hardly have become a major political force; with it they automatically were. In the early days of the revolution the Communists' home and chief base of operations was among the labor unions. Even after they became a legal party the labor movement provided their main source of mass support. Hence a thorough understanding of how the Communists came to control the labor movement is basic to an understanding of their political influence.

The outstanding characteristic of the Guatemalan labor movement was its involvement in politics. Born as the product of a drastic political change and surrounded by enemies who refused to recognize its right to exist, the Guatemalan labor movement could survive only by insuring the success of the revolutionary government and protecting it from the continual plotting of the intransigent opposition. The environment predisposed Guatemalan labor toward radicalism and extreme nationalism, a situation which the Communists were quick to exploit. In the years following the Revolution of 1944, they successfully won recognition as the spokesmen of the Guatemalan workers. The absence of an organized Communist Party prior to 1950 and the lack of knowledge of international affairs on the part of the laboring masses enabled the Communists to pose as nationalists and champions of the working class and gain a considerable degree of acceptance before coming into the open.

The working class in Guatemala was relatively unsophisticated and had no previous political commitments; thus the Communists met with little organized opposition or even competition among the workers. The Communists sought out the natural leaders among the workers and strove to win them over. In return the party bolstered their leadership positions. At the same time the Communists introduced an element of organization into a previously amorphous mass. By obtaining the support of key elements in the working class, the party prevented the Guatemalan workers from lending significant support to any other political movement.

EARLY HISTORY OF THE GUATEMALAN LABOR MOVEMENT

While it is not within the scope of this book to give a detailed history of the Guatemalan labor movement, it is impossible to understand the development of Communism or Guatemalan politics in general without a knowledge of the course followed by labor. Hence, before examining the ways in which the Communists utilized their control of organized labor, a brief survey of the Communists' rise to the control of a unified labor movement is in order.[1]

At the time of the overthrow of Ubico, no real trade unions existed in Guatemala. During the "Hundred Days" which preceded the October Revolution, the railroad workers, teachers and employees of the two United Fruit Company divisions formed their unions. The teachers were the most active in the work of organizing other unions, a task which they shared with radical labor leaders from other Central American nations who found a haven in Guatemala. In October of

---

[1] A very useful and detailed study of Guatemalan labor in the first half of this period is available in Archer C. Bush's *Organized Labor in Guatemala, 1944-1949: A Case Study of an Adolescent Labor Movement in an Under-Developed Country,* Colgate University Bookstore, 1950.

1944 the various unions banded together in the Confederation of Guatemalan Workers (CTG) headed provisionally by Carlos Raúl Alvarado of the Graphic Arts Union (SAG).[2] The formal establishment of the CTG came on December 5, 1944, with the moderate Gumercindo Tejada as Secretary General. Tejada was opposed to the idea of affiliating the CTG with the Communist-oriented CTAL and clashed with Lombardo Toledano when the CTAL leader made his first trip to Guatemala in December 1944. This provoked an open fight within the new labor organization, and Tejada expelled the bricklayers', carpenters' and leatherworkers' unions in June of 1945.[3] At the peak of the struggle the CTAL sent three organizers to Guatemala, and with their help Tejada was replaced on June 6, 1945, by a "Provisional Executive Committee" headed by Arcadio Ruíz Franco.

Friction within the CTG reached a new peak in the summer of 1945 over the activities of the so-called *Escuela Claridad,* which had been organized by Miguel Mármol, Virgilio Guerra and the Cuenca brothers, Abel and Max Ricardo. These Salvadorean Communists and Antonio Obando Sánchez, one of the "old" Guatemalan Communists who had survived Ubico's prisons, were teaching Marxist doctrines to the workers under the guise of "political orientation" and had the backing of the STEG, the teachers' union which was coming to play an increasingly important role in the CTG. The moderates had lost the first round in this dispute when on June 28, 1945, it was decided to continue the representation of the *Escuela Claridad* on the Executive Committee of the CTG. The provisional Executive Committee then issued an order that each union must send four members to the Marxist classes of the school.

In this heated atmosphere the "First Congress of Labor Unity" was held from August 15 to 20. At this meeting the CTG voted to join the Communist-dominated CTAL and adopted a resolution endorsing the *Escuela Claridad.*[4] No sooner had the new Secretary General Isaías Ruíz Robles taken office than the struggle was reopened. The Graphic

---

[2] For the declaration of principles of the CTG see 8017:1888, October 1, 1944, and Graciela García L., *Las Luchas Revolucionarias de la Nueva Guatemala,* Mexico, 1952, p. 59.

[3] *Ibid.,* p. 60.

[4] *Ibid.,* pp. 63-81. This contains the detailed story of the Congress as seen through the eyes of a Communist leader. Y-X-2:2406-37 contains the minutes of the Congress. The resolutions of the Congress were drawn up by Communists Antonio Obando Sánchez, Virgilio Guerra and Graciela García L.

Arts Union (SAG) led the fight against the *Escuela Claridad* while the defense of the school was championed by the rising young leader of the teachers' union (STEG), Víctor Manuel Gutiérrez. On November 4 the moderates again lost a motion to deny the *Escuela Claridad* representation and voting rights on the Executive Committee.[5] The vote was 13 for, 15 against and 3 abstaining, so by the narrow margin of two votes the Communists won a victory which was to prove far more significant than anyone thought at the time.[6]

Efforts to reconcile the two groups failed, and in January of 1946 ten unions which had withdrawn from the CTG banded together in a new organization, the Guatemalan Union Federation (FSG). As the moderate FSG contained the relatively stable and well-organized urban unions while the CTG was left with only the STEG and the poorly-organized agricultural unions, many observers felt that the moderate leaders would be able to steer the labor movement away from Communism and involvement in extremist activities.[7] These hopes were doomed to failure and the SAMF and FSG were eventually taken over by the Communists. As one student of the subject viewed this development:[8]

> In dealing with the social environment in which they dwelled, however, the FSG leaders were not so well equipped, nor did they have the grasp of the situation which personified the leaders of the CTG. The FSG never appeared to exercise a firm and well-formulated approach either to their internal or to the national problems. They were always reluctant followers unable to seize the initiative. Unhappy with the train of events and with the ascendancy of Communist leaders to the positions of political managers of the labor movement, they were unable to find a workable alternative.

The CTG: From Seedbed to Base of Communist Operations. After the split in the labor movement at the end of 1945, control of the CTG was taken over by an alliance of the young radical leaders of the

---

[5] 8036: Book 3, Acta No. 7, November 4, 1945.

[6] For the Communist side of the dispute see García L., *op. cit.*, pp. 83-98. The author was herself Secretary of Culture of the *Escuela Claridad*.

[7] Indeed, as late as 1950 one of the closest students of the labor movement in Guatemala felt that the moderates might be able to regain control of the labor organizations. See Bush, *op. cit.*, Part Four, p. 41.

[8] Edwin Bishop, "The Development of Unionism in Guatemala," MS., 1956.

STEG and the older Marxists of the *Escuela Claridad* group.[9] When the Arévalo government closed the Marxist school in January 1946 on the charge that it violated Article 32 of the Constitution, these leaders abandoned any immediate hope of forming a Communist Party and confined their activities to spreading their doctrines within the CTG.[10] The influence of Gutiérrez and his associates continued to increase until at the Second Congress of Trade Union Unity in October 1946 Víctor Manuel Gutiérrez was elected Secretary General of the CTG with such political extremists as Antonio Obando Sánchez, Francisco Hernández, Félix M. Ortíz, Ignacio H. Ortíz and Alfredo Pellecer on the Executive Committee.[11]

The young Marxist group within the CTG grew in size and influence during the succeeding years. Publicly members of the PAR, they secretly joined the clandestine Communist Party (VDG) headed by Fortuny. In 1948 Gutiérrez was reelected Secretary General with an Executive Committee composed almost entirely of Communists. José Luis Ramos, Pedro Fernández, Gabriel Alvarado, Antonio Sierra González, Ignacio H. Ortíz, Rogelio López, Félix M. Ortíz and Francisco Hernández made up the Executive Committee with Mario Silva Jonama and Virgilio Guerra on the Consultative Committee.[12] Two years later, after the Communists had withdrawn from PAR, and the PROG and PCG had come out into the open, the CTG was headed by Gutiérrez as Secretary General, Max Salazar as Secretary of Organization, Bernardo Alvarado Monzón as Secretary of Propaganda, José Luis Ramos as Secretary of Campesino Affairs and Pedro Fernández as Secretary of Communications. Gutiérrez, Fernández and Salazar were members of PROG and Alvarado Monzón of the PCG, while Ramos was active in both Communist groups. By this time the

[9] For the detailed story of the CTG in this period see 8036: Book 3, Actas 1-29, June 1945 to April 1946; 8026:1-98, Actas 30-53, April 25, 1946 to September 19, 1946; Y-X-2: Actas 54-88, September 26, 1946 to August 28, 1947.

[10] See 8019:256-8, Informe de los delegados de la CTG, ante la CTAL sobre el movimiento obrero, October 21, 1947.

[11] Document Y-377: CTG circular of October 31, 1946. For the political line adopted at this Congress see: 8026:401-7, Línea política de la Confederación de Trabajadores de Guatemala, aprobada en su 2o. Congreso de Unidad Sindical en 1946. For the statutes of the CTG see Document 1794 or 8017:1977-80, "Estatutos de la Confederación de Trabajadores de Guatemala." For the minutes of the Congress see 8017:2004-20, 2037-49 and 2127-56.

[12] Document Y-387: Manifiesto de la CTG, May 19, 1948.

political line of the CTG was indistinguishable from that of the Communist Party.[13]

The international Communist influence became increasingly evident in the latter part of 1949, when after Gutiérrez returned from a peace congress in Paris and the Second Congress of the WFTU in Milan, the CTG leadership endorsed the Soviet line on the cold war and propagandized it throughout the labor movement.[14] This intensified campaign of Communist propaganda among the workers caused a group of the few moderates who had remained in the CTG to break away and form a small rival organization, the Autonomous Labor Federation of Guatemala (FLAG), headed by Arcadio Chevez.[15] The withdrawal of the moderates freed the Communists of their last restraint, and as the tempo of the cold war increased, so did the volume and intensity of their pro-Soviet propaganda.[16]

The Communists were also in control of the CTG's chief affiliates. The Federation of Workers of the Department of Guatemala (FTDG) was headed by such Communists as Antonio Obando Sánchez, Antonio Ardón, Natzul Aguirre Cook, Alfredo Guerra Borges, Justo Rufino Argueta and Rafael Solís Barrios.[17] The FTDG leadership went all out for the Communist peace campaign and worked diligently to discredit anti-Communism.[18] Addressing the General Assembly of the FTDG, Secretary General Argueta blasted the United States and defended Communists as "our class brothers, honest workers and generally the

---

[13] Document 566: Víctor Manuel Gutiérrez G. to Congress of the Republic, September 12, 1950. The course of the CTG and its political line can be best followed in the reports of the Secretary General to the periodic General Assemblies. See 8026:369-72, January 31, 1948 for the First Confederal Assembly; 8026:412-5, November 20, 1948 for the Third Confederal Assembly; Y-X-4:337-342, August 27, 1949 for the Sixth General Assembly.

[14] See Document 1405: Resoluciones aprobadas por la VI Asamblea Confederal de la CTG, August 29, 1949; also point 6 of the "Declaración de Principios de la CTG," adopted at the 1949 Unity Congress.

[15] 8024:256-8, Informe rendido por el Secretario General ante la Novena Asamblea Confederal de la CTG, September 9, 1950.

[16] Por una lucha más efectiva, por una clase obrera más combativa! May 12, 1950; 8024:280-3, Informe del Secretario General de la CTG a la X Asamblea Confederal de la misma, celebrada el día 17 de Febrero de 1951.

[17] Y-X-1:894-5, Nómina de los Comités Ejecutivos de las entidades sindicales; also 8024:261, October 9, 1950.

[18] See Y-X-4:343-6, Informe de la Secretaría General de la FTDG a la Asamblea General en la sesión del día 29 de Marzo de 1951; 8024:412, Resoluciones tomadas en la Asamblea General de la Federación de Trabajadores del Departamento de Guatemala (FTDG) afiliada a la CTG, el Domingo 5 de Agosto de 1951.

best defenders of democracy and the best defenders of the workers' movement."[19] Anti-Communism was painted as the "flag of treason of crime and of war," and a cause to which only "people without intelligence and without a conscience" could be drawn. The members who listened to this speech were largely unaware of the fact that Argueta himself was a Communist.

Federación Sindical de Guatemala: From Anti-Communist to Communist. The FSG was founded in January 1946 by representatives of fifteen unions which had left the CTG over the issues of the *Escuela Claridad,* the role of foreign "advisers" and the dominance of the STEG. Formed by the better-organized unions centered in Guatemala City, it contained most of the urban proletariat. The typical FSG member had some formal education and at least a rudimentary awareness of the basic social and economic forces at work in Guatemala. Its backbone was the railroaders' union (SAMF) and its first Secretary General was Arturo Morales Cubas, the strong man of the SAMF.[20] The FSG started out with a moderate program and without any leanings toward Communism. However, after Pinto Usaga succeeded Morales Cubas as Secretary General in 1948, and as extremist leaders came to the fore in some of its member unions (such as José Alberto Cardoza in the Graphic Arts Union), the FSG moved steadily leftwards. Until the middle of 1950 the FSG was more important and influential than the CTG, but the withdrawal of the SAMF and the pains of internal dissension left it in a weakened position and it finally agreed to unity on terms favorable to the Communist leaders of the CTG.[21]

The original declaration of principles of the FSG was characterized by a desire to stay clear of Communist influence.[22]

---

[19] 8024:402-8, Informe a la Asamblea Federal del 5 de Agosto del año 1951 rendido por el Secretario General de la Federación de Trabajadores del Departamento de Guatemala (FTDG) afiliada a la CTG.

[20] For the early history and development of the FSG see "Actas de la Federación Sindical de Guatemala."

[21] By the end of 1949 the FSG could claim 54,000 members in 58 unions, some 20,000 more than the CTG. After the formation of the CGTG, the FSG existed only as a sub-unit of the larger organization and was slowly being squeezed to death by the formation of industry-wide federations.

[22] See Documents Y-217 and 1714: "Declaración de Principios Fundamentales."

The Federation will defend its ideological independence and will be energetically opposed to the meddling of exotic doctrines which do not fit into the Guatemalan social movement, in order that its final objectives may be reached without the intervention of foreign influences and guidance.

In its early years the FSG avoided the concern with international labor matters and the application of Marxist doctrine to Guatemalan problems which characterized the rival CTG. Unlike the CTG, the FSG did not affiliate with the CTAL or WFTU until 1950, and when the extremists did push this through, it provoked bitter opposition.

The First Convention of the FSG was held at the end of May 1947, at the very time that the moderate elements in the PAR were splitting away to reconstitute the FPL.[23] At the intervention of representatives of the CTG and Fortuny speaking for the PAR, the FSG agreed to pass over the motion of Jorge Morales Dardón which would have put them squarely on record as opposing Communism.[24] The final resolution embodied continued opposition to "exotic doctrines" and extremism of any kind. While the FSG continued to stress the "national" and "Guatemalan" nature of their program and work, Pinto Usaga began to push the theses that unity of the labor movement was necessary and that labor could not be apolitical nor neglect the fact that the "struggle of the workers is universal."[25]

After carrying on something of a struggle to gain governmental recognition under the provisions of the Labor Code, the FSG held its Second National Convention in January, 1948.[26] At this time Morales Cubas stepped down as Secretary General and was replaced by Manuel Pinto Usaga. The strategic post of Secretary of Organization and Propaganda went to the strongman of the Graphic Arts Union, José Alberto Cardoza, who was soon to develop into one of the leading Communists in Guatemala. Under this new leadership, Marxist doc-

---

[23] See Y-X-1:139, Temario de la Primera Gran Convención de la Federación Sindical de Guatemala, May, 1947.

[24] See Y-X-1:92-100, Acta número dos correspondiente a la segunda sesión plenaria de la Primera Gran Convención de la FSG, June 2, 1947; Y-X-1:67, Puntos de vista de la Confederación de Trabajadores de Guatemala sobre el problema de unidad sindical ante la comisión respectiva de la honorable Primera Convención de la Federación Sindical de Guatemala, May 31, 1947.

[25] Punto No. 1, Línea Política, June 3, 1947.

[26] See Y-X-1:39-42, Federación Sindical de Guatemala, Acta Constitutiva, June 25, 1947; Y-X-1:295-9, minutes of Second Convention of FSG, January 29, 1948.

trine was soon being disseminated through the official publications of the FSG. In nine "easy" one-page lessons the workers were introduced to the fundamental Marxist concepts, initiated into the Marxist interpretation of history, and shown how historical materialism could be applied to the Guatemalan situation.[27] Cardoza's own Graphic Arts Union (SAG), sponsored the publication of Lenin's *Tasks of Social Democracy in Russia*.[28]

On January 28, 1950, Pinto Usaga with the support of Communists Cardoza, Montenegro P. and other extremist leaders pushed through a resolution favoring affiliation with the CTAL and WFTU.[29] Pinto, who had attended the WFTU Second Congress in Milan the previous year, was talking and acting more and more like a Communist. His attitude was so objectionable to many non-Communists that his own union, SAMF, expelled him and withdrew from the FSG.[30] Though an extraordinary General Assembly gave Pinto a vote of confidence as Secretary General, the FSG had been irreparably weakened.[31] By this time Pinto had gotten the FSG on record as opposed to anti-Communism and was rivaling Gutiérrez in his denunciations of the Yankee Imperialists and warmongers and praise of the Soviet Union and Popular Democracies.[32] Pinto led his followers into the PROG, the Communist labor party of Gutiérrez, and agreed to unification of the labor movement. The Third Congress of the FSG in August of 1951 ratified the decision to merge with the CTG.[33] As a sub-unit of the CGTG, the FSG declined rapidly in importance, since union after

---

[27] Y-X-2:2368-76, *Boletín de Orientación y Capacitación de la Clase Trabajadora*, No. 1, August 31, 1948, through No. 9, January 7, 1949.

[28] Y-X-5:1535, April 29, 1950, and 1536, January 31, 1950.

[29] Y-X-1:307-9, La FSG resuelve afiliarse a la CTAL y a la FSM, January 29, 1950.

[30] See Y-X-3:3702, José Luis Alvarado and Tomás Yancos M. to Comité Ejecutivo y Consejo Consultivo de la Federación Sindical de Guatemala, October 19, 1950; Y-2: José Guillén to SAMF, September 29, 1950; Y-X-1: 870, José Luis Alvarado and Tomás Yancos M. to member unions, November 15, 1950.

[31] See Document 263:. Víctor A. Leal to Juan José Arévalo, December 26, 1950.

[32] See Y-X-1:274-280, Informe del Compañero Manuel Pinto Usaga con ocasión de la toma de posesión de los nuevos organismos directivos de la FSG para el período 1951/1953, presentado en la Asamblea Extraordinaria del 27 de Enero de 1951.

[33] See Y-X-1:1342-3, III Congreso de la Federación Sindical de Guatemala, diez importantes resoluciones, August 25, 1951; Document 2060: Llamamiento al Congreso, August 14, 1951.

union was taken away from it and put into newly-organized industrial federations.[34]

LABOR IN POLITICS

The Guatemalan labor movement from the beginning was deeply involved in politics. During the early years of the Arévalo regime, labor worked closely with the revolutionary political parties and particularly the PAR, which until 1950 contained the Guatemalan Communists. When the FPL broke with the PAR in 1947, labor leaders formed political action committees and later a network of workers' political committees in order to keep labor's voice united on political matters and to avoid the dispersal of its strength through a splitting into *Parista* and *Frente Populista* factions. The next stage was the creation of a Marxist labor party (PROG) and its eventual merger with other Communist elements to form a unified Communist Party of Guatemala. The final result was a labor movement whose leaders were members of the Central Committee of the Communist Party and which acted as an ally if not an arm of the party.

In the 1944 congressional elections labor ran its own candidates and succeeded in getting a number of them elected.[35] By the beginning of 1946 the situation had changed due to the split in the ranks of labor and the unification of the FPL and RN into the PAR. In January of that year the PAR promised to support Gutiérrez and several other labor leaders for Congress if the CTG would support the rest of the PAR slate.[36] The PAR-CTG ticket won a land-slide victory while the independent slate of the FSG ran a poor third. This lesson was not lost upon the FSG leaders, who subsequently abandoned independence for cooperation with the PAR.[37] On May 13 the leaders of the two labor

[34] See Y-X-2:1952, Resoluciones votadas en la Asamblea General de la Federación Sindical de Guatemala, March 20, 1954; Y-X-1:293 or Document 258: Guillermo Max González to Comité Ejecutivo; Y-X-2:1731 or 1951, Marco Cuellar Lorenzana to FSG unions, March 23, 1954; Y-X-3: 4248; Y-X-5:1397; Y-X-5:1407 and 1409; 8003:13 or 8024:273.

[35] See 8017:1892, Manifiesto del Buró Político, October 31, 1944.

[36] See 8036:Book 2, "Actas de las sesiones del Comité Ejecutivo Central del Sindicato de Trabajadores en Educación de Guatemala," No. 72, January 5, 1946.

[37] See Y-X-2:2903, Mario Monteforte Toledo to Secretary General of the FSG, April 22, 1946.

centrals and the PAR met to discuss the role of the PAR in working
for the Labor Code, which at that time was the prime concern of
organized labor.[38] The PAR Deputies, led by Fortuny and including
the Secretaries General of the CTG and of the FSG, served as the
champions of the labor movement in Congress, and *Parista* officials
acted as its intermediaries with the government. The PAR furnished
legal aid to the unions and supported them in many of the early labor
disputes.

In the January 1947 elections both the CTG and the FSG cooperated with the PAR, eight of whose 34 candidates were drawn from the
ranks of labor. Subsequently, however, a number of considerations
caused the leaders of the labor movement to turn toward a different
means of political participation which would assure the labor movement
somewhat more independence.[39] In the first place the PAR suffered a
rupture which led to the reconstitution of the RN and FPL and threatened to divide the support of the working class among the three
revolutionary parties. Secondly the Labor Code was passed and became
law on May 1, 1947, thus removing one of the purposes for the close
alliance of labor with the PAR. Finally, Article No. 204 of the code
prohibited labor unions from engaging in political activities. Hence
the CTG severed its organic connections with the PAR, but its leaders
remained active in that party.

In many respects the National Labor Unity Committee (CNUS)
functioned as the political spokesman of labor in the middle years of
the Arévalo regime, but by July 1948 division of the revolutionary
forces had gone so far the CNUS felt it was necessary to forge a new
political arm for organized labor. On July 28 the Political Action
Committee (CAP) came into being as an effort to restore the unity
of the revolutionary forces. Denying that it was "a political party of
the working class," the CAP pictured itself as "an organ of political
orientation of the workers, campesinos and broadest popular sectors"
and as "a vehicle of revolutionary national unity."[40] In part, its pur-

---

[38] See Y-X-2:2918-22, minutes of FSG, CTG, and PAR meeting, May 13,
1946.

[39] For the views of Gutiérrez see Document 996: Gutiérrez to Fortuny,
January 14, 1947.

[40] See Y-X-1:1120-2, Manifiesto del Comité de Acción Política de la Clase
Trabajadora, July 28, 1948; 8032:2907-8, Programa de lucha del Comité de
Acción Política de la Clase Trabajadora, August 17, 1948.

pose was to prevent workers who were alarmed by the Communist influence in the PAR from supporting the FPL, which was refusing to ally with the PAR and going it alone in the elections. The CAP, stressing that this division of the revolutionary forces was endangering the gains which labor had made since 1944, joined in an alliance with the PAR and RN for the congressional elections.[41] Its leaders took the relative success of the opposition as a sign that even greater unity among the revolutionary forces was needed. In the new Congress the PAR had 17 members, eight of whom were drawn from the ranks of labor.

The rash of anti-government plots in 1948 and 1949, particularly the army revolt of mid-July, which almost succeeded in overthrowing the Arévalo government, convinced the leaders of organized labor that it was essential to unify their support behind a single revolutionary candidate. As early as September 1948 the leaders of the PAR and most of the high command of organized labor secretly agreed upon Minister of Defense Jacobo Arbenz as their candidate. The leaders of organized labor were determined to exercise the maximum influence possible in the election and in November of 1949 began organizing a network of workers' political committees.[42]

The organ through which the leaders of labor intended to carry out their intensive program of political activity to unite all workers behind one candidate was the National Workers' Political Committee (CPNT). As the political committees of the various unions were legally distinct from the unions themselves, so the CPNT maintained the legal fiction of being distinct from the CNUS, although the composition of the two bodies was nearly identical. Gutiérrez, Pinto Usaga and their collaborators formed a provisional committee in the fall of 1949 and fostered the formation of workers' political committees in all the major unions.[43] On the 6th of January the top leaders of the labor federations gathered to make plans for a convention of all the workers' political committees to be held on the 21st and 22nd. Five of the dozen leaders present were secretly Communists, and four of them were elected to

[41] See 8032:2956, Manifiesto del Comité Político Ferrocarrilero.

[42] The CAP, whose final Secretary General was the Communist José Luis Ramos, had been allowed to slowly die out after the January 1949 elections. See 8024:568, Tomás Yancos M. and Eduardo Castillo H. to José Luis Ramos, March 10, 1949.

[43] See Y-X-1:1101 for the formation of the prototype Comité Político Ferrocarrilero in December, 1949.

the nine-member national committee.[44] The Convention adopted the Charter of the Workers (*Carta de los Trabajadores*), drawn up at the convention of the SAMF's political committee the preceding month, and confirmed Pinto Usaga as Secretary General, Morales Cubas as Secretary of Organization, and Gutiérrez as Secretary of Propaganda.[45]

On January 29, 1950, the new permanent CPNT began its work by issuing a warning to all committees that they should be on guard not only against the reactionaries, but also the "false revolutionaries."[46] This was followed up by bulletins denouncing the candidacy of Jorge García Granados and criticizing the FPL for dividing the unity of the Revolution. On February 24 the CPNT issued its "Agreement No. 1" declaring that "Citizen Lt. Col. Jacobo Arbenz Guzmán" was the candidate of the working class and the campesinos.[47] The task of the CPNT was to carry the Arbenz candidacy to the countryside and woo the workers and peasants away from the civilian candidates.[48] To accomplish this the CPNT first issued propaganda discrediting the assassinated Col. Arana as a reactionary traitor and tool of the United Fruit Company.[49] The candidacy of García Granados was attacked as divisionist and as being too much to the liking of the United Fruit Company. Next the *civilista* doctrine of the FPL was attacked as a "danger to national unity" and as endangering the revolution by separating the army and the people.[50] The FPL was called upon to

---

[44] See Y-X-1:1289-90, Acta No. 1, January 5, 1950; Document 327: Circular of the Comité Político Central de la Clase Trabajadora; Y-X-1:1291 or 8025:1588, Convocatoria a Convención Política de los Trabajadores, January 9, 1950.

[45] See Document 325: Comité Político Central Organizador, proyecto de reglamento para la Convención Nacional Política de los Trabajadores, January 9, 1950. The only change made from the provisional committee was the replacement of Mario Silva Jonama by José Luis Caceros. This marked the last time that Gutiérrez would take a backseat to Pinto or any other Guatemalan labor leader.

[46] Y-X-1:1163, Comité Nacional Político de los Trabajadores, Boletín No. 1, January 29, 1950.

[47] Y-X-1:1293, Y-X-1:1161 or Y-X-2:2931, Acuerdo No. 1, February 24, 1950.

[48] For the work of the CPNT and its delegates in making Arbenz known to the workers and particularly in introducing his candidacy to the rural areas see Y-X-3:3812-18 and Y-X-1:710-12.

[49] Y-X-1:1167-9 or 1283-5.

[50] Y-X-1:1162 or 1294, Comité Nacional de los Trabajadores, Boletín No. 4, March 6, 1950.

"rejoin the ranks of the revolution" and its members incited to turn against the party's candidate.[51]

As the principal task of the CPNT was to prevent the votes of the workers from being divided up among the several parties and candidates, it stressed to the working class and campesinos the need to oppose any attempts of the parties to work among them. The political committees were to be entirely independent of the parties and the sole political instrument of the working class.[52] The Convention had stated that the development of a working class party was the eventual goal, and that the role of the CPNT was a transitional one, that of the bridge between the stage in which the workers had belonged to the petty bourgeois revolutionary parties and the time when they would have their own class party.[53] Along these lines the CPNT participated in the coalition of forces supporting the Arbenz candidacy, instructed and got out the vote on election day, and ran six candidates in the congressional elections.[54]

Important changes in the Guatemalan political scene occurred during the life of the CPNT. While the withdrawal of the Communists from the PAR and their emergence into the open, the virtual disintegration of the FPL and the election of Jacobo Arbenz as President all impinged heavily upon the CPNT and affected its course, the most important development was the organization by Víctor Manuel Gutiérrez and other CTG leaders of the Revolutionary Workers' Party of Guatemala (PROG). (See Chapter IV, pp. 61-68.)

---

[51] Y-X-1:1155-6, Carta Abierta al FPL, March, 1950.

[52] See Y-X-3:4325; Y-X-3:4319; Y-X-1:549; Y-X-1:548; Y-X-1:546; Y-X-1:500; Y-X-1:851; letters from Pinto Usaga to workers explaining the nature of the political committees.

[53] See Y-X-1:1166 or 1140, circular of Manuel Pinto Usaga, June 16, 1950; Y-X-1:1164-5, CPNT circular, June 30, 1950; Y-X-1:1281-2, CPNT circular, August, 1950; Y-X-1:1170-1, CPNT circular, September 11, 1950; the so-called Program of National Unity of the CPNT, its formal statement of principles, can be found in the *Diario de Centro América,* of April 4, 1950 or in Bush, *op. cit.,* Part Four, pp. 23-7.

[54] See Y-X-3:3435, González Juárez to Secretary General of CPNT; Y-X-1:1154, Comité Político Nacional de los Trabajadores instrucciones urgentes para las votaciones, October, 1950; Y-X-1:1153 or 418, Resolución adoptada por la Asamblea de Comités Políticos del Departamento de Guatemala en su sesión del 1 de Noviembre de 1950; Y-X-1:1148 or 8031: 1590, CPNT circular on elections for deputies, November, 1950; Y-X-1: 1142, CPNT circular, December 11, 1950; Y-X-1:1146 or 1147, CPNT circular, December 31, 1950.

Since October of 1946 Gutiérrez and the majority of the CTG leaders had been stressing the eventual necessity of a party of the working class. Gutiérrez took the congressional elections of January 1947 as teaching that:[55]

> . . . it is necessary that there exist a party of the working class of revolutionary orientation, with a just ideological direction and an iron discipline. This party ought to aspire to bring together all the workers, many of whom are now active members of the existing parties.

In the meantime the workers should form factions within the existing parties to assure that these organizations would follow a policy which protected the interests of the working class. During 1948 and 1949 Gutiérrez came to distrust the bourgeois politicians and parties more and more, and the idea of a working class party became increasingly prominent in his thought, leading to his break with the PAR and the founding of the PROG.[56]

Gutiérrez and the CTG clearly got the jump on Pinto and his group by organizing the PROG in 1950 and claiming that this was the legitimate response to the resolution of the National Political Convention of the Working Class favoring the establishment of a working class party. Pinto had already moved considerably to the left in the preceding years, and the revolt against him in the SAMF forced him to turn to Gutiérrez for support. His expulsion from the SAMF in September 1950 and the subsequent withdrawal of that key union from the FSG removed Pinto as a serious rival to Gutiérrez. No matter what his attitude toward the PROG had been previously, this rapid deterioration of his position left him no course but to accept the PROG as *the* party of the working class. In March of 1951 Pinto and the other FSG leaders joined the PROG, and the CPNT came to the end of its existence.

During the single year of its life the CPNT had served the Communists well. Gutiérrez as Secretary of Propaganda had been able to disseminate Communist writings under the guise of the "most im-

---

[55] 8019:3-8, 8017:1907-10 or 1911-4, Informe de las actividades del Comité Ejecutivo del CTG del 28 de Diciembre de 1946 al 27 de Febrero de 1947, February 27, 1947.

[56] See Document 1315: V. Manuel Gutiérrez to Florentín Sánchez, December 26, 1949.

portant documents of the international labor movement."[57] Marxism-Leninism was accepted as the "only guide for the working class," and the disputes which occurred within the CPNT centered on the tactical issue of the degree to which the working class should cooperate with and be linked to the petty-bourgeois democratic parties.[58] The CPNT served the Communist labor leaders as a transitional stage in their efforts to win the support of the workers away from the bourgeois revolutionary parties to the Communist Party. This intermediate step of political independence of the working class eased the abruptness and absorbed much of the shock of this important development.

THE STRUGGLE FOR UNITY

In spite of the great political and ideological differences which divided the CTG and the FSG in 1946, they soon realized that they shared certain fundamental interests as the representatives of the working class. The uneasy political situation had caused the government to curb labor activities, a step which the union leaders saw as a threat to the continued development of the movement. Although both sides realized that continued division endangered the gains made by the working class, the CTG leaders held firm, and, while calling repeatedly for unity, waited for the FSG leadership to make the major concessions. In the end this waiting game was to pay great dividends to the Communist leaders of the CTG.

During this period the Chilean Communist Deputies Juan Vargas Puebla and César Godoy Urrutia acted as the CTAL's advisers to the Guatemalan labor movement. Arriving in Guatemala in the spring of 1946, Vargas Puebla went to work upon the FSG leaders in an effort to convince them that unity was more important than the differences which were dividing them from the CTG. Vargas' pet project was the "Pact of Common Action and Unity" which he pro-

---

[57] For the most useful statement of the political orientation of the CPNT see Document Y-355 or 8024:223-242, June 1950. Also Y-X-1:1173, Circular No. 14 of CPNT, May 1950; Y-X-1:1157-1160, "Guatemala denuncia la conspiración imperialista contra la Revolución de Octubre," Boletín No. 7 of the CPNT, March 29, 1950; Y-X-2:3214-31, *Boletín del Comité Político Nacional de los Trabajadores*, Año 1, No. I, May 13, 1950, which is a reprint of the Brazilian Communist leader Luiz Carlos Prestes' "The Fight Against Imperialism Demands a Fighting and Enlightened Vanguard."

[58] 8025:1763-4, Mario Silva Jonama to CPNT, December 27, 1950.

posed to the CTG, FSG and FRCT leaders at a meeting on April 29, 1946.[59] This pact provided that the signatories would organize a national labor congress at which the *Central Unica* would be created and that this confederation would be affiliated with the CTAL. The delay in the promulgation of a labor code and the seeming impasse to which the revolution had come made the FSG receptive to proposals of unity of action, if not organic unity. While both sides backed away from the Unity Congress which Vargas Puebla had proposed for May Day, two weeks later leaders of the CTG, FSG and the PAR came together to discuss the problem.[60] However negotiations for organic unity broke down when discussion got to specifics, particularly the question of affiliation with the CTAL.[61]

Comité Nacional de Unidad Sindical (CNUS). The failure of early talks on reunification of the labor movement and the precarious political situation led to the substitution of unity of action for organic unity as the immediate goal of the CTG leaders and their advisers from the CTAL. The CTAL sent the Cuban Communist labor leader Blás Roca to Guatemala in December 1946 with a plan for a degree of cooperation among the several labor organizations sufficient to permit them to present a united front to their enemies. On December 15, 1946, this was institutionalized in the CNUS, which, while working toward eventual unification of the labor movement, would in the interim act as organized labor's coordinating body.

Although the CNUS periodically developed plans for the unity of Guatemalan labor and even held several "unity congresses," it functioned primarily as the chief spokesman of labor on issues affecting the working class.[62] The CNUS was active on a wide variety of fronts

[59] See Document 2025: Proyecto de pacto de acción común y de unidad, April 29, 1946; also "Actas de la Federación Sindical de Guatemala," No. 14, April 29, 1946.

[60] "Actas de la Federación Sindical de Guatemala," No. 16, May 13, 1946.

[61] See Y-X-5: "Actas del Comité Ejecutivo de la Confederación de Trabajadores de Guatemala," No. 34, May 23, 1946; "Actas de la Federación Sindical de Guatemala," No. 17 through 22, May 20-June 10, 1946.

[62] Among the range of activities of the CNUS were the fight for the Labor Code, the fight for the removal of the Minister of Government after the suspension of the right to organize in rural areas, a threatened strike if Charnaud was removed as Minister of Economy and Labor, the request that the government arm the organized laborers in August 1948, support and coordination of the 1949 UFCO strike, presentation of a projected Agrarian

and spoke for organized labor on any subject upon which the leaders could reach agreement.[63] As time passed, the political line of the CNUS became indistinguishable from that of the CTG, and during 1950 it became more and more of a mouthpiece for the PROG.[64]

By 1949 conditions seemed ripe for a new attempt at reuniting the labor movement. The conflict with United Fruit Company taught the labor leaders that complete unity of action was required in successfully dealing with the powerful foreign corporations, and the revolt of July 1949 reminded them how close the opposition could come to overthrowing the government which had brought them great gains. With the elections for a successor to Arévalo approaching, the appeal of unity was strong. A unity congress met on May 1, 1949, but an impasse developed, so it was decided to try again on October 20.[65] Due largely to the delaying tactics of the SAMF, this was again postponed until the following May. At that time the unsettled political situation, the emergence of the Communist Party into the open and the dissension which wracked the SAMF and the FSG, dictated the postponement of this congress until after the presidential elections.

In spite of their failure to nail down unity in 1949, the Communists were close to victory as the two top leaders of the FSG, Pinto Usaga and Castillo Hernández, had been won over to the Marxist line. While the Communists may have been a minority among the Guatemalan workers, their "certainty" and discipline was triumphing over the

Reform law to Congress in September 1949, the creation of the Political Action Committee of the Working Class on July 5, 1948, and the establishment of the CPNT at the end of 1949. See Document 1490: Principales actividades del CNUS.

[63] See Y-X-1:338-9, Manifiesto del Comité Nacional de Unidad Sindical al Pueblo Trabajador de Guatemala, September 21, 1947; Y-X-1:1144, CNUS circular, July 12, 1950, Y-X-1:1152, Resoluciones de la Asamblea General de Comités Ejecutivos Sindicales aprobadas en la sesión del CNUS, el día 2 de Noviembre, 1950; 8025:1592, Plan de trabajo a desarrollar por el CNUS, January 5, 1948; also see Y-X-1:378, 381, 522 and 623; 8025: 1752, 1755, 1758 and 1759.

[64] See 8026:307-14 or Y-X-5:424-431, Unidad del movimiento obrero y función del Comité Nacional de Unidad Sindical (CNUS), April 1950.

[65] Y-X-1: 1233-4, Algunas bases generales para la formación de la central única de Guatemala, January 7, 1949. For the line of this congress see 8024:1223, Proyecto de declaración de principios de la nueva CTG (Central Unica) aprobado por el CNUS, March 24, 1949; 8024:33, Declaración de principios de la Confederación de Trabajadores (Central Unica) aprobados por el Primer Congreso de Unidad Sindical, April 30, 1949; 8024: 34-40, "Estatutos de la Confederación de Trabajadores de Guatemala (Central Unica)," May 1, 1949.

doubts and vacillations of their opponents. The events of the next year removed the FSG as a serious rival to the CTG and virtually assured domination of the labor movement by the Communist CTG leaders under Gutiérrez. The support of the new President and the help of the CTAL and WFTU leadership contributed to bringing this about sooner rather than later.

Unity Achieved: October, 1951. Since 1947 the CTAL had been working toward the unification of the Guatemalan labor movement.[66] Once the affiliation of the FSG to the CTAL was accomplished in early 1950, one of the main obstacles to unity had been overcome.[67] As soon as Arbenz became President, arrangements were made to hold a CTAL and WFTU-sponsored Conference of Transportation Workers' Unions of Latin America in Guatemala in May 1951. Such international Communist labor leaders as Louis Saillant, Maurice Carroué, Vicente Lombardo Toledano, Rafael Avila, Carlos Fernández, José Morera, and Rodolfo Guzmán took advantage of their presence in Guatemala to hold a meeting of the several Guatemalan labor organizations and impress upon them the necessity for unity.[68]

After this meeting, progress was rapid. A Preparatory Committee for the Unity Congress of Guatemalan Workers (CPCUTG) was immediately established with Gutiérrez at its head and the Cuban Communist José Morera, who was Secretary of Organization of the CTAL, as "advisor."[69] (To the Guatemalan labor leaders at this time, the "experienced guidance" of the CTAL seemed essential to make

[66] Documents 1712: Rodolfo Guzmán to Víctor Manuel Gutiérrez, February 11, 1949; 1711: Resolución número uno de la Comisión de asuntos Centroamericanos de la Confederación de Trabajadores de América Latina, February 12, 1949; 8015:115, Vicente Lombardo Toledano to CTG, April 13, 1949.

[67] Document 540: Gutiérrez to the Central Committee of the CTAL, January 5, 1950.

[68] Document 1308: May 11, 1951; also 8025:2083-4, May 12, 1951, which contains Gutiérrez's notes on the meeting; also Documents 486 and 401: Manuel Pinto Usaga to Vicente Lombardo Toledano, March 29, 1951, and April 10, 1951; Document 1308: Secretariat of the Central Committee of the CTAL to the Executive Committee of the CTG, May 11, 1951; Y-X-4: 327, April 24, 1951.

[69] Document 563: Gutiérrez to Lombardo Toledano, September 12, 1951; 8014:1605, Víctor Manuel Gutiérrez, Max Salazar and José Luis Ramos to Vicente Lombardo Toledano, September 19, 1951 which recognized the aid of Morera as "necessary to guarantee the success of one of the most important steps ever taken by the Guatemalan labor movement"; also Y-X-1:1378.

up for their relative lack of experience, and this gave the Communists an additional lever for their climb to the control of the labor movement.) Since Gutiérrez, José Alberto Cardoza, Pellecer, Max Salazar, José Luis Ramos and Pinto Usaga were members of this nine-member body, it was entirely under the control of the Communists.[70] In its report to the Congress, Gutiérrez made no effort to hide the fact that the CPCUTG had been set up in response to the advice of Saillant, Lombardo Toledano and Maurice Carroué and functioned in keeping with the line which the WFTU's executive bureau had established for Latin America.[71]

The Congress which met on October 12-14 was completely controlled by the Preparatory Committee. The chief working paper was the report of the "Commission on Organization, Statutes and Declaration of Principles" headed by Communists Max Salazar, José Luis Alvarado and Virgilio Guerra, which approved the statutes and declaration of principles drawn up in advance by the Preparatory Committee.[72] Pinto Usaga's report on the "Demands of the Workers, the Campesinos and the People," which was largely an attack upon the "voracity of the North American trusts" and the "powerful economic and political machine directed by Wall Street," received the endorsement of a commission headed by Pinto and the Communist Deputy Cardoza.[73] The Commission on Economic Development and National Independence, headed by Communist firebrand Carlos Manuel Pellecer and *Octubre* editor Alfredo Guerra Borges, produced a report which blamed the United States for the economic ills of Guatemala.[74] In the report on "Peace," the Communists pushed

[70] See Y-X-2:3170-2, Comité Preparatorio de la Unidad de los Trabajadores de Guatemala (CPCUTG), July 5, 1951.

[71] Y-X-2:3194-7, Y-X-5:694-7, or 8025:1498-1501, Informe de las labores del Comité Preparatorio del Congreso de Unidad de los Trabajadores de Guatemala, October 12, 1951.

[72] See Y-X-2:3202, Acta de la Comisión Número Uno, October 14, 1951; Y-X-2:3173-7, Resolución sobre el informe de organización presentado al Congreso de Unidad de los Trabajadores de Guatemala, October, 1951; Y-X-2:3104-13 or 8025:2106-19, Informe de organización al Congreso de Unidad de los Trabajadores, October, 1951.

[73] Y-X-2:3025-6, resolutions of the commission; Y-X-2:3078-88, Y-X-2:3185-93, 8025:1520-8 or 8026:386-92, Informe del compañero Manuel Pinto Usaga al Congreso de Unidad de los Trabajadores de Guatemala, sobre las demandas de los obreros, de los campesinos y del pueblo.

[74] 8033:55, minutes of Commission on Economic Development and National Independence, October 13, 1951; Y-X-2:3093-9, Y-X-2:3178-84 or

through a document depicting the "monopoly capitalists" of the "fascist" United States as plotting to impose tyrannical governments upon the Latin Americans in order to keep them in the position of colonies furnishing raw materials at low prices for the war machine of the U. S. and the profits of the Wall Street moguls.[75] The principles and program of the CGTG were a masterpiece of the Communists' ability to graft their program on to the aspirations of the nationalistic working class.[76] The Communists, owing to their careful preparation and groundwork, had their way on almost every point at the Congress.[77]

The slate of officers, ostensibly designed to give proportionate representation and influence to each of the organizations which were merging to form the CGTG, left the Communists in complete control. The Secretary General was Gutiérrez and the Vice-Secretaries General were the Communist Deputy Cardoza and the most amenable of the SAMF leaders, José Luis Caceros.[78] Pinto became Secretary of Propaganda, Max Salazar Secretary of Organization, and Communist Deputy César Montenegro Secretary of Campesino Relations with PCG Central Committee member José Luis Ramos as his assistant. Communists Pellecer and José Luis Alvarado were two of the five Secretaries of Conflicts. Even where the secretary was not a party member, loyal Communists were installed as vice-secretary such as the case of Antonio Obando Sánchez (Communications and Records) and Natzul Aguirre Cook (Social Welfare).

In looking back over the successful culmination of the Communists' desire to see Guatemalan labor unified on their terms and under their control, several points stand out. In the first place, the appeal of unity seemed to overcome any distrust or fear of Communism on the part

---

8025:1535-41, Informe del c. Carlos Manuel Pellecer al Congreso de Unidad de los Trabajadores; see also Y-X-4:349-51 for an intervention on the subject by Communist Deputy César Montenegro P.

[75] Y-X-2:3198-3201 or 8025:1531-4, Informe sobre la paz al Congreso de Unidad de los Trabajadores.

[76] Y-X-2:3091-2, Y-X-2:3203-4, 8025:1529-30 or 8026:396-400, "Principios y Programas de la Confederación General de Trabajadores de Guatemala," October, 1951.

[77] See Y-X-2:3071-6, Y-X-2:3164-9 or 8025:1502-7, Resoluciones del Congreso Constituyente de la Central Unica de los Trabajadores de Guatemala, October, 1951; 8025:2091-3, Resoluciones de la Comisión Número Cinco (de asuntos varios), 1951.

[78] See Document Y-345, 228, 8024:788 or 8021:1099, Planilla de Unidad.

of the workers. The Communists had done careful spadework in a successful effort to discredit the anti-Communists; had utilized the prestige of the CTAL and WFTU leaders; and had exploited the approval of President Arbenz. In addition, the entire congress was so carefully planned in advance that there was little chance of anything going wrong. Agreement had been reached previously by the leaders, and the congress was designed primarily to give an outward appearance of democracy as well as to afford the rank and file, through their delegates, a sense of participation.

1952: The Last Stand Against Communism in the Labor Movement. In the early part of 1952 the moderate elements in the labor movement, as in the political parties, made their last stand against the growing Communist influence. On February 19 the Regional Central Labor Federation (FRCT) headed by Carlos Marín withdrew from the CGTG stating that it was "not in agreement with the maneuvers of the Communist Party which is [identical with] the CGTG."[79] Arcadio Chevez, who felt that the policy urged by the CGTG leadership was politically motivated and did not take into account the interests of the workers, also left the CGTG and took with him the Autonomous Labor Federation of Guatemala (FLAG). The union of UFCO's workers at Tiquisate (SETCAG) was on the verge of withdrawing from the CGTG, and four of its Executive Committee members publicly charged that the CGTG leadership was trying to undermine the SETCAG since they "had been unable to plant seeds of Communism in its ranks."[80]

Fearing that Chevez would succeed in organizing a rival labor federation composed of the FRCT, FLAG, the two UFCO unions, and perhaps the SAMF, the CGTG leaders launched a concerted attack

---

[79] *El Imparcial,* February 19, 1952.

[80] Chevez, who had been appointed by the CGTG as legal advisor to the SETCAG, sought a court order of attachment against the UFCO properties to satisfy the claims granted by the labor courts for the time the workers had been suspended. The CGTG leaders publicly attacked Chevez's action and said that it would only lead to a protracted court battle. Instead they advocated the arrest of the General Manager of the UFCO's Tiquisate holdings for contempt of court. Chevez and the SETCAG leaders charged that the line of the CGTG leaders was illegal and designed to provoke an international crisis by the arrest of a United States citizen or to force UFCO to withdraw from Guatemala, causing the workers to lose their jobs.

against him. Gutiérrez's charges that Chevez had taken $40,000 from the union in legal fees discredited him in the eyes of many undecided workers. While Chevez was out of Guatemala in June 1952, the CGTG leaders persuaded the Secretary General of the FLAG to re-affiliate his unions with the Communist-controlled central and to declare that he had been misled by Chevez.[81] With this move the hopes of the moderates to organize a major federation free from Communist influence came to a dead end (as did the corresponding attempt to organize a revolutionary political party free from Communist influence). The moderates had failed in their efforts to curb the influence of Communism within the forces supporting the Arbenz regime. Any check on the influence of the Communists would have to come from the opposition or the army.

CONTROL OF THE CGTG: COMMUNIST LEVER TO POWER

It is impossible within the limitations of this chapter to portray the full variety of ways in which the Communists exploited their control of organized labor. In Chapter VIII we shall see how it gave them a lever to use upon the government and the role it played in their close relationship with the President. In Chapter X we shall see how the Communists used the CGTG as a front for many of their activities in a successful effort to gain the support of the non-Communist masses. Through the CGTG the organized workers of Guatemala were subjected to a constant bombardment of masked Communist propaganda designed to instill a favorable attitude toward the Soviet Union and various Communist causes. Here we shall first examine the leverage which control of labor gave the Communists in their relations with other parties and politicians.

The CGTG at the time of its founding was a formidable organization whose leaders would necessarily rank high in the councils of the revolutionary regime. At the end of 1951 the CGTG laid claim to over 60,000 members or at least six of every one hundred adult males in the country. Nearly half of the CGTG membership was centered around the capital in the Department of Guatemala where it could

---

[81] Evidence has been put forth that Clemente Soto Marroquín, the Secretary General of the FLAG, was offered a government position as an inducement to break with Chevez and return to the CGTG.

be quickly mobilized for demonstrations or fighting.[82] All parties and the government were well aware of the political importance of organized labor and coveted the votes of the working class. This need for working class votes placed the revolutionary parties in a position where they had to cooperate with and even court the favor of the Communist leaders of the CGTG. The Communists were not remiss in exploiting the great advantages afforded by their control of the organized sector of the working class.[83]

Outside of the Communists, the ties of organized labor were closest with the PAR. A considerable number of workers had affiliated with the PAR because their leaders had done so and could be led out of the PAR as they had been led into it. In other cases ties had developed which held them to the local PAR organization. Since it was not until 1953 that the Communists attempted to build a mass base, most workers were never faced with the necessity of choosing between following the CGTG leaders and their ties with local PAR organizations. Nor had they ever been forced to choose between the PAR or the Communists in an election. In general, the Communists contented themselves with skimming off the politically conscious elite who were ready for the demands of membership in a cadre party. Perhaps a majority of the workers considered themselves *Paristas,* but many of them placed union loyalty above party. The fact that the PAR was eager not to raise an issue on which the workers would have to choose between it and the CGTG was an important factor in its policy of cooperation with the Communists.

The pattern of CGTG-PRG relations paralleled that of the Communist Party with the PRG, in which the Communists first viewed the PRG as a possible threat and then treated them more cordially as the

---

[82] See 8013:265-281, Sindicatos hasta el 31 de Diciembre de 1951. Clasificados por departamentos y empresas.

[83] The reader interested in quickly following the internal story of the CGTG should look at the following: Y-X-1:1379-84, 1387-92, 8024:117-122, 8025:1508-13, or Y-X-2:2886-90, Resoluciones de la Primera Asamblea Confederal de la CGTG, October 13, 1952; 8024:1255-7, Resoluciones de la Segunda Asamblea Confederal de la CGTG, celebrada el día 11 de Abril de 1953, April 13, 1952; 8011:593-5 or Y-X-2:1739-41, Resoluciones de la Asamblea de Secretarios Generales y de Organización, celebrada el Sábado 28 de Noviembre de 1953, November 30, 1953. See also 8012:283, Tareas principales que tiene planteada el Comité Ejecutivo de la CGTG para el presente año, May 11, 1953.

PRG moved to the left. This leftwards movement of the PRG was combined with a policy of conceding the working class to the Communists and following the Communist lead on international affairs, the fight against anti-Communism and the constitution of the United Front of the Masses. In return the PRG leadership hoped for an end of PGT and CGTG opposition to their efforts to build a mass campesino base in the countryside.[84]

The overall impression obtained from an extensive reading of CGTG correspondence with members and local unions is that the hesitancy to accept Communism as the legitimate political expression of the working class was greatly reduced in the two years which followed the unification of the labor movement. This can be attributed to the revelation by an increasing number of labor leaders that they were Communists, to the acceptance of the Communists by the President and the leaders of the other parties, and to the intensive Communist propaganda campaign carried on within the ranks of labor. From late 1952 on, many local labor leaders left the other parties to join the PGT.[85]

The federations which comprised the intermediate level of CGTG organization were also controlled by the Communists, who were extending their control of labor downwards from the top. Communist Deputy Cardoza headed the Federation of Printing Industry Workers, PGT Central Committee member Efraín Villatoro Q., the Textile Federation, and Tischler the Federation of Workers of the Department of Guatemala. Within each union there functioned a Communist fraction which was under instructions to meet in advance to coordinate their work, to be the most active in the work of their union, and to insist that the directives of the CGTG, CTAL, and WFTU

---

[84] In addition to the discussion of PRG developments in Chapter IX, see 8008:6332, Alejandro Silva Falla to Víctor Manuel Gutiérrez, March 6, 1954 and 8008:6240, Augusto Charnaud MacDonald to Víctor Manuel Gutiérrez, March 10, 1954.

[85] For a prime example see 8016:1163, José Domingo Segura, Romeo Alvarado Polanco and Román Hinestroza L. to Víctor Manuel Gutiérrez, November 15, 1952; also 8016:1195, Oscar A. Moya Dubón to Víctor M. Gutiérrez, December 6, 1952; 8016:1196, Gutiérrez to Oscar A. Moya Dubón, December 9, 1952; 8005:2032, Marco Antonio Granados to Víctor M. Gutiérrez, July 31, 1953; 8003:434, Gregorio González G. to Víctor Manuel Gutiérrez, February 17, 1953; 8007:5330, Carlos Sánchez to Víctor Manuel Gutiérrez, February 27, 1954.

be carried out.[86] In this manner the less than 2,000 Communists in the CGTG were able to control its political line and speak in the name of its 100,000 members.

Second National Labor Congress: CGTG Convention or Communist Rally? On January 29, 1954, hundreds of delegates gathered in front of a stage upon which sat a majority of the members of the Central Committee of the PGT along with representatives of the Communist parties of France, Italy, Cuba and the Central American countries. A spectator could have been easily forgiven if he thought he had walked into the convention of the Communist Party of Guatemala. However he had not, for this was the opening session of the Second National Congress of the General Confederation of Guatemalan Workers.

Preparations for the congress began with the return of the Guatemalan delegates from the Vienna WFTU meeting and their subsequent pilgrimage to Moscow. At a series of rallies held ostensibly to explain the preparations for the Congress, the speakers devoted most of their time and effort to propagandizing the line of the international Communist labor movement and rallying support for the PGT's project of a united front of the masses.[87] Preparations were entirely in the hands of the Communists, whose plan was to bring together the "best" elements of the working class in order to subject them to a period of intensive Communist propaganda under the guise of a discussion of the problems of the working class.[88] The Congress was designed to give the delegates a sense of participation while keeping on the road planned in advance by the Communist leadership. The delegates were encouraged to voice their complaints with respect to labor matters, and some were given seats on the various commissions which ratified the resolutions of the Communist leaders while others

---

[86] See Chapter V, pp. 106-8. Also Y-X-2:2071-2072, Plan de trabajo de la fracción del Partido Guatemalteco del Trabajo en el seno de la Federación Nacional de Trabajadores en la Industria Alimenticia.

[87] Y-X-1:918-929 or Y-X-5:991-1001, Guión de orientación para los charlistas que participen en las asambleas sindicales de preparación del 2° Congreso Nacional Sindical de la CGTG.

[88] See Y-X-5:492, Y-X-3:3468 or 8025:1958, Proposiciones de la Comisión de Organización para el guión de los informes ante el Segundo Congreso Nacional, December 30, 1953; Y-X-5:1002-3, Proyecto de programa para el Desarrollo del Segundo Congreso Nacional Sindical.

read prepared "interventions" dealing with certain points of the major reports.[89] These interventions had been allotted to "safe" unions and served to reinforce the line taken by Gutiérrez, Pellecer, and Leal in their reports.[90]

In his report as Secretary General, Gutiérrez put forth a political line for the labor movement identical to that recently adopted by the PGT.[91] In glowing terms he described the joys of life in the "camp of peace, progress and socialism" where all forms of exploitation, oppression and misery had been abolished. In discussing the "camp of imperialism, war and death" Gutiérrez painted a dark picture of the "exploitation, ruin and pauperization of the majority of the population."

Pellecer began where Gutiérrez left off with the task of propagandizing the Communist line to the convention and managed to make the workers' lot under capitalism appear even more hopeless.[92] According to the fiery Communist orator, the high cost of living and rise in unemployment in Guatemala were the direct result of United States policy. Pellecer quoted U. S. Communist leader William Z. Foster as his authority for the contention that the lot of the worker in the United States was unbearable and that the capitalists were ready to bring destruction upon the peoples of the world in an attempt to stave off the effects of overproduction brought about by their own greed. Guatemala's only path to salvation depended upon a reduction of "our economic dependence upon the most aggressive and imperialistic

[89] See Y-X-2:1773-5 or Y-X-5:1004-6, Plan general de trabajo para el 2° Congreso Nacional Sindical de la CGTG, December 8, 1953; see 8016:81-126 for conflicts and 127-163 for agrarian matters; 164-196 gives the makeup of the various commissions and 260-351 the bulk of the interventions; 352-530 of the same reel contains the various messages of salutation from the political parties, government officials, and unions in other countries.

[90] See for example 8016:319-324, Intervention of the Federación Nacional de Trabajadores Gráficos, Publicitarios y Similares on Leal's report; 8039: 150-4, Intervention of the Federación Nacional de Trabajadores en la Industria de la Alimentación on the 4th Report; Y-X-5:1106-14 or 1097-1105, Intervención sobre el Segundo Informe presentado por el Compañero Carlos Manuel Pellecer, Secretario de Conflictos de la CGTG, by the Federación Nacional de Trabajadores en la Industria Textil, Vestido y Similares, January 29, 1954.

[91] Y-X-5:732-762 or 1052-1072, "Informe sobre el primer punto del orden del día del Congreso," by Víctor Manuel Gutiérrez.

[92] 8016:219-254 or Y-X-5:707-742, "Informe sobre el segundo punto del orden del día del Congreso" by Carlos Manuel Pellecer.

country in the world." Instead trade must be with the "camp of Socialism" where the planned economy left no room for economic crises. Borrowing almost bodily from Stalin's *Economic Problems of Socialism in the USSR,* Pellecer took for his peroration the theme that "peace kills imperialism and war cannot save it."

> Nor can war save imperialism from the imminent crisis because this, aside from producing death and greater misery and misadventures for the human species, is opposed by all the peoples, is hated by humanity and in the world millions of men of all tendencies and classes have organized to strengthen the invincible movement of the Partisans of Peace and because we can be sure besides that if the United States unleashes war against the countries of Socialism and Popular Democracy, this war would precipitate the internal contradictions of the regime, the subjected peoples of the colonies would obtain their liberation and, as in the case of Hitler, the armies of peace and Socialism will inexorably and definitely crush the fierce beast of Yankee Fascism.

After the verbal histrionics of the firebrand Pellecer, the address of Víctor Leal on the international labor scene was an anti-climax.[93] Lauding the CTAL and WFTU, Leal denounced the labor movements of the free world. Among his recommendations were the reinforcement of bonds with the organizations of the Soviet Bloc, which he termed the teachers of the Guatemalan labor movement, and the constitution of the United Front of the Masses, the chief immediate goal of the PGT. Even the final report, which was to deal with the conflicts and strikes engaged in by the CGTG, devoted the bulk of its time to the international scene.[94] Marco Cuellar Lorenzana stressed the necessity of solidarity of the international working class in the face of the international "united front" of the monopolies and their structure of reactionary governments, imperialist press and the "yellow" labor organizations. (It is interesting to note that the sinister organizations of the "international of exploiters" included the Rotarians, the Lions and the Junior Chambers of Commerce.)

The Congress gave rubber-stamp approval to the recommendations

---

[93] 8016:5-18, 19-32, 47-60, 208-218; Y-X-5:683-693 or Document 408: "Informe sobre el 3er punto de la orden del día" by Víctor A. Leal F.

[94] Document 390, 8016:197-207 or Y-X-5:476-486, "Informe al Congreso Sindical Nacional sobre el 4° punto de la orden del día," by Marco Cuellar Lorenzana.

of its Communist leaders.[95] The resolutions adopted stressed solidarity against the "foreign imperialist intervention" and the domestic reaction, "pushing with all vigor the creation of the united front of the masses," reinforcement of the alliance with the campesinos and collaboration with the petty bourgeoisie and patriotic sector of the national bourgeoisie, consolidation of relations with the international workers' movement, opposition to the economic policies of the United States, a joint attack with the campesino masses upon the landowners and foreign corporations, broadening the scope of agrarian reform to include lands which did not come under the present law, armed struggle against the "imperialist aggression," elimination of all opposition within the labor movement as "divisionist," and support for the (Communist) labor leaders of other nations. National sovereignty and foreign intervention were the main themes of its final manifesto.

In most cases the old officers were continued in power.[96] Communist control was consolidated with Max Salazar moving from Secretary of Organization to Secretary of Campesino Relations, César Montenegro P. going from Secretary of Campesino Relations to Secretary of Conflicts, Antonio Obando Sánchez moving up from Vice-Secretary to Secretary of Records and Virgilio Guerra taking over as Secretary of Organization. As all four Communist Deputies were high officers of the CGTG and a total of nine of its Secretariats were headed by members of the PGT Central Committee, Communist control of the labor movement, at the top at least, was as complete as possible.

Sindicato de Trabajadores de la Educación de Guatemala, (STEG).
One of the most important of all Guatemalan unions, both in size and strategic position was the teachers' union, the STEG. This union played a key role in the development of the labor movement and served as the seed-bed of Communism in Guatemala. It was in the STEG that many of Guatemala's leading Communists got their first

---

[95] See Document Y-394, 491, 8013:17-26, 8016:33-42 or 8024:1384-1393, Resoluciones del Segundo Congreso Sindical Nacional convocado por la CGTG, January, 1954; Y-394 A, 491 A, 8016:1-2, 3-4, 43-4 or 8024:1394-5, Manifiesto del II Congreso Nacional Sindical, January 31, 1954.

[96] See Document 262, 1643, 8024:417-8, 8016:45-6, 171-2 or 173-4, Proposición presentada por el Presidium al Congreso sobre integración del Comité Ejecutivo de la CGTG, January, 1954; Document Y-403, 403, or Y-X-4: 467-8, Circular of Secretaría de Organización listing new officers of CGTG, February 2, 1954; Y-X-5:668, list of outgoing officers.

real taste of Marxist doctrine, and it served as the Communists' base of operations in taking over control of the labor movement. Its approximately 5,000 members formed a net throughout the country and were, to a considerable extent, the opinion leaders of the communities in which they lived. The teachers were one of the most effective disseminators of Marxist doctrines and Communist propaganda among the youth of the country and participated actively in the various front organizations.

Much of the leadership and orientation of the labor movement was furnished by the STEG, which, after the moderate unions withdrew in November 1945, virtually took control of the CTG.[97] Many STEG leaders soon began to play major roles in other areas of labor and political activity such as Castillo Flores in the Campesino Confederation and Oscar Edmundo Palma in the Peace campaign. Within the Communist Party such leaders as Gutiérrez, Silva Jonama, Bernardo Alvarado Monzón, José Luis Ramos, Oscar Edmundo Palma, Edelberto Torres, Huberto Alvarado, Marco Antonio Blanco, Dora Franco y Franco, Hugo Barrios Klee, Rafael Tischler, Raúl Leiva, Elena Chávez Castillo, Hortensia Hernández Rojas, José Domingo Segura and Wenceslao Cordón y Cordón came from the ranks of the schoolteachers.

While a majority of the members of STEG were not Communists, PGT leaders occupied positions of control within the union and shaped its political line. After Gutiérrez ceased to take an active role in the day-to-day affairs of the STEG, Communist Rafael Tischler moved up to serve as Secretary General during the Arbenz regime. Indicative of the orientation of STEG during this period is its sponsorship and wide dissemination of Gutiérrez's *Apuntes de Economía Política*, a series of pamphlets designed to familiarize Guatemalans with the lessons of Marx's *Das Kapital*.[98] As early as 1946 the official bulletin of the Secretary of Culture and Technical Teaching Affairs spread a series of fourteen basic lessons in Marxism among the teachers.[99] In mid-1951 the 37 items in the STEG library contained seven books by

---

[97] See 8037:1065-1093, reports of Gutiérrez and Castillo Flores as STEG representatives on the CTG Executive Committee, November 1945 to January 1946.

[98] 8037:900, Enrique López Arriaza to Víctor Manuel Gutiérrez, December 1, 1952.

[99] 8037:1736-42 and 1748-54, August 24, 1946 to December 21, 1946.

Karl Marx, three by Lenin and fifteen by other Soviet and European Communist writers.[100] Some idea of the political orientation of the union can be seen from the fact that at the same time that Secretary General Tischler was visiting the "glorious" city of Stalingrad, the STEG National Assembly was asking the government to ban all publications, movies and toys from the United States as "harmful to our nation."[101] The Inter-American Cooperative Educational Service (SCIDE), which had been doing valuable work in the field of rural education, was attacked by the Communist leaders of the STEG as a "camouflaged form of North American imperialism" and a threat to the peace.[102] The propaganda put out by the STEG concerning the international situation and "foreign intervention" in Guatemala was identical with the line taken by the PGT.[103]

The STEG maintained close relations with the various front groups and Communist-oriented mass organizations, particularly the National Peace Committee.[104] Local STEG leaders served as a nucleus for the establishment of a system of departmental and municipal peace committees, while teachers who refused to sign pro-Soviet peace petitions

---

[100] 8039:920, Secretary of Culture of the STEG to Víctor Manuel Salán, November 30, 1949; Document 2073: Lista de los libros pertenecientes a la biblioteca de la Secretaría de Cultura, July 26, 1951; Document 1268; Lista de los libros pertenecientes a la biblioteca de la Secretaría de Cultura, June 3, 1953.

[101] See Document 1537: Rafael Tischler to Ruperto García Turcios, August 25, 1953; Document 1393: Acuerdo de la XI Asamblea del STEG, August 20, 1953; Document 714: Puntos de vista con respecto al plan sobre la política educacional en 1954, March 11, 1954.

[102] 8011:685-692, Lo que el Servicio Cooperativo Interamericano de Educación hizo en Guatemala y la postura del STEG para que fuera cancelado de operación, July 10, 1953.

[103] See 2029: El Sindicato de la Educación ante la denuncia de la ODECA y el retiro de Guatemala de la organización, April 9, 1953; 8011:319-322, Porqué el STEG se ha pronunciado contra la intervención extranjera y contra los traidores nacionales; Document 728: Llamamiento del Sindicato de Trabajadores de la Educación de Guatemala, STEG, a los países libres del mundo ante la amenaza de intervención en nuestra soberanía nacional por los Estados Unidos de América.

[104] See 8039:436-442, Informe del delegado del STEG al Congreso Mundial de los Partidiarios de la Paz, May, 1949; 8037:657-660, address of STEG delegate to Congreso Continental Americano por la Paz; Document 1574, Y-236 or 8037:449-553, Dictamen acerca de la lucha por la paz; also 8037:925 and 8037:934; Document 977: STEG circular of September 22, 1953; 8037:1579; 8037:1601; Document 1099: Por las negociaciones.

were hauled before the Commission of Discipline and faced with possible expulsion for "anti-union and anti-revolutionary activity."[105] The teachers' effectiveness in disseminating Communist propaganda stemmed from the fact that in many communities they were virtually the sole source of information in international affairs.[106]

The STEG was affiliated with the World Federation of Teachers' Unions, a professional department of the Communist-dominated World Federation of Trade Unions (WFTU), and acted as its agent in Central America.[107] The representatives of the STEG took advantage of their visits to teachers' congresses and educators' conferences in other Central American nations to spread Communist propaganda there.[108] Tischler and other STEG leaders toured the Soviet Union in September 1953 after the World Congress of Educators in Vienna and returned to spread stories of its greatness and progress.[109]

While there was some opposition to the Communist leaders of the

---

[105] Document 2036: Dictamen da la Comisión de disciplina en el caso de la profesora María Teresa Valdéz, March, 1953.

[106] See 8037:381-2, Julieta Sánchez Castillo to Secretario de Cultura, August 8, 1953; Document 1395 or Y-422: Llamamiento al Magisterio, January 19, 1954; also 8037:380, 383-4 and 386.

[107] See Document 1680: Virginia Bravo to Víctor Salán, January 16, 1950; Document 2012: Enrique Rodríguez J. to Juan José Arévalo, July 20, 1950; Documents 1125, 1126, 1128, 1146, 1321, 1322, 1337, 1341, 1532, 1932, 1936 and 1939 deal with Guatemalan participation in the World Congress of Educators in Vienna, July 21-25, 1953; Document 1329: José Ruperto García Turcios to Antonio Galindo de Portillo, June 20, 1953; Document 1239: José Ruperto García Turcios to Federación Sindical de Maestros de Nicaragua, July 1, 1953; 8037:1408-13, speech by Tischler at World Congress of Educators, July, 1953; also 8011:570, Rapport de la Comisión des Candidatures, July 26, 1953; also 8011:589-90; Document 310: Juan Pablo Saínz to Comrade Tischler, December 22, 1953 and Tischler to Saínz, December 30, 1953; Document 1116: C. Godoy Urrutia to José Ruperto García, December 24, 1953; Document 1119: José Ruperto García T. to César Godoy U., December 31, 1953; Document 1127: cable from César Godoy to STEG, June 20, 1953.

[108] See Document 1977 or 2031: Informe de la Delegación que fuera representando al Sindicato de Trabajadores de la Educación de Guatemala, ante el VI Congreso de la Federación Sindical de Maestros de Nicaragua, March 28, 1952; Document 1496: Adalberto Jiménez to Secretary General of STEG, September 13, 1951.

[109] 8037:1365-8, Rafael Tischler to STEG; 8011:302-6, Charla sobre el viaje a la Conferencia Mundial de Educadores; Document 1925: En los países capitalistas, coloniales y dependientes no se respetan las libertades democráticas del maestro; 8037:365-8, press interview with Rafael Tischler, November 28, 1953.

STEG in 1950-1951, with the election of Tischler as Secretary General Communist control was consolidated. Although some resigned from the union in protest to Communist influence, most teachers acquiesced in the face of the support which the Communist leaders enjoyed from the Ministry of Education.

In the preceding pages we have seen the extent of Communist control over the labor movement and how the Communists utilized this to increase their influence in Guatemalan national life. In the next chapter we shall examine more closely the way in which the Communists were able to take over native labor and peasant organizations and turn them to their own ends.

7

THE COMMUNIST TAKE-OVER OF LABOR:
THE CNCG AND SAMF

The story of Communist operations in the labor field is as many-sided as it is important. The last chapter portrayed the development of the Guatemalan labor movement from its first beginnings through consolidation under Communist control. Many important aspects of the labor movement, however, still remain to be treated—among others, rural labor in general and the campesino organizations in particular, opposition to Communism within the labor movement, and relations of the Guatemalan labor organizations to the international labor bodies. An examination of these aspects will help to explain how the Communists gained such great influence in the labor movement despite the fact that the great majority of the workers were not Communists.

Such an examination is made in the present chapter and we believe that it adds a new dimension to the story of the Communist take-over of labor in Guatemala. It offers two outstanding case studies. The first deals with the Campesino Confederation (CNCG) and shows how the Communist labor leaders converted this important organization from a rival and threat to the Communist position into their strongest ally. In the second case the story of the internal struggle within the railroad workers' union (*Sindicato de Acción y Mejoramiento Ferrocarrilero*—SAMF) sheds light upon the tragic failure of its non-Communist labor leaders and the way in which the Communists rallied from defeat to win control of this strategic and politically important union. Taken together, these two cases go far towards explaining why no strong revolutionary force capable of limiting Communist influence took root in Guatemala. Such a political force would have required a strong base among the workers and campesinos. This the Communists were able to prevent through their control of organized labor and their influence with the leaders of the campesino movement.

COMMUNISM AND THE CAMPESINOS

As Guatemala is largely an agricultural country and the campesinos outnumbered the urban workers by at least four to one, it was essential for the Communists to build support among the rural population. Although the Communist labor leaders had made substantial efforts to organize the rural wage workers during the last years of the Arévalo Government, they were unable to make any real progress among the campesinos themselves. With the enactment of agrarian reform legislation in June 1952, the Communists, as well as the other revolutionary parties, finally had a means of reaching the campesinos and interesting them in national politics. However, the Communists found their way partially obstructed by a rapidly growing campesino organization which was allied with the one group of revolutionary politicians whom the Communists viewed as a threat, the Socialist Party headed by Augusto Charnaud MacDonald. A year later the situation had changed drastically in favor of the Communists. Their goal of a Communist-led worker-campesino alliance was a reality. In the pages which follow we will attempt to see why this happened and how it was brought about.

One of the most important organizations in Guatemala during the last years of the Arbenz regime was the National Peasants' Confederation (CNCG), which by 1954 boasted of over 200,000 members. While the CNCG had its origin in 1950 as a counterweight to the Communist-controlled CTG, less than four years later it was an ally of the Communist labor movement and well on the way to becoming an integral part of the machinery by which the Communists were establishing their control over Guatemala. To understand the influence of Communism in Guatemala, it is necessary to study how the CNCG was converted from an actual or at least potential rival of the Communists into an instrument through which they were able to reach the peasant masses which made up the bulk of the country's population.

Leonardo Castillo Flores: Campesino Caudillo and Communist Collaborator. The leftward movement of the CNCG is bound up with the story of its founder and Secretary General, Leonardo Castillo Flores. In the Guatemalan context, where the peasant masses had never known any degree of organization and for whom leadership was highly personalistic, Castillo Flores became the *caudillo* of the peasant movement. Rivals were quickly disposed of, and the CNCG followed the line decided upon by Castillo Flores, a path which led the campesino masses step by step toward the Communist goal of an alliance of the workers and the peasants under the direction of the Communist Party. From his actions during the Arbenz regime it would appear that Castillo Flores was either a Communist sympathizer or an opportunist upon whose ambitions and weaknesses the Communists skillfully played, gradually converting him into a useful tool. Undeniably Castillo Flores appeared to go a very long way with the Communists. In 1953 he played their game to the extent of affiliating the CNCG with the CTAL, the WFTU, and several other Communist-oriented international organizations, attending the Vienna Congress of the WFTU, touring the Soviet Union with Gutiérrez and other Communist labor leaders, returning to Guatemala singing the praises of the USSR and virtually merging the CNCG with the Communist-controlled CGTG. Yet the possibility remains that Castillo Flores took these steps reluctantly, rather than eagerly, and that he saw no feasible alternative.

Tall, thin, mustachioed Leonardo Castillo Flores was a twenty-eight-year-old schoolteacher earning $65 a month when he joined the newly-formed teachers' union, STEG, in 1945. Along with Víctor Manuel Gutiérrez, five years his junior but a much abler leader in almost every respect, Castillo Flores served as the representative of the STEG on the newly-organized CTG. Under Gutiérrez, Castillo Flores rose to become Secretary of Records for the CTG and in January 1947 was elected to Congress as a PAR deputy from Chiquimula. Apparently tiring of living in the shadow of Gutiérrez, Castillo Flores turned to the nearly virgin field of organizing the campesino masses. Since he did this without their sanction, the CTG leaders criticized Castillo Flores as an opportunist and divisionist and threatened him with expulsion.[1] Shunned by the top labor leaders and with his seat in Congress expiring at the end of 1950, Castillo Flores allied himself with the ambitious Augusto Charnaud MacDonald and in May 1950 brought the CNCG into existence. Elected Secretary General at that time, Castillo Flores was reelected at each subsequent congress of the organization and rose to become a major figure on the Guatemalan political scene.

Founding of the CNCG. The National Campesino Confederation was born on May 28, 1950, at a meeting of the representatives of 25 campesino unions who felt that their interests were not being adequately served by the existing labor organizations. The CNCG was to fight for agrarian reform and to serve as the instrument of the class aspirations of the campesinos.[2] The "Minimum Program" agreed upon by its founders consisted largely of the struggle for the legitimate interests of the campesinos and was designed to lift the Guatemalan peasantry out of near feudal conditions.[3] The moving spirit of the organization was Leonardo Castillo Flores, a former schoolteacher turned labor organizer. Those who joined him as the founders and early leaders of the CNCG included Amor Velasco de León, Alejandro Silva Falla, Clodoveo Torres Moss, and José Joaquín García Manzo.[4] All of these,

---

[1] See Document 582: CTG Circular; Document 518: Gutiérrez to Comité Ejecutivo Nacional del Sindicato de Trabajadores en Educación de Guatemala, May 24, 1950; Document 612: Víctor Manuel Gutiérrez to Amor Velasco, May 31, 1950.

[2] 8026:357, Principios de la Confederación Nacional Campesina de Guatemala aprobados en la asamblea general de las organizaciones que la constituyeron, celebrada el 28 de Mayo de 1950.

[3] 8026:358-9, "Programa mínimo de lucha de la Confederación Nacional Campesina de Guatemala aprobado en la asamblea general de las organizaciones que la constituyeron, celebrada el 28 de Mayo de 1950."

[4] See Document 834 or 8052:3864-5, Cómo está integrado el Comité Ejecutivo Confederal.

along with the original political sponsor of the movement, Augusto Charnaud MacDonald, were eliminated one by one from the leadership of the CNCG as Castillo Flores carried the organization toward a policy of closer cooperation with the Communists.

At first the new organization had to face the opposition of the established labor centrals which resented it as an encroachment upon their spheres of influence and a threat to the Communist goal of unified control of the workers and peasants. As the urban working class in Guatemala was very limited in size, the CTG had undertaken much work in the rural areas, especially among the workers of the large fincas. The infant CNCG was careful not to infringe upon this preserve of the older organizations and abstained from organizing campesino unions on these fincas.[5]

In January 1951 the CNCG, by now a going concern, held a national convention at which Castillo Flores stressed that the Campesino Confederation was a response to the fact that the campesino had been left out of the gains which had been made by other groups and classes since the Revolution of 1944.[6] Decrying the hostility shown by certain labor leaders and politicians toward the new organization, Castillo Flores stated that the CNCG would organize only those field hands, small peasant owners, tenant farmers and others "who for their economic situation cannot be encompassed within the union organizations and therefore lack an adequate means of presenting their problems." The CNCG considered itself as "the functional ally of the proletariat" as well as the class instrument of the campesinos and would purge all those politicians who attempted to exploit and use the campesinos to their own ends rather than acting as servants of the interests of the class.[7]

Shift in Political Affiliation of CNCG from PRG to PAR. When the CNCG was first formed, the majority of its leaders, including Castillo Flores were members of the PAR.[8] During the intra-party power strug-

---

[5] Y-X-1:188, Alejandro Silva Falla to Secretary General of the FSG, July 31, 1950.

[6] 8051:2190-6, Informe del Comité Ejecutivo de la Confederación Nacional Campesina en el Primer Congreso de esta entidad, February 2, 1951.

[7] 8052:3637 and 3666, "Principios de la Confederación Nacional Campesina de Guatemala," Document Y-136 and 8050:1124-9, "Estatutos de la Confederación Nacional Campesina de Guatemala"; 8051-2185.

[8] 8052:1712, Carlos García Manzo to Leonardo Castillo Flores, January 5, 1951.

gle of 1951 they backed the leadership of Secretary of Organization Augusto Charnaud MacDonald and stood behind him and his associates Amor Velasco de León, Carlos García Manzo, Juan José Tejada Barrientos and Miguel García Granados—all of whom were members of the CNCG and the source of its influence in the government.[9] The CNCG leaders hoped that by affiliating with Charnaud's new Socialist Party (PS) they would gain the political influence and backing to become a major force in Guatemala, and at one time even had hopes that Castillo Flores would be named Minister of Interior.[10] When Charnaud broke with the PAR, the CNCG leaders followed him into the PS and worked actively to build a mass base for the new party by using the local campesino unions as a nucleus for local branches. While the fiction was maintained that the CNCG as an organization was apolitical, its members were urged by the leaders to affiliate with the PS as individuals.[11] The end result was that in many rural communities the local branch of the PS and the campesino union were for all practical purposes one and the same.[12]

Though the CNCG was still linked with the Socialist Party in the first half of 1952, some difficulties were developing. Alejandro Silva Falla, Secretary of Records and Communications of the CNCG and a member of the Political Commission of the PS, became critical of Castillo Flores' empire building and was purged in June.[13] Castillo Flores saw the opportunities which the agrarian reform program would open up for his organization and felt that continued affiliation to the PS of Charnaud might well cramp the expansion of the CNCG and with it his own personal influence, a feeling which was aggravated by

---

[9] Document 886: Leonardo Castillo Flores to Sr. Director de *La Hora,* June 18, 1951.

[10] 8052:4077, Amor Velasco de León to Juan B. Morán, November 27, 1951.

[11] 8051:823, Leonardo Castillo Flores to Florentín López Hernández, September 10, 1951; 8053:3457-8, Leonardo Castillo Flores to Salvador Ardón Arita, September 23, 1951.

[12] 8051:2504, Leonardo Castillo Flores to Abraham Salazar Serrano, December 27, 1951; 2505, A. Salazar Serrano to Leonardo Castillo Flores, December 17, 1951; 8050:493-4, Juan Velásquez Nova to Leonardo Castillo Flores, December 8, 1951; 494-5, Leonardo Castillo Flores to Juan Velásquez Nova, December 14, 1951; 497, Leonardo Castillo Flores to Martín Pérez Gutiérrez, December 26, 1951; 498-9, Martín Pérez Gutiérrez to Leonardo Castillo Flores, December 22, 1951.

[13] 8020:7, Alejandro Silva Falla to Leonardo Castillo Flores, February 2, 1952.

the fact that the PS was not becoming as powerful as Charnaud and Castillo Flores had hoped. The deciding factor may well have been the appointment of the *Parista* Alfonso Martínez as the chief of the National Agrarian Department, a post which Charnaud had sought.

The first sign of Castillo Flores' change in thinking about the relationship between the CNCG and the revolutionary political parties was a warning to all the parties that he felt it was harmful for them to attempt to organize the local agrarian committees and that this work should properly be left to the CNCG.[14] The new line of Castillo Flores was that the CNCG was to be considered as an apolitical organization which would not participate in party politics, but would enter a "United Front of the Democratic Forces."[15]

On August 14, 1952, Castillo Flores, Clodoveo Torres Moss, and Oscar Bautista G. resigned from the newly-formed PRG, a move which spelled an end to its hopes of becoming sufficiently strong to convince the President that he should dispense with the support of the Communists. As other CNCG leaders stayed with the PRG, this provoked a major dispute within the campesino confederation. Castillo Flores' emphasis upon the CNCG as an independent political force was merely a transition stage. He soon accepted the invitation of the PAR leaders to join forces. In September the CNCG began an all-out attack upon the PRG.[16] In less than two months Castillo Flores had shifted from a PRG leader to one of its chief opponents.

The main challenge to these political maneuvers came from Amor Velasco de Léon, one of the founders of the CNCG and its Secretary of Organization. After charging that Castillo Flores had sold out the campesinos to the Communists and that Castillo Flores, Torres Moss,

---

[14] 8051:2103, Leonardo Castillo Flores to Roberto Alvarado Fuentes, June 5, 1952; 8051:2599, Leonardo Castillo Flores to Rubén Castellanos F., June 21, 1952.

[15] 8051:1735-7, Declaraciones del Comité Ejecutivo Nacional de la Confederación Nacional Campesina de Guatemala, June 24, 1952; 8020:44, Circular from Castillo Flores to members of CNCG, August 22, 1952 and 8020:45, Castillo Flores to Secretaries of the PAR, PCG, RN and PRG, August 21, 1952.

[16] See 8020:47, Alvaro Hugo Salguero to Leonardo Castillo Flores, August 28, 1952; 8032:3189, Otilio Marroquín Ruano to CNCG branch at San José Nacahuiel, August 26, 1952; 8020:48 or 8051:2214, Castillo Flores to Secretary General of the PRG, September 2, 1952; 8052:1854 or 8020:61, Castillo Flores to the campesinos of Guatemala, September 5, 1952.

and Bautista González were Communists, Velasco was expelled on September 20.[17] Velasco and José Antonio Monroy continued organizational work among the campesinos in the name of the PRG.[18] As the PRG was unwilling to cease its efforts to organize the campesinos and to cede the field to the PAR-CNCG alliance, friction increased. Castillo Flores' attacks upon the PRG went so far as to accuse it of being "a party enemy of the campesino unions."[19] This rivalry and opposition of the PAR-CNCG with the PRG was so intense that it put the PGT right into the enviable position of the holder of the balance of power among the revolutionary parties.

In 1953 the ties between the PAR and the CNCG were tightened as Castillo Flores was named to the Political Commission of the PAR, and Torres Moss was elected its Secretary of Agrarian Affairs. However the leaders of the CNCG still stressed to the rank and file that their organization was not the affiliate of any political party, since Castillo Flores did not desire to split the membership or lose the support of those campesinos who were unwilling to change their political affiliations so suddenly. The strategy of the CNCG leaders was to win the campesinos away from their old political loyalties and to get them to place their CNCG membership above ties with any of the bourgeois parties. This would not only enable the leaders to weld the CNCG into a formidable political instrument, but would also encourage development of class consciousness.

Relations of the CGTG and CNCG. At the same time as the events which we have been discussing in the preceding section, a second major development was taking place in the relation of the CNCG to the major political forces in Guatemala. Early friction between the CNCG

---

[17] See Y-133: CNCG circular of September 8, 1952; 8022:343-6, manifesto of Amor Velasco de León; CNCG circular of September 22, 1952.

[18] 8050:324-5, Cirilio Aldana Morales to Comité Político del PRG filial de Chiquimula, May 5, 1953; 8052:3636, CNCG circular of October 27, 1952.

[19] 8051:2450, Oscar Bautista González to Francisco López Pérez, November 17, 1952; see 8052:3263, Leonardo Castillo Flores to Genaro Julio Reyes, September, 1952; 8051:2486, Leonardo Castillo Flores to Dionicio Chun R., October 13, 1952; 8052:3871, Leonardo Castillo Flores to Gerardo Barrientos E., December 12, 1952; 8052:3574, telegram from Jubal Cetino to Leonardo Castillo Flores, December 18, 1953; see Document 803: Leonardo Castillo Flores to Congreso Nacional, June 10, 1953 accusing PRG of sectarian and divisive efforts in the field of agrarian reform.

and the CGTG was gradually replaced by cooperation. The Communist leadership of the labor movement proved sufficiently flexible to reverse itself and seek to bring the CNCG into line with their program and goals rather than pursuing a futile policy of intransigent opposition. The Communist leaders of the CTG originally viewed the foundation of the CNCG as a maneuver by the PAR to weaken and divide the labor movement so as to retain control of the campesino masses.[20] In his desire to show the Communist labor leaders that they were wrong in considering him a divisionist and tool of the petty bourgeois politicians, Castillo Flores at the October 1951 Unity Congress put forth a proposal for a "functional alliance" of the CNCG and the newly-born CGTG and advocated cooperation to "liquidate the political exploiters of the working class."[21] Early in 1952 the CNCG proposed to the CGTG that arrangements be made to insure better coordination of their efforts.[22] The leaders of the two organizations, and particularly Leonardo Castillo Flores of the CNCG, strove to minimize the inevitable frictions at the local level.[23]

---

[20] See Document 514: Leonardo Castillo Flores to Víctor Manuel Gutiérrez, May 6, 1949; Document 582: Circular urgente de la CTG a las comunidades campesinas de Chiquimula; Document 579: Materiales del Congreso General de la Confederación de Trabajadores de Guatemala, a celebrarse los días 12, 13 y 14 de Mayo de 1950, el problema campesino, April, 1950; Document 518: Gutiérrez to Comité Ejecutivo Nacional del STEG, May 24, 1950; see Document 612: V. Manuel Gutiérrez to Amor Velasco, May 31, 1950 and Document 584: Amor Velasco de León to Secretary General of the CTG, June 1, 1950; Document 577 or 8026:325-9, Informe de la Secretaría de Acción Campesina de la Confederación de Trabajadores de Guatemala, a la IX Asamblea Confederal del 9 y 10 de Septiembre de 1950, by José Luis Ramos; also 8024:284-5, Informe de la Secretaría de Acción Campesina de la Confederación de Trabajadores de Guatemala, a la X Asamblea Confederal del 17-18 de Febrero de 1951.

[21] Document Y-42: message of CNCG to the Preparatory Committee, October 13, 1951.

[22] 8014:1129, Leonardo Castillo Flores to Víctor Manuel Gutiérrez, February 7, 1952.

[23] See 8014:1127, Clodoveo Torres Moss to Víctor Manuel Gutiérrez, March 11, 1952; 8002:1436, Víctor Manuel Gutiérrez to Leonardo Castillo Flores, August 26, 1952; 8002:1402 or Document 732: Leonardo Castillo Flores to Víctor Manuel Gutiérrez, September 2, 1952; 8002:1403, Leonardo Castillo Flores to Víctor Manuel Gutiérrez, September 4, 1952; 8002:1398, Víctor Manuel Gutiérrez to Leonardo Castillo Flores, September 9, 1952; 8016:744, Oscar Bautista González to Víctor Manuel Gutiérrez, November 18, 1952 and 8016:755, Víctor Manuel Gutiérrez to Oscar Bautista González, November 24, 1952; 8016:709, Leonardo Castillo Flores to Víctor Manuel Gutiérrez, December 3, 1952.

In pursuance of a resolution approved by the Assembly of Secretaries General, the CNCG sought a "firm and functional alliance with the CGTG."[24] After Castillo Flores returned from the Vienna WFTU Congress and a tour of the Soviet Union in late 1953, a Coordinating Committee was established to "strengthen the alliance of the workers and peasants."[25] The CNCG and CGTG delegates on the departmental agrarian commission were brought together and instructed to work as one.[26] The CNCG was invited to take a large role in the CGTG convention in January of 1954 and the CGTG helped in the preparations for the CNCG convention held the following month.[27] The CNCG leadership fully endorsed the Communist proposal for a united front of the masses which was to be built largely upon the foundation of the alliance of the workers and peasants. For political purposes the CGTG and the CNCG were virtually one and issued joint statements on national and international questions.[28]

While close collaboration between the CNCG and the CGTG was the order of the day on the national level, considerable friction arose at the local level over the rival claims of CGTG and CNCG members for the material benefits of agrarian reform. According to the agreement between the two organizations, CGTG affiliates were supposed to pass over into the CNCG when their members received land through

---

[24] 8016:667-9, Resoluciones votadas por la Asamblea de Secretarios Generales Federales, miembros de la CNCG, December 23, 1952.

[25] Document 762 or 8050:1328-9, Proyecto de manifiesto de la CGTG y de la CNCG.

[26] 8008:6271-2, Resoluciones presentadas por los delegados de las centrales CNCG y CGTG, ante la reunión que se lleva a cabo de tales delegados ante las distintas Comisiones Agrarias Departamentales de la República; also 8050:1239, March 12, 1954.

[27] See Document 1760: Plan de trabajo que se propone de parte de los Secretarios de Relaciones Campesinas y de Organización de la CGTG a la Dirección Superior de la CNCG para la organización del III Congreso Nacional de la Confederación Campesina en el curso del presente mes, February 4, 1954.

[28] 8050:839, Confederación General Trabajadores Guatemala and Confederación Nacional Campesina Guatemala to the President, January 15, 1954; 8051:1738-41, Carta de la CTAL a la CTG y a la CNCG, March 1954; Document 524: CTAL to Víctor Manuel Gutiérrez and Leonardo Castillo Flores, March 27, 1954; Document 339, 1579, 8024:1374-6, 8052: 4565-7, 8039:140-2 or Y-X-1: 1335-7, Llamamiento de la CGTG y de la CNCG, June, 1954; Document 1641, 8024:1370-3, 8032:2367-70, 8039:143-6, Carta de los obreros y campesinos de Guatemala dirigida a los trabajadores de Honduras y Nicaragua, en particular, y a todos los trabajadores de América Latina, June, 1954.

the agrarian reform program; in practice the Communist leaders of the CGTG were reluctant to give up their control over these campesinos. Although this placed a strain upon the CNCG-CGTG alliance, the campesino leaders felt they had nothing to gain from making an issue of it, as the National Agrarian Department and the President favored the Communist-controlled CGTG. In Escuintla, Chimaltenango and Chiquimula there was no such friction since the departmental CGTG, CNCG and Agrarian Department machinery were all directly controlled by the Communists.[29]

The CNCG Moves Into the Communist Orbit. The story of the CNCG from 1952 onward was one of rapid growth coupled with constantly increasing Communist influence. The leftward movement of the CNCG was brought about through the interaction of various forces, several of which have been discussed in the preceding sections. Here we will look at some of the evidence of CNCG-Communist collaboration.

In March of 1952 the CNCG joined with the Communists and the government parties to denounce anti-Communism as subversive.[30] On May Day Castillo Flores' speech followed the pro-Soviet line laid down by Gutiérrez.[31] At the June 1 CNCG Congress the Communist leader José Luis Ramos was elected Secretary of Training. After the CNCG leaders joined the PAR, relations with the CGTG became even closer and the CNCG began to participate more actively in the many Communist front activities and organizations which flourished in Guatemala during 1953.

As 1953 was marked by CNCG attempts to improve relations with the Communist-controlled CGTG, it likewise saw closer relations with the PGT.[32] The Communist leader Fortuny criticized the CNCG at

[29] See 8016:844-5, Pablo Morales S. and Andrés Barrera C. to Jefe del Departamento Agrario Nacional, December 26, 1952.

[30] See Document 2005: joint CGTG-CNCG telegram warning local leaders to boycott anti-Communist rallies and to keep a watch on anti-Communists, March 19, 1952; 8052:3250, Clodoveo Torres Moss to Bacilio Yos Bac, March 19, 1952. For CNCG opposition to anti-Communism see Documents Y-81: Leonardo Castillo Flores to Minister of Public Education, July 25, 1951; 651: Leonardo Castillo Flores to Chief of Department of Rural Education, January 29, 1952; 851: Manuel Monroy Flores to Leonardo Castillo Flores, July 20, 1951.

[31] 8025:2086-2090, joint CGTG-CNCG manifesto, April 1952; Y-44: May Day speech of Castillo Flores.

[32] See Document 924: report of Castillo Flores to General Assembly of CNCG, June 6, 1953.

the May session of the PGT Central Committee, and some CNCG leaders were concerned by the sectarian exploitation of agrarian reform by the PGT. However Castillo Flores sought closer relations with the Communists and directed a letter to Fortuny terming the PGT a "magnificent school for the national directors of the CNCG."[33] At a meeting celebrating the armistice in Korea, Castillo Flores pledged the support of the CNCG to the peace campaign.[34] With the support of the PGT, CGTG and PAR, the CNCG was admitted to the National Democratic Front (FDN) over PRG opposition. When the PGT issued its call for a united front of the masses, the CNCG leaders promptly endorsed this as their "patriotic duty."[35]

The "coordination" of the CNCG with the CGTG and the Communist leadership was capped by the affiliation of the CNCG with the international Communist labor organizations, the WFTU and the CTAL. As soon as the Communists had decided to try to work with and through the CNCG rather than attempt to destroy it, Gutiérrez put Castillo Flores in touch with the President of the Trade Unions International of Agricultural and Forestry Workers (UISTAF).[36] After Castillo Flores attended the Third Congress of the WFTU and completed his guided tour of the USSR, he began to participate in the activities of these three Communist-oriented bodies. Formal affiliation with these organzations was later approved by the National Congress of the CNCG.[37] The CNCG took no major action without consulting these Communist-controlled international organizations. As the CNCG was also bound to consult with the CGTG, the Communists had two lines of control over its policy.

In February of 1954 the CNCG held its Third National Congress, which was timed to take place just after the Second Congress of the

[33] Document 786: Roberto Montenegro to Secretary General of the CNCG, August 20, 1953; Document 637: Leonardo Castillo Flores to Secretary General of the PGT, July 27, 1953.

[34] Document 731: address of Leonardo Castillo Flores, July 31, 1953.

[35] Document Y-84: Otilio Marroquín Ruano to Alfredo Guerra Borges, November 4, 1953; 8051:1730-1734, Proyecto de manifiesto, probably proposed at the III National Congress of the CNCG.

[36] Document 457: Maurice Carroué to "Cher camarade Flores," November 30, 1951.

[37] On relations with the WFTU see: Documents 346, 574, 463, 475, 539, 470; 8050:1069, 1067, 1071, 1072; with the UISTAF see: Documents 347, 545, 222, 479, 531, 528; with the CTAL see: Documents 554 and 555; 8051:2303; Document Y-112.

CGTG so that the policy of the campesino organization could be adjusted to that of the ideologically more advanced workers' central. In the preparations for the meeting WFTU and CTAL agents such as the Italian Communist Guiseppe Casadei and Antonio Cabrera played a major role.[38] Among the groups invited to attend the congress were the Communist-dominated CTAL and WFTU, the International Union of Agricultural and Forestry Workers headed by the Italian Communist Ilio Bosi, and the Central Committee of Agriculture in Moscow.[39] In explaining the purpose of the Congress to a WFTU official, Castillo Flores stated that affirmation of the alliance with the CGTG, the peace campaign, the fight against foreign intervention (i.e. against the United States), and the strengthening of the united front of the masses were the major points to be treated.[40]

When the Congress was called, outside of Secretary General Castillo Flores, only one of the nine secretaries elected at the First Congress in 1951 and three of the ten elected at the June 1952 congress were still in the CNCG. The others had been purged by Castillo Flores when they objected to the path along which he was leading the CNCG, a path which "coincided" with that of the Communists. Late in 1953 Secretary of Organization Clodoveo Torres Moss, last of the CNCG founders to survive Castillo Flores' purges, was forced to resign after PGT leader Guerra Borges accused him of being an anti-Communist.[41]

The presidium of honor included the Secretary General of the PGT,

---

[38] Documents 1701: cable from Víctor Manuel Gutiérrez to Federación Sindical Mundial, January 12, 1954; 1700: cable from Saillant to CGTG; 621: Leonardo Castillo Flores to H. Jourdain, February 12, 1954; 205: Vicente Lombardo Toledano to Leonardo Castillo Flores, January 2, 1954; 471: Leonardo Castillo Flores to Vicente Lombardo Toledano, February 5, 1954; 623: H. Jourdain to Leonardo Flores, February 1, 1954.

[39] Documents 538: Leonardo Castillo Flores to Vicente Lombardo Toledano, December 28, 1953; 544: Leonardo Castillo Flores to Luis Saillant, December 28, 1953; 532: Leonardo Castillo Flores to Luis Saillant, February 5, 1954; 674: Leonardo Castillo Flores to Ilio Bosi, February 5, 1954; 533: Leonardo Castillo Flores to Comité Central de Agricultura, February 6, 1954; 530: Leonardo Castillo Flores to Lorenzo Azua, February 1, 1954; 526: Leonardo Castillo Flores to Secretario General de la CTG de Bolivia, February 12, 1954. Document 508 contains a list of others invited.

[40] Document 536: Leonardo Castillo Flores to Ilio Bosi, February 1, 1954.

[41] See *Tribuna Popular*, October 14, 1953; Y-103: Clodoveo Torres Moss to Alfredo Guerra Borges, October 23, 1953; 8051:2143, Clodoveo Torres Moss to Alfredo Guerra Borges, October 23, 1953; Document 611: Clodoveo Torres Moss to Comité Ejecutivo Nacional of CNCG, November 5, 1953; Y-89: Resoluciones votadas en el último consejo de Secretarios Generales Federales de la república.

the Communist heads of the AFG, AJDG, FUD and CGTG as well as five international Communist labor leaders from the CTAL and WFTU. The working presidium had as members such Communist firebrands as Carlos Manuel Pellecer and Jubal Cetino, Communist boss from Chiquimula.[42] In his report as Secretary General Castillo Flores pointed out that the CNCG had grown from 25 campesino unions in May of 1950 to 568 in May of 1952 and since the passage of the Agrarian Reform bill had more than trebled to 1785 local organizations.[43] Changed conditions required the establishment of three new secretariats—Rural Youth, Foreign Relations and Union Relations—to deal with the CTAL, WFTU, and CGTG respectively. These three Communist-controlled organizations were portrayed by Castillo Flores as "without a doubt our guides in the road toward the well-being of humanity." The strengthening of the alliance of the workers and peasants and the establishment of the "United Front of the Masses" were the two main tasks of the CNCG in the months ahead.[44] Was it merely coincidence that these had previously been declared the chief tasks and goals of the Guatemalan Communist Party?

The pro-Communist orientation of the CNCG leadership became even more apparent on May Day of 1954. Among the mottos which the campesinos were to use on the signs they carried were many which served the interests of the Communists.[45]

Long live the Soviet Union and the Peoples' China, defenders of the new life. The workers and peasants walk together in a united front of the masses . . . Long live the people of Viet Nam, who have defended themselves valiantly against the French and Yankee interventions. We condemn the atomic experiments of the U.S., which are a threat to life. Impose peace on the war mongers. Anti-Communism is the mask of feudalism. Who are the anti-Communists: The exploiters are. Salute the alliance of the workers and peasants. For the United Front of the Masses, upon the base of the alliance of the workers and the peasants.

---

[42] Document 253: proposals of the Comisión de Organización, February 19, 1954.

[43] Y-X-5: 1009-33 and Document Y-154: Informe del Secretario General Leonardo Castillo Flores, February 19, 1954.

[44] Y-147: Resoluciones del III Congreso Nacional Campesino, February 20, 1954.

[45] Y-141: various publications of the Secretary of Propaganda of the CNCG in preparation for the International Day of the Worker, April 1954.

In his May Day address Castillo Flores appeared more Communist than even Gutiérrez as he saluted the workers of the world who had been victimized by capitalist exploitations and described the plans of North American monopolies to commit mass murder in Guatemala. On the other hand "we salute with our spirit of brotherhood our companions in the Soviet Union, the Peoples' Republic of China, and all the countries of Popular Democracy, whose victorious march points out to us the path . . ."[46]

The participation of the CNCG in Communist front activities reached a peak with the organization of rural youth. When the World Federation of Democratic Youth invited the CNCG to participate in the proposed International Rally of Rural Youth, the CNCG gladly accepted.[47] At the 1954 CNCG Congress a Secretary of Rural Youth was appointed and plans made to launch a large-scale attempt to organize the campesino youth, an untapped source which had not been reached by any of the other "mass organizations."[48] The CNCG sent Marco Antonio Soto and Guillermo Ovando Arriola to the meeting of the International Organizing Committee in April and made plans to organize 150 "clubs" by the end of the year.[49] These organizations would join the other youth groups in the massive Festival of Friendship of Central American and Caribbean Youth which was scheduled for December.[50]

By 1954 the CNCG followed the lead of the CGTG on virtually every major question. Since the political line of the CGTG was determined within the PGT, and the CNCG leaders exerted considerable influence over the stand taken by the PAR, the end result of the CGTG-CNCG alliance was that the Communists had three and often

[46] *Nuestra Tierra*, No. 1, May 15, 1954.
[47] Document 464: O. Fischer and B. Bernini to CNCG, February 1, 1954; Document 476: Leonardo Castillo Flores to O. Fischer and B. Bernini, February 16, 1954.
[48] Documents Y-164: Reglamento de la uniones de la juventud rural, March 9, 1954; 222: Leonardo Castillo Flores to Ilio Bossi, April 12, 1954.
[49] Document 481: L. Petrov and B. Bernini to CNCG, March 4, 1954; Document 525: Leonardo Castillo Flores to Bruno Bernini and L. Petrov, March 20, 1954; 8050:1060, radiogram from CNCG to International Landungdon, March 30, 1954; See *Nuestra Tierra*, Epoca II, No. 1, May 15, 1954; Document 224: Plan organizativo de la Juventud Campesina; Y-143: Reglamento de los Clubes de la Juventud Campesina, May 22, 1954.
[50] Document 221: Luis Ronny Morales Chacón, CNCG Secretary of Rural Youth in a circular of June 16, 1954.

four votes within the National Democratic Front—that of the PGT itself, those of the CGTG and its ally the CNCG, and often that of the PAR.

SAMF: FOCUS OF THE STRUGGLE FOR THE CONTROL OF LABOR

What organized resistance there was to the Communist take-over and control of the Guatemalan labor movement came largely from within the ranks of the SAMF or Railroaders' Action and Improvement Union. One of the largest and most strategic unions in the country, the SAMF was in the early years of the Revolution the main rival of the Communistically inclined teachers' union (STEG) for the leadership of the labor movement. (Its members were relatively the most advanced and sophisticated in the Guatemalan proletariat and participated actively in union affairs.) If it had not been for the moderate elements in the SAMF, the unification of Guatemalan labor under Communist control would have come about years sooner. The opponents of Communism within the SAMF were a major source of support for attempts to form a revolutionary party which would champion isolation of the Communists, and constituted the potential backbone for a non-Communist labor movement. However, the SAMF could never play this role effectively until it settled the internal struggle between the pro-Communists and anti-Communists within its own ranks. For a variety of reasons the opponents of Communism lost this crucial battle. While it is far from certain that they could have decisively altered the course of Guatemalan labor and politics had they won control of the SAMF, their failure ended any hope of successfully challenging the Communist leadership of the CGTG. The developments within the SAMF were neither entirely a cause nor an effect, but rather an integral part of the growth of Communist influence in Guatemalan labor and politics.

To understand Communist success in Guatemala it is important to examine the internal power struggle within the SAMF to see why the anti-Communists failed and how the Communists first neutralized this nucleus of opposition within the ranks of labor and then brought the SAMF into line with the rest of the labor movement. The task of analysis is complicated by the fact that the long series of internal

battles which characterized the history of the SAMF had a number
of foci and the motives of the antagonists were often mixed. Personal
rivalries, dictatorial tendencies on the part of some leaders, corruption,
disagreement over policy and tactics, and politics all played a role.
That Communism was one of the main issues involved is evident, but
its relative importance and relation to the other causes of dissension
is not so easily ascertained. To a degree Communism was used as a
front to hide and cloud the real issues and differences; in other cases
the reverse was true and charges of corruption and dictatorship were
used to mask the real issue of Communism.

The SAMF descended from a mutual aid society which antedated
the Revolution of 1944. This organization, the Railroaders' Mutual
Aid Society (SAMF), which was converted into a trade union on July
6, 1944, was active in the struggle against Ponce. It was reorganized
as the Railroaders' Action and Improvement Union (SAMF) at a
General Assembly held on January 8, 1946. In July of that year a new
Executive Committee was elected with Arturo Morales Cubas as Secretary General, José Luis Caceros as Secretary of Organization and
César Montenegro Paniagua as Secretary of Propaganda. Of these
three, Morales Cubas was to become the leader of the anti-Communist
faction, Montenegro P. later served as Communist member of Congress, and José Luis Caceros was eventually to become an ally of the
Communist labor leader Gutiérrez. Another leading figure in the union
was Manuel Pinto Usaga, a Marxist-opportunist who became in
1949-50 the most important labor leader in Guatemala only to become
the center of the great SAMF controversy of 1950. The SAMF withdrew from the CTG in late 1945 over the issue of the Marxist school
Escuela Claridad and took a leading role in the formation of the rival
Guatemalan Union Federation (FSG) on January 23, 1946. The
leadership of the FSG came largely from the SAMF with Morales
Cubas as the first Secretary General and Pinto taking over the next
year. (See Chapter VI, pp. 129-32.)

As with other unions, the railroaders were quickly brought into
contact with Latin American Communists. The Chilean Communist
leader Juan Vargas Puebla was in close contact with SAMF in April
of 1946, and the First Railroaders' Convention of Central America and
the Caribbean in October of that year brought others such as the

Mexican Valentín Campa into close contact with SAMF leaders.[51] In these early years the SAMF successfully weathered a number of internal troubles stemming from personal and political differences.[52]

The first major political dissension within the ranks of the SAMF was over the question of presidential succession. In early 1949 the Railroaders' Political Committee (CPF) and the *Aranista* Railroaders' Union were formed.[53] The CPF secretly endorsed the candidacy of Col. Jacobo Arbenz in April of 1949, and a long internal struggle would have ensued had it not been for the assassination of Arana in July.[54]

1950: The First Battle: In 1950 Pinto Usaga was at the peak of his influence. As Secretary General of the FSG, the CNUS and the CPNT, member of Congress and a leader of the PAR, he seemed to be in an impregnable position. However, 1950 was a year of flux and uncertainties; Gutiérrez had formed the PROG, Fortuny and the other Communists were leaving the PAR, and the presidential elections were never far from the minds of the labor leaders and politicians. The coming of the Communists into the open had awakened people to the issue of Communism. Feeling secure in his newfound power, Pinto gave rein to his extremist views and continued to try to manage SAMF affairs in a high-handed manner. Many *Samfistas* were unhappy over the affiliation of the FSG with the CTAL and WFTU, an act for which Pinto was largely responsible. It was within the SAMF that Pinto was vulnerable, since his involvement in national politics and the burden of day-to-day management of FSG affairs left him little time to keep in touch with the internal politics of the SAMF or the sentiments and problems of its members. In all probability the rank and file members of the SAMF at this time were more concerned with the power and prestige of their union than with Communism, a term which had long been misused in Guatemala. While they knew little of

---

[51] See 8031:1481, April, 1946; 8031:1266-77, 1254-9, speeches of Campa and Pinto; 8031:1196, José Manuel Fortuny to Secretario General del SAMF, October 19, 1946.

[52] See 8032:3022-3; 8031:964-6; 8032:3025; 8032:1862.

[53] 8032:1863, 2039-41.

[54] See 8031:1347-8, members of CPF to Teniente Coronel Jacobo Arbenz, November 13, 1950.

the implications of Communism, a considerable number of workers felt that the interests of the union were being subordinated to this distant and poorly understood political goal by Pinto and his followers.

Friction within the SAMF between the moderate leadership and the younger Communist-influenced firebrands had been increasing, and the election campaign increased the tensions between the *Samfistas* of various political loyalties.[55] In July the first direct charges of Communism were launched against the extremist elements of SAMF.[56] The forces opposed to Pinto were led by Arturo Morales Cubas, Secretary General of the Railroaders' Political Committee (CPF) and a supporter of the Charnaud MacDonald faction of the PAR. On September 26 more than three hundred *Samfistas* petitioned the Executive Committee to expel Pinto and three days later the SAMF withdrew from the National Political Committee of the Workers (CPNT) over the formation of the Marxist labor party (PROG).[57] By now twenty-five hundred members had signed a petition accusing Pinto of wishing to put the SAMF in the hands of the "satellites of Stalin."[58] The union withdrew from the FSG and promised to return only when Pinto was no longer associated with that labor central. Following the expulsion of Pinto and three of his associates from the union, a series of short strikes were used to bring about his discharge by the railroad.[59]

The pro-Communist forces of Pinto had not taken this blow sitting down. The day after the CPF decided to withdraw from the CPNT, the Pintoists established a rump organization, the Political Committee of the Revolutionary Railroader's (CPFR), which affiliated with the

---

[55] See 8032:2913-14, José Luis Caceros to Alfonso Rivas Arroyo, Roberto López Porras and Armando Villaseñor, June 12, 1950, and 2932-4, Carlos López Sandoval to Sr. Editorialista de *Tribuna Ferrocarrilera,* June 29, 1950.

[56] 8032:1594 or 2937, editorial of *Vanguardia Sindical* and 8032:1596, *Vanguardia Sindical,* July 4, 1954.

[57] See Document 213 or Y-X-1:29, Adán H. Morales V. to Manuel Pinto Usaga, October 2, 1950, for the anti-Pinto petition and Y-X-1:30, Comité Político Ferroviario to miembros directivos del Comité Político Nacional de la Clase Trabajadora, October 2, 1950, for the withdrawal from the CPNT. Y-X-1:27-8, José Luis Caceros R. to miembros del Comité Político Nacional de la Clase Trabajadora, October 2, 1950; 8032:1979 or 2924; 8032: 2036-8.

[58] 8031:692, October 5, 1950.

[59] 8031:1601-3, Pinto Usaga expulsado del SAMF.

Communist dominated CPNT.[60] At the same time they demanded that the government investigate the activities of the Morales Cubas forces.[61] The weight of all the labor organizations controlled by Pinto or the Communists was thrown into the battle. Claiming that the Communist issue was a red herring used by reactionary opportunists, they depicted anti-Communism rather than Communism as the subversive movement.[62] Pinto and his supporters began an effort to discredit Morales Cubas in every way possible so as to prepare the way for their own eventual comeback. Dictatorship, graft, selling out to the employers, these and many more charges were made by the Pintoists within the ranks of the SAMF and echoed by the FSG.[63] Prominent Guatemalans such as the pro-Communist diplomat Enrique Muñoz Meany were called upon to support publicly the Pintoist line that "anti-Communism is the synonym of fascism" and that the moderates were really attacking the "elemental demands" and "legitimate aspirations" of the workers.[64] The workers were told that they should not oppose Com-

[60] See 8024:880-4, September 30, 1950; Y-X-1:33-4, numerous Samfistas to Secretario General del CPNT, October 2, 1950; Y-X-1:23, Mario Tejada to Comité Ejecutivo del CPNT, October 6, 1950; Y-X-1:21-2, 24-5 or 31-2, "Alerta Compañeros Ferrocarrileros!", October, 1950.

[61] Y-X-1:7, unidentified Samfista to Inspector General de Trabajo, September 30, 1950; Y-X-1:35-7, numerous Samfistas to Ministro de Economía y Trabajo, February 3, 1950.

[62] See Y-X-1:9-14, El problema del SAMF, visto por los trabajadores organizados de Guatemala, October 6, 1950, signed by representatives of 44 FSG unions and Y-X-1:777, Mensaje de Pinto Usaga a los ferrocarrileros, October 6, 1950; 8024:458-61, Federación de Trabajadores del Departamento de Guatemala, resolución tomada ante las agresiones a la unidad revolucionaria de los trabajadores de Guatemala por parte de dirigentes oportunistas alentados por altos funcionarios del gobierno, October 12, 1950; Y-X-1:1060-1, Boletín del Sindicato Artes Gráficas, November, 1950; see also 8026:157-162 for various telegrams of support for Pinto.

[63] See particularly Segundo mensaje de Pinto Usaga a los ferrocarrileros, November, 1950; Y-X-1:1150-1, Tercer mensaje de Manuel Pinto Usaga a los ferrocarrileros, November, 1950; Y-X-1:1141, Federación Sindical de Guatemala, December 10, 1950; also 8031:1605, "Dictadura sindical"; Y-X-1:1179, 1189, 1191, 1192, 1193, 1194 and 1195, "Boletín de la Federación Sindical de Guatemala a todos sus sindicatos," Comisión defensora de la unidad de los trabajadores FSG; Y-X-3:3648, Aclaración que hace el Señor José Luis Alvarado, October 9, 1950; Y-X-3:3575, Boletín de la Federación Sindical de Guatemala, October 25, 1950; Y-X-1:1-6, 8, 15-9, 577, 589, 590; 8025:1631.

[64] Y-X-2:2929, Carta elocuente de un eminente Guatemalteco, Enrique Muñoz Meany to Manuel Pinto Usaga, October 14, 1950.

munists until they had given it a hearing and urged to read and study Communist works so that they would not be sorry later. "There is no right to be mistaken against your own interests. . . . To be anti-Communist is to serve the interests of the reaction and your exploiters."[65]

This propaganda barrage was met head on by the moderate leaders and the supporters of Morales Cubas. The SAMF leaders raised the question of Pinto's eligibility to containue as Secretary General of the FSG, and the courts upheld his expulsion from the SAMF.[66] The Puerto Barrios branch of SAMF petitioned the President to expel Pinto from the country as an undesirable alien, and Pinto saved his position in the FSG only by getting the chauffers' union to accept him as a member.[67] Each bulletin or manifesto of the radicals was met by one from the moderates.[68] For the time being at least, the moderates seemed to have the upper hand.

1951: The Regrouping of Forces. In 1951 the Communists undertook a new approach to the problem of the SAMF. As Pinto was quite thoroughly discredited, the Communists quietly began to look for other SAMF leaders who could be influenced to look favorably upon Communism. The Communists were marking time in their political activities so as not to endanger the unification of the labor movement, which would be under their control, by giving cause for the raising of the Communist issue again. Within SAMF the pro-Communist elements restrained their propaganda to attacks upon Morales Cubas and the moderate leadership as agents of the railroad and pressing home the charges that they had sold the workers out to the management in their negotiations.[69]

---

[65] 8032:2921 or Y-X-1:20, "Obreros de Guatemala, Compañeros Samfistas."

[66] See 8032:1868-9 or 1902-3, "Boletín de Prensa," October 26, 1950; 8032:1841 or 2953, "Un mentis al traidor Pinto," October, 1950; 8032:1951, 1967 or 1872, "Boletín de Prensa del Sindicato de Acción y Mejoramiento Ferrocarrilero," November 6, 1950.

[67] 8032:2945-6, Comité Ejecutivo de la filial del SAMF en Puerto Barrios to Doctor don Juan José Arévalo, November 22, 1950; 8033:403, Adán H. Morales V. to Abel Recinos, February 15, 1951.

[68] See 8031:1616; 8032:1980, 1984, 2923 and 2948; Y-X-1, 419.

[69] See Y-X-1:768-9, "Por sus actos los conoceréis, carta de recomendación para las elecciones: MORALES: sinónimo de INMORALIDAD," June 1, 1951; Document 1227: "Los líderes del SAMF y su Eterna demagogia," Efraín González, October 14, 1951.

The first major development of the year was the election of officers which took place on June 15. The slate headed by Aristeo Sosa, José Luis Caceros, and Rolando Calderón won; but the railroad refused to recognize them until after an appeal by the defeated ticket headed by Víctor Merlos had been thrown out by the authorities and the union had threatened a strike.[70] Such tactics by the company as consciously fostering division within the union played into the hands of the Communists and lent support to their claim that unity in the face of the exploiters was more important than political differences, i.e. opposition to Communism.[71]

The issue of Communism could not be kept submerged, and soon a dispute broke out over the proposal of newly-elected Secretary of Organization José Luis Caceros to attend a meeting in East Berlin to which he was invited at WFTU expense.[72] Caceros, who only a year earlier had been exasperated by the young Marxists who presumed to tell the old fighters what course they should follow, had gradually been won over toward cooperation with the Communists through his participation as Secretary of Records of the Communist-dominated CPNT. Although his political affiliation was with the PAR, Caceros answered criticism of his desire to attend this "Communist" meeting with an impassioned defense of his right to visit Berlin, Moscow, China or any other country "to see with my own eyes if Communism is good or not."[73]

---

[70] For Merlos' long reputation as a divisionist see Document 1233: Aristeo Sosa h. to Víctor Merlos, September 18, 1951.

[71] See 8031:933, "Atención Compañeros de Agencia"; 957, telegram Aristeo Sosa h. to Teniente Coronel Jacobo Arbenz Guzmán, July 12, 1951; 859-65, Puerto Barrios Filial de SAMF to Ejecutivo Central del SAMF, July 14, 1951; 908, Waldemar Barrios Klee to Adán H. Morales Vielman, July 16, 1951; 903, Aristeo Sosa to Presidente de los F.I. de C.A., July 18, 1951; 874, T. Bradshaw to Aristeo Sosa h., July 20, 1951; 896, Aristeo Sosa to E. S. MacDonald, August 20, 1951; 883, Varios Samfistas to compañeros ferrocarrileros, July 24, 1951; Documents Y-221 and Y-222: Boletín de la filial del SAMF en Escuintla, July 25, 1951.

[72] 8032:1855, Adán H. Morales V., and Manuel Antonio Morales B. to Director del Periódico *La Hora*, July 3, 1951; 8031:948, Zacapa Filial to Ministro de Economía y Trabajo, Inspector General de Trabajo and Secretario General del SAMF, July 10, 1951; Document 652: Humberto Bocaletti M. to José Luis Caceros R., July 24, 1951; 8015:306, Louis Saillant to SAMF, September 11, 1951.

[73] Document 652A: José Luis Caceros R. to Director del *Imparcial*, July 10, 1951; Document 670: José Luis Caceros Rodríguez to Domingo Orantes A., August 25, 1951.

In this changed environment the SAMF was racked by dissension and disagreement which rivaled if it did not surpass the trouble of the previous year. The question of participation in the unification of the labor movement raised ambivalent feelings in many *Samfistas*—the desire for unity versus the fear of Communist domination. On the one hand, Morales Cubas, with strong support from several branches and particularly Puerto Barrios, was calling for cooperation with the CNCG and several small organizations to assure that the unified labor movement would not be under the control of the Communists, while at the same time attempting to build a broad base among labor for the newly-organized Socialist Party in an effort to cut the ground out from under the Communists by offering them some real competition within the revolution.[74] On the other hand, Caceros and such Communists within the ranks of SAMF as Deputy César Montenegro P. and Secretary of Propaganda Rolando Calderón B. were determined to bring the SAMF into a Communist-led CGTG.[75]

At a General Assembly held on the 16th of October the SAMF decided to join the CGTG on the condition that it would put off the question of affiliation with the Communist-led CTAL and WFTU.[76] The desire for unity had apparently been stronger than the fear of Communism. However hundreds of *Samfistas* resigned in protest, while many more hesitated, torn between the desire for unity and the fear that the Communists would manage somehow to turn the newly-unified labor movement to their sectarian ends.[77] Hoping to allay the fears of the moderates, the Communists and their sympathizers agreed in principle that the CGTG would be apolitical, knowing that this would be impossible to enforce.[78]

---

[74] See 8031:1351, A. Morales Cubas to la directiva del SAMF, September 17, 1951; 8031:1420, "Boletín del Gran Partido Acción Socialista."

[75] See 8032:2090 or 8014:1498, "Qué es la CGTG?" by Rolando A. Calderón B., October 1951; 8014:1497, R. A. Calderón B. to Compañeros Samfistas, October 25, 1951.

[76] Document 1191: Arnoldo Otten Prado to Aristeo Sosa h., October 19, 1951.

[77] See Y-408 for a listing of 452 resignations and Y-402 for the names of 159 who rejoined after the leadership agreed to certain conditions; 8033:299-301, Jorge Morales Dardón to Secretario General del SAMF, October 26, 1951; 8032:2291, Humberto González and Ricardo Oliveros L. to compañeros ferrocarrileros, October 31, 1951.

[78] 8033:53, "Compromiso Solemne," December 23, 1951; 8032:2230-4, meeting of SAMF Executive Committee, June 12, 1951.

To shift the attention of the members away from their internal troubles, the SAMF leadership, particularly the Communists of the Defense Commission, launched a campaign for the expulsion of the Vice-President of International Railways of Central America (IRCA) and the dissolution of the Union of Railroad Workers (STF), a small rival railroad union which had long been a thorn in their side.[79] The STF had been organized in 1946 by a small group of *Samfistas* who were disturbed by the influence of the Communist CTAL leader Lombardo Toledano with the leaders of SAMF. In 1950 it had gained members who left the SAMF during the dissension over Pinto, and in July of 1951 many of the supporters of the defeated slate in the SAMF elections joined the STF. Now many other moderates were leaving SAMF for the smaller anti-Communist union, which had grown to about 750 members while the SAMF was shrinking from a high of 4850 in 1949 to about 4000. When Arbenz ordered the STF dissolved at the end of the year, it greatly helped the extremist leaders.[80]

1952: Victory and Defeat. The pro-Communist and extremist elements in SAMF began 1952 with an attempt to place the blame for the dissension upon the shoulders of the railroad company and the Morales Cubas faction.[81] Unity was stressed as a primary value and the necessity to remain within the CGTG pictured as the only way to prevent the railroad from destroying SAMF or the reaction from destroying the revolution and its gains. On the other hand, the moderate elements were dissatisfied with the pro-Soviet line of the CGTG and the closeness of the leaders of SAMF to the Communists.[82] On March 3, the Puerto Barrios local forced its Executive Committee to resign on

[79] See 8031:1772, "Boletín de Prensa de la Comisión de Defensa del SAMF," November 3, 1951; 8031:1771, "Boletín de Prensa de la Comisión de Defensa del SAMF," November 6, 1951; 8031:1342-6, various letters of support from the CNCG.

[80] See Y-196: copy of decree extinguishing STF, December 21, 1951. For the story of the STF see Y-272, 8033:71, Y-398, 8025:1661.

[81] See Document 1651 or Y-205: "Manifiesto de los Samfistas a las valientes bases de la línea alerta trabajadores Samfistas de las filiales, la unidad es la base de la fortaleza"; also 8031:698-700, report of commission named to study the internal situation of the SAMF, January 9, 1952; 8031:713, Línea política; 8031:718, proposals to Comité Ejecutivo of SAMF to combat "disorientation," March 8, 1950.

[82] See 8031:1434-6, Act 139 of Puerto Barrios filial of SAMF, February 16, 1952.

charges of placing the interests of Communism above the interests of the union. Under the leadership of Morales Cubas and Adán H. Morales V., both of whom had served as Secretary General of the union, four locals joined in demanding that the SAMF withdraw from the CGTG unless its Communist leaders were removed from office.[83]

Early in March Communist chief Fortuny launched a public attack against Morales Cubas and sought to have him expelled from the Socialist Party.[84] Morales Cubas in return blasted Communism as "anti-revolutionary and anti-national," stating that his only fault had been telling the Communists to keep their hands off the SAMF.[85] Elections were called for the days June 30 to July 3. In spite of the fact that the Communist-backed slate was considered by most observers to have the support of the Executive Committee, the anti-Communists won by a surprising margin of 1321 to 720.[86] Nevertheless the five officers elected the preceding year still formed the majority of the Executive Committee and controlled its three most important posts.[87] From the office of Secretary of Propaganda Rolando Calderón B. and from the fortnightly paper which was in the hands of the Communist deputy Montenegro P., Communist propaganda was still diffused throughout the SAMF.

When the anti-Communists demanded the expulsion of Calderón and Caceros, the pro-Communist leadership countered with an investigation of the tangled affairs of the SAMF-owned transportation company CONDETSA headed by moderate leader Adán Morales V. and the Consumers' Cooperative managed by Morales Cubas himself.[88] In the confusion of these investigations Morales Cubas, the leader of the

---

[83] See 8031:1437-43 and 8031:1580-2.

[84] *El Imparcial,* March 19, 1952.

[85] 8033:268-82, Arturo Morales Cubas to Charnaud MacDonald, President Arbenz, SAMF national leaders, and branches, March 15, 1952; 8032:2975, "A los reaccionarios y a los Comunistas," Arturo Morales Cubas.

[86] See 8031:785, Aristides Mota H. to Arturo Morales Cubas, April 1, 1952; Y-X-1:317-9, 301, 320-2, 1081-2, Y-X-3:3914-5, various attacks upon Morales Cubas by Juventud Revolucionaria Ferrocarrilera, April, 1952; see 8031:1056, Acuerdo No. 14, June 21, 1952; 8031:1059, 1063-6, propaganda of the Celada-Villaseñor slate; *El Imparcial,* June 30, 1952; 8032:1745-6, Aristeo Sosa h. and José Luis Caceros to David Vela, July 2, 1952.

[87] See 8031:1654 and 1692-5.

[88] 8031:1651, "La verdad en torno al caso del compañero Rolando A. Caldéron," August, 1952; 8031:1670-5, Asamblea local en Puerto Barrios, August 21, 1952; *El Imparcial,* October 8, 1952.

opposition to the Communists, was quite thoroughly discredited. On October 5 Morales Cubas was removed by a newly-elected Administrative Council; his attempt to fight this action was thwarted by the President who appointed Col. Anselmo Getella as "interventor" of the cooperative. Apparently the government had decided to help the pro-Communist forces by discrediting Morales Cubas.[89] As the year closed the opponents of Communism were on the defensive and their leader was facing congressional investigation.

1953: The Final Round. In the elections scheduled for June 6, 1953, Arturo Morales Cubas headed the moderate slate supported by the Puerto Barrios, Zacapa, and Mazatenango locals. He was opposed by the extremists, who had the backing of the Executive Committee and the CGTG.[90] Claiming that the government and the administration political parties had intervened in support of the pro-Communist Caceros-Calderón faction, the Morales Cubas forces set up a rump Executive Committee headed by Secretary of Relations Gonzalo Gutiérrez Juárez.[91] The outgoing officers countered with the charge that Morales Cubas was not a bona fide member of the SAMF.[92]

The candidates of the pro-Communist group (*Frente Ferroviario*

---

[89] See 8032:2981, "Boletín maniobras ilegales de Celada y compañeros," Comité de Defensa y Unificación del SAMF, September 5, 1952; also 8032: 2979-80, 2985 and 2992.

[90] 8033:178, Comité Ejecutivo to members of SAMF, March 20, 1953; 8031:219, Aristeo Sosa h. and José Luis Caceros R. to Roberto Loyo Díaz, Ricardo Saavedra Cerna and Rolando A. Lemus P., March 28, 1953; 8033: 41, José Luis Caceros Rodríguez, "Los dinamiteros, los complotistas, tratan de penetrar las líneas sindicales," May 1953; Y-X-5:852-61 or 1082-4, Y-X-1:1065-8 or 8032:2758-11, 272 Samfistas to Víctor Manuel Gutiérrez, May 6, 1953; Y-X-1:1062-3, Y-X-5:866-7 or 8013:520-1, 522-3, and 524-5, "Llamamiento a los compañeros del SAMF," Víctor Manuel Gutiérrez, May 22, 1953.

[91] 8013:223, "Compañeros dirigentes de las organizaciones sindicales, compañeros sindicalizados, miembros de base," May 22, 1953.

[92] See 8013:518-9, *SAMF, Organo del Sindicato de Acción y Mejoramiento Ferrocarrilero,* Año VII, No. 139, May 22, 1953; 8033:151, Aristeo Sosa h. to members of SAMF, May 9, 1953; 8032:2812, José Maria Celada C. and José Félix Mendizabal Leiva to Secretario General del SAMF, June 12, 1953; 8032:2811, Aristeo Sosa h. and José Luis Caceros R. to José Félix Mendizabal Leiva and José María Celada Corzo, June 16, 1953; 8032:2813, José Félix Mendizabal Leiva to Aristeo Sosa h., June 18, 1953; 8032:2814-5, Aristeo Sosa h. and José Luis Caceros R. to José Félix Mendizabal Leiva, June 19, 1953.

Democrático Electoral—FFDE) defeated the Morales Cubas slate by a reported vote of 2008 to 1024.[93] While new Secretary General Jaime Zavala had not been prominent in union affairs or politics, Secretary of Organization José Félix Mendizabal Leiva was a leader of the extremist wing, and the guiding spirits of the FFDE included Communist leader Armando Villaseñor and the heads of the pro-Communist slate which had been defeated in the 1952 elections. The young Marxist zealots who had been scorned by the older pragmatic leaders less than three years before were now in a position to shape the political line of the most important union in Guatemala. The leaders of the Communist youth group within the SAMF, the *Juventud Democrática Ferrocarrilera,* had masterminded the victory of the Zavala slate. In Armando Villaseñor, Mario Tejada, Abelardo Ruíz Rizzo and Humberto González the PGT had a nucleus within the SAMF which had been able to rebound from two setbacks to engineer the crushing defeat of Morales Cubas and all but destroy organized opposition to Communism within the union. Their political activities received the rubber stamp approval of the new Secretary General who owed his election to their efforts.[94] (In June 1954 the anti-Communists prepared to challenge the official slate of candidates headed by PGT leader Armando Villaseñor, and some members threatened to resign if he were elected to the Executive Committee. However, the Arbenz regime fell before these elections could be carried out.)

Retrospect: Communist Success or Anti-Communist Failure? We have seen that the Communists were able within the span of a few short years to take control of the well-organized and relatively democratically run railroad union, the majority of whose members were, originally at least, unfavorably disposed to Communism. In several respects this was a victory for Communist tactics and propaganda. The anti-Communist tendencies of many members were neutralized by playing upon their fear of serving the interests of the reaction and their suspicion of the foreign-owned railroad company. The Communists concentrated upon making Communists out of the SAMF leaders rather than making

---

[93] 8032:2816-9, IGT scrutiny of votes, June 22, 1953.

[94] See 8031:1076, "Llamamiento del Frente Ferroviario Democrático Electoral," June 23, 1953; 8031:1341, "La juventud ferrocarrilera se dirige a los jóvenes del país"; 8031:1105-6, July 29, 1953; 8031:1104; 8033:206, 456 and 506-10; Document 1379.

leaders out of the Communists and in this way managed to bring victory out of defeat after the 1952 elections. Control of the Secretariat of Education and Propaganda and of the union paper enabled the Communists to spread their propaganda. The Communists played upon the desire of the workers for a unified labor movement to bring the SAMF into the Communist-led labor confederation. A Communist-oriented youth organization within the railroading brotherhood served to make allies or converts out of the promising younger union activists.

The greatest step toward victory was in identifying anti-Communism with opposition to the revolution and the gains of the workers as well as in making the anti-Communists appear as tools of the company and the reactionary elements in Guatemala. In this way anti-Communism was branded as subversive in the eyes of many workers and Communism identified with their interests. The ability of the Communists to become accepted as an integral part of the Arbenz regime served to win tolerance from many workers who were not favorable to Communism but felt an intense loyalty to the Arbenz government for its support of organized labor and its championing of the interests of the working class.

The opponents of Communism within the SAMF were in a difficult position. As supporters of the Revolution of 1944, they were unable to join forces with the more conservative anti-Communists. They were hampered by the lack of a strong non-Communist leftist party upon which they could rely for political support and which would offer a feasible alternative to cooperating with the Communists. On the other hand, the pro-Communist faction of SAMF could count upon the aid of the Communist-led labor movement, and, as it proved, of the President himself.

Unfortunately, the opponents of Communism within the SAMF, along with the management of the railroad and the enemies of the Arbenz Government, were to a certain degree responsible for the success of the Communists. The attitude and actions of the conservative elements in Guatemala were often such as to discredit the anti-Communist movement in the eyes of Guatemalan workers who were stanch supporters of the Revolution of 1944 and the program of the Arbenz Government. The intransigence of the railroad company and its obstructionist tactics in dealing with the union, added to its efforts to split the union and foster division among the workers, led to an atmosphere which lent credence to the Communist claim that the moderate leaders of SAMF were really tools of the railroad who were selling out the interests of the workers.

The moderate leaders themselves must bear partial responsibility for their failure and hence for the success of the Communists. The tragedy is that Morales Cubas and his followers discredited themselves by taking advantage of their positions for personal gain at the workers' expense. Even when there were no sins of commission on the records of the opponents of Communism, they partially defaulted to the Communists and their allies. Many of the moderate leaders were too interested in their own economic well-being and job advancement to devote as much time to union affairs as did the extremists. Some moderate leaders stagnated once they tasted the better things of life and others gave up the fight and resigned to care for their personal or family interests. These actions and attitudes lost them the support of such dedicated leaders as José Luis Caceros R., who began to see in the Communist labor leaders a model more worthy of emulation. The Communists did not overlook these opportunities. By making Caceros an officer of the CGTG they not only created a new tie with the SAMF, but also brought him into physical proximity with the Communist labor leaders, a contact which grew into political and ideological agreement. While the Communists seemed able to regroup and bring victory out of apparent defeat, the moderates too often took the negative road of resignation in protest, thus leaving the field to the extremists.

The case of the CNCG differed materially from that of the SAMF. Anti-Communism was never a significant issue within the campesino organization, whose members were unequipped to take an active part in shaping its policies. The CNCG's professedly non-Communist leaders, either incapable of providing positive guidance or seeking the path of least resistance, allowed their organization to come under the domination of the more experienced CGTG, and hence indirectly of the PGT. The willingness of its leaders to let themselves be carried along with the tide allowed the CNCG to serve Communist ends. The road to Communism, as well as that to hell, is often paved with good intentions.

8

COMMUNIST PENETRATION OF THE GOVERNMENT

It has frequently been pointed out by those who wish to minimize the influence of Communism in Guatemala that there were relatively few Communists holding high governmental offices under the Arbenz administration. The classic example which they use is the fact that none of the Cabinet Ministers were Communists and that only four of the members of Congress were affiliated with the PGT. While these facts are literally true, to conclude from them that the Communists were not influential in the government is to ignore the basic political realities of the Guatemalan situation under the Arbenz regime.

The key characteristic of the Communist penetration of the Guatemalan government and influence over its policies was the principle of indirect control. As a matter of fact Communists did hold key positions in certain strategic agencies which administered vital governmental programs and shaped public opinion. In most cases, however, they were satisfied to have the top offices filled by their political allies. They were not particularly concerned with the ministries which carried on the work of routine government administration, for they realized that the policies and programs of these agencies could be controlled through the President, who dominated the government. The Communists' influence with the leaders of the other political parties and their control of organized labor also gave them added leverage over the governmental bureaucracy. All these influences were institutionalized in the National Democratic Front, which, composed of representatives of the government parties, the labor confederation, and the peasant confederation and presided over by the President himself, became the top policy-making organ and the seat of political and governmental decisions. (This institution is further discussed in Chapter IX, pp. 218-19.)

The examination of the extent and means of Communist influence upon government policy and its implementation necessarily begins with a study of the relationship between the President and the Communists. The latter part of the chapter will attempt to portray the actual degree of Communist penetration of certain government agencies and programs and the use to which this was put. It should be borne in mind that in most cases the actual extent of Communist penetration of the government bureaucracy will be understated, since the names of a considerable fraction of the PGT membership have never become public. In addition it is known that the Communists made a practice of keeping secret the affiliation of many government officials with the PGT, as they made themselves more useful to the party by posing as members of other revolutionary parties or professing no party ties. The author knows of no government, short of an openly Communist one, in which the Communists were so influential as they were in the Guatemalan government during the last two years of the Arbenz regime.

RELATIONS WITH THE PRESIDENT

Jacobo Arbenz Guzmán, President of Guatemala during the years in which Communism gained its greatest influence there, continues to be an enigma. Many observers, including some of the closest students of the Guatemalan political scene, expected his administration to follow a centrist line and to bring respite from the radicalism of Arévalo. Yet within two years of his inauguration the Communists were a major factor in shaping government policy and were looked upon by many as the President's favorites. It is difficult to ascertain just what were the political beliefs of this reserved, tight-lipped soldier or fully to understand his motivations. Nevertheless several lines of inquiry have led the writer to certain conclusions concerning the nature of his relationship with the Communists.[1]

Arbenz was born in Quezaltenango, the second city of Guatemala, on the 14th of September, 1913. His father, a Swiss pharmacist who migrated to Guatemala in 1901, killed himself while Jacobo was in his teens. His mother was of mixed Spanish and Indian blood, but he grew into a European-appearing blond of medium build, whose impression of coldness was enhanced by a tendency to say as little as possible. Appointed to the *Escuela Politécnica,* Guatemala's West Point, Arbenz proved an excellent student and an accomplished athlete, particularly as a boxer. Graduated as a sub-lieutenant of Infantry in 1935, he returned to the school two years later as an instructor, first in science and then in history. A competent and intelligent soldier, his lack of personal magnetism seemed destined to hold him to a routine military career.

A turning point in the life of the future president came in 1939 with his marriage to María Cristina Vilanova Castro, the daughter of a wealthy Salvadorean coffee planter. The match was opposed by her family and friends, who felt that she was marrying beneath her station. In the end, Guatemalan and Salvadorean society alike snubbed the young couple. Their resentment against the existing order grew as the lively, cultured Sra. de Arbenz took to tinting pictures to supplement the slim pay of her husband.

On July 4, 1944, Captain Jacobo Arbenz, by then the father of two baby girls, resigned his post and went to El Salvador to begin his efforts to overthrow the dictatorship of Ponce. (See Chapter I, pp. 13-14.) Returning to Guatemala on September 29, Arbenz played a key role in the October 20 revolution and was one of the three members of the junta which governed Guatemala until March 15, 1945. As Minister of Defense in the cabinet of President Arévalo,

---

[1] In addition to the material published on Arbenz and interviews with a variety of persons who knew him, the author has studied the public statements of Arbenz himself. In the final analysis all this material has been weighed and analyzed in the light of his actions. While few who knew him will agree with everything said here and many will violently dissent from the author's conclusions, only Arbenz, his wife, Fortuny and a handful of his closest confidants could serve as qualified judges.

Arbenz began to maneuver toward election to the presidency in the 1950 elections. At the same time his access to loans from government banks enabled him to become a large-scale and rather wealthy agriculturalist.

Arbenz and Communism. A great divergence of opinion exists as to Arbenz's private political beliefs and to the nature of his relationship with the Communists. If he did not actually embrace Communism, Arbenz at least numbered the Communist leaders among his closest friends and advisors and turned over to them the implementation of major social and economic programs of his administration as well as following their lead in shaping the international policy of his government. How much of this was due to sympathy for Communist doctrine and what proportion was due to his trust in the Communists and feeling that they were best able to strengthen his regime and implement his policies is extremely difficult to ascertain. While not discounting the possibility that he became or was becoming a convinced Communist, the author believes that there was a strong rational element in his original choice to accept the Communists as collaborators in his government. There can be little doubt that the relation between Arbenz and the Communists was a changing one. Nor are there many students of the subject who can deny that the Communists played their cards shrewdly in winning first his tolerance and then his trust. At the end their influence with Arbenz was undoubtedly great, but attempts to paint him as nothing more than a dupe of the .Communists or a puppet in their hands are probably as erroneous as the claims of Arbenz partisans that the President was merely using the Communists.

While it is impossible to substantiate the many stories told by leading Guatemalan political figures of the Arévalo period who claimed that Arbenz was trained in Communist doctrine before reaching the Presidency, a close study of the life of the Arbenzes during the late 1940's indicates that their circle of friends included a large proportion of Communists. (It must be remembered that the Communists had not yet come into the open and that several of them were prominent politicians, labor leaders and government officials who were on close terms with President Arévalo.) During this period Marxism was something of a vogue among the younger revolutionaries, while only the conservative opposition was much concerned over the issue of

Communism, and they tended to use the term indiscriminately. Looking to the future, the Communists, along with other leaders of the extreme left such as Charnaud MacDonald, wisely gathered around Arbenz and began cultivating him as their candidate for President. While the Arbenz's house may have been something less than the "Marxist salon" which has been pictured by some writers, there is little doubt that Fortuny, Gutiérrez, the Chilean Communist intellectual Eduardo Hubner and other Communists were their frequent and welcome visitors. The Minister of Defense probably just sat and listened, but his wife became an avid reader of Marxist books. The presence of the Chilean Communist Virginia Bravo Letelier as her secretary and confidant facilitated the task of introducing Sra. de Arbenz to the glittering generalities of Communism. Ever ambitious for her husband, María listened carefully to the proposals of the leftist leaders and their promises of support for his candidacy.

Activities of María Vilanova de Arbenz. Since it has been repeatedly argued that Sra. de Arbenz was one of the chief Communizing influences upon her husband, it is important to examine her political activities and her relations with the Communists. Of her close friendships and associations with a number of leading Communist figures, there can be no doubt. Her association with the Chilean Communist leader Virginia Bravo Letelier was long and close, as was her friendship with Matilde Elena López, a Communist exile from El Salvador and close associate of Gutiérrez. These two served at different times as her private secretary and are usually credited with helping Sra. de Arbenz get started with the study of Communism. The Chilean Communist Eduardo Hubner was another friend and frequent guest of the Arbenzes. Among the Guatemalan Communists, Fortuny, Gutiérrez, Silva Jonama and Guerra Borges were frequent visitors at the Arbenz home from at least 1948 on.[2]

The Arbenzes' private library was well stocked with the works of

---

[2] See Document X-72: List of "amigas y amigos" from the papers of María Vilanova de Arbenz; Document 1262: María de Arbenz to Víctor Manuel Gutiérrez, asking him to place Matilde Elena López on the Preparatory Commission for the 1951 Unity Congress "so that we can work together"; Document 2092: María de Arbenz to Víctor Manuel Gutiérrez, June 14, 1950 offering to trade some pamphlets for a copy of PROG statutes; Document 770: memorandum on discussion between Eduardo Hubner and the Arbenzes on international politics.

Marx, Lenin, Stalin, Mao and other Communist writers. While some of these were autographed copies received as gifts by Arbenz as President, most were purchased by Sra. de Arbenz in 1948 and 1949.[3] Aside from her participation in the *Alianza Femenina Guatemalteca,* the first lady of Guatemala sponsored and financially underwrote a number of Communist front groups and activities.[4] Through Virginia Bravo the President's wife lent her name to Communist front activities among the women of Latin America.[5]

Arbenz's Public Statements on Communism. In spite of the fact that Arbenz's statements intended for public consumption cannot be taken at face value, they do serve to give some indication of the relations between the President and the Communists. In many of his statements, and particularly his answers to the questions of reporters and the memorial of the officers' corps of June 5, 1954, the most revealing thing is the fact that they were drafted by José Manuel Fortuny, the head of the Communist Party.[6] Nevertheless, taking into account what these statements admit and what they do not deny, the picture which emerges shows that the Communists did have a substantial influence in the government and were numbered among his closest friends and advisers by the President.

In his March 1953 Report to Congress, Arbenz stated that acceptance of the Communists as a legitimate political movement was "an

---

[3] See Document 773: list of the books of María Vilanova de Arbenz; also bills from the Librería Guatemala seen by the author while in Guatemala.
· [4] Document 117: José Solís Rojas, Vice-Secretary General of the Comité de Solidaridad con el Pueblo Dominicano, to María V. de Arbenz, June 17, 1951 requesting financial aid to send the Communist Juan Ducoudray to the Berlin Youth for Peace Festival and a receipt for $50. signed by Elena Leiva de Holst on June 29, 1951; Document 1612: receipt in favor of María Vilanova de Arbenz for paying the rent for the Grupo Saker-Ti, May 30, 1950; Document 315: Jacobo Rodríguez Padilla to María Vilanova de Arbenz; Document 410: Luis Cardoza y Aragón to Jacobo Arbenz, March 30, 1950 and Document 370: *Revista de Guatemala* to Señora María de Arbenz, May 15, 1951, a group of Communist intellectuals headed by Huberto Alvarado, Raúl Leiva and Otto Raúl González obtaining financial support for their publications from the Arbenzes.
[5] Document 170: Virginia Bravo Letelier to María Vilanova de Arbenz, April 4, 1954, and Document 171: Virginia Bravo L. to María Vilanova de Arbenz, March 23, 1954.
[6] Autocriticism of José Manuel Fortuny written in Mexico, February 15, 1955.

unalterable norm" of his government from which he would not retreat a single millimeter.[7]

> . . . we have maintained inviolate the respect for democratic principles which involves the adequate guarantee of all beliefs, opinions and forms of organization of all, of absolutely all the social sectors and classes.

The most useful of Arbenz's public statements on Communism can be found in his March 1, 1954 Report to Congress.[8] As he professed to view the situation, those whose economic interests had been hurt by agrarian reform were calling for the isolation of the Communists as a means of dividing the "democratic forces." This policy of "quarantining" the Communists could not be seriously considered as "it would be equivalent to the suicide of the democratic and revolutionary movement of Guatemala."[9] The preservation of democracy required equality of opportunity for the PGT with the other parties.[10]

> It is well known that during the regime of Doctor Arévalo no party of the extreme left gave visible signs of its existence. There was not then a Marxist party, like that which now exists in Guatemala, and which participates in the political activities of the country, because the Constitution does not prohibit, but rather guarantees to all the citizens the rights of organization, of assembly and of affiliation with the ideas of their sympathies. The Magna Carta of the Republic prohibits in a final manner all types of political discrimination.

To Arbenz the phrase "intervention of international Communism" was meaningless and the ODECA anti-Communist proposals were anti-democratic. Were the rights of one Communist interfered with, Guatemala could no longer call itself a democracy.[11] He pointedly stressed that it was not the Soviet Union which had designs upon Guatemalan sovereignty and that they "have not intervened nor are they now intervening in the domestic affairs of Guatemala."[12]

---

[7] See *Octubre,* March 5, 1953.

[8] *Informe de Ciudadano Presidente de la República, Coronel Jacobo Arbenz Guzmán al Congreso Nacional en su Primer Período de Sesiones Ordinarias del Año de 1954,* Guatemala, 1954.

[9] *Ibid.,* p. L.

[10] *Ibid.,* p. LIX.

[11] *Ibid.,* p. LXI.

[12] *Ibid., p.* LXIII.

President Arbenz would never discuss Communism with reporters, but would require them to put their questions in writing and would return their questionnaires with brief written replies. In most cases he turned the requests over to his Communist advisers and allowed them to draft the replies. The questionnaire from the officers' corps was important enough to receive the attention of Fortuny himself; in other cases it might be Raúl Leiva or some other Communist in the Publicity Office of the Presidency.[13]

In answer to a question by a Mr. O'Leary, President Arbenz had this to say for public consumption.[14]

"Everyone" knows that Communism is a philosophic and economic doctrine, which has its corresponding political conclusion, which a great part of the proletariat of the entire world has made theirs. In this sense it should not be surprising that a part of the Guatemalan workers have adopted the ideas of Communism. I firmly believe that no idea is dangerous for a true democracy, sufficiently strong for itself when democracy means government of the people and for the people.

However when asked if he considered anti-Communism a threat to the country, Arbenz answered:

While it defends only the particular interests of those who visibly direct it, no. As soon as it tries to break lances in the name and defense of foreign and anti-national interests, my reply is affirmative.[15]

According to Arbenz, Communism was an idea which was no threat to Guatemala, but anti-Communism was a tool of a foreign power and a threat to the nation.

The latest recorded public statement of Arbenz on Communism is embodied in his interview with Ronaldo Ramírez, who interviewed him in Prague, Czechoslovakia after his overthrow.[16]

The political parties which aided the government were of the most varied tendencies. Among them were found some moderates and some extreme leftists. My government counted also on the

---

[13] See Document 121: Seven questions asked by a *Visión* reporter, a memorandum from the Communist advisers in the Publicity Office, and the replies which they prepared.

[14] Y-282: Respuestas al Cuestionario del Señor O'Leary, March, 1953.

[15] Y-291: Respuestas al Cuestionario del Corresponsal de *Time* y *Life*.

[16] *La Prensa Libre,* San José, Costa Rica, October 25, 1955.

aid of the Guatemalan Labor Party (Communist). There was a great stir over the participation of this party in the activities of my government, but this was only the external excuse for the aggression. Among the parties, among them all, the Communists had the same opportunities as the others. I ought to declare the fact that through their activities the Partido Guatemalteco de Trabajadores was always distinguished by the intransigent defense of every action of the Government which was in benefit of the working classes. It never hesitated to criticize firmly all that seemed inconsistent and it was its decisive action which always maintained without deviations the unity of the workers in support of the government.

In the rest of the parties the situation was not of the same firmness, for frequently, through their work, you could see their party interests come to the forefront. . . . There were, and it ought to be said and denounced firmly, vacillations and fears in the moderate parties which retarded the development of our activity.

Arbenz criticized the proposals of "the political parties of the center" that the government should follow the tactic of the "step backwards" and outlaw the Communist Party "to demonstrate to the imperialists that the Guatemalan government was not at all Communist."

Our negative was final. Outside of what such a step would signify for Guatemalan democracy, of which we were so proud, to outlaw the PGT would have meant breaking up the internal democratic bloc and abandoning one of the strongest cornerstones of fight against imperialism and the landowning national reaction.

When asked to explain why he had chosen Czechoslovakia for his place of exile, Arbenz replied:

My intention to visit Czechoslovakia was very old. . . . Politically I am a man without a party, but I believe that every person who is concerned with the destiny of humanity ought to be interested in familiarizing himself with the Socialist countries. Guatemala as a nation was always aligned, in the international sphere, on the side of the countries which defended liberty, national independence and peace. In the eyes of some that was another of our sins.

On June 5, 1954, the General Staff of the Guatemalan Army presented Arbenz with a list of twenty questions and proposals concerning his relations with the Communists and their influence in his government. José Manuel Fortuny, according to his own statements made in Mexico early in 1955, was given the task of preparing the reply which the President then gave to the officers as his final word on the subject.[17] (For the significance of this action on the part of the officers see Epilogue, pp. 313-17.) In reply to the Army officers' suggestion that the government did not need the PGT and that known Communists should be removed from all official posts, Arbenz answered that this would be undemocratic. Concerning the Communists in the National Agrarian Department, Arbenz stated that they were "precisely the most effective and those who do not sell out to the landlords."[18] In the President's eyes there were no reasons for considering the Communist Party as part of an international movement and hence coming under the constitutional ban against such organizations.[19] When the officers stated that the Communist Party controlled the masses of the workers and campesinos in spite of the fact that most of them were not Communists, the President retorted that:[20]

> This is the first time that I have heard that the members of the PGT use such means, but the great demonstrations (May Day, etc.) give the impression that leaders such as Gutiérrez are beloved and that the influence of the Communists depends upon their activities and their willingness to guide the workers and campesinos.

Conclusions on Nature of the Arbenz-Communist Relationship. Since the Guatemalan Communists owed much of their influence and success to their acceptance and endorsement by the President, it is necessary to define the nature of this relationship. In the following pages we shall try to provide a coherent picture of Arbenz's dealings with the Communists.

When Arbenz first cast his eye upon the Presidency, it seems safe to assume that he cared little about Communism one way or the other.

---

[17] See Document 1037: Pliego de consultas de la Oficialidad del Estado Mayor del Ejército, preparado por sugestión del Señor Presidente de la República, para los efectos de la plática que dictará el propio alto funcionario oportunamente, en este cuerpo, June 5, 1954. See Document 1034: replies of Arbenz to the memorial cited above.

[18] *Ibid.*

[19] *Ibid.*

[20] *Ibid.*

During 1948 he probably became acquainted with the outlines of Marxist doctrine, but his personal contacts with the individual Communist leaders such as Gutiérrez and Fortuny were more important in shaping his attitude. As he had a dislike for the United States and no real knowledge of the U.S.S.R., the international implications of Communism did not bother or concern him. While he was the underdog in the race to succeed Arévalo, the Communists were among the first to give him their support and hence remained among his favorites after it became obvious that he would be the probable victor in the 1950 elections. In the eyes of Arbenz, the Communists seemed valuable allies owing to their great influence in the labor movement. If the workers chose them as their leaders, Arbenz saw no reason not to accept them as the legitimate spokesmen of the working class.

In the presidential campaign the Communist leaders proved their usefulness to Arbenz. Through the National Workers' Political Committee and the network of local committees which it controlled, the Communist labor leaders contributed extensively to his election. The Communists handled much of the organizational and propaganda work of the campaign[21] and impressed Arbenz as the most honest and trustworthy, as well as the hardest working of his supporters. As Fortuny himself had to say of the Communist role in the campaign, "our party was a very influential factor in the elaboration and development of the strategy and tactics of the democratic and revolutionary forces in the presidential electoral campaign, as it was in the formulation of the program for this campaign."[22] Since the Communists chose the middle of the campaign to come into the open, it would seem that they had reached an understanding with the heir apparent. Indeed, Arbenz, unlike Arévalo, agreed with the Communists that Article 32 of the Constitution did not apply to them.

When Arbenz took over the Presidency, it was apparent that the Communists were accepted by him as a useful and legitimate support for his regime. The Communists were still far from dominant in the government and Charnaud MacDonald and perhaps González Juárez were nearly as influential as Fortuny with the President and more

---

[21] See *Proyecto de Organización de la Propaganda* by Juan Miguel de Mora, May 2, 1950.

[22] *Informe del Comité Central del Partido Comunista de Guatemala,* December 11, 1952, p. 52.

important on the national political scene. However Arbenz afforded the Communists an opportunity to compete freely with the other government parties. With the consolidation of Communist control over a unified labor movement and the rapid growth of the party, their influence with the President grew. As the politicians of the other revolutionary parties lapsed into opportunism and concentrated upon getting the lion's share of the spoils of office, the Communists' stock rose in the President's eyes.

The Communists worked hardest in support of the President's pet project, agrarian reform, and were able to provide the background studies, technical advice, mass support and enthusiasm which the project required. The struggle for the enactment of agrarian reform became a dividing line in the eyes of Arbenz; those who opposed it were his enemies and those whose support was only lukewarm dropped in his esteem. By mid-1952 he began to look upon the Communists as his most reliable supporters and the truest interpreters of the wishes of the people. As this became evident, he lost the support of some moderate elements, such as Avila Ayala and the Najera Farfán brothers; nevertheless he went ahead with the view that the Communists were to be accorded the full rights of a legal party and incorporated into the government coalition on an equal basis with the much larger PAR and PRG.[23]

By 1953 it seemed to many Guatemalan politicians that the Communists were the President's favorites, and the Communists did whatever they could to confirm this belief. Fortuny would arrive late at meetings and give the impression that he had come straight from the President. Non-Communist government officials began to go to the Communists seeking to find out what the uncommunicative President desired. The National Agrarian Department was virtually in the hands of the PGT, and the party doubled its membership in the first eight months of 1953. The National Democratic Front increasingly became the seat of major political decisions, and the Communist-controlled CGTG and its sister group the CNCG were given equal representation in it with the parties. A steady stream of Guatemalans travelled to Communist-sponsored meetings behind the "Iron Curtain"; in many

---

[23] For a detailed treatment of the support of Arbenz for the Communists in the spring of 1952 see a series of articles by Manuel María Avila Ayala in *Diario de Centro América,* May 7-25, 1957.

cases the President paid their expenses.[24] Fortuny, Gutiérrez and Guerra Borges rose increasingly higher in the President's "kitchen cabinet."[25]

It would appear that Arbenz favored the Communists more for their abilities and virtues than from any belief in Communism. Although Marxist doctrine did serve to give his regime some degree of ideological underpinning, he was more concerned with the immediate problems than with the shape of things to come. There was nothing in the program of the PGT which was objectionable to him and he was at least openminded toward the Communist model for the future and looked favorably upon the development of China and the Peoples' Democracies under Communism. In contrast to the other politicians, the Communists brought him answers and plans rather than problems and constant demands for the spoils of office. The discipline and businesslike attitude of the Communists were apt to impress the career military officer more favorably than the constant bickering and dissension of the *Paristas*. In picturing Arbenz as the "soldier of the people," suggesting that he could go down in history as another Cárdenas, and perhaps even hinting that the working class considered him indispensable and might demand that he be given a second term —in all these ways the Communists were not doing their cause any harm. (Lázaro Cárdenas, President of Mexico from 1934-1940, has a reputation in Guatemala as well as his own country as a great champion of the common man.)

Communist Mobilization of Support for the President: Pressure Group Techniques. One of the key elements in the Communists' relationship with the President was their ability to mobilize support for his actions and to organize mass demonstrations in favor of the government or against its opponents. Given his desire to be a "popular" president and not just another military dictator, the "soldier of the people" felt a need for the manifestations of popularity which his personality was not sufficient to generate. In addition, with constant pressure being put upon the government by the opposition, demonstrations of support

---

[24] See Document 1189: receipt for $1500 from the Presidency for expenses as FUD delegate to Bucharest Youth meetings signed by Carlos Castañeda, June 19, 1953.

[25] Fortuny's own statements on the subject can be found in his autocriticism written in Mexico City on February 15, 1955.

were a virtual necessity to show the opponents of the government and those whose loyalty might be wavering that the regime had a mass base of support among the people. It is the author's conclusion that these Communist-organized manifestations of support for the government did have a considerable deterrent effect upon groups which might have been tempted to try their hand at overthrowing the Arbenz government.

While the Communists never demonstrated against the Arbenz government, they occasionally found it necessary to pressure the government in favor of certain policies or actions concerning which the President was hesitant. In many cases the Communists would use their control of organized labor to mobilize manifestations of support for policies urged upon the government by the Communist leaders. These demonstrations served to make it appear that the Communists were the true spokesmen for labor and most closely attuned to the aspirations of the working class. When the President adopted their policies or when the pressure of the opposition mounted, the Communists would organize mass rallies and demonstrations in support of the government. The indispensable prerequisite for the success of this tactic was the Communists' control of organized labor. With nearly 40,000 union members in and around the capital, Gutiérrez and his associates could fill the streets in short order. A telegram from Gutiérrez to the CGTG affiliates could bring hundreds of messages pouring into the National Palace. During vital sessions the galleries of the National Congress were filled with shouting, banner-waving workers, whose placards made clear their support of Communist-favored legislation.

The usefulness of the Communists in this respect first became apparent to Arbenz during the last year of the Arévalo government. Organized labor had played a major role in putting down the July 1949 army revolt and in breaking up the "minute of silence" campaign which threatened the Arévalo government a year later. During the 1950 presidential campaign the Communists had shown him their organizational and propaganda abilities; at the same time they had proven able to mobilize sufficient support to neutralize the attack upon *Octubre* and the reaction to the emergence of Communists into the open. As the Communists grew stronger and consolidated their control over a unified labor movement, their usefulness turned into something more: in the eyes of Arbenz they became indispensable.

The first efforts of the Communist labor leaders to use their control of the CGTG to affect the policy of the Arbenz government came only a few months after the inauguration.[26] Labor had besieged the Government with messages of support in mid-July when the President was uneasy about the opposition's plans to demonstrate on the second anniversary of the assassination of Arana.[27] Four months later a flood of messages was sent from the unions to Arbenz requesting the expulsion of a top IRCA official.[28] In early 1952 the unions sent messages of approbation for the President's firm attitude in the face of the United Fruit Company.[29] The first major mobilization came in March of 1952 when the anti-Communists were planning a series of mass rallies throughout the country and a major demonstration in the capital. The CGTG and the CNCG sent orders to their affiliates to boycott these demonstrations and to flood the President with messages of support. In line with the Communists' policy of discrediting anti-Communism as subversive, the workers were informed that these anti-Communist rallies were intended as part of a plot to "overthrow the constitutional government and install a criminal dictatorship."[30] This manifestation of labor's repudiation of anti-Communism did much to neutralize the effect of the anti-Communist rallies held on the 23rd.

Naturally the unions congratulated Arbenz upon the enactment of the agrarian reform bill,[31] but the major effort of the Communist-led organizations in this field came at the end of 1952 and beginning of 1953 as part of the Communist plan to exploit agrarian reform to

[26] The connection of these campaigns with the policies of the Communist Party is evident from a study of the party papers *Octubre* and *Tribuna Popular* for the corresponding dates.

[27] See 8032:1851, Julio A. Veras P. to Director of *La Hora,* July 14, 1951; 8033:133, Gustavo Adolfo García A. to President Arbenz, July 13, 1951; *Octubre,* July 29, 1951 and August 2, 1951.

[28] 8014:288, 289, 290, 737 and 738.

[29] Y-X-4:515.

[30] 8014:1541, telegraphic circular from Gutiérrez, March 19, 1952; 8014: 1537, telegraphic circular in the name of the CGTG, March 19, 1952; 8026: 231, joint CGTG-CNCG telegraph to member organizations, March 19, 1952. For messages sent to the President see: 8012:1538, 1539, 1540, 1109, 1241, 1242, 1039-42; 8024:1091; 8026:220 and 222.

[31] 8026:223, 191, 192; Y-X-5:773.

the advantage of the PGT. The first phase of the campaign was criticism of the National Agrarian Department for going too slowly and of the lower courts for agreeing to hear the appeals of expropriated land owners.[32] To back up these demands which he had made "in the name of the working class and campesinos," Gutiérrez mobilized a stream of messages demanding that the lower court judges be removed.[33] Following Gutiérrez's statement that: "The people can live without courts, but not without land," the second phase of the campaign was aimed at the removal of the Supreme Court judges who had favored consideration of the appeal. The hand of the Communists can be seen in Pellecer's instructions to the PGT-CGTG leader in Escuintla.[34]

> Mobilize organizations to reject firmly "amparo" conceded by Supreme Court against President Arbenz whom we will back to the end, increase vigilance and prepare to mobilize to repress the reaction if they provoke it. Alert.

The Communists published a special edition of *Octubre* attacking the Supreme Court justices as large landowners, while the CGTG organized a rally in support of Arbenz. In addition the Communists spark-plugged the movement in Congress to remove the justices. This backing encouraged Arbenz to issue a challenge to the opposition saying that: "if they want to provoke civil war, we, on the other hand, will be prepared to give them the answer they deserve. . . . Cost what it may cost, agrarian reform will go forward."[35] Days later

---

[32] See Document 1480 or 8016:1183, series of five telegrams sent by Gutiérrez in the name of the CGTG, December 18, 1952; *Octubre,* January 2, 1953.

[33] 8024:106, CGTG circular, December 27, 1952; 8016:533-5, messages of SAG; 8016:1020 and 1021, workers on National Finca "El Porvenir" to Congress and Supreme Court, January 9, 1953; 8016:1105, response of United Fruit Co. workers, January 2, 1953; 8003:153.

[34] 8024:1058, telegram from Carlos Manuel Pellecer to Manuel Sánchez, February 5, 1953. For the Communist party views see *Octubre,* January 30, 1953.

[35] Statement of the President to a rally organized by the CGTG and CNCG, February 7, 1953 as reported in *Octubre,* February 12, 1953. For other messages calling for the dismissal of the judges and commending Arbenz on their subsequent removal see 8003:52, 60, 76, 78, 123, 125, 126, 158, 160, 161, 203, 235, 242, 251, 252, 283, 289, 291, 293, 294, 344, 346, 377, and 391; 8024:1059; 8026:225 and 227; 8021:1085, CGTG and CNCG Boletín a la Radio y a la Prensa, February 5, 1953.

the government expropriated a large segment of the United Fruit Company holdings, a move which had long been advocated by the Communists.

When the anti-government uprising at Salamá occurred on March 29, 1953, the Communists immediately pledged the support of the workers to the government.[36] This was immediately followed by streams of telegrams supporting the proposal of the Commmunist leaders that Guatemala retire from the ODECA. The campaign was based on the claim that the proposal to include the question of Communism on the agenda of ODECA was aimed at the internal affairs and sovereignty of Guatemala and that the organization had been converted into a tool of the State Department. This effort to disrupt ODECA had begun the preceding September with a concerted attack upon the anti-Communist proposal of Salvadorean Chancellor Canessa.[37] When the government withdrew from ODECA, a second stream of messages was directed to the President commending him upon the patriotic act.[38]

The close relations of the President and the Communists was apparent in September of 1953. The Communists had been in consultation with the President on the diplomatic negotiations with the United States over the expropriation of UFCO holdings and had urged him to reject the United States notes.[39] They exploited this incident in their anti-United States propaganda campaign and mobilized a flood of messages praising the action of the President.[40] Their strategy was to represent the action of the United States in this case as an attack upon the whole agrarian reform program as well as an example of "yankee intervention." Rallies were held throughout the country with

[36] 8003:664, telegrams from José Luis Cáceros to President and Chief of Armed Forces, March 30, 1953.

[37] See Document 1761: Comité Ejecutivo de la CGTG to Embajador de El Salvador, October 10, 1952; CGTG circular of September 2, 1952; CGTG Bulletin of March 26, 1953.

[38] 8003:657, 659, and 660, CGTG to Arbenz, April 9, 1953.

[39] See 8005:2695-2694/14, September 4, 1953, letter from Humberto González Juárez, Private Secretary of the President, to Víctor Manuel Gutiérrez enclosing copies of United States notes and Foreign Ministry confidential reports to the President on meetings with U.S. Ambassador.

[40] See 8005:2567, 2565, 2566, 2139, 2627, 2751, 2647, 2646, 2087, 2136, 2140, 2141, 2143, 2144, 2326, 2377, 2433, 2449, 2450, 2458, 2527, 2532, 2571, 2572, 2657-2657/5, 2383, 2679, 2389, 2628, 2380, 2669; messages from unions to President.

the cooperation of the CNCG and the various front groups.[41] A campaign to form "Committees for the Defense of National Sovereignty" was climaxed by a rally on September 14, 1953, repudiating the State Department memorandum.[42]

COMMUNIST PENETRATION OF THE BUREAUCRACY

While the relationship between the Communists and the President was the key to their influence in the government, they also occupied positions within the bureaucracy which enabled them to control the administration of certain strategic programs. The Communists were not interested in positions and patronage as the spoils of political victory, but rather for the influence which certain key posts would give them over the molding of public opinion.

Congress. The representation of the PGT in the National Congress was four out of 56. While this figure has been used to play down the influence of the Communists in Guatemala, a closer examination indicates that the PGT deputies played a far more important role in the work of the Congress than their numbers would indicate. In the first place, this disciplined bloc of four often held the balance of power between the two larger administration parties. Secondly all four of the PGT deputies were among the small group of a dozen to eighteen deputies who formed the elite controlling group of the Congress in contrast to the party hacks who composed the rest of the revolutionary coalition. Then it must be remembered that in the last year or so of the Arbenz regime decisions as to the position of the government parties on legislation were made within the Communist-dominated FDN, while Congress merely ratified these decisions made by the party leaders. In addition the PGT could count upon the fact that the other congressional delegations contained a number of deputies who were close collaborators of the Communists.

In the last Congress of the Arbenz regime, which began its work in

---

[41] See 8051:2111, September 7, 1953 and 2112, September 8, 1952, circular telegram sent from Castillo Flores to Secretaries General of Departmental Campesino Confederations, and instructions by Otilio Marroquín Ruano to local Secretaries General.

[42] See 8005:2602-2602/8, collection of CGTG documents planning this rally of the "working forces."

March 1954, the PGT was represented on all fourteen of the commissions within which the bulk of the legislative work was conducted.
On each of the ten commissions which paralleled the executive departments, there was one PGT deputy and six members of the other
parties. However on the politically important Extraordinary Commission on Reforms of the Labor Code, all four of the PGT deputies
were members and Cardoza served as President. Gutiérrez was President of the Agrarian Reform Commission on which Cardoza was also
a member. While the average number of committee assignments for
non-Communists was 1.7, each of the PGT deputies served on at least
four commissions and Gutiérrez and Pellecer on five. In addition
Gutiérrez held the post of First Secretary of Congress and served on
the steering committee.[43] This contrasts sharply with the situation of
the five anti-Communist deputies who held no committee assignments
and who eventually were forced to leave the Congress and flee the
country.

Without exception the Communists controlled the politically important Extraordinary Commissions such as those that wrote the Labor
Code, Agrarian Reform Law and Rent Law and handled the amend-
ments to these laws. This provided the Communists with an opportunity to appear in the eyes of the common people as "giving" the
law to them and to get credit in the public mind as the champions
of the common people.

Education. As indoctrination of the youth of Guatemala was one of
the primary goals of the Communists, they made a particular effort
to infiltrate the Ministry of Education and the schools. The early
success of the Communists in this field contributed to their rapid rise
to power. The Chilean Communist Virginia Bravo Letelier, along with
her countryman César Godoy Urrutia, played an important role in
this process. Holding various positions in the Ministry of Public Education during the late 1940's, Virginia Bravo worked closely with the
Communist leaders of the STEG to spread Communism among its
members. Most of the time she travelled through the country giving
lectures to the teachers and seeking to establish a training school
for them which would further their knowledge and appreciation of

---

[43] See Document 1549: Comisiones Ordinarias y Extraordinarias del Congreso de la República para el ciclo 1954-55.

Marxism.[44] An example of the type of "advice" she was giving to the teachers was the proposal that they build their library up with 90% Communist books and "10% of modern educational works in order to mislead."[45] At this same time the young Communist leader Mario Silva Jonama was appointed Under-Secretary of Public Education, while the Spanish Republican exile Rafael de Buen y Lozano and the Nicaraguan Communist Edelberto Torres (father of the PGT leader of the same name) were appointed advisors to Minister Raúl Osegueda.[46] A number of Marxist exiles from Central American countries and Spain taught at San Carlos University.

During the Arbenz regime, the Communists' hold over education was strengthened considerably. The Communist leaders of the STEG, working with the Minister of Education, Héctor Morgan of the pro-Communist wing of PAR, were able to bring all but the staunchest anti-Communists into line. The women's normal school was directed by the wife of one of the Barrios Klee brothers, herself active in the ranks of the Communist women. While Gutiérrez was too busy to continue the teaching of Marxism in political economy classes as he had done in the normal school during the earlier years of the revolution, his Spanish Republican friend and collaborator Gabriel Alvarado became Chief of the Normal School section.[47]

In January of 1953 the PGT's candidate to replace Carlos González Orellana as sub-Secretary of Public Education was appointed over those of the other parties.[48] By this time the Communists controlled the textbooks, the courses and examinations of the teachers, and the Ministry of Public Education was publishing a number of books by avowed Communists.[49]

---

[44] See Documents 2020-2023; also 1373 and 1394.

[45] Document 1679: letter signed by Virginia Bravo and dated December 29.

[46] See Document 120 for a diagram of the Communist control mechanism in the field of education.

[47] See Document 1390: Enrique A. Rodríguez J. to Presidente Jacobo Arbenz G., March 27, 1951.

[48] See *Prensa Libre,* January 5, 1953 and *Nuestro Diario,* January 13, 1953.

[49] The most comprehensive treatment of the Communist control of education during the Arbenz regime can be found in a series of three articles by Frank Reynolds in the Mexican magazine *TODO,* No. 1103, October 23, 1954, pp. 36 ff; No. 1104, November 4, 1954, pp. 27 ff; No. 1105, November 11, 1954, pp. 20 ff.

The official text in political economy used by all normal schools was Gutiérrez's *Breves Resúmenes de Economía Política,* a simplified abridgement of Marx's *Capital.* Examinations were written so that only Marxist answers would be acceptable; hence, if not believers in Communism, the teachers of Guatemala at least had been taught Communism and had to teach from Communist texts. It has been estimated that by 1954 some 1600 of the country's 8,000 teachers were actual Communists; that this was so should not be surprising since the Communists controlled the flow of materials sent out by the Ministry to "orient" the teachers of the country. It should be remembered that the average teacher in Guatemala was much younger and had only a fraction of the schooling possessed by his counterpart in more advanced countries. For this reason he was much more dependent upon the "training" courses and materials furnished by his union and the Ministry of Education. With both of these in the hands of the Communists, he was all but cut off from conflicting sources of information and ideas. The Nicaraguan Communist Edelberto Torres (senior) was in charge of the press of the Ministry of Education, which put out the *Revista del Maestro.* This publication furnished the teachers with many articles by Russian and Guatemalan Communists: "On the Attitude of the Intellectuals" by Guerra Borges, PGT Secretary of Propaganda; "The Mission of the Teacher" and "Politics, Democracy and Education" by César Godoy Urrutia, Chilean Communist leader; and "Youth and the Revolution of October" by the Communist Secretary of Youth Affairs Huberto Alvarado. Such articles supplemented the regular contributions of Silva Jonama, the PGT Secretary of Education. *Alegría,* a Marxist primary school text, and the *Biblioteca Popular* series of books by Communist and pro-Soviet writers such as Raúl Leiva and Luis Cardoza y Aragón were also published by the Ministry of Public Education.

National Agrarian Department (DAN) and Communist Exploitation of Agrarian Reform. Aware of the great advantages which would accrue to those who controlled the implementation of the agrarian reform program, the Communists sought and received virtual control of the machinery set up for its administration. The nominal head of the DAN was Major Alfonso Martínez Estévez, a crony of the President who had been serving as his private secretary and whose political affiliation was with the fringe of the PAR.[50] Behind the front provided by Martínez, the Communists controlled the key positions in the DAN. The head of the Lands Section and Deputy Chief of the Department was Waldemar Barrios Klee, while María Jérez de Fortuny, the wife of the PGT leader, was the Secretary General of the Department. Other members of the PGT to hold positions within the DAN were Augusto Cazali Avila, Eugenio Arrivillaga Veliz, Roberto Bran Maldonado, Jorge Villavicencio Marroquín, Eduardo Sosa Montalvo, Pedro Noubleau, Abraham René Figueroa, Raúl Alarcón, Humberto de León, Arnulfo Parada, Luis López, Carlos Rodríguez, José Reyes, C. Humberto González Ordóñez, José Helindo Castañeda, Alberto Guzmán Estrada and Luis Felipe González.[51] At least 35% of the full-time DAN employees were PGT members.[52] The *Sindicato de Trabajadores del Departamento Agrario Nacional* was controlled by the Communists, with Humberto de León serving as Secretary General and Augusto Cazali as Secretary of Organization.

The Inspector General of the DAN was Mario Sosa, a Honduran Communist known to have been a collaborator with the Communists while they operated within the PAR. The 20 inspectors operating under his supervision included PGT members Natzul Aguirre Cook, Marco Antonio Blanco, Florencio Méndez, Roberto Cabrera, Juan Rafael Vittorazzi, Andrés Barrera, Justo Rufino Argueta, and probable Communists Jorge Alvarado Monzón (brother of Bernardo Alvarado Monzón), Rubén Castellanos, Víctor Girón Cabrera, Claudio Miranda, Luis Rozzotto, and Roberto Gaitán. These Communist Agrarian Inspectors played a strategic role in the actual execution of agrarian reform and were able to help Communist campesinos get land, as well as to aid local Communists gain control of the agrarian committees.

The Agrarian Reform Law established, in addition to the DAN,

---

[50] Martínez, a political opportunist, was generally held to be responsible for the assassination of Col. Arana in 1949. As a tool of the President who had aspirations to the presidency himself, he had no desire to break with the Communists.

[51] These last four joined the party on the same day, July 9, 1953. See Document 49: Lista de solicitudes de ingreso, Guatemala 9 de Julio de 1953.

[52] *El Espectador* of September 8, 1953 put the figure at 85%, which is probably an exaggeration.

Local Agrarian Committees (CAL), Departmental Agrarian Commissions (CAD) and the National Agrarian Council (CAN). These committees carried out much of the actual work of deciding what land was to be expropriated and who were to benefit. The law as amended provided that three of the five members of the local committees would be representatives of the CGTG and CNCG, that the three-man Departmental Commissions would be composed of the Governor of the Department and one representative from the CGTG and one from the CNCG, and that the National Agrarian Council would have one CGTG representative and two from the CNCG. As the Communists controlled the CGTG and the CNCG came to function as their closest ally, they were virtually assured of having the strongest say, if not the actual control of these committees. José Luis Ramos, the PGT Secretary of Campesino Affairs sat on the eight-member National Agrarian Council along with fellow Communists Otto Raúl González and Augusto Cazali. The Departmental Agrarian Committees of the most important Departments were fully controlled by the Communists. In Escuintla, where its impact was the greatest, Communist Deputy Pellecer became the virtual czar of the Agrarian Reform program, with the CAD representatives and the head of the peasant organizations all Communists. In Chimaltenango the machinery was entirely in the hands of the Communists, since the Agrarian Inspector, the CGTG and CNCG representatives on the CAD and the Secretary of the CAD were all members of the PGT.[53] In these Departments as in Guatemala, San Marcos, Santa Rosa and others, the Communists' control of the administration of agrarian reform enabled them to build a mass campesino base which more than trebled the party's membership. Those who got land felt they owed it to the Communists and those who wanted land felt that the wisest thing was to join the party.[54] Pellecer presided over the dis-

---

[53] See 8005:2114, Telegram from Andrés Barrera C. to Víctor Manuel Gutiérrez, August 15, 1953; 8002:462, Natzul Aguirre Cook to Víctor Manuel Gutiérrez, March 3, 1953; 8003:22, María Jérez Rivera to Víctor Manuel Gutiérrez, January 9, 1953; 8003:54, Pablo Morales S. to Víctor Manuel Gutiérrez, February 13, 1953; 8005:2290/2, Personas Propuestas ante el Comité Agrario Departamental; Document 44: Nómina de los Secretarios Generales de las Federaciones Campesinas.

[54] See 8003:654, Pedro Fernández P. to Víctor Manuel Gutiérrez, April 9, 1953.

tribution of UFCO's Tiquisate land and Virgilio Guerra was a member of the commission which was to divide up the same company's Bananera holdings.

Banco Nacional Agrario. This important institution, established to provide credit for campesinos receiving land under the agrarian reform program was headed by Alfonso Bauer Paíz, a left-wing PRG leader who espoused the view that the Communists "are as much Guatemalan as we" and should be allowed to compete freely with the other parties.[55] As the CGTG was represented on the board of directors of the bank, the Communists had a voice in its policy.[56] They occupied their full share of positions in the bank at least on a level with the PAR and PRG. For example, the makeup of the branch in Chiquimula was: Chief, Luis Carlos Avendaño, proposed by the CGTG and a member of the PGT; Vitorio Lemus of the PAR; Roberto Cabrera of the PGT; Manuel Vicente Castañeda of the PRG; and Antonio Andrino of the PAR.[57]

Ministry of Economy and Labor. The chief levers of Communist influence over this key ministry and the role it played in Guatemalan national life were: 1) the President; 2) the Communists' control of organized labor; and 3) their acceptance by the other revolutionary parties and the sympathetic attitude of many "progressives." The Minister was always a politician who was sympathetic toward and acceptable to organized labor and its leaders. As these leaders were chiefly Communists, he was of necessity more or less of a collaborator with them. Most important to the Communists were the Administrative Department of Labor (DAT) and the office of the Inspector General of Labor (IGT), since these agencies administered the government's controls over organized labor. When the Labor Code was adopted in 1947, Alfredo Guerra Borges was appointed the first Inspector General of Labor. While nominally a member of PAR, there is little doubt that Guerra Borges was one of the original members of the clandestine Communist party (VGD) established by Fortuny and

[55] Interview with Alfonso Bauer Paíz, Mexico City, June 25, 1957.

[56] 8005:1991, Gutiérrez to President Arbenz, June 1953, proposing Hugo Barrios Klee and Max Salazar as substitutes for José Luis Caceros.

[57] 8008:6423-4, Alfonso Bauer Paíz to Private Secretary of the President, April 14, 1954.

his followers in September of that year.[58] Most of the Labor Inspectors, whose primary task was to investigate labor disputes and advise the labor courts as to the "facts" and relative responsibility of the workers and the employers, were appointed from among those nominated by the CGTG. Communist domination of that labor organization meant that these inspectors would be sympathizers and in many cases party members. Often they reported to the CGTG and the PGT as well as to the government.[59] In Escuintla for example, the office of the *Inspección General del Trabajo* was the nucleus of the Communist Party in the days before the Communists spread their influence throughout the campesino communities.[60] PGT leader Hugo Barrios Klee occupied the key position of Secretary of the Administrative Department of Labor in a move which was typical of the Communists, that of controlling the real nerve center which was one step removed from the public eye.[61] In addition the Congressional Special Committee on Reform of the Labor Code was always headed by a Communist deputy, usually Gutiérrez or Montenegro P.

Instituto Guatemalteco de Seguridad Social, (IGSS). The social security institute was politically important both because of the wide variety of services which it dispensed and because of the large number of vehicles it possessed and which were often used for electioneering purposes. Its head during the Arbenz regime was Alfonso Solórzano, its office manager Abel Cuenca, and Chilean Communist Laura Mallol de Bermúdez its Chief of Maternity Services.

An indication of the degree of Communist penetration of the IGSS comes from a study of the STIGGS, the Union of the Employees of

---

[58] See Y-X-1:341, Arturo Morales Cubas to Alfredo Guerra Borges, October 10, 1947.

[59] See 8003:726, José Domingo Segura to Víctor Manuel Gutiérrez, March 18, 1953 enclosing "Informe del Inspector de Trabajo, José Domingo Segura a rendir a la CGTG y al Partido Guatemalteco del Trabajo, a las cuales me es muy orgulloso a pertenecer," March 17, 1953; 8003: José Domingo Segura to Víctor Manuel Gutiérrez, March 20, 1953; 8005:1683, José Domingo Segura to Secretario General de la CGTG, July 1, 1953; 8008:6207, CGTG to Jaime Díaz Rozzotto, March 26, 1954.

[60] Document 1399: Francisco Hernández Alvarez to Carlos Manuel Pellecer, June 19, 1952.

[61] See Y-X-2:1970, Presupuesto del DAT, 1953-4; Y-X-5:1455, Hugo Barrios Klee to Secretario General del Sindicato Artes Gráficas, October 30, 1952.

the Social Security Institute. A strong Communist fraction or colony operated within the IGSS and managed to elect Communists to the posts of Secretary of Education and Propaganda, Secretary of Conflicts and two posts on the Consultative Council of the union.[62] While the majority of the IGSS employees were *Paristas,* they "considered indispensable the presence of the Communists in the Executive Committee." The Communist faction included employees in responsible positions such as Hortensia Hernández Rojas, Oscar René Cruz, Alberto Piñeda, Luis Felipe Gómez, Luis Felipe Sierra, Flavio Rojas Lima, Roberto Ortega and René Araujo.

Press and Propaganda Agencies. The Communists placed a high priority upon positions from which they could help mold and shape public opinion. During the Arévalo administration, many of the young Communists obtained high positions in the national radio station TGW. Mario Silva Jonama, Alfredo Guerra Borges and Huberto Alvarado headed the station at various times during the period when the Communists were in ascendancy within the PAR. In the last years of the Arévalo government Guerra Borges served as editor of the official paper *El Diario de Centro América.* Under the Arbenz regime the Communists continued their control of the national radio with Carlos Alvarado Jérez as its Director.[63] In addition to writing for the semi-official *Nuestro Diario,* Communist Raúl Leiva was appointed Chief of the Publicity Office of the Presidency in 1953. His successor in that position was Carlos González Orellana, another Communist. Among the other prominent Communists in the Department of Propaganda, Information and Tourism were Otto Raúl González and Medardo Mejía. A study of the official paper *DCA* and semi-official *ND* shows that by 1953 the international line of these papers coincided with that of the Communist organs and that they took news and leads from the Soviet news agency *Tass.*

Ministry of Foreign Affairs. As the foreign policy of the government was largely shaped by the President, the Communists did not par-

---

[62] See Document 1039: report of the PGT fraction within the STIGGS to the Comisión Sindical del PGT, December 7, 1953.

[63] For the efforts of the Communists to place members in the TGW, see 8005:2529, J. A. Cardoza to C. Alvarado Jérez, October 9, 1953.

ticularly seek positions in the ministry or the foreign service. In fact, the embassies abroad were most frequently used as places of exile or rewards for politicians and army officers for whom there was no suitable place in the bureaucracy in Guatemala City. The Communists were most prominent in the diplomatic service during the middle years of the Arévalo government when their presence in Guatemala would have embarrassed the government. Hence Pellecer's tour of duty as Chargé d'Affaires in France. Guerra Borges' assignment in El Salvador in 1949 may or may not fit in this category, as he took advantage of the stay to help the El Salvadorean Communists rebuild. Arévalo's Minister of Foreign Affairs, Enrique Muñoz Meany, was at least a Communist sympathizer who as a teacher had started many of the young Communists on their study of Marxism. During the Arbenz government the Foreign Ministers and most of the diplomatic personnel were picked from among the ranks of the left-wing nationalists who were predisposed to cooperate with the Communists, particularly if that was the way the President wanted it. Guatemalan citizenship and corresponding papers were arranged for Communist exiles from neighboring countries and many other types of favors shown them, ostensibly for the benefit of the CGTG, but actually in the interest of the Communists.[64]

One development worthy of close examination was the sending of Manuel Pinto Usaga to Mexico City as Consul General in 1952, which was followed up a year later by the appointment of Roberto Alvarado Fuentes as Ambassador to Mexico. While on the surface it appears that Pinto may have been sent there to get him out of Gutiérrez's way and Alvarado Fuentes appointed to relieve Charnaud of the hindrance of having a co-Secretary General in the PRG, their behavior in Mexico suggests another purpose.[65]

In the case of Pinto Usaga, there is strong evidence that he acted as a contact between the Guatemalan Communists and the agents operating out of the Czechoslovakian and Soviet embassies in Mexico City. This evidence is corroborated by a careful study of Pinto's political relations. While it would seem that Pinto had too much of an

---

[64] See 8003:244, Foreign Minister Raúl Osegueda to Víctor Manuel Gutiérrez, January 27, 1953, consulting Gutiérrez on the agenda for a proposed ODECA meeting.

[65] On Pinto see Y-X-3:3457-9, CGTG reply to *La Hora*, January 8, 1952.

opportunistic streak in him to be entirely trusted by the Communists, he had a reputation of long and close collaboration with them. In addition to the key role which he played in delivering the *Federación Sindical de Guatemala* into the hands of the Communists and his participation in the short-lived Communist workers' party PROG, Pinto's own words show him to be at least a sympathizer with the cause of Communism. His May Day speeches of 1949 and 1952 were among the most impassioned denunciations of the United States and of anti-Communism to be heard in Guatemala.[66] This latter address in particular followed closely the Communist line on the international situation. Early in 1951 he had chastized the editors of *Octubre* for "passions which I consider unworthy of Communists" and termed Communism "a doctrine which, it is necessary to repeat, deserves all our respect."[67] Previously he had been praised by Fortuny and Bernardo Alvarado Monzón for his "indefatigable fight" on the floor of Congress against the ratification of the Río Pact. [68] In addition Pinto received letters referring to him as "the only person capable of giving me an exact and sincere idea of the principal bases and of the content of Communism."

Once in Mexico, Pinto kept up a steady correspondence with the Guatemalan Communist leaders. We have already seen how he reacted to the attack by Fortuny on the formation of the PRG and the advice which he offered as to the proper tactics for the Communists to follow in Guatemala.[69] After making it plain that he considered the Communist Party the proper directive force in Guatemalan politics, Pinto suggested that the party base its tactics upon the "valuable experience of the C.P. of China, which knows how to maintain the united front with the bourgeoisie." A note appended to the letter makes it plain

---

[66] See Y-X-1:1299-1304 or Y-X-3:3819-3824, Discurso pronunciado por el compañero Manuel Pinto Usaga en el Gran Mitín del Primero de Mayo de 1949; Y-X-1:785-790 or Y-X-1:1688-1693, Intervención del C. Manuel Pinto Usaga, May 1, 1952.

[67] Y-X-1:579, Manuel Pinto Usaga to Director of *Octubre,* February 3, 1951.

[68] Y-X-3:3449, José Manuel Fortuny to Manuel Pinto Usaga, September 22, 1950; Y-X-3:3450, Bernardo Alvarado Monzón to Manuel Pinto Usaga, September 26, 1950.

[69] See Chapter V, pp. 120-21. Also Document 1066 or 1370: Manuel Pinto Usaga to Chemanuel [Fortuny], July 30, 1952.

that Pinto had been sending Fortuny and the Communists "materials which I believe would be useful for you" and wished to receive *Octubre* in return. As Consul General in Mexico, Pinto passed on messages from the Hungarian commercial mission to Arbenz, acted as a middleman between the Guatemalan Communists and Communists of various nationalities in Mexico, kept the Guatemalan Communist leaders posted on the activities of their enemies, helped organize the Society of Friends of Guatemala to spread the propaganda line on "yankee intervention," and generally made himself useful to the cause of Guatemalan Communism.[70]

Pinto's frequent trips between Guatemala and Mexico were ideally suited to the role of a contact with the Communists in the Mexican capital. He is reported to have attended the session of the PGT leadership on January 28, 1954 which discussed the Central American political situation and to have recommended greater aid for the Communists of Honduras and El Salvador.

Civil Guard and Judicial Guard. The police forces of the nation were for all practical purposes an instrument of the executive, and their relations with the various parties and organizations were largely determined by the attitude of the President. Thus it is difficult to say whether Rogelio Cruz Wer, the Director General of the Civil Guard, or Major Jaime Rosenberg, the Chief of the Judicial Guard were Communists or whether they merely took their lead from the President. However we can say that in the last years of the Arbenz regime these officials cooperated closely with the Communist-controlled CGTG and with Castillo Flores' CNCG. The local organizations of the CGTG and CNCG furnished the police with the names of reactionaries, anti-Communists and "opponents of agrarian reform," while Cruz Wer and Rosenberg reciprocated by appointing nominees of the labor

---

[70] See Document 1513: Manuel Pinto Usaga to President, October 9, 1952; 543: Manuel Pinto Usaga to Leonardo Castillo Flores, December 31, 1953; 8007:5349, Manuel Pinto Usaga to Víctor Manuel Gutiérrez, December 31, 1953; 1074: M. Pinto to José Manuel Fortuny, January 16, 1954; 8003:703, Manuel Pinto Usaga to V. M. Gutiérrez G., January 30, 1953; 8005:2000, Manuel Pinto U. to V. M. Gutiérrez G., June 2, 1953; 8005:2414, M. Pinto to Gutiérrez, August 17, 1953; Document 945: M. Pinto to Gutiérrez, August 30, 1952.

organizations to the local civil guard posts.[71] The tone and substance of the communications between Gutiérrez and the heads of the two national police organizations were extremely cordial.[72] The Communist labor organization and the police grew closer as time went on, and in the last months of the regime the leaders of the CNCG and CGTG were virtually auxiliary police with credentials and arms furnished by the Civil Guard.[73] In communities where Communist influence was strong the local Civil Guards often joined the PGT in order to avoid harassment.[74]

The Army. Communist infiltration of the army was perhaps less successful than in any other area of the government; that the army tolerated the Communists as long as it did was largely out of loyalty to the President. This is not to say that the Communists did not try, nor that they did not have success with some of the younger politically ambitious officers. (The greatest success of the Communists was of course with Arbenz himself.) The Communists did not have time to infiltrate the army from below; and with the exception of Arbenz and perhaps Paz Tejada and Aldana Sandoval, their wooing of the top officers proved to be far less effective than they had hoped. Many of the professional soldiers saw in the plans of the Communists a threat

---

[71] See the following letters from Castillo Flores to Director General de la Guardia Civil: Documents 893, June 26, 1952; 613, February 1, 1952; 597, February 12, 1952; 615, April 21, 1952; 595, November 20, 1952; 607, December 13, 1952; 606, June 9, 1953; 588, December 4, 1953; 883, December 24, 1953; 614, February 26, 1954; 756, June 20, 1954; 874, May 31, 1954; Y-36, February 1, 1954; 8051:2313, February 18, 1954; also 311, Leonardo Castillo Flores to Mayor Jaime Rosenberg, January 4, 1954; 8016:815, Víctor Manuel Gutiérrez to Jaime Rosenberg, January 8, 1953; 8003:137, Gutiérrez to Rosenberg, January 19, 1953; 145, Víctor Manuel Gutiérrez to Director de la Guardia Civil, February 19, 1953; 535, V. M. Gutiérrez to Director de la Guardia Civil, April 9, 1953.

[72] See 8003:180, 919, 921, 927; 8004:966; 8005:2267; 8007:4499; 8008: 6667; 8012:477; 8002:1245, 1548, 1551, 1554-5.

[73] Document 756 or 8051:1709, Leonardo Castillo Flores to Director General de la Guardia Civil, June 20, 1954; 8050:464, Víctor Fernando Guzmán Rojas to Leonardo Castillo Flores, May 4, 1954; 561; V. M. Gutiérrez to J. Rosenberg, June 25, 1954. For other documents on CNCG and Civil Guard see 8050:428, 430, 859, 1581-3; 8051:1869, 2097, 2113-4, 2244-5, 2312-5, 2319, 2424; 8052:3924, 4086-7, 4320.

[74] 8007:5603, Rodrigo A. Bautista Soto to Víctor Manuel Gutiérrez.

to the favored and strategic position which they had traditionally occupied in the political process of Guatemala. *Civilismo* was a doctrine abhorrent to the officer corps, and the lesson of July 1949 had taught them that the continued growth of organized labor might eventually reduce the army to a negligible factor and cost them their political perquisites. In addition a good number of the officers were from the upper middle class and naturally moderate in their political views.[75]

Aside from using the President's control over the army, the Communists sought to influence it in two ways. First they attempted through the CNCG and CGTG to infiltrate the local *Comisionado Militar* positions much as they had filled the ranks of the Civil Guard with sympathizers. The other arm of their tatcic was to woo and win the Chief of the Armed Forces, Col. Carlos Enrique Díaz, much as they had Col. Arbenz—including dangling the presidency before his eyes. In the early years of the Arbenz regime the Communist labor leaders seemed to have reached something of a "you scratch my back and I'll scratch yours" relationship with Díaz.[76]

The first record of the dismissal or appointment of *Comisionados Militares* at the request of Gutiérrez, Castillo Flores, or Pellecer came at the beginning of 1951.[77] When the officer at Tiquisate got in their way, Pellecer and Gutiérrez persuaded Díaz to remove him on the charge of organizing anti-Communist committees.[78] Such removals and replacements continued until Castillo Flores demanded a large scale purge in June of 1954.[79] CNCG officials toured the departments looking for anti-Communist officials and forwarded their names to the

[75] In the epilogue the Army-Communist friction is examined more closely.

[76] See 8014:1263, 1301, 1477; 8001:33-5; 8002:2291; 8003:565, 948-9; 8031:150.

[77] 8050:883, Carlos Enrique Díaz to Señor Presidente de la Confederación de Campesinos de Guatemala, January 25, 1951.

[78] Y-X-2:1913, Víctor Manuel Gutiérrez and Carlos Manuel Pellecer to Col. Carlos Enrique Díaz.

[79] See 8050:462, Leonardo Castillo Flores to Simón Morales, May 10, 1954; 8050:841, Otilio Marroquín Ruano to Secretarios Generales of all the Campesino Unions in the Department of Guatemala, June 16, 1954. Also 8052:3927-31, August 15, 1951; Document 650, February 25, 1952; Document 753, April 11, 1952; 805:3268, June 13, 1952; 8031:2049-51, June 13, 1952; 8050:299-300, April 15, 1953; 8050:258-9, April 23, 1953; 8051:1907, December 3, 1953; 8052:4101-3, January 5, 1954; 8052:3959-62; 8052:3995-7; 8051:2327-8; Document 862, February 27, 1954.

Chief of the Armed Forces along with suggestions for their replacements.[80] At the same time hundreds of CNCG and CGTG unions in response to orders from Gutiérrez and Castillo Flores were sending a barrage of messages to the President and Chief of the Armed Forces pledging their support to the regime and seeking arms and military instruction.[81]

Patronage and Favors. In many ministries and agencies the bulk of patronage and employment was handled through the CGTG and there is little doubt that this redounded to the advantage of the Communists in several ways. In the first place, it was possible to place many members and sympathizers in the government bureaucracy; in the second place, many who got jobs or other favors in this manner felt indebted to the Communist labor leaders such as Gutiérrez and Pellecer; finally, many opportunistically inclined individuals strove to be of service to the Communists or even to join the party in order to gain the support of the CGTG's patronage influence. The Communists had a double leverage in this respect as Gutiérrez, Pellecer, Cardoza and Montenegro P. would second the CGTG proposals with their endorsements as Deputies.[82] As a majority of the employees in many agencies were affiliated with the CGTG, governmental officials found it advantageous to cooperate with its leaders and grant most of their requests. This was another of the many ways in which control of organized labor greatly contributed to Communist influence. In addition to patronage matters, the CGTG leaders could obtain from the government a wide variety of favors such as railroad passes from the Ministry of Communications and Public Works, use of jeeps from the IGSS, firearms licenses from the Minister of Government or even loans from the INFOP. Government agencies also aided the several Communist front organizations in such ways as furnishing meeting places and free transportation for

---

[80] 8052:4610-11, José María López Valdizón and Otilio Marroquín Ruano to Leonardo Castillo Flores, June 14, 1954; Document 158, Leonardo Castillo Flores to Jefe de las Fuerzas Armadas, June 21, 1954; Document 159, Otilio Marroquín Ruano to Leonardo Castillo Flores, June 21, 1954; also 8051: 2135-40.

[81] These messages mount into the hundreds and can be found throughout the files of the CGTG and CNCG and their affiliates particularly on reels 8024, 8027 and 8052.

[82] This patronage correspondence is found throughout reels 8001 to 8008 and is so abundant that it is unnecessary to cite in detail here.

their agents.[83] In turn the Communists used these favors to consolidate their hold over the workers and peasants.

Communist penetration of the government was closely related to another area of Communist operations in Guatemala, infiltration of and influence over the revolutionary political parties. Once again the two developments interacted. The position of the Communists in the government both depended upon their influence in the revolutionary parties and contributed to its growth. The National Democratic Front (FDN), in which the Communists had the greatest voice in shaping national policy, was both the highest political and governmental decision-making body. In the next chapter we shall study these parties and the ways in which the Communists used them.

[83] Document 2017: José Enrique Torres to Carlos González Orellana, October 14, 1952.

9

MANIPULATION OF THE REVOLUTIONARY PARTIES

To understand how the relatively small Communist Party came to exert such great influence, it is necessary to study its relations with the other revolutionary parties. In addition, an examination of the nature ·of these parties is essential to explain why they were so ineffectual in contrast to the Communists. As political parties came and went in Guatemala with considerable frequency and were as much the product of personal rivalry as they were of ideological differences, the story is necessarily complex. In general, the Communists skillfully exploited the shortcomings of the revolutionary parties and took advantage of the inter- and intra-party rivalries in order to strengthen their own position as the holder of the balance of power.

The long-term aim of the Communists, even before they emerged into the open, was acceptance as part of a coalition of the revolutionary political parties. This they finally achieved through the National Democratic Front (FDN), which was founded at the end of 1952.[1]

---

[1] Document 1095: Julio Estrada de la Hoz to Secretary General of the Partido Comunista de Guatemala, November 5, 1952.

The FDN became institutionalized after the legal registration of the PGT in December, 1952. In the summer of 1953 the CGTG and CNCG were added to its membership and the FDN became the chief policy-making body in Guatemala. To a considerable extent the cabinet was reduced to a purely administrative body and the Congress merely ratified the decisions reached by the leaders at the sessions of the FDN, which were presided over by the President.

With the decline of the RN and the alliance between the two labor organizations (CGTG and CNCG), the Communists came to dominate the FDN. Early in 1954 it was composed of five Communists (Fortuny and Guerra Borges for the PGT; Gutiérrez and Pellecer for the CGTG; Alfonso Solórzano for the PRG), three fellow travellers (Castillo Flores for the CNCG; Julio Estrada de la Hoz and Marco Antonio Franco for the PAR), and two other leftists who frequently cooperated with the Communists (Oscar Bautista for the CNCG; Charnaud MacDonald for the PRG). With such sympathizers heading the other parties, it is no wonder that the Communists were able to exert an influence over the national and international policies of Guatemala far out of proportion to their numbers. In the following pages an attempt will be made to show how the Communists rose to such a favorable position within the Arbenz coalition.

PARTIDO ACCION REVOLUCIONARIA (PAR)

In discussing the PAR, and particularly its relation to the Communist movement, it is necessary to bear in mind that there were a number of very distinct periods in the life of this party. What was true of it at a particular moment may not be at all applicable a year later or earlier. Within this limitation it is still possible to make several valid generalizations concerning the PAR. For the greater part of its existence the PAR was, if not the majority party in Guatemala, at least the one with the most extensive electoral support. However, each time it approached a position of dominance, internal dissension among its rather heterogeneous elements led to the resignation of some considerable portion of its membership and the formation of a rival party.

At one time or another almost all the political leaders and government officials of the Arbenz coalition had been affiliated with the PAR. Of particular interest is the fact that for a period of several crucial years (November 1946 to March 1949) the PAR was led by Fortuny and other Communists who were at the same time members of a clandestine Communist Party. Even after the Communists withdrew, there remained within the PAR at all times a colony of Marxists who strove to keep the party following a course of cooperation with the PGT. This Communist influence was much stronger among the controlling circles of the PAR than among the rank and file. With but brief exceptions, the PAR was an ally rather than a rival of the Communists. Other than the PGT, the PAR can be considered as the most radical of the Guatemalan parties.

The Early Years of the PAR. The PAR was founded in November of 1945 through the merger of the two main revolutionary parties, the *Renovación Nacional* (RN) and *Frente Popular Libertador* (FPL).[2] Although Julio César Méndez Montenegro was its first Secretary General, Fortuny soon became the most influential single leader of the new party. As Secretary of Education and Propaganda and editor of the party paper, *El Libertador,* as well as a leader in Congress, Fortuny was in a position to increase his influence and propagate Marxism within the PAR.

In November 1946, one year after its founding, the PAR held a national convention at which its "progressive" or radical wing won a victory over the moderate faction composed of some of the ex-leaders of the FPL.[3] Shortly before the convention Fortuny had become interim Secretary General replacing Mario Monteforte Toledo, and at the convention he was confirmed in this post. Augusto Charnaud Mac-Donald as Secretary of Propaganda and Humberto González Juárez as Financial Secretary completed the Executive Committee of the party. These three men were later to become the leaders of the three

---

[2] The merger of the RN and FPL seems to have been at least partially the result of President Arévalo's automobile accident and the so-called "Pacto de la Barranca" in which the leaders of the revolutionary parties agreed to support Colonel Arana for the presidency in case Arévalo should die. For background on the founding of the PAR see 8021:45. For the minutes of the Executive Council of the PAR see: 8021:292, November 5, 1945; 8021: 275-77, November 10, 1945; 8021:294-5, November 12, 1945; 8021:281-4, November 17, 1945; 8021:285, November 21, 1945; 8021:273, November 22, 1945; 8021:287-8, November 25, 1945; 8021:274, December 3, 1945; 8021: 271, December 8, 1945; 8021:268, December 19, 1945; 8021:266-7, February 20, 1946; 8021:264-5, February 23, 1946.

[3] 8021:191-193, José Manuel Fortuny to Carlos Manuel Pellecer, January 27, 1948.

major parties of the Arbenz regime. The statement of principles adopted by the convention was mildly Socialist in tone, and several of its seventeen points were obviously compromises into which much or little could be read.[4] Although the statutes of the party envisaged a greater degree of organization and discipline than was usual for Guatemalan parties, they were not Communist inspired.[5] At this stage the PAR contained a heterogeneous collection of left wing political beliefs and tended toward factionalization over ideological and personal differences.

The convention did not settle the control or policy of the PAR for long. By early February the moderate wing of the party publicly declared that the leadership which had come into power through the convention had followed a "demagogic, extreme and violent" conduct which had adverse effects upon the work of the government and the prestige of the nation, government and party.[6] The demand that those responsible for the extremist policies of the party resign touched off a bitter and prolonged intra-party struggle. Eventually a compromise was reached with Ricardo Asturias Valenzuela of the dissidents replacing Fortuny as Secretary General, Fortuny moving to Secretary of Propaganda (his old post), and Charnaud becoming Secretary of Organization.[7] This compromise, a last ditch measure to preserve unity, was short-lived. On the thirty-first of May, 1947, the dissension within the PAR again came to a head with a large number of its leading figures withdrawing to reconstitute the *Frente Popular Libertador*. Along with PAR Secretary General Ricardo Asturias Valenzuela, former Secretary General Mario Monteforte Toledo, Mario Méndez Montenegro and Alfonso Bauer Páiz of the political commission, Ministers Manuel Galich and Víctor Giordani, and twenty-eight members of Congress left the PAR. One of the reasons publicly given for this action was their disagreement with "theories which only have as their object placing us at the service of foreign interests."[8] Within

---

[4] "Declaración de principios y bases fundamentales del programa político del 'PAR' aprobados en sesión plenaria de la convención nacional celebrada el 18 de Noviembre de 1946."

[5] "Estatutos del Partido Acción Revolucionaria adoptados en la Primera Convención Nacional."

[6] *El Imparcial,* February 10, 1947.

[7] Document A-22: José Manuel Fortuny to the Political Commission of the PAR, March 7, 1947.

[8] *El Imparcial,* May 31, 1947.

the inner circles of the government the moderates charged that the PAR leadership was becoming Communist dominated.[9] As a result of the split the FPL became the leading party in Congress and the Cabinet, while the PAR was relegated to a secondary position.

The PAR was now fully in the hands of the extremist wing headed by José Manuel Fortuny, who became Secretary General once again. Four months later Fortuny and his closest followers founded a clandestine Communist party (VDG) and began a two-year attempt to convert the PAR into their tool.[10] Within the PAR at this time were many young radicals who, although they never joined the Communist Party, could never completely free themselves from the influence of Fortuny. For example, Julio Estrada de la Hoz, who served as President of Congress in 1952 and as Secretary General of the PAR in the crucial 1953-54 period, was always indebted to Fortuny, who had served as his political sponsor when he was trying to get a start in politics.[11] As Secretary General of the PAR, Fortuny was one of the most influential politicians in Guatemala and built up a following, prestige and reputation which he was later at least partially able to transfer to the

---

[9] 8021:46, J. Manuel Cordón C. to Compañeros del Partido Acción Revolucionaria, June, 1947.

[10] The situation in which Fortuny found himself when he took over control of the PAR is described in a revealing letter to the Communist firebrand Pellecer, who had been exiled by Arévalo to the Legation in Paris. (8021: 191-3, José Manuel Fortuny to Carlos Manuel Pellecer, January 27, 1948). In analyzing the developments of the past three years, Fortuny felt that Manuel Galich and the other moderates of the old FPL were motivated by hate of "the world currents" and particularly by hate for Vicente Lombardo Toledano, leader of the CTAL who had played an important role in fostering Communism among the labor leaders of Guatemala. This group, which later had battled Fortuny within the PAR and had finally reconstituted the FPL, had been attracted to the doctrines of Haya de la Torre and his *Aprista* movement and the "other nationalist conservatives of America," rather than to Communism. Now that the FPL had broken with the PAR, the latter would concentrate upon the workers and campesinos as well as the progressive elements of the middle class. Fortuny wished Pellecer to return to Guatemala to help with the task of rebuilding the PAR along the lines of a "working class" party.

[11] 8021:207, Julio Estrada de la Hoz to José Manuel Fortuny, August 7, 1947; 8021:200, Julio Estrada de la Hoz to José Manuel Fortuny, August 29, 1947; 8021:208, José Manuel Fortuny to Julio Estrada de la Hoz, September 4, 1947; 8021:160, Eliseo Zelada Martínez to Fortuny, July 5, 1948; 8021:163, Fortuny to Eliseo Zelada Martínez, July 15, 1948; 8021:202-3, Alvaro Hugo Salguero to José Manuel Fortuny, September 1, 1947; 8021: 204-6, Fortuny to Alvaro Hugo Salguero, September 4, 1947.

Communist Party. When the Communists eventually came into the open, the relative ease with which they won acceptance from the revolutionary parties and a large segment of the people was due largely to the fact that leaders had already attained prominence within the PAR, the government, and the labor movement before they publicly announced that they were Communists.

PAR Round Table on Charnaud's Proposals. The extent of Communist control of the PAR and the Marxist orientation of its leadership during this period is evidenced by the reaction to a proposal made in 1948 by Augusto Charnaud MacDonald, PAR Secretary of Organization and Propaganda and, until May 31 of that year, Arévalo's Minister of Economy and Labor. Charnaud had addressed a letter to the General Association of Agricultural Producers (AGA), the Chamber of Commerce and Industry (CCI), and the National Committee for Labor Unity (CNUS) inviting them to participate in a joint discussion of national problems in the political-economic spheres. Since the first two of these organizations represented the vested interests of the country, such a conciliatory measure upset those leaders of the PAR who were closely wedded to the Marxist concept of class struggle. At a meeting of the party's political committee, these leaders raised serious objections to Charnaud's actions, and it was decided to hold a round table (*mesa redonda*) on the question. This extraordinary meeting began on Saturday, August 28, 1948, and ran through the following Tuesday. Included among its active participants were José Manuel Fortuny, Secretary General of the PAR and of the clandestine Communist Party (VDG); Augusto Charnaud MacDonald, PAR Secretary of Organization and Propaganda and later Secretary General of the Socialist Party and of the PRG as well as a leading member of the Arbenz cabinet; Mario Silva Jonama, later Secretary of the Central Committee of the Communist Party; Alfredo Guerra Borges, likewise a Secretary of the Central Committee of the Guatemalan Communist Party when it emerged into the open; Víctor Manuel Gutiérrez, number one Communist labor leader; and Abel Cuenca, Salvadorean Communist who was to serve as Charnaud's deputy in the PRG. At least four of these top leaders of the PAR were at that time militants of the yet clandestine Communist Party. In addition to the specific task of criticizing Charnaud's letter, this meeting was to "study the tactics of the party in the present moment."[12] Much of the discussion hinged around the question of whether or not the PAR was to become a Marxist working-class party.

Quoting liberally from Marx, Lenin, and Stalin, the Communists attacked Charnaud as a "reformist" and demanded that he submit to party discipline.[13] In the face of the concerted attack by Fortuny, Silva Jonama, Cuenca, Carlos Arias, and Guerra Borges, Charnaud defended his proposal on the grounds that he had not called for a pact or cooperation between the classes and had considered the round table as a battlefield in the class struggle. Héctor Morgan García, José Joaquín García Manzo, Chita de Balcarcel and González Juárez attempted to defend Charnaud but were unable to match the Communists' dialectical skill. The ideological extremes within the party were evident in Cuenca's speech which stressed that Marxism was the official philosophy of the PAR and Chita de Balcarcel's statement that the entire episode was "another schism of the party provoked by the Marxists." However several of Charnaud's defenders, and even Charnaud himself, resorted to quoting from Lenin to justify their stand.

After the debate the Communist faction headed by Fortuny presented a set of proposals as to the future tactics of the party.[14] While accepting the view that the PAR was the instrument of "revolutionary national unity" and hence could not become strictly a class party, they insisted that the immediate and concrete object of the party should be "definitely defeating the feudal, landholding reactionaries in the political arena and in the economic field." Severely criticizing the "petty bourgeois mentality" manifested by those who supported Charnaud, Fortuny contrasted the true Marxist position with the "insecurity, vacillation, fear, and above all, lack of confidence in the combative

---

[12] See 8031:584-8 or Document 1417: Relación de la mesa redonda efectuada para hacer una crítica a la carta que el Secretario de Organización y Propaganda dirigió a la AGA, CCI y CNUS, y estudiar la táctica del partido en los actuales momentos; Document 1421: Puntos de referencia de crítica que se hará al compañero Charnaud por la carta que dirigió a la AGA, a la CCI y al CNUS; Document 1420: José Manuel Fortuny to members of the Political Commission of the PAR, August 27, 1948.

[13] See Document 1416: continuation of the minutes of the round table; Document 1418: Intervención de Abel Cuenca, August 30, 1948; Document 1419: Intervención de Enrique Rodríguez, August 30, 1948; Document 1413.

[14] Documents 1414 and 1415: Algunas consideraciones sobre la táctica del partido.

power of the great exploited masses" shown by those who disagreed
with the Communists. The program of the PAR should not be socialis-
tic because "socialism is not the order of the day in our country." The
"confused marriage of semi-feudalism, incipient capitalism and imperialist penetration" which prevailed in Guatemala called for a program of "Revolutionary National Unity." As outlined by Fortuny, this
included: an intensification of the class struggle; agrarian reform;
strengthening of the PAR and its conversion into the "great party of
the masses"; an organic alliance between the PAR and organized labor;
and the public repudiation of Charnaud's round table proposal.[15]

Although they were victorious in the dispute with Charnaud, it appears that the Communist faction within the PAR may have over-
extended themselves and, by trying to go too far too fast, have touched
off a reaction against their continued dominance of the party. Whatever
the proportions of ideological and personal differences which went
into the mixture, the end result was that the Communists were defeated
in their attempt to take over the PAR and reshape it in their own
image. The battlefield was the Second National Convention of the
PAR.

PAR Convention of March 1949. This convention of the PAR marked
a turning point in the development of that party and led to a major
change in the strategy being followed by the Guatemalan Communists.
The extremists' attempt to take over the PAR and convert it into a
Communist party was defeated by the combined forces of the non-
Communist Marxists and the non-Marxists. The faction led by Charnaud and González Juárez called for a critical reevaluation of the
political line followed by the PAR while under the leadership of Fortuny. While important changes in the ideology and position of the party
on alliances with the other revolutionary parties (i.e. a rapprochement
with the FPL and RN) were expected, the center of interest was the
election of the officers who would direct the party for the next two
years. In an attempt to win the support of the undecided by presenting
a ticket which represented the entire range of opinions within the

---

[15] There is considerable evidence that even this statement was a modifica-
tion and substantial toning down of the original program of the Communist
faction. If so, this was brought about by the adverse reaction of the less
Marxist wing to the extremist statements of Silva Jonama and Cuenca.

party, González Juárez and Charnaud included a number of the popular young Communists on their slate and proposed the Marxist Roberto Alvarado Fuentes for Secretary General in place of Fortuny.

When the showdown session arrived tempers ran hot and the atmosphere was explosive. Results of the balloting showed that the Communists had received a resounding defeat by a vote of 372-120.[16] The Statutes and Statement of Principles adopted made it plain that, although the PAR was still a revolutionary party with a general Marxist orientation, it was not going to become a "class" party.[17]

> The Partido Acción Revolucionaria (PAR) is a party of the masses which expresses the interests of the workers, peasants, employees, intellectuals, democrats, small proprietors, small businessmen, indigenous nuclei and the progressive industrialists.

PAR and Communism, 1949-1954. As the FPL went into decline after the middle of 1949, the PAR rose to be the number one political force in Guatemala. However, it was at the same time weakened by the withdrawal of the Communists in 1950. After reaching a new peak of strength and influence early in 1951, the PAR received a major setback as the supporters of Charnaud MacDonald split off to form the new Socialist Party. In the following year the PAR was again badly split as many of its leaders joined with Charnaud in founding the PRG. This last loss was offset in 1953 by the switch of Castillo Flores and many of the CNCG leaders from the PRG to the PAR, so the PAR was still the largest single party in Guatemala and had the lion's share of the spoils of office. On the other hand, it had in the PRG a formidable threat to its dominant position and lost the control of the labor movement to the Communist Party.

The net result of both of these developments was that the PAR found itself being pushed farther to the left and into the arms of the Communists. On the one hand, Communist support was necessary to stand off the challenge of the rival PRG; and on the other, the PAR had to move leftwards in order not to lose the votes of the working class to the Communists. Added to this were the increasing closeness between the

---

[16] The figure was given by Roberto Alvarado Fuentes in a letter to *El Imparcial,* March 21, 1949. For a list of the new officers see Document 289: Roberto Alvarado Fuentes to Secretario General de la FSG, March 19, 1949.

[17] See "Estatutos del Partido Acción Revolucionaria aprobados por la Segunda Convención Nacional," March 15, 1949.

President and the Communist leaders and the internal dissensions which racked the PAR. In this environment the PAR, during 1953 and early 1954, was being reduced to an ally of the Communist Party on terms increasingly favorable to the Communists. In spite of the difference in the size of the two parties and their representation in Congress, it seems clear that by 1954 the Communists were the dynamic element in the relationship and the initiative was in their hands.

To appreciate more fully the relationship between the PAR and the Communists, it is necessary to examine several episodes and aspects of the development of the PAR during the Arbenz regime. The Second Extraordinary Convention of the PAR met in March 1951 and re-elected Roberto Alvarado Fuentes as Secretary General over a determined bid by Charnaud. The statement of principles which was adopted at this convention was progressive, nationalistic and anti-imperialistic, in general similar to that of the previous convention.[18] A notable addition was the statement that:

> The Partico Acción Revolucionaria (PAR) recognizes the necessity of fighting against all the means of foreign ideological penetration, which tend to deform the meaning of our nationality, culture, and revolutionary process.

On the other hand, the international portion of the program, while calling for friendship with the United States on the basis of the good neighbor policy, also:

> Repudiates and denounces the campaign undertaken by imperialism to discredit "popular democracy" and socialism, since this campaign constitutes a serious threat against the peace.

Remarking nearly a year later on the relations of the PAR to the Communists, the Secretary of Propaganda stated that those who called the PAR a Communist Party were mistaken and that there was no reason to confuse the two.[19]

> The Communist Party of Guatemala, like the Communist parties of every country, has its own program and its own tactics. And, if its program and tactics coincide with the tactics and program of the PAR, it is due to the fact that both organizations

---

[18] See: "Partido Acción Revolucionaria: Principios, Estatutos, Programa," March 11, 1951.

[19] 8022:579-83, *Boletín del Partido Acción Revolucionaria (PAR)*.

have as a common objective, in this epoch of our history, the fight against feudal backwardness and against imperialism.

During the same period there were repeated charges by members of the party that the leadership was too heavily influenced by the Communists.[20]

Communist inroads into the youth of the PAR had reached the point where many of them were relatively well indoctrinated with Marxism and accepted the Communist line on international developments. The *Parista* youth group, *Juventud Parista*, participated actively in the work of the AJDG and other Communist-controlled youth groups, and in this way were exposed to a great amount of "masked" Communist propaganda. The youth were a particularly ready target for the Communists since they were by nature more radical than their elders and had been growing up in the environment of the revolution and the Arbenz regime. *Acción*, the paper of the young *Paristas*, took on a Marxist orientation with articles on historical materialism and the evils of capitalism.[21]

The most famous statement of a PAR leader on Communism was that of Secretary General Francisco Fernández Foncea on the floor of Congress on October 6, 1953.

> I am in support of the PRG which presently is expelling four young gentlemen from its ranks, and of the most logical, decent, honest and patriotic party of Guatemala: the *Partido Guatemalteco del Trabajo!* I fight for my party in spite of the fact that I know that it is a transitory party which necessarily will have to be swallowed up, like all the other revolutionary parties of Guatemala, in the great world socialist party.[22]

While Fernández Foncea was removed from his post after making this remark, it would appear that not all of those who acted against him disagreed with the sentiments expressed. Some PAR leaders merely considered its public utterances rash and untimely. In any case the PAR continued to cooperate with the Communists in the 1953 munici-

---

[20] Document 1031: 11 *Paristas* to the Secretary General of PAR, September 19, 1951; Documents 1491 and 1492; 8022:38, Augusto de León to *El Imparcial*, January 28, 1952.

[21] See *Acción*, Año I, No. IV, August 14, 1953; Año I, No. XI, February 20, 1954; also 8051:1913-6 or Y-X-5:988-90, Manifiesto de la Juventud Parista al Pueblo de Guatemala, January, 1954.

[22] *El Imparcial*, October 6, 1953.

pal elections. All in all, there would seem to be little doubt that the
Communists had a considerable number of allies and sympathizers
within the PAR, and that at least a strong faction of its leaders advocated a policy of close cooperation with the PGT.

Dissension Within the PAR. One of the factors which made it possible
for the Communists to exert a great influence over the much larger
PAR was the fact that the latter was constantly weakened by internal
dissension. Even after the expulsion of Alvarado Fuentes, Abel Cuenca
and Alfonso Solórzano in July 1952, the PAR with Alvaro Hugo
Salguero as provisional Secretary General was unable to find any real
degree of stability. Early in August the party purged those elements
most closely connected to the leaders who had entered the PRG.[23]
With the local readjustment occasioned by individuals and branches
switching from the PAR to the PRG and others from the PRG to the
PAR already disrupting the work of the party, the impending elections
and an internal power struggle brought the PAR to the verge of chaos.
Efforts by provisional Secretary General Alvaro Hugo Salguero to
purge his enemies led to local revolts which greatly weakened party
discipline.[24] In Quezaltenango the departmental officials were suspended by the national leaders when they attempted to show independence, but in Alta Verapaz the local PAR organization successfully
scuppored the candidacies of René Rubín and Ricardo Barrera over
the selections of the national leadership. Entire local branches resigned
in protest at Salguero's highhanded actions. Finally in April 1953,
Francisco Fernández Foncea was named Secretary General over Julio
Estrada de la Hoz. Although Fernández was reportedly the choice of
Salguero, backers of González Juárez became Secretary of Organization
and Financial Secretary. By September those persons purged by Salguero the previous year were reinstated and the González Juárez faction
appeared to be coming back into power.[25]

All hell broke loose in the PAR after Secretary General Fernández
Foncea, who had sought a rapproachement with the Communists in
an attempt to strengthen his position, stated on the floor of Congress

---

[23] *El Imparcial,* August 12, 1952.

[24] *El Imparcial,* October 18, October 23, October 24, November 12 and
December 12, 1952.

[25] *Diario de Centro América,* September 10, 1953.

that the PAR would eventually be absorbed into the "great world Socialist Party."[26] His statements were immediately repudiated by other party leaders and an extraordinary session of the National Council was summoned. The González Juárez-Estrada de la Hoz faction made use of Fernández Foncea's slip to purge the Salguero leadership.[27] In addition to Fernández Foncea, seven other members of the National Executive Committee and five of the eight members of the Political Commission, including Salguero, were removed from office, in many cases being replaced by those whom they had purged a year earlier. Estrada de la Hoz was recalled from the United Nations to take over as Secretary General less than a year after he had been forced to petition abjectly for readmittance to the party. An ex-protégé of Fortuny, he appeared to be on even closer terms with the Communists than had his predecessor.[28]

The displaced faction attempted to fight the action of the new leadership and appealed to the local organizations, but the Civic Registrar ruled in favor of the new officers.[29] In March, after the election of the officers of Congress, two deputies were expelled and three more suspended, bringing the total of ousted deputies to ten and leaving the PAR with only fifteen.[30] In an attempt to resolve this crisis an extraordinary convention was held on March 26-28. It appeared that the party might be further disrupted as the dissatisfied elements gathered behind Alfonso Martínez as their choice for Secretary General.[31] When it was rumored that a serious split was developing between González Juárez and the present and past presidents of Congress, Marco Antonio Franco and Guillermo Ovando Arriola, Arbenz took the matter to the FDN for settlement, thus affording the Communists an opportunity to conciliate the internal disputes of the

---

[26] *El Imparcial,* October 6, 1953. For Fernández Foncea's relations with the Communists, see *Tribuna Popular,* September 3, 1953 and September 4, 1953.

[27] *El Imparcial,* October 12, 1953.

[28] Document 519: Antonio Sierra González to Julio Estrada de la Hoz, April 21, 1949; Document 520: Julio Estrada de la Hoz to José Luis Ramos, April 15, 1949.

[29] *El Imparcial,* October 13, 1953. 8037:409, telegram, Francisco Fernández Foncea to Secretarios Generales, October 15, 1953; 8037:405-8, various telegrams to the branches announcing this ruling.

[30] *El Imparcial,* March 8 and March 9, 1954.

[31] *El Imparcial,* March 10, 11 and 12, 1954.

PAR.[32] Martínez renounced his ambitions and Estrada de la Hoz was confirmed as Secretary General. On the other hand, five purged deputies were restored to the party's good graces, leaving only Salguero, Fernández Foncea and three others on the black list. González Juárez became Secretary of Organization and was recognized as the party's strong man.

The PAR was so weakened by this unending dissension that it was unable to risk conflict with the Communists and forced to lean upon the PGT as a support against the challenge of the PRG. In addition, many local leaders and promising younger politicians were alienated by the undisciplined behavior of the PAR leadership and turned their eyes toward the PGT.[33]

FRENTE POPULAR LIBERTADOR (FPL)

The FPL, or "students' party" was one of the first to emerge from the Revolution of 1944. In November of 1945 it joined with the RN to form the PAR, but withdrew in May of 1947 over the influence of the Marxist extremists within the PAR. In comparison with the PAR, the FPL was more moderate. The progressive decline of the FPL in the 1949-1951 period was important in opening the way for the acceptance of the Communists as an integral part of the Arbenz coalition.

After the FPL was reconstituted in the summer of 1947, it became

---

[32] *El Imparcial,* March 13 and 16, 1954.

[33] Since the timing of events within the PAR made it appear that Fernández Foncea was being removed for his "indiscreet" and public manifestation of pro-Communist sentiments, the PGT spokesmen attempted to dissociate the two developments. Writing in *Tribuna Popular* on October 14, 1953, Editor Alfredo Guerra Borges denied that this was either a victory or a defeat for the Communists and that the PGT had any role in the matter. As the PGT saw it, the dispute climaxed a long rivalry within the PAR. The removal of Fernández Foncea must be considered as a continuation of the González Juárez-Salguero rivalry and not as a matter involving the issue of Communism. According to the PGT pundit, González Juárez was just raising a smoke screen when he stated that "the change of the national leadership was necessary because the members who were removed were not responding to the aspirations of the party . . . and also for their radical deviation toward the extreme left." This made it appear that developments in PAR all revolved around the speech of Fernández Foncea. Guerra Borges denied that the Communists tried to influence internal matters of the other parties.

the leading Guatemalan political party. However the majority of the labor leaders remained close to the PAR and sought to discredit the FPL in the eyes of the workers. The FPL leaders denied the charges that they had been moving toward the right, and argued in turn that the PAR was following a "suicidal tactic" in failing to adjust its demands to the historical reality of Guatemala.[34]

At a National Convention in April 1949 the FPL decided that it was too early to consider the question of presidential succession and strictly forbade campaigning for any candidate within the party.[35] From this point on, the position of the FPL steadily deteriorated, and it was soon eclipsed by the more radical PAR which embraced the candidacy of Col. Arbenz. In less than two years the FPL lost its position as the majority party in Congress and the Cabinet, and was reduced to a negligible political force. One of the factors which must be taken into consideration in understanding the disintegration of the FPL is that at its peak of size and influence it encompassed a heterogeneous collection of elements. Drawing upon both labor and the middle class for support, and with a leadership composed of young lawyers, the party fell prey to its own internal contradictions. Each major step forward with the legislative program of the party and of the government alienated some elements who felt that this was not the course the revolution should follow. In the final analysis the party was unable to satisfy the wide variety of political viewpoints and economic interests which it attempted to represent.

The internal contradictions of the FPL were brought sharply into focus by the question of presidential succession. Early in 1949 a group of FPL moderates supported Arana. After Arana's assassination the party officially informed Arbenz that they could not back his candidacy, since they felt that he would be dependent upon the army for his real support.[36] A few days later, and apparently with the encouragement of Arévalo, a group of FPL leaders headed by Alfonso Bauer Paíz decided to endorse Arbenz. This split within the FPL was

---

[34] Y-X-3:3496-3501, Ricardo Asturias Valenzuela and Marco Antonio Villamar to Comisión de Defensa de la FSG, January 7, 1948.

[35] 8032:3063-6, pp. 7-10 of what appear to be condensed version of the minutes of the convention, April 4, 1949.

[36] The author has had an opportunity to discuss the decline of the FPL with many of its leaders including Mario Monteforte Toledo of the moderate anti-Communist wing and Alfonso Bauer Paíz of the more radical faction.

skillfully exploited by the Arbenz forces, who utilized Manuel Galich as their instrument. A group of *Frente Populistas* threw their support to Jorge García Granados, but the party convention nominated Dr. Víctor Giordani, Arévalo's Minister of Health, as the official FPL candidate. In August of 1950 Secretary General Manuel Galich announced that he would run for the presidency in competition with Giordani.[37] As a result of this split the National Election Board cancelled the party's registration. After the first day of the three-day presidential elections, Galich withdrew in favor of Arbenz. As his reward, Galich was named as Arbenz's Foreign Minister; the FPL, still badly split, did poorly in the congressional elections and had only seven members in the new Congress. Thus the FPL had fallen from the majority party to a tie for fourth place in the Congress. Eventually the FPL was swallowed up in the formation of the PRG in the summer of 1952, but it was already dead as a real political force after the 1950 elections. As the Arbenz administration got under way the PAR was the strongest political party in Guatemala.

RENOVACION NACIONAL (RN)

The RN was one of the original revolutionary parties and managed to survive until the end of the Arbenz regime, although it was virtually destroyed by internal dissension and rendered impotent by early 1954. The course of its development and decline shows most of the defects and deficiencies from which Guatemalan parties suffer. The RN was founded by a group of the more mature young revolutionaries on the day that Ubico fell, July 1, 1944. Carlos Leonidas Acevedo, Juan José Orozco Posadas, Oscar Benítez, and Mario Efraín Najera Farfán were among its founding fathers and took for its motto "A New Country in Social Justice."[38] Known to many as the "teachers' party" to distinguish them from the FPL or "students' party," the RN soon developed into a personalist party composed of friends of President Arévalo. Once Arévalo was off the political scene, the RN deteriorated into a collection of rival factions, office holders, and politicians who stuck with the party in an effort to control the patronage and financial subvention which it received as an administration party. In November

---

[37] See *El Imparcial,* August 17, 19, 21 and 24, 1950.
[38] See Najera Farfán, *op. cit.,* pp. 49-50.

of 1945 it merged with the FPL to form the PAR; but in less than a year the RN was reconstituted, although with a considerable loss in membership. Throughout the rest of the Arévalo administration the RN ranked as the smallest of the three government parties and was not a dynamic or particularly significant political force.

Factionalism weakened the RN even more during the Arbenz regime, as one dispute followed another. By the end of August 1951, three separate wings of the party were clamoring for recognition by the Civic Registrar with the nod going to Oscar Jiménez de León's clique.[39] In the early part of the following year the party was still paralyzed by the existence of three feuding factions—the *auténticos, antiguas* and *Sexta Avenida*.[40] After some hesitation the RN joined the PRG in June 1952, but withdrew a month later. By this time its Secretary General, Jaime Díaz Rozzotto, was working closely with the Communists, going as far as to salute the end of the Korean War as a step toward the establishment of the Socialist world order.[41] Díaz Rozzotto was active in front groups such as the CNP and attended some meetings of the PGT, and may have been a secret member of the party.

In the final crisis which broke into the open in the latter part of December 1953, the behavior of its so-called "leaders" was such as to completely discredit the party. RN Deputy Alejandro Revolorio was beaten by Díaz Rozzotto and Virgilio Zapata Mendía, Secretary General of the Presidency and a Justice of the Supreme Court respectively.[42] Zapata was removed by Congress from the Supreme Court and a group headed by Deputy Héctor Fión Garma took over the party headquarters. When Díaz Rozzotto and his backers attempted to seize the party offices by an armed attack, seven of them ended up in court.[43] The FDN attempted to resolve the impasse and reconcile the factions, but the effort backfired when the convention was interrupted by gunfire and had to be suspended.[44] A new compromise made Roberto Cabrera Guzmán Secretary General, but soon the party was

[39] See *El Imparcial,* August 30-31 and September 1, 1951.
[40] *El Imparcial,* February 26, 1952.
[41] See Document 938: Jaime Díaz Rozzotto to Alfredo Guerra Borges, April 7, 1952, for an example of their cooperation.
[42] *El Imparcial,* December 19, 1953.
[43] *El Imparcial,* December 21, 1953.
[44] See *El Imparcial,* March 17, 20 and 22, 1954.

split into four factions and for all practical purposes ceased to exist.[45] By the end of the Arbenz regime it was said that the RN could have held its national convention in a bus.

The RN, to an even greater extent than the PAR and PRG, was racked by internal dissension and virtually falling apart at the same time that the PGT was rapidly growing in strength and influence. The Communists stood to pick up most of the Congressional seats which would become available due to the disintegration of the RN, and probably would have won over many RN members who were disillusioned at the behavior of their own leaders and saw the PAR leaders as little better.

PARTIDO INTEGRIDAD NACIONAL (PIN)

This party, which had its headquarters in Guatemala's second city of Quezaltenango, played a short and not very distinguished role in the political life of the country. PIN was launched late in 1949 to sponsor the presidential candidacy of that city's favorite son, Col. Jacobo Arbenz. Headed by Nicolás Brol Galicia, the PIN was composed of moderately well-to-do and progressive land-owners and considered itself to be "nationalist," defining this as opposition to "exotic theories which come to disturb our tranquility."[46] As the PIN interpreted it, Article 32 of the Constitution barred Communism as well as Fascism. In March of 1952 they rejected an alliance of revolutionary political parties which would have included the Communists, since the statutes of the party "reject energetically doctrines which have international connections of a Stalinist type."[47] When the PRG was formed, the PIN joined it and generally formed its more conservative wing.

PARTIDO SOCIALISTA (PS)

The Socialist Party to Guatemala was born in the summer of 1951 as a result of a major schism in the PAR. While the motivations of

---

[45] See *Tribuna Popular,* May 7, 1954.

[46] Y-381: Manifiesto del Partido "Integridad Nacional" al Pueblo de Guatemala, July 13, 1951.

[47] 8039:724, Enrique Galindo to Humberto Rodríguez G., March 5, 1952.

its founders were mixed and involved personal ambitions as well as matters of principle, ideology and political line, the *Partido Socialista* may be considered as the major effort to bring together those elements of the left-of-center political forces which felt that it was necessary to put some curb upon the growing influence of the Communists. For a short time it appeared that the PS might possibly succeed in its effort to guide the Guatemalan Revolution along the lines of an indigenous national social revolution and hence to counteract and contain the influence of the Communists.

Aside from the support of the moderate wing of the PAR, this new movement was launched with the endorsement of some elements of the virtually defunct FPL, which had been partially successful in its earlier attempt to play a similar role. In addition, the PS originally counted on the support of the National Confederation of Campesinos (CNCG) and the moderate leaders of the railroad union, the SAMF. If this support could have been consolidated and strengthened, the PS might have been successful in its aim of counter-balancing the influence of the Communists *within* the nationalist coalition of parties which backed the government and program of President Arbenz. At no time did the PS consider allying with the so-called "anti-Communist" forces which were in opposition to the Arbenz government; the leaders of this new movement fully endorsed the Revolution of 1944 and the work of the Arévalo government. What they desired to do was to keep the revolution developing along the same lines and to prevent it from being diverted into the channels of class warfare by the Communists. In a sense the PS represented the embodiment of the views expressed by Charnaud at the PAR round table in September of 1948 and opposed then by the Communists.

To a certain degree the PS was also a personal instrument of Charnaud, and, while his prestige and friendship with the President was one of its chief assets, his ambition and opportunistic nature were a weakness which may have kept the party from coming closer to succeeding as a rallying point for non-Communist revolutionaries. As it was, the PS never developed into a real threat to the aims of the Communists, nor was it for long an effective brake upon their aspirations.

At the PAR Convention on March 10 and 11, 1951, Roberto Alvarado Fuentes was elected Secretary General over Francisco J.

Silva Falla in an election which was really a duel between the two *caudillos* of the PAR, Humberto González Juárez and Charnaud MacDonald. With his candidate's defeat, Charnaud lost the position of Secretary of Organization which had been his source of strength and influence within PAR for almost five years. Upon his subsequent resignation from the PAR, Charnaud was followed by thousands of its members.

When the PS made its appearance on July 11, its manifesto stated that the new party would follow a "socialist ideology of the left."[48] One of the reasons for the formation of the new party was apparently the opposition of some of its members to the efforts of the Communists, aided and abetted by Alvarado Fuentes, to form the PAR, FPL and RN into a National Democratic Front.[49] At first the PS grew rapidly, as its moderate leftist doctrine held appeal for many Guatemalans.[50] It took as one of its professed aims the task of bringing back into politics those leaders of the Revolution of '44 who had abandoned the political arena when the opportunists and extremists took over control of the revolutionary parties.[51]

Early in September the new party held its first national convention and elected Charnaud as Secretary General, Juan José Tejada Barrientos as Secretary of Organization, and Emilio Zea González (who had been Secretary General of the *Partido del Pueblo* which had supported García Granados for President in the 1950 elections) as Secretary of Propaganda. Mario Morales Vielman of SAMF was Secretary of Labor Affairs, while Clodoveo Torres Moss of the CNCG served as Secretary of Campesino Affairs. In addition Arturo Morales Cubas and José Luis Caceros, leading figures in the SAMF, and Leonardo Castillo Flores and Amor Velasco de León of the CNCG held posts on the Political Commission, thus linking those two important organizations to the party.[52]

Those who viewed the new party as a threat soon brought pressure to bear upon it. Deputies of the PAR, FPL, and RN began agitation for Charnaud's removal as Minister of Finance. Although the Presi-

---

[48] *El Imparcial,* July 11, 1951.

[49] *Ibid.*

[50] See *El Imparcial,* August 3, 1951 for a discussion of its ideology.

[51] *El Imparcial,* August 8, 1951.

[52] See "Estatutos del Partido Socialista" for a list of all officers of the PS.

dent retained Charnaud, the Socialist leader took the episode to heart as a warning not to go too far in trying to alter the political balance. By October 10, 1951, the PS joined in defending the government against the charges of the anti-Communists.[53] The PS continued to work closely with the moderate elements in the SAMF and CNCG, while the same time undertaking secret discussions with the leaders of the other revolutionary parties looking toward organic unity.

PARTIDO DE LA REVOLUCION GUATEMALTECA (PRG)

The relations between the PS and the other revolutionary parties remained in a state of flux throughout late 1951 and early 1952. Dissension within the SAMF and the growth of Communist control over the unified labor movement kept the PS from developing into as strong and independent a force as its founders had expected. In addition, the relations between Charnaud and CNCG leader Castillo Flores were becoming strained. On the other hand, the PAR was suffering from a continuation of its internal difficultes with supporters of Alvaro Hugo Salguero feuding with the González Juárez faction. Against this background of mutual frustrations the PAR, led by Alvarado Fuentes, and the PS, headed by Charnaud, undertook to unite the revolutionary parties.

On February 4, 1952, these two leaders signed an alliance between their parties pledging them to support a common program.[54] On the 13th of March the PAR and PS were joined in an alliance by the FPL and RN, and the four parties agreed upon a common program including support of the agrarian reform bill which was before congress.[55] At this time the Communists, who were calling for a National Democratic Front in which they would be included, apparently approved of the action taken by the other parties as a step in the right direction. Meanwhile Arturo Morales Cubas, a member of the Political Commission of the PS, was leading a strong fight against the Communists within the important railroad workers' union SAMF.[56] Morales Cubas stirred up the ire of the Communists by

---

[53] *El Imparcial,* October 10, 1951.

[54] See *Octubre,* February 7, 1952, for the text of this pact.

[55] See *Octubre,* March 20, 1952 for the text of the joint statement.

[56] See *El Imparcial,* March 19, 1952, for Morales Cubas' statement against Communists who were trying to take over control of the union.

declaring publicly that Communism was anti-national and anti-revo-lutionary.[57] When the Executive Committee of SAMF gave a vote of confidence to Morales Cubas,[58] the Communists pressured the PS to repudiate him. However the party refused to expel him and by so doing rekindled Fortuny's suspicions that it harbored anti-Communist designs.

At this time the fear that the implementation of agrarian reform would lead to "fratricidal struggle" among the revolutionary parties and the need to present a united front to the opposition in the up-coming congressional elections led some of the leaders of the adminis-tration parties to consider merging the several parties into one. Organic unification rather than just unity of action had been one of the aims of the PS since its birth not quite a year earlier. Now, in the face of a lack of enthusiasm among the rank and file members of the party, Secretary General Roberto Alvarado Fuentes of the PAR decided in favor of such a merger.[59] On June 10, 1952, this move was made public and the PRG or Party of the Guatemalan Revolution came into existence.

The exact motives of the several parties involved in the formation of the PRG have never been too clear. It has been claimed that the impetus came from the President in order to have unified backing for the agrarian reform bill. Anti-Communists have claimed that it was a move to give the Communists a chance to exert more influence over the nationalist politicians.[60] However the Communists seemed to see in it a threat, and at least one anti-Communist analyst felt that the PRG was an effort to "bring about the elimination of Communist influence from the government of Jacobo Arbenz."[61] The truth of the matter seems to be that the purposes of the several individuals who brought about the formation of the PRG were mixed. While

---

[57] *El Imparcial,* March 20, 1952.

[58] *El Imparcial,* April 1, 1952.

[59] It is interesting to note that nearly a year earlier Alvarado Fuentes had proposed to the other revolutionary parties, including both the PCG and PROG, as well as the AFG, AJDG, CNCG and labor leaders that they join in a National Democratic Front. 8022:888, Roberto Alvarado Fuentes to Secretaries General of FPL, RN, PRUN, PIN, PROG, PCG, AFG, AJDG, CNCG, CPCUTG, July 3, 1951.

[60] See James, *op. cit.,* pp. 81-2.

[61] Josefina de Wiche, "El Comunismo en Guatemala," in *Estudios Sobre el Comunismo,* Año I, No. 1, Santiago de Chile, Julio-Septiembre, 1953, p. 95.

some of the PS leaders may have looked on it as a brake upon the Communists, certain non-party Communists such as Cuenca, Solórzano and Alvarado Fuentes played a prominent role in its formation. The bulk of the PRG's founders came from between these two extremes and probably hoped for an end to the disunity and bickering among the administration parties. Some leaders apparently agreed to the merger of their parties as a means of neutralizing the influence of the PS.

Whatever the motivations of its founders were, the PRG did not survive in its original form for more than a single month. The joint PAR-PS manifesto was issued by Charnaud and Alvarado Fuentes on June 10, and for the next week the other parties debated affiliation. At this time Charnaud was rumored as the probable chief of the National Agrarian Department, a factor which may have weighed heavily in the minds of many politicians.[62] On the 17th a provisional Political Bureau of the new party was established with four representatives of the PS and four of the PAR.[63] The FPL, RN and PIN soon agreed to the merger and the PRG seemed a going concern. On the first of July the PRG received a blow when Alfonso Martínez rather than Charnaud was appointed to head the National Agrarian Department (DAN).[64] While the task of organizing PRG branches began on the 2nd of July with the formal inscription of the new party, opposition was soon felt from local PAR officials.[65] On July 18 the rump leadership of PAR on the initiative of Alvaro Hugo Salguero withdrew from the PRG and expelled Cuenca, Alvarado Fuentes, Solórzano and Héctor Morgan García.[66] The reasons given for the action were the excessive influence of *Aprista* doctrine and the dominance of the Socialist Party leaders within the PRG.[67] The RN also withdrew from the PRG, leaving only the Socialists, the FPL, the PIN and a portion of the PAR. The PRG suffered another blow when

---

[62] See *El Imparcial,* June 10, 1952.

[63] Charnaud, Morales Cubas, Juan José García Manzo and Francisco Silva Falla for the PS; Estrada de la Hoz, González Juárez, Cuenca and Solórzano for the PAR.

[64] *El Imparcial,* July 1, 1952.

[65] 8020:27, telegram sent by Secretaries of Organization of PAR, PS, RN, FPL, and PIN to local Secretary General, July 2, 1952; 8022:745, Arturo Fernández to Augusto Charnaud MacDonald, July 9, 1952.

[66] *El Imparcial,* July 19, 1952.

[67] *El Imparcial,* July 21, 1952.

CNCG leaders Castillo Flores, Torres Moss and Oscar Bautista González left the party and moved over to the rival PAR.[68]

Communist Reaction to the Founding of the PRG. While it is difficult to prove that the Communists were directly responsible for the break-up of the PRG, their attack on it coincided with the first manifestations of opposition from within the PAR and RN. A study of the reaction of the Communist leaders to the formation of the PRG bears out the contention that this was more than coincidental. The PCG had approved of the alliance between the PAR and the PS signed on February 4, 1952, by Alvarado Fuentes and Charnaud.[69] At the same time the PCG was carrying on preliminary discussions with the PAR, PS, FPL and RN in an attempt to reach agreement on a minimum program so that work could be begun toward the establishment of the National Democratic Front.[70] Accord was reached among the parties on a five-point program of agrarian reform, resistance to UFCO, industrialization and improvement of the economic situation of the masses, defense of national sovereignty and peace, and the unity of the democratic forces.[71] When the PAR, FPL, PS, and RN formally signed such an alliance, the Communist Party approved of it as "an important positive step."[72]

The immediate reaction of the Communists to the founding of the PRG was noncommittal.[73] However, on July 3 *Octubre* carried the first of a series of articles by PCG Secretary General Fortuny on "Elements for the Analysis of the Unification of the Democratic Parties of the Arbenz Government." Fortuny interpreted the formation of the PRG as a regrouping of the bourgeois and petty bourgeois political forces in the face of the growing strength not only of the rightist opposition, but of the working class and the Communist party as well. The Communists feared that if the bourgeoisie were united in one party they would be able to control the government and isolate

---

[68] Interesting light upon this situation and the purposes and position of the PRG can be found in *Boletín Informativo del PRG,* No. 1, August 9, 1952, and 8022:795, Alfonso Rodrigo Trangay to Juan José Tejada Barrientos, July 28, 1952. See Chapter VII, pp. 160-63.

[69] *Octubre,* February 7, 1952.

[70] *Octubre,* February 14, 1952.

[71] *Octubre,* February 21, 1952.

[72] *Octubre,* March 20, 1952.

[73] *Octubre,* June 19, 1952.

it from "the influence of the leadership of the labor movement in the bourgeois revolution, and separate it, therefore, from the masses." Such a development would conflict with the Communist goal of "proletarian leadership of the bourgeois revolution." In short the Communists saw the PRG as a possible threat and preferred to keep the bourgeois parties separated and fragmentized so that they could apply divide-and-rule tactics if necessary. In particular they saw in the PRG's emphasis upon the non-sectarian administration of agrarian reform a threat to their fundamental goal of reaching the campesino masses and converting them eventually to the Communist cause. As use of the agrarian reform machinery was a prime requisite in the Communist program, it would not do to have one strong united rival for control of this machinery. How much better it would be to be able to exploit the rivalry of several parties.

In his second installment Fortuny charged that the formation of the PRG could be interpreted as a step towards "the isolation of the Communists, both from the masses and from the direction of the revolutionary movement."[74] The following week he warned that it was a mistake to think that the bourgeois revolution could be brought to completion without the guidance of the Communist Party.[75]

> . . . only the working class, 100 per cent revolutionary and therefore, its political expression, its vanguard expression, its organized forefront, its party in other words, that is to say, the Communist Party, possesses the theory, discipline, organization and tactics necessary to carry the democratic-bourgeois revolution and national liberation to victorious culmination of all its tasks.

In his fourth article, which appeared just as the PAR was withdrawing from the PRG, Fortuny stated that the Communist Party considered the manner of unification to have been an error and felt that the parties should participate in talks concerning the unity of *all* the democratic forces. The root of the Communist Party's concern was whether the bourgeois parties would still be willing to sign an alliance with the Communists and to run joint slates with the PCG in the elections. The Communists were not willing to see their cherished project of a National Democratic Front, with their party as a full member, endangered by the formation of a unified bourgeois party

---

[74] *Octubre,* July 10, 1952.
[75] *Octubre,* July 17, 1952.

which might feel strong enough to go it alone without or even against the Communists.

On July 31, *Octubre* published an article by Fortuny on "The Rupture of the PRG." According to him the three causes of the breakup were the fear of being led by members of other classes, the failure of the PAR leaders to insist upon a leading role for PAR, and the orientation toward *Aprismo* or socialism of the right. Fortuny appeared to gloat over the fact that, in his eyes at least, developments had borne out the suspicions and dire forecasts of his first two articles. Whether or not the breakup of the PRG as the "only party" was a positive step hinged upon the formation of a "true united front" of the democratic forces, one in which the Communists would be included. Guerra Borges amplified the attitude of the PCG by stating that they favored unity of action but felt that organic unity among diverse elements and classes was not then desirable.

While it is not possible to prove that the Communists were directly responsible for the breakup of the PRG as a coalition of the native Guatemalan revolutionary forces, the consensus of opinion of the observers with whom it was possible to discuss this point held that the Communists had at least encouraged their friends in the PAR to work for the withdrawal of that party from the PRG and had played upon the fears of some *Paristas* and members of the RN that their interests and influence would suffer from immersion in the larger entity. Hints were widely circulated that the President did not approve of the PRG in its present form. In any case the subsequent course of events worked out advantageously for the Communists, who obtained co-operation of the other parties on their terms and saw the successful establishment of the "National Democratic Front." Likewise it appears to have been a decisive lesson to the ever ambitious Charnaud, who after this blow and the subsequent loss of CNCG support, followed a policy of working with the Communists rather than attempting to challenge them.

Relations Between the PRG and the Communists. The relations of the PRG with the Communists are complex and difficult to evaluate. The PRG was, on the whole, not as far left as the PAR, and in the rivalry between the two parties the Communists usually sided with the PAR. In addition, the PRG and PGT as young growing parties occasionally clashed in their efforts to build a mass base in the countryside. While the PRG leadership contained Marxists and Communists such as Solórzano, Alvarado Fuentes, and Abel Cuenca, these individuals had in the past differed with the tactics proposed by Fortuny and disagreed with the Communist Party leadership. Also, the Communists were somewhat wary of the shrewd opportunist Charnaud MacDonald, who dominated the PRG. However, it appears that during 1953 and 1954 the PRG leadership moved sharply to the left and sought to win the approval of the Communists. This was chiefly a political maneuver of the national leaders and did not correspond to the sentiments of the rank and file. The ambiguous nature of the relations between the PRG and the Communists can be seen in the fact that, while the two parties ran joint slates in some communities during the 1953 municipal elections, in other places there was bitter rivalry between the two parties.

Dissension Within the PRG. In the last year of its short life the PRG was shaken on several occasions by severe internal dissension. While each of these disputes involved several factors, all were related to the question of Communism and Communist influence in the PRG.

On May 23, 1953, Alvarado Fuentes, Cuenca and Solórzano asked for the expulsion of Arturo Morales Cubas from the PRG, claiming that his actions within the SAMF had endangered the unity of the labor movement.[76] Morales Cubas, who felt that the real reason for this attack was his opposition to the Communist take-over of the SAMF, fought back and accused his enemies of being "external agents" within the party.[77] The moderates among the PRG leadership, headed by Carlos García Bauer, one of the few deputies of the revolutionary parties who had refused to participate in the "minute of silence" as a memorial to Stalin, sought in turn to have Alvarado Fuentes, Cuenca and Solórzano expelled.[78] They charged these extremist leaders of being Communists and of trying to eliminate the ex-leaders of the PS from the controlling organs of the PRG. Charnaud deserted his old comrades and sided with the allies of the Communists.[79]

---

[76] Document Y-249: Comunicado del PRG a todos los hombres y mujeres de la Revolución Guatemalteca, June, 1953.

[77] 8033:262-3, Arturo Morales Cubas and G. Gutiérrez J. to Augusto Charnaud MacDonald, May 23, 1953.

[78] *El Imparcial,* May 27, 1953.

[79] 8020:77, El Partido de la Revolución Guatemalteca ante el conflicto del SAMF, June 18, 1953.

Dissension within the PRG continued as Charnaud was unwilling to tolerate any real opposition or challenge to his dominant position. Secretary of Organization Juan José Tejada Barrientos was preparing to run against Charnaud for the Secretary General's post at the convention which was to be held late in 1953. Charnaud, with the backing of Alvarado Fuentes, Solórzano, Cuenca, Héctor Morgan García and Bauer Paíz, railroaded through the expulsion of Tejada Barrientos on charges of having "threatened the unity of the party." Deputies Carlos García Bauer, Emilio Zea González, and Abundio Maldonado opposed Charnaud and argued that the expulsion of Tejada Barrientos should be left to the convention to decide.[80] In the debate which followed, Zea González openly charged co-Secretary General Alvarado Fuentes with being a Communist.[81]

After the expulsion of Tejada Barrientos and the subsequent reorganization of the national leadership, the radical, pro-Communist wing was in the driver's seat.[82] The moderates saw no alternative than to withdraw and split the party.[83] The matter came to a head in September 1953 with the resignation of a group of deputies led by Carlos García Bauer, Emilio Zea González, and Abundio Maldonado. While opposition to the dictatorial actions of Charnaud was the reason given to the public, disagreement with the policy of close cooperation with the Communists was equally important.[84] The resignation of the six deputies cut the PRG congressional representation down to nine. One of its results was the replacement of the moderate Carlos García Bauer by Alfonso Solórzano on the FDN, which meant that yet another Communist sympathizer and collaborator was placed upon the most important political decision-making body in Guatemala. Behind all the surface discussion of unity, discipline, dictatorship and democratic centralism, there lay the basic political difference over the policy of collaboration with the Communists. Once again those who felt that

---

[80] See Document 988: Sesiones de la Comisión Política del PRG, July 29, 1953.

[81] 8022:554-6, Sesiones de la Comisión Política del PRG, August 5, 1953.

[82] Y-235: Sesiones de la Comisión Política del PRG, August 7, 1953.

[83] The leader of this faction argued with the author that his group could have taken over control of the party from Charnaud and his supporters, but that they could not have successfully bucked the opposition of the President, so they chose instead to withdraw.

[84] See *El Imparcial,* September 26, 1953 for the declaration of the dissidents.

Communism was perverting the course of the revolution went down to defeat.[85]

The PRG in 1954. By January 1954 the PRG leaders felt they could safely hold a national convention. Charnaud's report to the convention revealed the extent to which he was willing to go in order to achieve a modus vivendi with the Communists.[86] Bitter as he was over the way the PRG was being squeezed out of the agrarian reform program, Charnaud preferred to put the blame upon the PAR and the CNCG, and not the Communists; Martínez and Castillo Flores rather than Pellecer were his villains.[87]

With respect to the Communists, Charnaud held that they had "enriched" the field of democratic political organization.[88] As he felt that "a party is only the political expression of the predominant economic interests of a specific class," the PRG's leader readily conceded to the Communists the role of representative of the workers, including the salaried rural laborers. The campesinos he held to be more properly a portion of the petty bourgeoisie and hence should be represented by the PRG. Since the necessity of an alliance between the workers and the peasants was obvious, according to Charnaud, it was necessary for the PRG to work closely with the PGT.[89] As the multiplicity of petty bourgeois parties served no useful purpose and confused the masses, the proper step would be for all the middle class parties to merge into one (the PRG), which would function as an ally of the PGT.

In what was very nearly an open bid for Communist preference for the PRG over the PAR, Charnaud stated that a petty bourgeois revolutionary party such as the PRG leaders desired to build would be "a better ally with which they [the Communists] could arrive at very

---

[85] The Communists reported in *Tribuna Popular,* October 23, 1953, that Maldonado was travelling about telling the local organizations and campesinos that the PRG was in the hands of the Communists. See also Augusto Charnaud MacDonald to Eugenio Bolanos de León, October 13, 1953 and the attached documents: *Boletín del Partido de la Revolución Guatemalteca,* No. 1, September 25, 1953, No. 2, October 1, 1953, No. 3, October 2, 1953.

[86] Y-248: *Informe a la Primera Convención Nacional del Partido de la Revolución Guatemalteca,* January 15, 1954.

[87] *Ibid.,* pp. 22-27.

[88] *Ibid.,* p. 36.

[89] *Ibid.,* pp. 37-39.

positive revolutionary understandings.[90] Charnaud endorsed the strengthening of the FDN and pledged the party to overcome the "anti-unitary," *i.e.* anti-Communist, tendencies among some of its branches. In this respect he specifically mentioned the case of the "underhanded anti-Communist" Juan José Tejada Barrientos, who had been expelled from the party for accusing Charnaud of "handing the party to the Communists."[91]

The statutes adopted by the convention marked a conscious effort to model the party along Leninist organizational principles. The use of the cell as the basic structural unit, adoption of the principle of democratic centralism, and the acceptance of "criticism and self-criticism" as a means of tightening discipline were all part of an attempt to bring the PRG up to the organizational efficiency of the PGT.[92] The party secretariats were professionalized and Abel Cuenca was elevated to the key position of Secretary of the Central Committee.[93]

In 1954 the PRG leadership adopted an extremely nationalistic and anti-United States propaganda line. By the time of the Caracas Conference the PRG was going as far as the PGT itself in their denunciations of the United States and its motives. In one of their regular series of radio programs the PRG stated that the United States, whose goal was to dominate the world, was preparing to unleash aggression against Guatemala on the pretext of Communist influence.[94] At the same time, when it was suggested that the Communists be curbed in

---

[90] *Ibid.,* p. 41.

[91] *Ibid.,* p. 53.

[92] The statutes were drawn up by Abel Cuenca, a long-time Communist, and Marco Antonio Villamar and Guillermo Palmieri of the extremist wing of the party, all of them admirers of Communist techniques, if not always of their doctrine. Document 1773: Ante-proyecto de Estatutos del Partido de la Revolución Guatemalteca, December 21, 1953; Estatutos del Partido de la Revolución Guatemalteca, January 17, 1954; Partido de la Revolución Guatemalteca, Materiales de discusión para la Primera Convención Nacional, December 21, 1953; El Partido de la Revolución Guatemalteca (PRG) como partido democrático de nuevo tipo en Guatemala, September 10, 1953.

[93] For the officers as of August 8, 1953, see Document 1918 or 8013:184, PRG Comunicado de Prensa del Partido, August 8, 1953. For the Central Committee see Y-234 or Document 162: Precandidatos para el Comité Central, January 1954. For the outgoing Central Committee see Document 1795: Comité Central del PRG. See also Y-358: Comisión Ejecutiva and Y-315: La Comisión Política del Partido de la Revolución Guatemalteca.

[94] 8002:68-80, Script 12 of radio series "El Partido de la Revolución Guatemalteca a paso firme," March 20, 1954.

order to save the Arbenz government, Charnaud defended them saying that "to isolate the Communists would be to open the doors to Fascism."[95]

Communist influence within the PRG was perhaps strongest among the youth of the party, many of whom participated in the Communist-led youth organizations which will be discussed in the following chapter.[96] In 1954 the youth arm of the PRG was reorganized as the *Juventud Perregista,* and the party leadership gave considerable attention to defining its role and increasing the scope of its activities.[97] In a document dealing with the role of youth drawn up by the three top leaders of the PRG—Charnaud, Cuenca, and Villamar Contreras—the PGT was held up as the only party in Guatemala which had paid attention to the problem of educating its youth.[98] Stating that Marxism was the "only revolutionary ideology of our time" the PRG leaders instructed the youth of the party to continue participating in the Alliance of Democratic Guatemalan Youth (AJDG) in spite of the fact that it had become a "peripheral organization" of the PGT.[99] At the First Congress of Perregista Youth at the end of April 1954, it was decided to affiliate directly with the Communist-controlled World Federation of Democratic Youth and to send delegates to the rural youth rally in Ravena, Italy. Among the resolutions of this Congress was the "intensification of the fight against anti-Communism" as well as the fight against "imperialist aggression."[100] The PRG youth were thrown fully into the peace campaign and the creation of Youth Committees against Foreign Intervention. In every case the party leadership en-

[95] See *Tribuna Popular,* June 16, 1954.

[96] See 8022:916, Marco Antonio Villamar Contreras to Alfonso Marroquín Orellana, September 1, 1952; Document 1811, Hoja de instrucciones; Document 1750: Alfonso Castellanos and Francisco Muralles to Comisión Política del PRG, October 1, 1953; 8022:696, J. Humberto Carrillo L. to Secretary General of Juventud Perregista, June 8, 1954. For more of Juventud Revolucionaria Guatemalteca see 8022:762, Carlos García Manzo to Marco Antonio Villamar Contreras, February 26, 1954; also Documents 767, 768, 28, 29, Y-231, Y-276, Y-280, Y-333 and Y-350.

[97] See 8022:123-31, Plan de Organización de la Juventud Perregista.

[98] 8022:226-246, Qué papel corresponde a la juventud dentro del PRG, qué papel corresponde a la juventud en partidos políticos.

[99] 8022:851-4, Plan de trabajo sobre el frente de lucha de las relaciones que la Juventud Perregista debe guardar con las organizaciones internacionales y nacionales de la juventud, Comisión Nacional de Trabajo de la Juventud Perregista.

[100] 8022:148-153, Dictámen de la Comisión de Asuntos Políticos, May 1, 1954.

dorsed and supported moves which would bring their youth groups under greater Communist influence.[101]

To recapitulate briefly, the Communists brought to Guatemalan politics a degree of organization, discipline and purposefulness previously unknown. The most moderate of the revolutionary parties, the FPL, opposed the Communists, but lost out to more radical groups by the end of Arévalo's presidency, chiefly because of its inability to work effectively at the grass roots level. The PAR, although the country's largest party, never freed itself from the effects of a two-year domination by the Communists (1947-1949) and suffered from internal dissension which caused the loss of many of its most effective leaders. It was a typical "official" party, concerned chiefly with patronage and doing what the President wanted.

The best hope for a strong non-Communist revolutionary party was the Socialist Party (PS) founded by Charnaud in the summer of 1951. Having strong support from the Campesino Confederation and the moderate unions led by the SAMF, the PS gave promise of becoming an effective rival of the Communists. However, the President chose to side with the PAR and the Communists, thus preventing the PS from developing into a major force. In 1952 Charnaud and a number of moderate leftists made another attempt to form a unified revolutionary party which would exclude the Communists. Thwarted a second time, Charnaud decided that to stay in business the PRG had to build a popular base and an effective organization. To accomplish this, he rebuilt the party along Communist lines and paid lip service at least to Communist policies. Whether Charnaud planned on beating the Communists at their own game, or whether he was merely following the old political adage—if you can't beat them, join them—is not certain. The end result of these factors and Arbenz's insistence upon unity and conformity was that the Communists set the tone for the revolutionary forces.

In the next chapter we shall study the mass organizations through which many of the non-Communist revolutionaries and nationalists were subjected to Communist propaganda and lent their support to pro-Soviet causes.

---

[101] 8022:421-3, La Lucha por la Paz, PRG Comisión Nacional de Trabajo de la Juventud, May 3, 1954; 8022:416-20, Informe a la Secretaría de la Juventud Perregista sobre la lucha de la juventud contra la intervención extranjera y por la defensa de la soberanía nacional, Comisión Nacional de Trabajo, June 1, 1954.

10

FRONT ORGANIZATIONS AND THE COMMUNIST LINE

Front organizations and propaganda campaigns carried out through them have been accorded a prominent place in Communist theory and practice.[1] In Guatemala, where these organizations and activities played a major though not decisive role in the success of the Communists, one of their chief advantages was apparent independence from the Communist Party.

---

[1] In Communist theory there is a distinction between the functions of "front" groups and those of the so-called "mass" organizations. In Guatemala the same entities could best be characterized as "front" groups at one time and as "mass" organizations at a later stage of the Communist movement's development. For further discussion of this distinction, see Bernard S. Morris, "Communist International Front Organizations: Their Nature and Function," *World Politics,* Vol. IX, No. 1 (October, 1956), pp. 76-87. See also Stephen King-Hall, *The Communist Conspiracy,* London, 1953; and *Organizaciones Internacionales Comunistas de Fachada,* Mexico, 1956. For a general understanding of Communism, R. N. Carew Hunt's *The Theory and Practice of Communism: An Introduction,* New York, 5th Revised Edition, 1957, is a good place for the layman to begin.

Before examining the case of Guatemala, let us recapitulate briefly Communist theory on the nature and purposes of front organizations and their relation to the Communist movement. Such organizations are designed to act as instruments of Communist policy while masking their real purposes behind an ostensibly non-political facade of social and economic goals which have wide acceptance and appeal to progressive public opinion. Communist emphasis upon the role of these so-called "mass organizations" predates the Russian revolution as Lenin in his *What Is To Be Done* distinguished between the function of the party itself and the role which could be played by organizations such as the trade unions which, though under hidden control of the party, could attract broader mass support for Communist causes. "We must go among all classes of the people as theoreticians, as propagandists, as agitators and as organizers. . . . The principal thing, of course, is propaganda and agitation among all strata of the people."[2] To Stalin the Communist Party was the "general staff" of the revolution while the mass organizations acted as "transmission belts" which linked the party and the masses.

The function of these organizations is to spread Marxist-Leninist doctrine, to mobilize support for the immediate foreign policy objective of the Communist bloc, and to recruit and test potential party members. In addition they serve as a training ground for future party leaders. Most of these groups also function as a non-governmental channel for sponsoring free or low-cost trips to Communist countries for groups and individuals whom the party or the Soviet Union are interested in wooing. Their meetings furnish an opportunity for international Communist leaders to get together without arousing undue attention.[3]

In Guatemala during the Arévalo administration the front groups had the added advantage that, as there was no open organized Communist Party, the fear of Communist control did not arise and many persons who would have had nothing to do with Communism as such

---

[2] Lenin, *Selected Works,* Vol. II, New York, 1935, p. 101.

[3] For example, many Guatemalans who might have opposed the idea of the leaders of the French, Italian, Cuban, Mexican and other Communist parties gathering in Guatemala to counsel the PGT felt honored by the fact that leaders of the World Federation of Trade Unions and the Confederation of Latin American Workers attended the Second Congress of the General Confederation of Guatemalan Workers. However, the end result was the same.

took an active part in these groups and their activities. Soon, however, the disciplined Communist faction within each organization, aided by the influence of the international parent organization, began to take control and turn its activities away from exclusively social and economic ends and into the realm of politics.

The pattern was similar in almost every case. The organization would be founded to champion some social or economic cause or the interests of some broad group such as women or youth, and would claim to be non-sectarian and apolitical. The Communists would first capture the position of Secretary of Organization and Secretary of Propaganda while letting others have the more glamorous posts of Secretary General and President. This was usually easy, since many considered these posts undesirable because of the amount of work involved. From these strategic positions the hard-working Communists would spread their propaganda and entrench themselves in the organizational structure of the group. Converts would be made and the Communists would use their balance of power position to see that friendly elements remained in control. Eventually a Communist, whose membership in the party was usually not widely known, would be elevated to the Secretary General's post. If objection was raised that the group was following a Communist line, they would point out that they were only following the policy "democratically" formulated by the representatives of millions of their companions in other countries of the world. The small group of Communist activists and their allies would soon be in a position where they could pose as the spokesmen for all the "democratic" youth, women, peace-lovers, etc., and throw the support of their organization behind the programs and propaganda of the party.

The success of the Communists in controlling these front organizations was such that the party occasionally had to warn the Communist leaders to move out of the public eye and mask their pro-Communist activities so as to be able to draw even more of the unsuspecting into their net. The culmination and apex of these activities was to have been the constitution of the "United Front of the Masses," a sort of super-front organization built upon the fusion of all the mass organizations. The Arbenz regime collapsed before this could be implemented.

In many respects the most important front group was the labor movement, which we have examined in Chapters VI and VII. The CGTG and, particularly in the later years, the CNCG as well constituted a major support for the activities of the other front groups. In this chapter we shall examine the full array of specialized front groups and study how the Communists used them as a facade through which to carry on their propaganda activities and to gain recruits to the Communist cause, particularly among the bourgeoisie. To a considerable extent these front groups or "mass organizations" served to strengthen the alliance between the Communists and the revolutionary parties by bringing their members into contact and cooperation.

THE PEACE CAMPAIGN

Of all the propaganda campaigns and front activities carried on in Guatemala by the Communists, those grouped around the peace theme were broadest in scope and involved the greatest number of people. The wide appeal of this theme gained a sympathetic hearing for the Communist propaganda which was aimed at creating a favorable attitude toward the Soviet Union while undermining trust in the United States. The peace campaign was led by a National Peace Committee (CNP) and its subsidiary committees, but the CGTG played a major role in it, and all the other so-called mass organizations participated. The device of the peace committees was used by the Communists to reach many individuals and groups who could not be reached through the more specialized organizations such as labor unions, youth and student groups, and the Women's Alliance. It was in this field that the Communists were most successful in capitalizing upon the idealism and naïveté of many non-Communist "progressives."

While many well-meaning individuals of various political viewpoints participated in the peace activities, the controlling positions were held by Communists and fellow-travellers who saw that the directives of the Communist-dominated international organizations were faithfully implemented. The importance of this campaign to the Communists can be seen from the fact that the Cominform gave it precedence over all similar activities.[4]

---

[4] "Resolution of the Information Bureau of the Communist Parties," *For a Lasting Peace, for a Peoples' Democracy,* November 29, 1949, p. 1.

1949-1951. The peace movement in Guatemala made little headway before mid-1951. In April, 1949, Gutiérrez and Fortuny represented the CTG and the PAR at the Paris meeting of the World Congress of Partisans of the Peace and along with Pinto Usaga attended the Second Congress of the WFTU in Milan, a meeting at which the peace campaign was given heavy play.[5] Although a number of Guatemalans, including Fortuny and Francisco Hernández, attended the Continental Peace Congress in Mexico City, the PAR refused to send an official delegation.[6] A National Peace Committee was founded in 1950 by Fortuny, Solórzano, and other Communist intellectuals. Efforts to convince labor organizations and political parties that the peace campaign was important to Guatemala aroused little popular interest.[7]

In 1951 the CNP was reorganized and stepped up its activities. With the pro-Communist intellectual Luis Cardoza y Aragón as President, and the Communists Alfonso Solórzano, Marco Antonio Blanco, and Mario Silva Jonama as Secretary General, Secretary of Organization, and Secretary of Relations respectively, the CNP undertook a campaign to obtain signatures on a petition demanding a peace pact among the five great powers, including Communist China. As the movement had not yet developed a real popular following, the burden of the campaign fell upon the labor unions.[8] On April 27 a major peace rally was held in Guatemala City with Solórzano, Gutiérrez and Guerra Borges among the speakers.[9] A National Youth Committee for Peace was set up under the leadership of Communist Hugo Barrios Klee to sponsor Guate-

---

[5] 8019:113-9 or 8039:436-442, "Informe del delegado del STEG al Congreso Mundial de Partidarios de la Paz," May 1949; 8024:167-175, notes of Manuel Pinto Usaga dated July 4 from Milan and July 12 from Rome.

[6] 8019:120-3, Resoluciones generales del Congreso Continental por la Paz, November 1949; 8050:1200, credential of José Manuel Fortuny as delegate to the Congreso Continental por la Paz.

[7] 8025:1637-9, April 27, 1950; Document 322: Gutiérrez to National Executive Committee of the PAR, September 18, 1950, Y-X-1:645, Gutiérrez to Executive Committee of the FSG, September 18, 1950.

[8] 8024:9, La Lucha por la Paz: una tarea de honor, CTG circular of March 30, 1951; Y-20 or Y-21: Gran Campaña de la CTG en favor de la Paz en apoyo del Comité Nacional de los Partidarios de la Paz de Guatemala, March 30, 1951; 8031:1431, Circular de la Secretaría de la Paz en el Comité Central Pro 1° de Mayo; 8014:105, CPCUTG circular of June 28, 1951.

[9] Document Y-10: Handbill of peace rally.

malan representation at the Third World Festival of Youth and Students for Peace which met in Berlin.[10]

1952. This was a year of great activity for the peace movement in Guatemala. In March the American Continental Congress for Peace in Montevideo was attended by Communists Raúl Leiva and O. E. Palma along with Haydeé Godoy and Castillo Flores.[11] This meeting stressed germ warfare charges against the United States; in Guatemala the Communists operating through the CNP showed a germ warfare picture and spread these charges throughout the country.[12] Soon after the first of the year a call was issued for the First National Assembly for Peace. The actual work of organizing the assembly was in the hands of a preparatory committee whose officers were all Communists.[13] Much of the burden of propagandizing and of making the assembly a success fell upon the shoulders of the labor movement, which by then had been unified under Communist leadership.[14]

The assembly convened on May 23 and listened to a report from the preparatory committee which followed the international Communist line in stressing that the "Fascist" North Americans were the aggressors in Korea and had unleashed the horrors of germ warfare against the innocent people of that country. This warlike behavior was pictured as a natural and inevitable result of monopoly capitalism which threatened to involve the entire world in the horrors of atomic and bacteriologic warfare. Only the concerted action of the peoples of

---

[10] 8033:225, Adán H. Morales to César Montenegro P., June 12, 1951; Document 971: Hugo Barrios Klee to Víctor Manuel Gutiérrez, November 21, 1951; 8014:1157, handbill for peace rally.

[11] Document Y-444: Conferencia Continental Americana por la Paz, April, 1952.

[12] 8029:581, permit from governor of Guatemala to show the film and carry out meetings on this subject, September 26, 1952.

[13] Y-X-1:1685, Llamamiento a Una Asamblea Nacional por la Paz, February, 1952.

[14] See 8014:1382-3 and 1414-1418 for the coordination of the CGTG's efforts with the work of the preparatory committee. Also Document 562: Hugo Barrios Klee to Aristeo Sosa h., April 14, 1952; Document 565: Aristeo Sosa h. and Rolando Calderón B. to Hugo Barrios Klee, April 17, 1952; Document 854: Hugo Barrios Klee to Leonardo Castillo Flores, April 14, 1952; Document 585: Wenceslao Cordón y Cordón to Secretary General of SAMF, May 13, 1952.

the world in support of the Soviet Union's peace policy could curb the greedy imperialists and prevent this disaster.[15] The resolutions called for the affiliation of the National Peace Committee with the Communist-dominated World Peace Council and condemned United States foreign policy as a threat to world peace. This support of Soviet foreign policy was immersed in a sea of pious platitudes concerning "the spirit of cooperation and understanding among all the peoples of the world" and a description of the horrors of atomic war in such a manner that many of the Guatemalans were unable to discern any bias or propagandistic intent. Indeed, a majority of those who were drawn into the work of the peace movement were not sufficiently informed on world affairs nor politically sophisticated enough to realize that there was another side to the story. The workers seemed willing to accept as the truth whatever their highly respected leader Gutiérrez had to say on the subject.

With the CNP safely in Communist hands—Palma was Secretary General, Blanco was Secretary of Organization and Alvarado Jérez was Secretary of Relations—participation in international activities was accelerated. The highlights of the year's activity were the Peace Conference of the Asian and Pacific Regions, which met in Peking in October, and the Vienna Congress of Peoples for Peace in December. Silva Jonama attended the preparatory meeting of the Asian Conference in July, going and returning by way of Moscow. Others to go to Peking were the Communist leaders Cardoza and Alvarado Jérez, labor leader Víctor A. Leal, Carmen Morán of the Women's Alliance (AFG) and newspaperman Francisco Galicia.[16]

1953. In this year the tempo of the peace campaign in Guatemala reached a new high. With Silva Jonama as Secretary General, Palma as Secretary of Propaganda, Leiva as Press Secretary, and Alvarado Jérez as Secretary of Relations, the Communists were able to handle the CNP virtually as an organ of the PGT. As part of the CNP's plan for greatly intensified efforts, peace committees were organized on the departmental level. The First Assembly of Peace for the Department of Guatemala met July 3-5 and was used to introduce the World Peace

---

[15] 8039:430-5, Informe del Comité Preparatorio a la Asamblea Nacional por la Paz, May 24, 1952.
[16] 8002:1877; Y-X-3:4237; Y-X-3:3933-5; 8002:2037.

Council's new campaign to collect signatures on a petition demanding negotiations among the great powers.[17]

Organized labor climaxed its participation in the peace movement by holding a National Assembly of Unions in Defense of Peace which met in the capital on July 25.[18] To gain the support of the rank and file, the peace campaign was linked to the theme of national sovereignty. The workers were told that the failure of the campaign for negotiations might enable the United States to turn Guatemala into another Korea. Peace, anti-imperialism, national sovereignty and anti-interventionism were tied together and the United States pictured as the fly in the ointment.[19] According to the chief speaker, Víctor A. Leal, only the fascists and criminals who wished to plunge the world into war for their own selfish gains were opposed to the peace campaign. American capitalists were pictured as placing their huge profits above the welfare of humanity and willing to unleash the horrors of germ warfare upon the "inferior" peoples of Asia, Africa and Latin America.[20]

The Campaign for Negotiations. The last major effort of the peace movement was to collect signatures on a petition calling for negotiations among the great powers. The revolutionary parties, labor unions, and front organizations all participated, and competition was established on the Communist pattern of "socialist emulation."[21] The cam-

---

[17] Document Y-14, 8013:505-7, 8013:508-510, 8039:591-3, Y-X-1:1054-6 or Y-X-5:465-7, Resoluciones de la Cuarta Plenaria del Comité Nacional de la Paz, February 14, 1953; Document Y-11, Document Y-229, 8013:465-9 or 8032:2516-9, Report by Alvarado Jérez in the name of the CNP; Document 1050: Sugerencias a las Comisiones; Document 1053: Sugerencias para el Trabajo de las Comisiones; Document Y-230: CNP reproduction of the Llamamiento del Consejo Mundial por la Paz.

[18] See Document 404: Una Nueva Campaña para Alcanzar la Paz; Y-X-5: 1261, CGTG circular of December 2, 1952; 8024:426, Plan de Trabajo para la realización de la Asamblea Nacional de los Sindicatos en Defensa de la Paz, June 26, 1953; Y-X-1:1048, CGTG circular of July 1, 1953; 8005: 2033, 8013:242 or Y-X-1:1049, Llamamiento para la Asamblea Nacional de los Sindicatos por la Paz, July 2, 1953.

[19] 8024:535-7, memorandum of Víctor A. Leal, July 19, 1953.

[20] For Leal's report see Document 1511, 8013:350-7, 8024:1176-83, 8039: 459-466, Y-X-1:1327-1334, Y-X-1:1251-8, or Y-X-5:1087-1094, August 1953.

[21] See Document 967: Circular from Jean Laffitte, July 1, 1953; 8005: 2392, *PAZ: Boletín Quincenal del Comité de la Paz del Departamento de Guatemala*, No. 1, August 19, 1953; 8005:2396, Augusto Cazali Avila circular, August 24, 1953; 8051:2354-6, PAR circular.

paign, which opened on September 19 and closed five months later, was termed "the Guatemalan Pronouncement in Favor of Negotiations and National Sovereignty" in order to take advantage of nationalist sentiment. It is doubtful if many of the illiterate campesinos who put their thumbprints to the petitions were aware that they were doing any more than express their support of the sovereignty of Guatemala. Nevertheless the 175,974 signatures obtained marked a considerable achievement in a country the size of Guatemala.[22] In their report to the President, the CNP interpreted the results of the campaign as an endorsement of his policies.[23]

Conclusion. While the control of this movement was in the hands of the Communists, they were able to disguise the Communist orientation of its work from the masses and to obtain the participation of individuals who might have hesitated at openly serving the interests of international Communism. Particularly in the earlier years, the Communists in the peace movement appeared in their guise of labor, youth and student leaders. In this respect the cooperation of the leaders of other revolutionary parties and the support of the government were useful in masking the Communist orientation of the movement from the masses. Many people accepted the repeated claim of the leaders that the campaign was part of a world-wide humanitarian drive and were unaware of its political ends and international implications. In particular Gutiérrez was able to shape the views of many of the Guatemalan workers.[24]

YOUTH, STUDENTS AND WOMEN'S GROUPS

One of the primary target groups for the Communists in Guatemala, as elsewhere, was the younger generation. As the majority of the Communist leaders in Guatemala were in their 20's and early 30's and had

[22] For the variety of methods used to collect these signatures see Document 936 or 8052:3708-9; for other material on the campaign see Y-X-3:4008; 8050:373-4; Document 149; Document Y-95; 8039:974.

[23] 8051:1847-50, letter CNP to President, March 9, 1954; Comunicado del Comité Nacional de la Paz, March 2, 1954; Declaración de las organizaciones y entidades participantes en la recogida de firmas por las negociaciones y la soberanía de Guatemala.

[24] See 8039:590, Gustavo A. Aguilar to Víctor Manuel Gutiérrez, February 15, 1954, in which he requests a copy of Gutiérrez's "En la Unión Soviética, Capital de la Paz."

only recently become Communist militants themselves, they were particularly adept at proselyting and propagandizing among the generation which was coming of age during the revolution. Attuned to the needs, motivations, aspirations and frustrations of the middle class and working class youth, the Communists soon gained control of a number of active and useful organizations among the youth and students of Guatemala.

Alianza de la Juventud Democrática Guatemalteca (AJDG). The AJDG was founded on December 21, 1947, as an affiliate of the World Federation of Democratic Youth.[25] Since the Communists in Guatemala had not yet come into the open, and the international parent group did not split over cold war issues until 1949, the AJDG was able to operate under the guise of a non-political youth group and built up a considerable following among the young revolutionaries. The leadership came from the group of young *Paristas* who were followers of Fortuny and had recently joined the clandestine Communist Party (VDG). Among the early officers of the AJDG were Bernardo Alvarado Monzón, Carlos René Valle, Mario Silva Jonama, Huberto Alvarado, Octavio Reyes, Edelberto Torres and Carlos Manuel Pellecer—all future leaders of the PGT.[26] Through close connections with the CTG some working class youth were brought into the organization, which in its early days was predominantly made up of students and intellectuals.[27] In September 1948 Pellecer represented the AJDG at the Congress of Working Youth in Warsaw.[28]

By the middle of 1949 the AJDG had grown to nearly 3500 members. While ostensibly still a nonsectarian organization working to further the legitimate interests of the middle and lower class youth, the AJDG assumed the task of raising the political level of the Guatemalan youth and particularly of the incipient proletariat.[29] Edelberto Torres and Huberto Alvarado occupied the post of Secretary General,

---

[25] See Y-X-1:1267-8, Llamamiento a la Juventud de América, March 31, 1947, for the initiative in Latin America.

[26] See 8039:98 and 8039:100; credentials as founding members of the Consultative Committee of the AJDG, April 18, 1948.

[27] See 8024:1226-8, Manifiesto en el Primer Aniversario de Fundación de la AJDG, December 21, 1948; Document 1301: Enrique Adolfo Rodríguez J. to Secretary General of CTG, April 14, 1948.

[28] Y-X-2:3387, AJDG circular, November 15, 1948.

[29] Document Y-317: Situación y organismo de la juventud de Guatemala, report of the Secretary General of the AJDG, June, 1949.

and Carlos René Valle was Secretary of Organization during the 1949-1950 period, giving the young Communists complete control of the organization. Cooperating closely with the Communist-controlled labor organizations, the AJDG served as a base for the Communists' operations in the period between their withdrawal from the PAR and acceptance as a legal party.

In an attempt to strengthen its organization and to prepare to play the role assigned to it by the Communists as a "mass organization," the AJDG held its first congress in March of 1951. Now that the Communist Party was free to operate in the open, the AJDG was to serve as a point of contact between the Communists and the youth of the country rather than as an organization monopolized by the Communists.[30] A National Committee for the Berlin Festival was established under the leadership of Octavio Reyes to arrange sending a Guatemalan delegation to the Third World Festival of Youth and Students for Peace, a rally sponsored by the Communist-dominated World Federation of Democratic Youth and International Union of Students.[31] The six Guatemalan delegates included five Communist leaders—Huberto Alvarado, Edeleberto Torres, Hugo Barrios Klee, Octavio Reyes and Elena Chávez—who returned from the conference and a tour of the Communist countries to propagandize the Communist line at a public rally sponsored by the newly-established National Youth Committee for Peace.[32]

In February 1953 the AJDG sponsored the First National Conference for the Defense of the Rights of Youth. To mask its Communist inspiration, the call was first issued by the newly-established Railroaders' Youth headed by the Communist Armando Villaseñor.[33] Gutiérrez and

---

[30] This development has been fully discussed in our treatment of the Youth Commission of the Communist Party. See 8021:145-150, Sobre el trabajo de la Juventud, draft from the papers of Fortuny; also Document 2082 or 8039:688-693, Partido Comunista de Guatemala: Puntos de vista acerca de la organización de la Juventud, April 1951.

[31] Document 1303: Octavio Reyes to Víctor Manuel Gutiérrez, May 12, 1951.

[32] See *Octubre*, November 15, 1951; Document Y-12: handbill of the Comité Nacional del Festival de Berlín; Document 971: Hugo Barrios Klee to Secretary General of the CGTG, November 21, 1951; 8014:1955, Huberto Alvarado to Secretary General of CGTG Youth, November 8, 1951; 8014:1157, handbill announcing public meeting on November 22.

[33] 8002:2074, Llamamiento de la Juventud Ferrocarrilera para una Conferencia de Defensa de los Derechos de la Juventud; 8002:2073, Huberto

the CGTG closely cooperated with the conference, since one of its major aims was to bring the youth of the working class into the activities of the AJDG.[34] Two delegates were sent to the First International Conference for the Defense of the Rights of Youth held in Vienna the next month.[35]

Frente Universitario Democrático (FUD). Since the Communists were unable to capture control of the Association of University Students (AEU) and were faced by the challenge of the growing Committee of Anti-Communist University Students (CEUA), they founded the FUD in order to give organized support to the Marxist current in the National University.[36] Augusto Cazali Avila and Ricardo Ramírez served as Secretary General, while their fellow Communists Edelberto Torres, Luis Morales Chua, and Otto Peñate were among the most active members of the FUD. Its activities were chiefly associated with the theme of "defense of national sovereignty."[37] On May 11 it took the initiative in the formation of the Youth Committee Against Intervention, which sponsored rallies in support of the Arbenz regime.[38]

Confederación de Estudiantes de Post-Primaria (CEPP). Under the leadership of Communists Otto Peñate and Julio René Estevez, sec-

Alvarado (AJDG), Augusto Cazali (FUD), Otto Peñate (CEPP) and Armando Villaseñor (CJF) to CGTG, November 6, 1952.

[34] See 8016:729, Augusto Cazali Avila to Secretary General of CGTG, November 28, 1952; 8016:730, Gutiérrez to Augusto Cazali, December 2, 1952; 8016:725, Ricardo A. Ramírez to Gutiérrez, December 1, 1952; 8016:865, Ricardo Ramírez to Secretary General of CGTG, December 9, 1952; 8003:755; 8003:64; 8003:490; 8003:755.

[35] 8003:73, R. Knaak to Gutiérrez, January 12, 1953; 8003:680, R. Knaak to CGTG, March 9, 1953; 8003:681, Alberto Cardoza to R. Knaak, March 23, 1953.

[36] 8014:1049, Hugo Barrios Klee, Secretario Coordinador to SG of CGTG, December 14, 1951; 1050, Hugo Barrios Klee to Secretary General of CGTG, December 12, 1951.

[37] 8001:237, Augusto Cazali Avila to VMG, April 23, 1953; 8001:871, Carlos Menéndez h. to Secretary General of CGTG, June 26, 1952; 8005:2021, Ricardo A. Ramírez to Víctor Manuel Gutiérrez, July 13, 1953; 8003:939-40 or Y-X-1:1032-3, FUD circular to various revolutionary groups, February 2, 1954; 8051:1821-35, Manifiesto del Frente Universitario Democrático, sobre Décima Conferencia Interamericana.

[38] Document 1580: Raúl Santacruz Morales to Secretary General of Sindicato de Trabajadores del Instituto Guatemalteco de Seguridad Social, March 14, 1954.

ondary school students were organized into the CEPP, which functioned as a little brother of the FUD.

Grupo Saker-Ti of Young Artists and Writers. This group of young radical intellectuals, founded at the beginning of 1947, served as a focus of efforts to create a new "revolutionary" art and literature. (Saker-Ti is the Indian word for the dawn.) By 1953 it was headed by such Communists as Huberto Alvarado, Otto Raúl González, Raúl Leiva, Augusto Cazali and Melvin René Barahona. In addition to bringing the arts into the ideological harness of Communism, the group sponsored such political activities as the Committee of Friends of the Cuban People, an organization founded to aid the Cuban Communists, and participated in many pro-Communist activities sponsored by other front groups.[39]

Youth Activities in the Last Half of 1953. The climax of international activity for the Guatemalan youth groups came in the summer of 1953. The several youth groups sent three delegates to the Third World Congress of Youth (Bucharest, July 16-31), eight to the Fourth World Festival of Youth and Students for Peace (Bucharest, August 2-16), and eleven to the Third World Congress for Students (Warsaw, August 27-September 3). The delegation, which included six young Communist leaders, toured the U.S.S.R. and Communist China before returning home.[40]

Fiesta de la Amistad. The major activity of all youth groups in late 1953 and 1954 was the Festival of Friendship of the Youth of Central America and the Caribbean, which was to be held in Guatemala in December 1954. The initiative for this came from the international youth and student organizations, and the moving spirits were the Guatemalan delegates to the Bucharest and Warsaw gatherings. At

---

[39] See Document Y-40: Huberto Alvarado to Leonardo Castillo Flores, August 6, 1953. The Communist leaning of the group can be seen in their publications, particularly "Por un Arte Nacional, Democrático y Realista" by Huberto Alvarado in the name of the Executive Committee, October 31, 1953.

[40] See 8013:171-2, Circular of Comité Guatemalteco pro IV Festival Mundial de Juventud, May, 1953; Document 941: Circular of Comité Guatemalteco pro IV Festival Mundial de Juventud; *Octubre,* May 28, 1953; *Tribuna Popular,* September 5, 1953.

the end of 1953 these individuals formed an Organizing Committee of the First National Festival of Youth and Students headed by PGT youth leader Hugo Barrios Klee.[41] Rallies were held, departmental committees were set up, and a national festival was held on February 21 at the rural normal school "La Alameda" in Chimaltenango.[42]

Left-wing figures readily lent their support to the project for the international rally, and financial support came from the PGT and the government.[43] The festival was to last from December 5th through the 12th and to have 500 delegates from other countries as well as over 3000 from Guatemala. The President's wife contributed to the festival by pledging the aid of government departments to furnish lodgings and guaranteeing the cooperation of the Guatemalan Embassies abroad. The Organizing Committee was enlarged to include delegates from other Latin American countries and from the international Communist-dominated youth organization. The strategic positions on the various commissions were held by such Communist leaders as Hugo Barrios Klee, Virgilio Guerra, Otto Raúl González, Huberto Alvarado, José Luis Ramos, Bernardo Lemus, Luis Morales Chua and Ricardo Ramírez; however, efforts were made to bring the youth of all the "revolutionary" organizations into the work of the Festival.[44]

Alianza Femenina Guatemalteca (AFG). Founded in 1947, this women's organization was affiliated with the Communist-controlled International Federation of Democratic Women and was led and directed by members of the Communist Party. In 1954 Secretary General Dora Franco y Franco, Secretary of Organization Irma Chávez

[41] Document 223: Hugo Barrios Klee to Leonardo Castillo Flores, February 15, 1954.

[42] Document 1930: manifesto of Quezaltenango Comité Departamental Pro-Festival de la Juventud, November 30, 1953; letter of Hugo Barrios Klee to youth leaders, November 7, 1953 found in files of Chimaltenango PGT headquarters; *Tribuna Popular,* January 6, 1954.

[43] See Document Y-121: handbill of the Comité Internacional Preparatorio de la Fiesta de la Amistad, March 31, 1954; Document Y-98: Hugo Barrios Klee to PGT Secretary of Finance, April 19, 1954; Document Y-15: Programa de la Fiesta de la Amistad de la Juventud Centroamericana y del Caribe y estimación de gastos que puedan hacerse; Document 355: Hugo Barrios Klee to María Vilanova de Arbenz, June 15, 1954.

[44] Document 830: list of commissions of the Comité Organizador de la Fiesta de la Amistad de la Juventud Centro Americana y del Caribe, **April, 1954.**

de Alvarado, Secretary of Propaganda Elsa Castañeda de Guerra Borges, Secretary of Finance María Jerez de Fortuny, Secretary of Communications Laura de Piñeda, and Secretary of Labor Matters Concepción Castro de Mencos were all prominent Communists. Most of these officers were either members of the Feminine Commission of the Central Committee of the PGT or wives of PGT leaders.[45]

Originally the AFG, as did the other front groups, posed as non-political, nonsectarian and interested primarily in the problems of women and the betterment of society. This initial stress upon recognized and legitimate objectives served to facilitate the task of recruitment and growth.[46] The AFG leadership soon began efforts to develop a political consciousness among the members and to "inform" them on national and international affairs. During the presidential campaign of 1950 the AFG stepped into politics, using as justification the claim that only the victory of Arbenz would insure the preservation of the political gains made by women since 1944.[47] At the same time its publications began to laud the U.S.S.R., China and the Peoples' Democracies and to denounce the "warlike designs of the North American imperialists."[48] On the international front the AFG was represented at the Second Interamerican Congress of Women and Peace, the Peking and Vienna Peace Congresses of 1952 and at the World Congress of Women in Copenhagen in the fall of 1953.[49]

In November 1953 the AFG held its First National Congress.[50] For the Communists, the purpose of this meeting was to bring the AFG into line with its projected role as one of the mass organizations which would enable the party to come into closer contact with the people.[51]

---

[45] For the leadership of the AFG see Document 415: Aliancistas, April 5, 1950; Document 1640: Planilla que propone el Presidium para integrar el Consejo Nacional de Alianza Femenina Guatemalteca.

[46] See Y-X-2:3027-53 and 3132-56 for the First National Congress on the Defense of Infancy held on December 12-15, 1951.

[47] Llamamiento a las Mujeres de Guatemala, AFG, 1950.

[48] *Mujeres*, June 20, 1950; Document Y-328: *Tina Modotti: Suplemento de Mujeres, vocero de Alianza Femenina Guatemalteca*, Año I, No. 1, June 20, 1950; 8039:20-24, Informe de la Secretaría General de AFG.

[49] Document 942: "El Segundo Congreso Interamericano de Mujeres y la Paz" by Hortensia Hernández Rojas, November 5, 1951; 8002:2038; AFG circular of October, 1952.

[50] Y-X-3:3409 or 8024:542, Temario del Primer Congreso Nacional de Alianza Femenina Guatemalteca, November 26, 1953.

[51] 8006:3700-1, Comisión Femenina del Comité Central del PGT.

The AFG, which had been essentially a middle class organization centered in Guatemala City, had recently carried on extensive organizational efforts in Escuintla and Santa Rosa among the agricultural workers. Together with the many women members from the textile industry, these new recruits were to give the AFG the mass base and more representative character which was considered necessary as preparation for the establishment of the united front of the masses.[52]

PROPAGANDA CAMPAIGNS

Guatemalan Reaction to the Death of Stalin. When Stalin died on March 5, 1953, the Guatemalan Communists strove to convert it into a virtual national day of mourning. The CGTG immediately sent out a circular lauding Stalin and calling upon member unions to send messages of condolence to the Soviet people.[53] The messages sent in the name of Guatemalan unions waxed even more eloquent in their praise of Stalin and the U.S.S.R.[54] The PGT published a special edition of *Octubre* on March 12 dedicated to the praise of Stalin. At a meeting in honor of Stalin which was held on the 14th at the Central Normal Institute for Girls, the leading political figures of the PAR, PRG and RN joined the Communists in singing the praises of the "immortal" Stalin and stood at attention while the Internacionale was played. The National Congress observed a minute of silence in honor of Stalin as fourteen PAR, ten PRG, and four RN deputies joined the Communists in according this honor to the leader of world Communism.[55]

Solidarity with the Korean and Viet Namese People. Following instructions from the Communist-dominated WFTU, in June 1952 the CGTG took the initiative in sponsoring a week dedicated to propagandizing the international Communist line on the Korean War. With the coop-

---

[52] 8018:34, Dora Franco y Franco to Federación de Textiles, May 31, 1954; 8018:75, Irma de Alvarado to Federación de Textiles, June 5, 1954.

[53] Document 468, 1523, 8013:538, 8013:539, 8024:91, or Y-X-1:1345, CGTG circular of March 6, 1953.

[54] Y-X-5:470, Comité Ejecutivo del Sindicato de Costureras de Guatemala to Consejo Central de los Sindicatos Soviéticos, March 12, 1953; also 8003:460, 461, 504, 506, 618, 622, 729, 736, 765 and 766; 8024:89; Y-X-2:3379.

[55] See *Octubre,* March 19, 1953.

eration of the various front groups, the week of June 22-28 was dedicated to the "second anniversary of the Yankee aggression and the heroic resistance of a heroic sister people."[56] The line taken by the Communists and their collaborators was that the imperialists would not hesitate to do in Guatemala what they had already done in Korea unless curbed by world public opinion.[57] When the armistice was signed in July 1953, the Communists treated it as a major victory for their peace campaign and held a series of mass rallies in Guatemala City.[58] With the end of the Korean War, Indo-China replaced Korea in the Communist propaganda scheme.[59]

"Save the Rosenbergs" Campaign. This propaganda effort, which lasted from November 1952 to June 1953, was designed primarily to build the Rosenbergs into martyrs by making it appear that they were condemned to die for their political beliefs. The propaganda which was disseminated through the labor unions, the revolutionary political parties, and the several front groups completely ignored the fact that they had committed acts of espionage and claimed that "Ethel and Julius Rosenberg have been falsely accused by the Fascist reaction in the United States with the end of sowing fear among the North American people who fight for peace and seek the immediate end of the war in Korea."[60] The CGTG and its affiliates were mobilized to send streams of protest messages to President Truman, while the Communists gave the campaign a heavy play in their press and twenty

[56] See 8001:74, 164,·265, 266, 566, 567 or Document 541, June 13, 1952; also Y-344: Manifiesto del Comité de Solidaridad con el Pueblo Coreano.

[57] See 8032:2088-9, Y-X-1:281-2, 1077-8, 1235-6 or 1241-2, CGTG circular of June 14, 1952; 8002:1126, Gutiérrez to Trygve Lie, June 27, 1952; Document 1906 is a message of sympathy from the CGTG to the President of North Korea, June 28, 1952.

[58] See Y-X-1:955, CGTG circular of July 30, 1953; 8004:1773, Gutiérrez to Antonio E. Santa Cruz, August 8, 1953; Document 860: Proyecto de mensaje al Presidente de la República, para firmarse en el acto de celebración del armisticio, July 31, 1953.

[59] See 8013:9, H. Jourdain to V. Manuel Gutiérrez, February 6, 1954; 8008:6228, memorandum of PAR Secretary of Organization, December 7, 1953; 8006:3993, Ernesto Carrillo O. to Víctor Manuel Gutiérrez, December 9, 1953; 8006:4079, Dora Franco y Franco to Gutiérrez, December 16, 1953; Y-X-3:4032, CGTG-CNCG circular of December 17, 1953; 8006: 4039, Campesino Federation of Sacatepequez Manifesto, December 19, 1953.

[60] Pamphlet sent on November 19, 1952 to the PRG.

members of Congress signed a letter of protest.[61] On the eve of the execution the full array of front organizations joined in a protest to the United States Ambassador.[62] A year later the Communists were still exploiting the Rosenbergs as martyrs for the cause of peace.[63]

Social Security Assemblies: Communist Propaganda Platforms. The Communists were constantly looking for opportunities to disseminate their propaganda in such a manner that it would not appear to be coming from the party. In addition to gaining a hearing from those who might be suspicious of views coming from the Communist Party, this propaganda, apparently originating from independent and non-political source, would break the ice for future Communist proposals. One of the smoothest of these operations was developed around the theme of social security, a subject which had broad appeal to the workers and middle class white-collar groups.

The First National Assembly of Social Security which was held in Guatemala City on November 7, 8 and 9, 1952 was designed to pave the way for Guatemalan participation at an international conference. While the conference was ostensibly sponsored by the CGTG, its course was planned by a commission of the Communist Party composed of Gutiérrez, Fortuny and Ramos.[64] Behind a facade of proposals to improve social security in Guatemala, approval was obtained to send the Communist labor leader Natzul Aguirre Cook and Marco Cuellar Lorenzana of the CGTG to Vienna for the international meeting sponsored by the WFTU. The Communists also succeeded in getting the assembly to approve a resolution linking social security to the number-one propaganda theme of international Communism, the "peace" campaign.

Upon the return of the Guatemalan delegates to the International Conference for the Defense, Improvement, and Extension of Social

---

[61] See 8002:2192; 8002:399-400; 8003:759; 8005:2737; 8016:768; 8016:1185; 8016:1023; 8026:166; 8026:218; 8032:2381; Y-X-1:865; Y-X-2:2084; *Octubre,* December 4, 1952, December 10, 1952, and January 30, 1953.

[62] Y-X-2:2075, June 16, 1953; also *Octubre* June 4, 1953; 8013:261 or 262, CGTG circular of June 27, 1953; 8004:1767; Y-X-5:472.

[63] Y-X-5:1077-9, speech of Concepción Castro de Mencos to a meeting of the AFG, March 6, 1954.

[64] See Document 951: series of notes on meetings of PCG Political Commission in November, 1952.

Insurance and Social Security, held in Vienna on March 2-6, 1953, a second meeting was called in Guatemala City. This Extraordinary Assembly on Social Security met on the 27th and 28th of June and, under the leadership of Gutiérrez, accepted the Communist-inspired line of the international meeting.[65] According to this propaganda, social security in the capitalist world had been neglected in favor of the economic burden of rearmament. Only in the Communist countries were the interests of the workers protected by an adequate system of social security. Unaware of the realities of the situation, most Guatemalans believed that the Vienna meeting had been representative of the peoples of the world, while in reality at least 17 of the 27 members of the presidium had been Communists and the conference followed a course charted in advance by the Communist leadership of the WFTU.

Conference Against the High Cost of Living. In conjunction with the campaign undertaken by the Communist press, the CGTG and other so-called mass organizations sponsored a Conference Against the High Cost of Living, Rent and Unemployment. This activity had the three-fold purpose of creating discontent against the capitalists and middlemen of Guatemala, linking these problems to the international policy of the United States, and helping the Communists appear as the champions of the interests of the people. The Communists, who were upset by the fact that organizations of the unemployed and victims of high rents had been formed by non-Communists, were determined to regain the initiative and establish a monopoly on the role of champions of the underdogs.[66] Behind a facade of "representatives" of the various mass organizations and a "presidium of honor" composed of public figures willing to lend their prestige, the Communists dominated the conference with Gutiérrez as Secretary General and Virgilio Guerra as Secretary of Organization.[67]

In the materials circulated by this committee and in the accompanying publicity campaign, the commercial treaties with the United States,

---

[65] See Document Y-30 or Y-X-1:1200-1227, pamphlet of the major documents of the meeting printed and distributed by the Sindicato de Trabajadores del Instituto Guatemalteco de Seguridad Social.

[66] See 8013:247-8 or 8024:1437-8, circular of CGTG, June 13, 1951.

[67] See Document 723: Gutiérrez to members of Preparatory Committee of the Conference Against the High Cost of Living, July 21, 1953; 8005: 2192.

the U.S. corporations in Guatemala, the international policies of the warlike United States, and the Guatemalan middlemen were blamed as the factors responsible for the high cost of living.[68] The findings and resolutions of the conference, whose 350 delegates met on August 27-29, adhered to the Communist-inspired line of the preparatory committee and advocated policies which would have borne heavily upon the foreign corporations and native capitalists in Guatemala.[69] A permanent vigilance commission was set up with five Communists included among its twenty-three members. This was later replaced by a 9-member committee on which the Communists had a majority. Once again the Communists were able to take control of an originally broad-based organization.

League of Renters (Liga de Inquilinos). The Communists lost little time in taking over control of the movement of dissatisfied renters. While the Communist Deputies put themselves in the forefront of the battle for the Rent Control Law, Gutiérrez sponsored a meeting on August 22, 1953, at which the League of Renters of Guatemala was reconstituted with PGT leader Antonio Ardón at its head.[70] Although this move had been carefully planned within the party, in order to allay suspicions of the non-Communist members it was executed under the guise of fraternal aid from the CGTG.[71] Communist Deputy Cardoza was named to head the extraordinary Commission on Reforms of the Rent Control Law, and the Communists got credit for its passage.[72] While the law was before Congress, the Communists mobilized the renters to demonstrate in front of the Congress and packed the galleries

---

[68] Y-126 or Y-168: Llamamiento a la Conferencia Contra el Alto Costo de la Vida, July 27, 1953.

[69] See Resoluciones de la Conferencia Contra el Alto Costo de la Vida, August 29, 1953. A comparison with the resolutions on "Comercio y Transporte" of the Second Congress of the PCG shows a striking similarity.

[70] See Y-X-2:2164-5, Organizada la Liga de Inquilinos de Guatemala: magnífico éxito de la CGTG; Y-X-2:2162-3, Ante-proyecto de estatutos de la Liga de Inquilinos de Guatemala. For the role of the Communist press and Congressmen see *Octubre,* June 4, 1953, July 7, 1953 and August 13, 1953.

[71] See Document 659: Proposiciones para la reunión de la Liga de Inquilinos, a document presented by Gutiérrez for the approval of the PGT leadership.

[72] *Tribuna Popular,* October 13, 1953, October 14, 1953, and November 13, 1953.

with sympathizers.[73] After Communist control was consolidated, the organization was used as another mass organization of the party and its members called upon by their president, a PGT Central Committee member and Secretary General of its Departmental Committee, to participate in the various mass demonstrations organized by the Party.[74] At one such demonstration, the League mobilized 5000 demonstrators, a valuable addition to the ranks of the mass organizations.[75]

Unión de Compradores de Lotes. In their role of champions of the masses, the Communists missed no opportunity. When the purchasers of lots in the "colonies" on the outskirts of Guatemala City became dissatisfied, the Communists stepped in.[76] In line with the policy of stimulating the "class struggle," Communist Deputy Cardoza advised them to refuse to make further payments.[77] On December 19, 1953, a mass meeting was held and the Union was formally established with the Communists Justo Rufino Morales Chua and Bernardo Lemus at its head. Morales Chua informed his fellow members that only the PGT had their problems and interests at heart.[78]

May Day: From Labor Holiday to Communist Rally. During the Arbenz era the Communists succeeded in converting the May Day celebration into what was for all practical purposes a Communist rally. Control of the labor organizations put the Communists in a position of dominating the preparatory commission and determining the slogans and propaganda line for the celebrations. In addition to diffusing Communist propaganda and the pro-Soviet international line, the Communists utilized the May Day demonstrations to impress upon the government and the other political leaders the fact that they could control and mobilize the mass of workers. The Communist-dominated organizing committee would pass out to the workers banners and

---

[73] Y-370: CGTG circular of October 26, 1953.

[74] See Document 1396: Todos los inquilinos a la gran manifestación del día Viernes 18 de Junio.

[75] *Tribuna Popular,* April 28, 1954.

[76] See *Tribuna Popular,* September 26, 1953, September 30, 1953, and October 9, 1953.

[77] *Tribuna Popular,* November 1, 1953.

[78] *Tribuna Popular,* April 4, 1954.

placards which would endorse Communist policies and campaigns, thus making it appear to observers that the workers were solidly behind the PGT.

Communist exploitation of May Day in 1951 and 1952 was partially restrained by political considerations, but it still afforded them a major opportunity to spread pro-Soviet and anti-United States propaganda.[79] In 1953 the Communists had consolidated their position in Guatemala and were able to exploit May Day to the utmost.[80] The May Day Committee was securely in the hands of the Communists, who also had charge of organizing the demonstrations in the departments.[81] The international line for the propaganda was taken from the directives of the WFTU and blended with Guatemalan developments into a guide for speakers throughout the country.[82] The demonstrations were carefully planned in advance and accompanied by a large-scale propaganda campaign involving over a half million circulars and handbills. All the front groups were brought into the work and the President agreed to deliver a major address.[83] Denunciation of the Korean War, support of the Soviet Union's peace proposals, opposition to the plans for Western European defense, denunciation of ODECA and the demand for Guatemala's withdrawal, opposition to anti-Communism, and support of the various Communist propaganda campaigns were embodied in the May Day plans. The approved slogans for the demonstrations included the following:[84]

[79] Y-X-2:3013-9 or 8024:1442-8, Comité Nacional Pro Primero de Mayo to President Arbenz, May 1, 1951; Document 288, Y-X-1:161 or Y-X-3: 3774, circular of May Day Committee, April 2, 1952; Y-X-1:785-790 or 1668-1693, Intervención del C. Manuel Pinto Usaga, May 1, 1951; Y-X-4: 489, Max Salazar to Comisión de Propaganda del Comité Pro Primero de Mayo, April 17, 1952; Y-X-1:1085-7, Exposición de los trabajadores y campesinos de Guatemala al Presidente Constitucional, Coronel Jacobo Arbenz Guzmán, May 1, 1952.

[80] See *Octubre,* May 1, 7 and 14, 1953.

[81] 8013:477, CGTG circular, April 9, 1953; Document 285: Comisiones Pro Primero de Mayo a los Departamentos.

[82] See 8013:459-61, CGTG circular reproducing the Llamamiento de la Federación Sindical Mundial a los trabajadores y trabajadoras de todo el mundo en ocasión del Primero de Mayo de 1953; 8013:387 or Y-X-5:874, Guía para un discurso del Primero de Mayo.

[83] See 8013:472-6 or Y-X-1:1036-1041, Plan general de trabajo para la celebración del Primero de Mayo de 1953.

[84] Y-X-1:1034-5, Leyendas para cartelones para el Primero de Mayo.

We salute the propositions of Chou En-lai to put an end to the bloody Korean War. We demand that the UN and Eisenhower accept the proposals of Peoples' China for a prompt peace in Korea. For the diversification of the external market of Guatemala and commercial interchange with the Soviet Union and the countries of popular democracy. Imperialist hands off Guatemala. Liquidate with an iron hand the reactionary fifth column at the service of the imperialist companies. Crush the national traitors who ask for foreign intervention.

The efforts of the Communists on May Day 1954 dwarfed even those of the previous year, both in size and in the intensity of the Communist propaganda.[85] Nearly a million pieces of propaganda were printed and distributed in advance of the celebration and all the Communist-oriented mass organizations participated in the seventy-one May Day celebrations at the side of the organized workers.[86] The official line for the demonstrations was dictated by the Communists and emphasized the contrast between the existence of the workers in the capitalist world and the joyous life under Communism.[87] In addition to stressing the need to unite in the face of "imperialist intervention" and the "criminal aggressive intentions" of the United States, the official themes of the celebration included support of the "United Front of the Masses" and the other planks of the Communist program adopted at the two preceding meetings of the PGT's Central Committee.[88] The Communists claimed 70,000 participants in the demonstration in the capital, which was addressed by the President, Gutiérrez, and Castillo Flores. In his address the President thanked the workers for their support and assured them that:

We will increase our firmness and resolution to carry forward the Guatemalan Revolution, cost what it may cost, it will always

---

[85] For Communist control of the demonstrations see Documents 391 or 163; Y-X-2:1988, circulars of the Comité Central Pro Primero de Mayo, March 30, 1954; Document 1769: list of delegations to the departments, April 23, 1954; Y-155: list of delegations to the departments, March 31, 1954.

[86] See Document 624 or Y-X-5:1049-51, Plan general de trabajo del Comité Central Pro Primero de Mayo de 1954; Y-X-2:1985-6, Orden del desfile del Primero de Mayo.

[87] See Document 407, Y-X-1:1261-3 or 1680-2, Llamamiento para el Primero de Mayo, March 25, 1954.

[88] See Document 396 or 8024:1489-91, Plan general de trabajo para la preparación de la gran jornada del Primero de Mayo, March 16, 1954.

cost less than to bow our necks. We will triumph in the enterprise. No people has ever been defeated when they unite with determination and courage and present a united front to the enemy.

After denouncing the opposition as traitors and backing the Communist line on the imperialist threat to peace, Arbenz saluted the alliance of the workers and campesinos as the "indispensable condition for victory" and "the base for our triumph."[89]

Most of the front groups which we have discussed were primarily oriented toward the international scene and provided one of the chief linkages between the Guatemalan Communists and the international Communist movement. In the following chapter we shall examine other aspects of the relationship between developments in Guatemala and those in the international sphere.

---

[89] *Discurso del Presidente Jacobo Arbenz, en el Mitín del 1° de Mayo de 1954,* published in pamphlet form by the Secretaría de Propaganda y Divulgación de la Presidencia, Guatemala, 1954.

11

INTERNATIONAL ASPECTS OF GUATEMALAN COMMUNISM

In spite of the claims of the Arbenz government, Communism in Guatemala was not merely a domestic matter. The actions of the Guatemalan Communists were conditioned by the international situation and attuned to the aims of the world Communist movement directed and dominated by the Soviet Union. Guatemala played a definite and significant role in the plans of international Communism, particularly during the last year or eighteen months of the Arbenz regime. The leaders of world Communism exploited the Guatemalan situation to disrupt hemispheric unity, used Guatemala as a base for Communist operations in the Central American area, and presented that country as a model for the other Latin American Communists to copy. Above all, the international leaders attempted to use developments in Guatemala to picture the United States as an "imperialist" power. In this respect even the fall of the Arbenz-Communist regime served the propaganda interests of the Soviet Union and world Communism. Not only in Latin America, but throughout the Middle East,

North Africa and Asia as well, the Communist and nationalist press stressed the issue of "Yankee intervention."

In Latin America the Communists were able to play upon the apprehension concerning the "Colossus of the North" and to reopen old sores which even the "Good Neighbor" policy had never fully healed. Their aim was to stir up visions of a return by the United States to the policies of "dollar diplomacy" and the "big stick."

International connections of the Guatemalan Communists are important in yet another way. The various international Communist front organizations and particularly the World Federation of Trade Unions (WFTU) and Latin American Confederation of Workers (CTAL) were instrumental in the growth of Communist influence and the dissemination of pro-Soviet propaganda in Guatemala. Many Guatemalans accepted these organizations at face value and believed that they represented the views and aspirations of the working class masses throughout the world. By and large the Guatemalan workers did not realize that the WFTU and CTAL were dominated by the Soviet Union and its Communist allies. Nor did they realize that only those relatively few labor organizations in the free world which were controlled by the Communists were affiliated with these international labor bodies. (Frequently the Guatemalans even accepted the Communist leaders of small dissident labor groups in the United States, the United Kingdom, and Australia as the true spokesmen for the laboring masses of these countries.)

The pages which follow are intended to show the nature of the relationship of the Guatemalan Communists to the international Communist movement, the extent of Communist influence over the foreign policy of the Arbenz regime, and the degree to which this was felt by Guatemala's neighbors. While the treatment of this subject is intended to be suggestive rather than exhaustive, it should be sufficient to show that Communism in Guatemala was not entirely a native development nor exclusively the concern of the Guatemalans.

CONNECTION OF THE GUATEMALAN COMMUNISTS WITH THE INTERNATIONAL COMMUNIST MOVEMENT

One of the factors which contributed to the Communist success was that in the eyes of Guatemalan nationalists and workers the Communist leaders did not appear as instruments of an international movement. While the opposition exaggerated the degree of the Guatemalan Communists' dependence upon the Soviet Union, they were correct in holding that the PGT was an integral, if relatively minute, part of the world Communist movement. The Guatemalan Communists looked upon themselves as part of that movement, and their actions were at all times conditioned by the international situation. In addition to having close relations with the other Communist parties of Latin America and particularly those of their neighboring countries, they closely followed the international line as established by the Soviet Union. The international ties of the Communist Party were so apparent that even Arévalo, sympathetic as he may have been toward its doctrine, had to recognize that it contravened the constitutional ban on "parties of an international or foreign character."[1] From their words and actions it is apparent that the interests and aims of the international Communist movement and of the Soviet Union were given the highest priority.

During the 1952-54 period Guatemala played a not insignificant role in the plans of the Soviet Union and the international Communist movement which it controlled. Even before the problem of Communism in Guatemala came to a head in the last half of 1953, the Cominform journal, *For a Lasting Peace, for a Peoples' Democracy,* paid close attention to the Guatemalan Communist Party.[2] The primary role of Guatemala in the plans of the Soviet Union was as a showcase. The task of the Guatemalan Communists was to disrupt hemispheric unity, create a sore spot in the backyard of the United States, and aid in the penetration of the other Central American countries. As Communism was losing ground throughout the rest of Latin America during these years, Guatemala became the chief focus of Soviet hopes in the western hemisphere.

Ideological Subordination to the Soviet Union. The subordination of the Guatemalan Communists to the aims of the Soviet Union is apparent from the fact that one of the main tasks of the PGT was to propagandize the "truth" concerning the new society and life in

---

[1] See Chapter IV, p. 72.

[2] See the issues of January 25, 1952, February 22, 1952, April 4, 1952, July 17, 1952, February 6, 1953, and July 3, 1953.

the USSR while another was to refute the charges brought against Russia by the Western nations.[3] We have already seen how the decisions of the XIX Congress of the Communist Party of the USSR conditioned the work of the Second Congress of the PCG and determined the line taken by the party in the months which followed.[4] As exemplified by the question of "collective leadership," which we have already discussed, the Guatemalan party slavishly followed every twist and turn of the Kremlin's line.[5] Scarcely an issue of the party paper ever appeared without an article lauding Stalin and the "peaceful construction of Socialism in the USSR," as well as at least one article taken from a Soviet publication.

On the 34th anniversary of the Russian Revolution the circular sent out by the party described the USSR as an "illuminating torch," "invincible" and the "bulwark of peace." In rendering "homage to the Soviet Union," the Guatemalan Communists should include "among our principal tasks" the refutation of the "lies and calumnies" about the USSR.[6] Upon returning from their frequent trips to the USSR, the PGT leaders would publish laudatory articles and pamphlets upon what they saw in the "invincible" fatherland of the Socialist revolution. The Communist paper ran as regular features the "Review of the Soviet Press" and the "truth about the Soviet Union."

One of the clearest examples of the subordination of the Guatemalan Communists to the policy line of their "teacher," "guide" and "torch," the Communist Party of the USSR, can be seen at the II Congress of the PCG.[7] This was held shortly after the XIX Congress of the Russian party, and the documents of that meeting served as study materials for the delegates to the PCG Congress. *Octubre* published the speeches of Molotov, Malenkov, Stalin and Voroshilov.[8] Guerra Borges in his editorial comment upon the speech of Stalin

---

[3] See Chapter IV, p. 79.

[4] See Chapter IV, p. 77.

[5] On the case of Beria the Communist papers twisted and turned in an effort to show that Beria was a long-time imperialist spy. Shortly before, they had been giving prominent display to the words of that "grand leader of the Soviet people." See *Octubre,* November 22, 1952, and July 17, 1953, and *Tribuna Popular,* December 18, 1953.

[6] 8013:379-381. See also *Octubre,* November 8, 1951, November 6, 1952, and *Tribuna Popular,* November 7, 1953.

[7] See Chapter IV, pp. 77-79.

[8] *Octubre,* October 16, 23, and 30, 1952.

made it plain that the policy of the Guatemalan Communists would have to be adjusted to the new interpretations of Stalin with respect to the role of the bourgeoisie.[9] A week before the Congress opened, *Octubre* published several excerpts from Stalin's *Economic Problems of Socialism in the USSR* on the "deepening of the general crisis of the world capitalist system" and "the inevitability of wars among the capitalist countries." Guerra Borges required all party members as a duty to study these materials as an "invaluable source of experience, teachings and orientation," and to use them in arriving at a proper line for the Guatemalan party.[10] At the Congress itself Guerra Borges delivered an appeal to the members to study the work of the Communist Party of the USSR and particularly the words of Stalin as the torch to light their way to the eventual construction of a Communist society in Guatemala.[11]

> We will light our way with the inexhaustible teachings of this Congress and with the wise indications of comrade Stalin. We bear always in mind that the destinies of humanity are today indissolubly linked to the genius of Stalin.

Six months after the Congress, the report of Malenkov was still being studied by the cells in the outlying departments as "a duty as a true militant of the party of the working class."[12]

Contacts with Iron Curtain Countries. A majority of the leaders of the Guatemalan Communist Party had made one or more trips to the Soviet Union, and in most cases to China and the Peoples' Democracies as well. Pellecer had served in the Guatemalan Legation in Moscow during 1945 and travelled behind the Iron Curtain in the summer of 1949. Fortuny went to Moscow in the summer of 1949 and again from November 1953 to January 1954. Gutiérrez spent two and a half months in East Germany, Poland, and the USSR at the end of 1951 and the beginning of 1952, and returned to the USSR for six weeks in the fall of 1953. Silva Jonama and Cardoza travelled to Moscow and China twice in the summer of 1952. Central Committee member Virgilio Guerra was in Moscow for the Soviet labor congress

---

[9] *Octubre,* October 30, 1952.
[10] *Octubre,* December 4, 1952.
[11] *Octubre,* December 26, 1952.
[12] 8013:419, Circular a los Comités de Base del PGT en Escuintla, June 5, 1953.

in May 1954. José Luis Ramos, Oscar Edmundo Palma, Dora Franco y Franco, Otto Raúl González and many lesser Communists also visited the Soviet Union and the other Communist countries. In all, nearly 130 Guatemalans travelled to Communist countries during the Arbenz regime, 70 in 1953 alone.

Two related incidents testify to the degree of Soviet influence over the Guatemalan Communists. During Fortuny's trip behind the Iron Curtain in 1949, he was informed of the decision against backing agrarian reform in countries such as Guatemala.[13] Returning to Guatemala, Fortuny put this policy change into effect even at the cost of destroying the unity of the party. (See Chapter IV, p. 59.) At a meeting held in Berlin in November 1951, the Communist-controlled World Federation of Trade Unions (WFTU) reversed this line on agrarian reform. Immediately Fortuny and the Communist Party of Guatemala adopted agrarian reform as the key plank in their platform. (See Chapter IV, p. 73.)

In addition to the frequent and varied contacts provided through the World Federation of Trade Unions, its subsidiary organizations, the various international front organizations and visits by more than one hundred Guatemalan labor leaders and politicians to Communist bloc countries, a considerable amount of correspondence passed between Guatemalan organizations and individuals and their counterparts in Communist countries. Taken as a whole, this material sheds light upon the nature of the relationship between the Guatemalan Communist movement and that portion of the world which the Communists already governed. Cordiality and curiosity are the outstanding characteristics of this correspondence, and, if any one point emerges clearly, it is that the Guatemalan Communists looked upon these countries, particularly the U.S.S.R., as a guide and a model. For their part, the organizations in the Communist countries were eager to take advantage of this friendly disposition on the part of the Guatemalans.[14]

---

[13] A leading member of the agrarian reform commission of the Guatemalan congress told the author that Fortuny said to him: "It has been approved in Warsaw that advanced parties will never be in favor of agrarian reform in small Latin American countries, for it creates a small propertied middle class and castrates the revolutionary impulses of the masses."

[14] See Documents 1475: P. Vutov to Alfredo Guerra Borges, April 20, 1953; 1571: C. Petrov to Alfredo Guerra Borges, March 18, 1953; 1476: C. Petrov to Alfredo Guerra Borges, March 4, 1953; 1505, April 17, 1953; 1506, July 2, 1953; 1530; 8024:52-3, cable from Leipzig workers to Gutiérrez, June 23, 1954; 8024:724-6, European Labor Conference to Gutiérrez, June

Relations of the Communist leaders with the USSR were close, as evidenced by the trip of Virgilio Guerra as a "fraternal delegate" to the Second Congress of Soviet Trade Unions in 1954 and the invitation by the Soviet propaganda magazine *New Times* to Gutiérrez to write an article on the "Struggle of the Guatemalan people against the American Monopolies' Oppression."[15] Most of the correspondence with China concerned the magazine *China Reconstructs,* the Foreign Language Press and its magazine *Peoples' China,* and the All-Chinese Federation of Trade Unions, which sent a steady stream of pamphlets and other propaganda into Guatemala.[16] The government of Bulgaria, through the Committee of Friendship and Cultural Relations with the Exterior, kept up a steady flow of propaganda materials into Guatemala from June of 1952 until the fall of the Arbenz Government. Gutiérrez reciprocated by furnishing them with an ever-increasing list of names to which they should send their materials and by starting a reverse flow of Guatemalan materials to Sofia.[17] The Communist labor leaders maintained "fraternal" relations with the unions in all the Communist countries.[18]

21, 1954; 8024:647, cable from José Manuel Fortuny to Central Committee of the Communist Party of the Soviet Union, March 4, 1953; 8024:648, Central Committee of the PGT to Central Committee of the Communist Party of the Soviet Union, March 5, 1953; 8024:649, Central Committee of the PGT to the Central Committee of the Communist Party of Czechoslovakia, March 13, 1953.

[15] See 8007:5485, cable from Berezhkov to Gutiérrez, January 29, 1954; 8007:5486, Gutiérrez to Berezhkov, February 16, 1954; 8008:7137, V. Berezhkov to Víctor Manuel Gutiérrez, April 16, 1954; Document 1697: cable from N. Shvernik to Gutiérrez, April 28, 1954; Y-X-6:2202, cable from CGTG to Consejo Sindicatos Soviéticos, April 28, 1954; 8008:7478, Gutiérrez to Mihail Vasilievich Sirof, May 14, 1954.

[16] See Y-X-1:869, T. K. Cheng of Foreign Languages Press to Sindicato de Artes Gráficas, April 1, 1954; 8006:3193, All-China Federation of Trade Unions list of publications sent to Guatemala, August 19, 1953; 8003:455, 8005:2013, 8006:3156, Y-X-6:2207, correspondence of Gutiérrez with Li Ping of *China Reconstructs.*

[17] See 8009:91, R. Georgieva to Secretario de la Confederación General de Trabajadores de Guatemala, June 2, 1952; also 8009:92; 8016:625; 8009:5; 8002:2058; 8009:6; 8016:630; 8016:626; 8003:428; 8010:1896.

[18] Document 1703: cable from Conseil Central Syndicats Tchecoslovaques to Confederación de Trabajadores de Guatemala, April 30, 1954; 8032:2357, Timotei Seripnic to Aristeo Sosa h., March 26, 1952; also Documents 1702 and 1900; 8003:812, 8025:2058; 8003:852; 8007:5660; 8008:6445; 8014:1264-6.

Relations with Other Latin American Communist Parties. The Guatemalan Communists enjoyed close contact with their counterparts in the other Latin American countries. In the early years these parties advised and counseled the inexperienced Guatemalans; in the 1950's the roles were reversed.[19] The Chileans Virginia Bravo, Eduardo Hubner and César Godoy Urrutia were of particular help to the Guatemalan Communists from 1947 to 1950. Many of the leaders of Communism in the Central American republics spent most of this decade in Guatemala. A few including the Salvadorean Abel Cuenca, the Nicaraguan Manuel Pinto Usaga, and the Honduran Mario Sosa played important roles in Guatemalan politics without openly joining the PGT. Many others such as the Nicaraguan Edelberto Torres h. Salvadoreans Virgilio Guerra and Miguel Mármol or Dominican Juan Ducoudray were active within the PGT. Others devoted their efforts to plans concerning their own countries and formed such organizations as the Salvadorean Democratic Association (*Asociación Democrática Salvadoreña*), the Movement of Nicaraguan Partisans of Democracy (*Movimiento de Nicaraguenses Partidiarios de la Democracia*), and the Democratic Revolutionary Party of Honduras (*Partido Democrático Revolucionario Hondureño*). These groups and the Spanish Republican exiles formed the Democratic Front of American and Spanish Exiles (*Frente Democrático de Exilados Americanos y Españoles*).[20] A number of these exiles aided the Guatemalan Communist movement by their participation in various front organizations, teaching positions, and the governmental bureaucracy.

Cooperation between the PGT and the Communist parties of Mexico, El Salvador, Costa Rica and Cuba was particularly close.[21]

---

[19] Document 1657: Fortuny (?) to Blas Roca, December 18, 1947; Documents 1573: C. Godoy Urrutia to José H. Zamora, February 17, 1950; 1572: C. Godoy Urrutia to Rafael Tischler, February 17, 1950; 1465: Celso Nicolás Celano to Fortuny, January 16, 1950; 1488: Juan Marinello and Blas Roca to José Manuel Fortuny, January 14, 1952.

[20] See Documents 1731; 366; 1504; X-157; 8003:24; 8003:801; 8010:1626-7; 8010:1654-5; and *Tribuna Popular,* January 27, 1954.

[21] Documents 1256: Comisión Política del Comité Central del PCG to Dionosio Encinas, June 6, 1950; 986: J. Antonio Díaz to José Manuel Fortuny, August 20, 1950; 987: J. Antonio Díaz to José Manuel Fortuny, September 20, 1950; 1094: Mensaje Fraternal del Partido Vanguardia Popular de Costa Rica a los Comunistas de Guatemala, August 11, 1950; 1069: Galo González a los camaradas del Comité Central del Partido Comunista de Guatemala, November 2, 1950.

The leaders of these parties played an important role in mediating between the Gutiérrez and Fortuny factions during the 1949-1950 period. The Guatemalan Communists were also in constant communication with the other Communist parties of the hemisphere.[22]

INTERNATIONAL RELATIONS OF GUATEMALAN LABOR

The international connections of the labor movement are of the greatest importance in understanding the Communist pattern of operations in Guatemala. Foreign organizers were largely responsible for making the first converts to the Communist cause among Guatemalan labor leaders. The advice, experience and prestige of these international labor leaders greatly aided the young Guatemalan Marxists in their rise to control of organized labor. Before each labor congress or convention, representatives of the Communist-controlled CTAL came to Guatemala to advise and aid Gutiérrez and his associates. Communists such as the Chileans Virginia Bravo, César Godoy, Eduardo Hubner and Juan Vargas Puebla, or the Cubans Lázaro Peña, Blas Roca and Juan Marinello fanned the Marxist embers among the leaders of the STEG into life and helped the young Communist converts take control of that union as a base for extending their control over the entire labor movement.[23]

Until 1949 or even later, the only contact most of the Guatemalan Communist leaders had with the international Communist movement was through these labor leaders and organizations. During the Arbenz regime the labor movement served as a façade for Communist propaganda efforts and pro-Soviet activities. The instructions for these campaigns came chiefly through the World Federation of Trade Unions

[22] For the wide variety of Communist contacts in other countries see Document 1555: Lista de Direcciones de Organizaciones Revolucionarias; 269 or Y-X-3:4066-7, Lista de Organizaciones y Personas de Exterior de la República para el envío de correspondencia o periódicos; Document 807: Lista de direcciones donde se envía *Correo de Guatemala;* also Y-X-2:1732-6; Documents 599; 955; 1355; 1729; 576; 1131; 1080; 559; 6; 1598; 510; 517; 112; 1263; Y-449; 694; 172 and 173.

[23] For the role of these individuals see Documents 1297: FSG-CTG invitation to lectures by Hubner, October 1948; 1314: Manuel Eduardo Hubner to Víctor Manuel Gutiérrez, May 25, 1949; 1302: Lázaro Peña and José Morera to Secretary General of CTG, February 18, 1947; 1298: Lázaro Peña to V. Manuel Gutiérrez, February 12, 1948.

(WFTU) and the Latin American Confederation of Labor (CTAL) rather than through party channels.

Relations of Guatemalan Labor with the WFTU and CTAL. The pattern of relationships between these Communist-controlled international labor organizations and Guatemalan unions varied as the Guatemalan Communists and their labor organizations became stronger and more important. At first the Guatemalans were little brothers to be guided and helped by the CTAL and of only casual interest to the WFTU and its subsidiaries. With the coming of Arbenz to the Presidency and the unification of the labor movement under Communist control, the WFTU began to take notice of the Guatemalans. As the CTAL shrank in size and influence in the face of the challenge of the Inter-American Regional Labor Organization (ORIT), Guatemalan labor became of great importance to it. At the same time, the international Communist movement awoke to the full propaganda and strategic potentialities of the Guatemalan situation and Gutiérrez was elevated in 1953 to the Executive Council of the WFTU. As industrial federations replaced geographic divisions in the internal organization of the CGTG, they were affiliated with the corresponding "professional departments" of the WFTU. By 1954 many links tied Guatemalan labor to the Communist-controlled international labor movement.

The early contacts of the Guatemalan labor leaders with the CTAL and WFTU were important in shaping the course which the labor movement would follow. Due to the almost complete absence of trained and experienced labor organizers which faced Guatemala after the overthrow of the Ubico dictatorship, the way was open for labor leaders from other Latin American countries to step in and mold the newborn labor movement in their own image. Indeed, the services of such individuals were essential if the Guatemalan labor organizations were to get on their feet. Unfortunately, those persons who did move in to fill the vacuum were in most cases Communists. In addition to the many political exiles who flocked into Guatemala, the main organizational efforts and influence came from the CTAL and its leader, Vicente Lombardo Toledano. After the original organizational work, the CTAL served as an advisor and reservoir of experience upon which the Guatemalan leaders could call when in trouble. With the rise of Gutiérrez to the top of the CTG, the CTAL turned its attention to bringing about unity in the labor movement. The Chilean Communist Deputy Juan Vargas Puebla was sent by Lombardo Toledano to Guatemala in May 1946, and Lombardo Toledano himself made periodic visits.[24] Through the CTAL the CTG of Gutiérrez was brought into contact with the WFTU and its work.[25] By 1949 Guatemala was important enough in the thinking of the WFTU for it to pay the expenses of Gutiérrez and Pinto Usaga to the Second Congress of the WFTU in Milan,[26] where Gutiérrez delivered a short report and was elected to the Executive Committee as an alternate.[27]

As the Communists became more important in Guatemala, Guatemala in turn became more important to the CTAL and of considerably greater interest to the WFTU.[28] In November of 1950 Gutiérrez was called to Paris for a joint meeting of the CTAL Central Committee and the high command of the WFTU to consider the labor situation in Latin America.[29] He returned to propagandize the WFTU line on Latin America, which consisted of a concerted attack on all aspects of United States prestige and influence based upon a theme of "North American Imperialism" as the cause of economic backwardness, lack of political freedom, and the danger of war. Resistance to United States aims, unity of the labor movement, "solidarity and reciprocal aid," and support of the policies of the CTAL and WFTU were put forth as the primary tasks of Latin American labor.[30]

---

[24] See Y-X-2:2904, V. L. Toledano to Federación Sindical de Trabajadores de Guatemala, April 22, 1946.

[25] Document 1309: V. L. Toledano to V. M. Gutiérrez, January 7, 1947.

[26] See Document 1260: cable from Fortuny to Gutiérrez, June 17, 1949.

[27] Y-X-4:520-2, Informe rendido por el delegado de la CTG ante el Segundo Congreso de la Federación Sindical Mundial, en la ciudad de Milán, Italia, Junio de 1949.

[28] See Documents 434: Enrique Ramírez y Ramírez to V. M. Gutiérrez, March 9, 1950; 769: V. Lombardo Toledano to V. M. Gutiérrez, April 10, 1949; 465: José Luis Ramos to Enrique Ramírez y Ramírez, April 20, 1950; 771: Gutiérrez to V. Lombardo Toledano, April 27, 1950; 503: C. Aparicio to M. Gutiérrez, February 3, 1950; 504: C. Aparicio to M. Gutiérrez, February 16, 1950; 1083: C. Aparicio to J. M. Fortuny, October 20, 1950.

[29] Document 1351: V. Lombardo Toledano to V. M. Gutiérrez, October 17, 1950; Y-X-4:48-9, CTAL circular 21/50, November 2, 1950; Y-X-4:51, V. Lombardo Toledano to V. M. Gutiérrez, November 2, 1950.

[30] 8001:272-7, "La situación del movimiento obrero Latinoamericano y la unidad continental."

In the spring of 1951 the WFTU and CTAL held two conferences which were of great importance to the Guatemalan labor movement. These were the Latin American Regional Agricultural Conference which was held in Mexico on May 2 to 6[31] and the Conference of Unions of Land and Air Transport Workers that opened in Guatemala City four days later, with leading Communist international labor figures in attendance.[32] Both these meetings afforded the Guatemalans an opportunity to confer with the WFTU leaders and gave the latter a chance to apply face-to-face persuasion on the recalcitrant Guatemalan leaders.[33] The WFTU attempted to work upon the SAMF, which was wary of Communism, by inviting one of its leaders to the Berlin meeting of the Executive Committee.[34] Though technically the CGTG, founded in October 1951, was not affiliated with the CTAL or WFTU, the Communist leadership proceeded exactly as it had before and regularly paid its dues to both organizations. Early in 1952 Gutiérrez was requesting CTAL and WFTU aid in the dispute with United Fruit Company and keeping them fully informed on Guatemalan developments.[35] The CGTG took part in the International Conference for the Defense, Extension and Improvement of Social Insurance and Social Security held in Vienna under WFTU

[31] Document 1815: CTAL to V. M. Gutiérrez, March 27, 1951; 8026: 320-4, "Informe del delegado de la Confederación de Trabajadores de Guatemala a la Conferencia Regional de Agricultura," June 1951.

[32] Documents 493: CNUS to Arbenz, March 22, 1951; 1814: CTAL to V. M. Gutiérrez, March 14, 1951 and to Stelian Moraru, March 9, 1951; 397: CTAL to Manuel Pinto Usaga, March 14, 1951; 398: CTAL to FSG, April 6, 1951.

[33] See Carlos Fernández, "Transport Workers' Conference and Trade Union Unity in Guatemala," World Trade Union Movement, July 20, 1951; V. M. Gutiérrez, "The Road to Unity in Guatemala," World Trade Union Movement, January 1-15, 1952.

[34] 8015: 305, Louis Saillant to V. M. Gutiérrez, September 11, 1951; 8015:306, Louis Saillant to SAMF, September 11, 1951.

[35] Document 1708: CGTG to V. Lombardo Toledano, February 5, 1952; 1709: CGTG to Louis Saillant, February 5, 1952; 8015:195, Louis Saillant to V. M. Gutiérrez, February 19, 1952; 8024:348, S. Rostovsky to V. M. Gutiérrez, March 15, 1952; 8002:1181, Natzul Aguirre to Louis Saillant, July 16, 1952; 8009:721, CGTG to FSM, August 23, 1952; 8001:677, Natzul Aguirre to V. M. Gutiérrez, July 24, 1952; 8014:1399, CTAL to SAMF, February 24, 1952; 8009:719, CTAL to V. M. Gutiérrez, August 11, 1952; 8001:714-5, CTAL circular 15/52, August 13, 1952; 8009:102, Gutiérrez to V. Lombardo T., August 3, 1952; 8009:89, V. Lombardo T. to V. M. Gutiérrez, August 25, 1952; 8005:2590, V. Lombardo T. to CGTG.

auspices from March 2 through March 6, 1952.[36] Throughout this period the CGTG took its international line from the directives of the CTAL and WFTU.[37] Through these international labor organizations the Guatemalan unions were brought into specific Soviet propaganda campaigns such as the germ warfare charges, the peace campaign, and the so-called "International Day of Solidarity with the People of Viet Nam."[38]

Third World Labor Congress. For the Communist leaders of the CGTG, the major international activity of the year 1953 was the Third World Labor Congress held in Vienna on October 10 to 21. While the CGTG had never ceased to be active in the WFTU and CTAL in spite of the pledge made to the SAMF in October of 1951, (See Chapter VII, p. 178), its Communist-dominated leadership saw the successful take-over of the SAMF by their allies as removing the last obstacle to the formal affiliation of the CGTG with the international labor fronts. The project was propagandized heavily during the May Day celebrations and a stream of requests from member unions mobilized. In response to this manufactured "grass roots" demand, the Executive Committee affiliated the CGTG with the WFTU and CTAL in August 1953.[39]

---

[36] 8009:106, Gutiérrez to Jan Dessau, February 18, 1953; 8003:95, Jan Dessau to CGTG, January 9, 1953; 8003:157, cable Henri Jourdain to Gutiérrez, January 30, 1953; Y-X-5:1115-1120, report of Marco Cuellar L. to CGTG, June 27, 1953. For CGTG relations with CTAL and WFTU in 1953 see 8009:1031; 8005:2646; 8005:2645; 8009:1089; 8009:1085; 8005:1877; Y-X-6:2145 and 2160.

[37] See Document 1536: H. Jourdain to V. M. Gutiérrez, April 14, 1954; 1642: CTAL circular 15, March 1953; Y-X-6:2210-2211, WFTU instructions for May Day 1954; 8024:2-5, Llamamiento de la Federación Sindical Mundial a los trabajadores del mundo entero con motivo del Primero de Mayo, fiesta internacional del trabajo; Y-X-5:444-6, Llamamiento de la FSM a los trabajadores y trabajadoras del mundo entero con ocasión del séptimo aniversario de su constitución, September 18, 1952.

[38] 8024:1080-5, "A las centrales nacionales y departamentos profesionales de la FSM sobre el arma bacteriológico," April 15, 1952; 8009:791, S. Rostovsky to V. M. Gutiérrez, May 29, 1952; Y-X-6:2187-8, WFTU circular 12/54, April 30, 1954; 8014:1159-1161, CTAL circular No. 17/51, October 6, 1951; Document 2068: "Con la FSM los trabajadores defienden la Paz," reprint of editorial by Henri Jourdain from *Movimiento Sindical Mundial,* No. 14, July 16-31, 1953; 8009:903, WFTU circular 12/53, May 27, 1953.

[39] 8003:891 or Y-X-1:310, Víctor A. Leal to Secretary General of the CGTG, May 11, 1953; Y-416, 8013:167 or Y-X-1:1306, Histórico acuerdo

The preparations for the congress and the reports on its work provided the Communist leadership of the CGTG with an opportunity to carry on an extensive propaganda campaign among the member unions. This campaign was based on the theme that it was necessary to attain unity of the working class in the face of the "furious capitalist offensive against the rights of the workers."[40] As the situation was pictured in the pro-Soviet propaganda of the congress, the "American imperialists" were converting Germany into a "focus of Fascism and militarism" in line with their role as the "instigators of war." The capitalists were willing to bring unspeakable horror upon the peoples of the world in order to "procure collosal gains," and the only solution was for the workers of the world to aid the peaceful policies of the Communist countries.[41] This propaganda repeated over and over, under the guise of an objective discussion of the conditions of the working class throughout the world, the Communist propaganda theme that:[42]

. . . there are forces and groups in the world who oppose the cessation of international tension. Peace does not interest them. In search of the maximum profit, they speculate with a new aggravation of international tension, they speculate with war.

For a country of its size, Guatemala played a prominent role in the congress. While Guatemala's normal representation would have been two delegates and an alternate, no less than eleven Guatemalans attended the congress. Leal and Pellecer were elected to the General Council of the WFTU and Gutiérrez to the more select Executive Committee.[43] At this same time, three other Guatemalan Communist

de afiliación de la CGTG a la CTAL y a la FSM, adoptado por unanimidad en el comité ejecutivo de la CGTG, el día 18 de Agosto de 1953; Document 1677: H. Jourdain to CGTG, August 26, 1953.

[40] Document 2063: Soviet trade union magazine *TRUD* quoted in CTAL publication *Hacia el 3er Congreso Sindical Mundial*, No. 2, June 20 to July 5, 1953.

[41] Document 2052 or Y-X-5:924-6, Proyecto de la Primera Comisión, also produced in a pamphlet circulated by the thousands in Guatemala by the CGTG on the eve of its January 1954 convention.

[42] See Document 1577: "Por considerar la gran importancia para la lucha por la paz y la unidad de los trabajadores transcribimos el llamamiento a los trabajadores y a los sindicales de los países Europeos," November 4, 1953.

[43] See Y-X-1:952, Lista de los delegados de Guatemala y El Salvador al III Congreso Sindical Mundial; Y-X-1:953-4, "Intervención de Guatemala para el Mitín del día 22" by Víctor Manuel Gutiérrez; for the propaganda

labor leaders were attending a three-month course at the WFTU's training school in Vienna, *at WFTU expense.* Gutiérrez had nominated nine candidates from whom the CTAL had selected three.[44] Among the subjects which they studied were imperialism, historical materialism, history of the labor movement and various courses in union organization and propaganda taught by Marxists from the USSR, China, France, Italy and other countries. After their course was finished, they attended the Third Congress of the WFTU and went to the USSR as guests of Soviet labor organizations.[45]

Guatemalan Unions and WFTU "Trade Departments." One of the steps in consolidating the influence of the WFTU over the Guatemalan labor movement was the affiliation of its member unions with the appropriate "trade department" of the WFTU. For this reason the CGTG, since its birth in October 1951, had striven to establish industry-wide federations as the intermediate level of organization in place of the older geographic groupings. By 1954 progress along this line had been nearly completed and each federation was actively participating in the work of the international parent organization.[46]

Communist propaganda was masked behind the guise of "interchanges of experience" and the "peace" campaign was woven into virtually every activity of these organizations.[47] In addition the several

---

exploitation of the "typical" Guatemalan workers see *Boletín del III Congreso Sindical Mundial,* "resúmen de la sesión del Lunes 12 de Octubre de 1953," p. 2; for other correspondence on the congress see Documents 1710, 2065, 1687, 2064, 2050, 2066, 2051, 2054, 2067, 2049, 1682, 1688, 2048, 1686, 1411, 1383, and 1567.

[44] See Y-X-2:2147, Víctor Manuel Gutiérrez to Guillermo Max González, Armando Villaseñor, Rodolfo Aguilar, Calixto Morales, Antonio Sierra González, Concepción Castro de Mencos, Juan Cabrera López, Santiago Reyes and Felícito Alegría, May 21, 1953; 8009:1035, radiogram from CGTG to CTAL, May 28, 1953; 8004:1321, Felícito Alegría H. to Víctor Manuel Gutiérrez, May 21, 1953; 8007:4398-4400, Felícito Alegría H. to Secretary General of CGTG, December 31, 1953.

[45] Document 2039: Felícito Alegría H. to Secretary General del Sindicato de Trabajadores en Madera y Vidrio, December 31, 1953.

[46] See Documents 196: CTAL to Guillermo Max González, April 15, 1954; 1618: CTAL to Gutiérrez, April 15, 1954; 194: CTAL to Gutiérrez, May 10, 1954.

[47] See Documents 1998: Fernand Maurice and Karl Pfeiferova to José Antonio Flores Domínguez, December 31, 1949; 2074: "Los Sindicatos Soviéticos luchan activamente por la paz," by A. Aslanov (This is a bitter denunciation of the Marshall Plan and other proposals for Western European defense.); 1993: Alois Hochfelder to Manuel Alfonso González, December

Communist-controlled Latin American unions in each industry were urged to cooperate with each other and to act jointly.[48] These trade departments of the WFTU, which almost without exception had their headquarters in the Eastern European countries, exploited their relationship with the Guatemalan unions to further the ends of international Communism and acted as yet another means of organizing and propagandizing the various Communist front causes discussed in the preceding chapter.[49]

The main contribution of these organizations to the growth of Communist influence in Guatemala was as a cloak for Communist and pro-Soviet propaganda. The Communist labor leaders who had gained control of most of the industrial federations in Guatemala were enabled to spread the Communist line behind the claim that it was the objective findings of the organization which represented all the workers in that particular industry or trade throughout the world. The fact that the views of the international body agreed with those expressed by the Guatemalan Communists reinforced the workers' confidence in their Communist leaders.

The propaganda disseminated through these organizations painted the beauties of life in the Socialist countries and the evil lot of the workers under the warmongering capitalists and imperialists.[50] The carpenters and brick layers were told that:[51]

29, 1951; 1999: A. Hochfelder to SCTIC, April 10, 1952; 1989: De las experiencias de la huelga de los trabajadores Italianos del ramo del cuero; also Documents 1994 and 2009.

48 Documents 1990: F. Konecny to Manuel Alfonso González, August 3, 1951; 1991: Domingo Agostini to José Ortiz Prado, September 6, 1951.

49 Document 1992: A. Hochfelder to José Ortíz Prado, November 1, 1951 and Manuel Alfonso González to Alois Hochfelder, February 4, 1952; Document 1997: Unión Internacional de los Sindicatos de Trabajadores de Cuero, Calzado, Pieles y Productos de Cuero circular of August 27, 1953; Document 2044: Unión Internacional de los Sindicatos de Trabajadores de Cuero, Calzado, Pieles y Productos de Cuero circular of May 4, 1953; also Documents 512, 513, 1603, 511 and 1597; Y-X-5:1095 and 1132-4; Y-X-2:3375-6 and 3377-8; 8024:344-6.

50 Y-X-4:474, Irena Piowarska to Federación Nacional de Trabajadores en la Industria de Textiles, Vestuarios y Similares, April 9, 1953; Y-X-6: 2164, Irena Piowarska to Federación Nacional de Trabajadores en la Industria de Textiles, Vestuarios y Similares, September 16, 1953; Unión Internacional de los Sindicatos Textiles y del Vestuario: *Boletín de Información,* No. 17, March 1953.

51 Document 1929: Unión Internacional de los Sindicatos de Trabajadores en Madera y Materiales de Construcción, circular No. 3/1952, March 27, 1952.

In the Soviet Union, in the countries of popular democracy, in the Democratic Republic of Germany and in the Peoples' Republic of China, the workers are celebrating their conquests in the construction of Communism and Socialism. . . .

In order to save themselves money, the imperialists of the United States of North America have transformed the propaganda war into the Korean War and in other parts of the world into the same kind of wars. Each day the capitalists wish war upon the world and agitate against the partisans of peace.

The United States economy was still standing only because of the Korean War, but the workers there looked longingly at the USSR and would not long put up with the tax burden imposed upon them by the warlike plans of the profit-mad capitalists. When the Korean War ended, it was due to the "constant efforts of the Soviet Union, the popular democracies and the peoples of the world," and the workers were to accelerate their efforts to bring peace in Viet Nam through the Soviet-sponsored campaign for negotiations. While in the capitalist and colonial countries economic stagnation had put many building trades workers out of work, their Soviet counterparts were enjoying unparalleled prosperity.[52]

According to the Trade Unions International of Workers of the Food, Tobacco and Beverages Industries and Hotel, Cafe and Restaurant Workers, the "modern cannibals" who wished to convert Korea into a "colony of the New York Bankers" and use it as a "springboard to attack the Peoples' Republic of China and the Soviet Union," had unleashed a campaign of bacteriological warfare which threatened the lives of every man, woman and child in Asia and Europe.[53] The Guatemalan workers were treated to a picture of the miners in the capitalist and colonial countries as "harshly exploited" and their lives "each day more sorrowful." On the other hand, the miners in the Communist countries lived better and more freely as time went on.[54]

While it is difficult to judge the impact of this propaganda upon the rank-and-file workers, there is little doubt that it helped create an atmosphere in which the Communist labor leaders could work more effectively.

---

[52] Document 1606: "Resolución" de la IV Sesión del Comité Administrativo de la Unión Internacional de los Sindicatos de Trabajadores en Madera y Materias de Construcción, January 14-16, 1954.

[53] 8024:344-6, circular from Anton Ditchev, March 24, 1952.

[54] Document 1381: Unión Internacional de los Sindicatos de Mineros circular, 1954.

Perhaps the most important of these linkages was that of the CGTG and the CNCG with the Trade Unions International of Agricultural and Forestry Workers. The Guatemalan organizations ranked relatively high among the affiliates of this body, and in 1953 they were asked to nominate a member to serve as Latin American representative on the Secretariat and to deliver one of the main reports at the World Conference in Vienna during October of that year.[55] José Luis Ramos, PGT Central Committeeman and one-time official of both the CNCG and CGTG, accordingly delivered a report on "The Importance of the Organization of the Peasants of Latin America and the Aid of the Working Class in the Struggle for their Demands" in which he blamed most of Latin America's ills upon the "warlike rearmament policy of North American monopoly capital." The resolutions of this conference went even further in blaming the ills of the agricultural workers of the world upon the "warlike policies" of the United States and holding the USSR, Communist China and the Eastern European Popular Democracies up as examples to be emulated.[56] The international also carried on the usual mobilizations of messages for the "victims" of the capitalist and colonial governments.[57]

WFTU and CTAL Interest in and Use of Guatemala. Guatemala was of more than routine interest to the leaders of the Communist international labor organizations, since at a time when they were losing ground in the rest of Latin America, it was their one bright spot. They held Guatemala up as an example to be emulated by other Latin American nations as well as "colonial and semi-colonial" countries in general. Gutiérrez was called upon frequently to contribute articles to the WFTU magazine, and Guatemalan events were heavily played up in the *Noticiero de la CTAL*.[58] In addition, Guatemala was given a

[55] 8009:1014-5, CTAL to CGTG, April 24, 1953; Documents 1676: Ilio Bosi to Guatemalan affiliates, August 21, 1953; 1685: Ilio Bosi to CGTG, September 8, 1953; 1684: Luigi Grassi to CGTG, August 14, 1953; 206: CTAL to Gutiérrez, September 10, 1953.

[56] "Proyecto de resolución general" and "Conferencia mundial de los trabajadores agrícolas y forestales y campesinos laboriosos: textos adoptados," supplement to No. 10-11 of the UISTAF's *Information Bulletin.*

[57] See Document 549: UISTAF circulars of February 15 and March 31, 1954.

[58] Documents 1671: H. Jourdain to CGTG, December 21, 1953; 1673: F. Leriche to Manuel Gutiérrez, January 28, 1954; 1535: Director del servicio de Edición y de Propaganda de la FSM to Manuel Gutiérrez, April 17, 1954; 1534: Gutiérrez to Director del servicio de Edición de Propaganda de la

prominent place in the WFTU propaganda film, *The Great Appointment* (*La Gran Cita*). It was the idea of the Executive Committee of the WFTU that the section on Guatemala should:[59]

. . . show the workers and people of Guatemala struggling against the United Fruit Company and its subsidiaries, the railroad company, Puerto Barrios, etc.

The case of Guatemala is essential to the motion picture, because it will show the aggression of Yankee imperialism everywhere; yesterday in Korea, armed aggression; today in Guatemala, political aggression at the other end of the world.

The WFTU and CTAL, as did the Communist line press and organizations everywhere, exploited the "intervention" issue to the utmost.[60]

Guatemala was extremely valuable to these international labor organizations as their middleman or contact with the labor movements of the other Central American nations. Gutiérrez kept the WFTU informed of developments in these countries and passed on messages and propaganda material from the international organization to the extremist leaders in El Salvador, Honduras and Nicaragua.[61]

FSM, April 27, 1954; 8002:2223, cable from Leriche, chief editor of Revista FSM to Manuel Gutiérrez, September 26, 1952; 8005:2642 or 8009: 1031, Antonio García Moreno and Lourival Villar to V. M. Gutiérrez and C. M. Pellecer, May 14, 1953; 8005:2643, José Alberto Cardoza to Lourival Villar, June 8, 1953; 8009:726, H. Jourdain to V. Manuel Gutiérrez, July 9, 1952.

[59] Documents 200: Vicente Lombardo Toledano to V. M. Gutiérrez, April 15, 1954; 207: radiogram from Vicente Lombardo T. to V. M. Gutiérrez, April 15, 1954.

[60] 8009:965, H. Jourdain to CGTG, May 22, 1953; Document 2056: CTAL circular No. 19/53, "Situación de Guatemala," April 24, 1953; Document 1391 or Y-X-6: 2146, cable from José Alberto Cardoza to FSM, November 14, 1953; 8024:539-40, José Alberto Cardoza to Buró Ejecutivo de la Federación Sindical Mundial, November 14, 1953; 8007:5278, radiogram from Morera to V. M. Gutiérrez, January 23, 1954; Y-X-6:2131, CGTG and CNCG to FSM, June 25, 1954; also *Noticiero de la CTAL*, Vol. IV., No. 240, February 1954, No. 241, March 1954, No. 242, April 1954, and No. 243, May 1954.

[61] See 8009:240, H. Jourdain to Víctor Manuel Gutiérrez, October 21, 1952; 8013:1401, CTAL to Víctor Manuel Gutíerrez, January 21, 1953; 8013:13, CTAL to Víctor Manuel Gutiérrez, January 31, 1953; 8003:98, CTAL circular, January 7, 1953; 8016:658, Comité de Edición en Español de la Revista *El Movimiento Sindical Mundial* to Víctor Manuel Gutiérrez, January 7, 1953; 8016:660, *Noticiero de la CTAL* to Víctor Manuel Gutiérrez, January 9, 1953; 8005:2171, CTAL to Víctor Manuel Gutiérrez, August 6, 1953; Documents 1566, CTAL to Víctor Manuel Gutiérrez, May 28, 1954; 505: L. Saillant to Manuel Gutiérrez, February 3, 1950; 502: Gutiérrez to

International Working-Class Solidarity. Faithful to their concept of the unity of the world proletariat, the Communist labor leaders saw to it that the CGTG participated fully in the international propaganda campaigns instigated and coordinated by the CTAL and WFTU. The pattern in these campaigns was usually similar: instructions would come from the WFTU or the CTAL, Gutiérrez would send a telegram in the name of the CGTG and circularize the member unions to do the same, the campaign would be picked up by the Communist press, and, if the cause had broad enough appeal, other front groups would be brought in and a rally organized. At the same time the Communist press gave heavy emphasis to these causes. While the ostensible purpose was to mobilize public opinion to force the government under attack to change its policies, the real value of these activities was to reinforce the Communist propaganda picture of tyrannical, warlike, imperialist governments persecuting "peace lovers" and "beloved leaders of the working class," i.e. Communists.

The archetype of these campaigns was the propaganda attack upon the Cuban government undertaken in 1953. The Cuban Communist labor leaders had played a major role in the early days of the Guatemalan labor movement and were among the most valuable instruments of international Communism in the Western Hemisphere. When the Cuban government interfered with the activities of Marinello, Blas Roca, Lázaro Peña and the other leaders of the Popular Socialist Party (the Cuban Communist Party), their Guatemalan comrades raised a storm of indignant protest.[62] In response to the calls of the WFTU and

---

Louis Saillant and G. Aparicio, March 7, 1950; 107, Rodolfo López, Humberto Laitano and Carlos Bernhard to Víctor Manuel Gutiérrez, May 5, 1950, and reply of June 13, 1950.

[62] See Y-X-1:581, Eduardo Castillo H. to Ministro de Cuba en Guatemala, June 15, 1951; 8003:284, Gutiérrez to General Fulgencio Batista, February 20, 1953; 8001:730, Gutiérrez to Gen. F. Batista, June 27, 1952; 8001:804, Gutiérrez to Gen. F. Batista; 8010:1867, H. Jourdain to V. M. Gutiérrez, February 10, 1953; Documents 1605, 1658 or 1683, WFTU circular No. 25/53, August 2, 1953; 1659, H. Jourdain to V. Manuel Gutiérrez, September 8, 1953; 1818, Víctor A. Leal to Buró Ejecutivo de la Federación Sindical Mundial y de la Confederación de Trabajadores de América Latina, August 19, 1953; 8005:1893, telegram from CTAL to Gutiérrez, August 2, 1953; 8005:2156, CTAL circular No. 47/53, August 4, 1953; Document 1346, Y-X-5:1303 or 8013:187; 8005:2394; 8005:2402; 8004:1650; 8005:2680/3; 8005:2095; 8005:1966; 8005:1967; 8005:2474; 8005:2178; 8005:2680/4; Y-X-5:1136; 8005:2381/1; 8005:2295; 8005:2700; 8005:2561; 8005:2680/2; 8005:2680/1; 8005:2680; 8005:2368-70; 8005:2206; 8005:2159; 8005:2662; 8005:2205; and 8005:2230.

CTAL, the Guatemalan labor leaders came to the defense of the Communist labor organizations in Argentina, Nicaragua, Dominican Republic, Costa Rica, British Guiana, Ecuador, Brazil, Chile, Venezuela and El Salvador.[63] They also directed messages to such far-off governments as Japan, the Philippines, France and Great Britain. While it is doubtful that these messages had any effect upon the government to which they were directed, they were printed in the Communist press and served the propaganda purpose of picturing these governments as "unconditional servants of imperialism" or "of a marked Fascist tint."

COMMUNIST INFLUENCE ON GUATEMALAN FOREIGN POLICY

Throughout the life of the Arbenz regime Communist influence over Guatemala's foreign policy was increasing. One indication of this was the government's response to their repeated demand for closer relations with the countries of the Communist bloc. The Czech and Polish Ministers in Mexico City were accredited by their governments to Guatemala as well. In March 1953 Lubor Zamlar, the Commercial Attaché of the Czechoslovakian Legation in Mexico, visited Guatemala for an extended stay.[64] In October of the same year Mikhail K. Samoilov, Soviet Commercial Attaché in Mexico, arrived in Guatemala and had a three-hour private interview with the President. On January 29, 1954, a Czechoslovakian Minister presented his credentials to President Arbenz. (It was at this time that Major Alfonso Martínez was reportedly in Prague completing arrangements for a shipment of Czech arms to Guatemala. See Epilogue, pp. 309-10.)

Disruption of Hemispheric Solidarity. Further insight into the growth of Communist influence over Guatemala's foreign policy comes from its actions in the Inter-American movement. The Organization of

---

[63] For Argentina see 8002:1815, 8002:1816 and 8016:614. Nicaragua—8026:197. Dominican Republic—Y-X-5:1138 and 8024:275. Costa Rica—Document 546 and Y-X-4:514. British Guiana—8024:921-2 and 8007:5064. Ecuador—Y-X-6:2203, Y-X-6:2204 and 8032:3088. Brazil—8009:19, Y-X-4:282-3 and Document 1601. Chile—Document 1565. Venezuela—Document 2057, Document 435, Document 1704; 8026:419; 8002:2502; 8008:7101. El Salvador—8002:1852, 2205, 2200, 1609, 2534 and 2399; Y-X-1:1359-70; 8026:102; Y-X-5:1144; Y-X-2:1723.

[64] See 8003:594, Lubor Zamlar to the CGTG, March 18, 1953 and 8003:597, CGTG to Lubor Zamlar, March 16, 1953.

Central American States (ODECA) was formed in December 1951 with Guatemalan Foreign Minister Manuel Galich playing a major role. On the eve of a meeting of the new organization scheduled for Guatemala City in September 1952, Salvadorean Foreign Minister Roberto Canessa proposed that the question of Communist infiltration be placed on the agenda. Immediately the Guatemalan Communists began a propaganda attack against the Salvadorean government as a tool of "North American imperialism" and mobilized all the organizations which they controlled or could influence to pressure the Arbenz government to reject the Canessa anti-Communist proposal. (See Chapter VIII, p. 201.) The Arbenz government as host postponed the meeting until the following May. Galich, who was closely tied to the ODECA idea, was removed as Foreign Minister and replaced by Raúl Osegueda. On April 1, 1953, Arbenz's Foreign Minister protested to the Secretary General of the United Nations that Guatemala was the victim of a "vast international conspiracy" involving the United States, the Dominican Republic and her Central American neighbors. This move was only a prelude to an act which marked a signal victory in the Communists' efforts to shape Guatemalan foreign policy. On April 7, Guatemala withdrew from the Organization of Central American States (ODECA), charging that it had been converted into an "aggressive bloc" against Guatemala and that its proposal to study the influence of Communism in Central America constituted unwarranted interference in the domestic affairs of Guatemala. This thesis, which the Communists had been propagandizing for over six months, now became the official policy of the Guatemalan government.[65]

Throughout 1953 the Communist press, both within Guatemala and in other parts of the world, placed increasing emphasis on the "imperialist threat" to Guatemala and the slogan "hands off Guatemala." After the return of Communist leaders Gutiérrez and Fortuny from Moscow, the latter on January 8, 1954, the Communist press throughout the hemisphere began to "warn" the United States against turning Guatemala into a "second Spain" or a "second Korea." On January 29, the same day that Arbenz was entertaining the Soviet diplomat Samoilov, the government announced the discovery of a subversive plot

---

[65] The Communists had been strongly advocating this action for several months, and the reasons given by the Arbenz government were identical with those outlined by the Communists a few days earlier. See *Octubre,* April 4, 1953.

which it claimed was supported by the Dominican Republic, Nicaragua, El Salvador, Venezuela, and "a government of the North."

By the beginning of February 1954, Guatemalan attention was focused upon the Tenth Inter-American Conference scheduled for Caracas, Venezuela, the following month. On November 11, 1953, Guatemala had cast the lone vote against the inclusion of the question of "Intervention of Communism in the American Republics" on the conference agenda. Rather than withdrawing from the OAS or boycotting the conference, the government followed the Communists' advice to attend and attempt to use it as a platform for an attack upon the United States. Guillermo Toriello was called back from his post as Ambassador to the United States to replace the rather colorless Raúl Osegueda as Foreign Minister and chief delegate to the conference.

Toriello was eminently fitted for the role which he was to play. A young, personable nationalist, he had no known political affiliation. In addition to being a fiery orator, "el Globo" (the Balloon), as he was called by his detractors, was a natural actor. His emotion-charged pleas and denunciations were calculated more to arouse the nationalistic sentiments of the Guatemala people and Latin Americans in general than to move the delegates at Caracas.

The line which Toriello was to follow had been determined at a meeting of the National Democratic Front (FDN), composed of the Communists, the three other government parties, and the labor and campesino confederations. This arrangement gave the Communists disproportionate influence as they controlled the votes of the labor representatives as well as those of the PGT itself. Stripped to its barest essentials, the Guatemalan position at Caracas was that Communism was a purely internal concern of the country and that Guatemala was the victim of an international plot to overthrow her government on the pretext that it was Communist and to replace it with one subservient to the United Fruit Company.[66] Guatemala not only cast the lone vote against the anti-Communist resolution, but also abstained from voting on the Panamanian resolution on racial discrimination on the ground that it included the phrase "as one means of combatting international Communism." In addition the Guatemalan delegates absented themselves during the tribute to the United Nations war dead.

Many supporters of the Arbenz regime felt that they had won a

---

[66] For the text of Toriello's speeches see Toriello, *op. cit.,* pp. 259-282.

moral victory at Caracas. The Communists had achieved their goal of using the Conference as a propaganda platform, and their claims had gained a sympathetic hearing from many Latin American nationalists, leftists and intellectuals who bore a deep suspicion of United States' motives.[67]

Communist influence over Guatemalan foreign policy continued to increase. Immediately after the close of the conference the Guatemalan Congress withdrew its ratification of the 1947 Rio Treaty on collective defense of the hemisphere. When the attack headed by Castillo Armas came on June 18, 1954, the Arbenz government sought support in the United Nations Security Council where the USSR could exercise its veto power and play a determining role, rather than taking the dispute to the Organization of American States (OAS). Throughout the first half of 1954, the foreign policy of the Arbenz regime enabled the international Communist movement to reap a propaganda harvest.

Guatemala and Her Neighbors. The foreign policy followed by the Arbenz government and the extra-curricular activities of many of its diplomatic representatives involved Guatemala in a series of disputes with her neighbors. During the period from 1951 to 1954 many Guatemalan diplomats were declared *persona non grata* by neighboring governments on the charge that they were disseminating Communist propaganda and giving aid and encouragement to groups plotting against the duly constituted authorities. In Panama, Guatemalan Ambassador Oscar Benítez Bone was declared *persona non grata* after he was discovered working with Communist-dominated workers' organizations. In Colombia it was Ambassador Virgilio Rodríguez Beteta who was caught disseminating Communist propaganda. In Costa Rica Ambassador Jorge Arankowsky was expelled after addressing a Communist labor rally. Alfredo Chocano had the distinction of being declared *persona non grata* by both Nicaragua and Honduras, while Ambassador Gabino Santizo was accused of transporting Communist

[67] The strength and persistence of anti-Yankee feeling in Latin America is often underestimated by people in this country. While this sentiment is frequently latent, it can be fanned into life by those who have an axe to grind. The Communists with their appeals to nationalism and anti-imperialist sentiment have been able to exploit this potential and fan it into open hostility toward the "colossus of the North." The situation within Guatemala under Arbenz and the exploitation of the Latin American reaction to the fall of the Arbenz regime are classic examples of this.

propaganda into Nicaragua under cover of his diplomatic pouch and of being involved in a plot to assassinate President Somoza.

Salvadorean Communists aided by the PGT made considerable progress in infiltrating labor and student groups. While the Communist and government press attacked El Salvador President Osorio as a "fascist," a vast amount of propaganda demanding immediate agrarian reform found its way across the Guatemalan border. In September of 1952 the Salvadorean government felt forced to close its border with Guatemala and to expel 1200 Guatemalans living in El Salvador.

When a strike broke out in the spring of 1954 among the workers of the banana plantations on the north coast of Honduras, it was widely believed that the inspiration and example came from Guatemala.[68] Just how deeply the Communists were involved in efforts to exploit the strike and turn it against the Honduran government remains a moot point. At the time most observers accepted the fact that the strike was beyond the capabilities of the Honduran labor leaders. The Honduran government felt that three Guatemalan Consuls appointed shortly before the strike began to posts at Tela, Puerto Cortes and Nueva Ocatepeque were involved in giving propaganda, funds and advice to the strikers. (There is some evidence, however, that the primary or at least original task of these consuls had been to check upon the activities of Castillo Armas and his supporters.) Since by mid-May between 50,000 and 70,000 workers were involved in the stoppage, which had attained the proportions of a general strike, the Honduran government was extremely upset by rumors that a portion of the arms shipment which the Guatemalans had just received from behind the Iron Curtain was intended for the Honduran strikers. The obvious financial and moral aid which the strikers were receiving from Guatemalan labor organizations added to the apprehensions of the Honduran authorities.[69] Under these conditions the Honduran authori-

---

[68] For a detailed story of this incident see James, *op. cit.*, pp. 195-6 and 218-22. James holds that the strike was probably not instigated by the Communists, but that they attempted to take over its leadership and turn it to their political ends. Robert J. Alexander, in his book *Communism in Latin America* (Rutgers University Press, 1957), 375, reports that President Gálvez claimed that the strike was inspired and directed by the Guatemalan Communist leaders and was designed to overthrow his government. However, the Communists could not retain control of the strike, and an anti-Communist group of leaders came to the fore.

[69] For the support and encouragement given by the Guatemalan labor movement to the Honduran strikers see: Documents 3, 4, 5, 7, 8, 23, 406,

ties felt justified in closing their eyes to the activities of the Guatemalan exiles under Castillo Armas and may even have felt that a change in the Guatemalan government was necessary for their own safety. How the attack launched by these exiles contributed to the overthrow of the Arbenz government is told in the next chapter.

105, 1526, 1533, 1590, 1662, 1663, 2071 and 2072; 8008:7287, 7422, 7459, 7475, 7473, 7476, 7514, 7601, 7617, 7674, 7722; 8026:109 and 110; 8029:227 and 228; 8050:786 and 845; Y-X-1:8051; Y-X-3:4044, 4064-5 and 4083; Y-X-5:423 and 796; Y-X-6:2121 and 2122. The amount of money collected by the CGTG to aid the Honduran strikers was well up into the thousands of dollars.

EPILOGUE

Our story would be incomplete without a discussion of why the Arbenz regime fell in June 1954.[1] The immediate cause of the sudden collapse of so outwardly impressive a regime is to be found in the attitudes and actions of the small group of professional soldiers who headed the regular army. However, the decisions of the officer corps were conditioned by a number of considerations. In the following pages we will attempt to depict the interaction of these factors.

The Guatemalan people as a whole played a relatively small role in the events of June 1954. In this respect both the expectations of the leaders of the Arbenz regime and the hopes of Castillo Armas and his "Liberation" movement were disappointed. The spontaneous wave of uprisings for which Castillo Armas hoped when he crossed the frontier from Honduras with his makeshift army of a few hundred campesinos led by a handful of professional officers and eager but inexperienced students never materialized. On the other hand, the Communists and their allies were unable to produce the thousands of workers and campesinos who had supposedly been ready to lay down their lives for

[1] For a detailed treatment of the international aspects see Philip B. Taylor Jr.'s "The Guatemalan Affair: A Critique of United States Foreign Policy," *American Political Science Review*, Vol. L, No. 3 (September 1956), pp. 787-806. A useful chronology of the fighting can be found in *The New York Times* of July 5, 1954. See also the official story of the liberation movement, *Así se Gestó la Liberación*, cited above.

the Arbenz government. If not apathetic, the bulk of the Guatemalan people were at least so torn by ambivalent feelings that they took no active part in shaping the course of events.

Indecision characterized the behavior of the people, the army, and the government itself during the crucial ten days from the initial attack by the Liberation Army until the resignation of Arbenz. Even after Arbenz had left the presidency and led the flight to the Mexican Embassy, a week passed before the governmental vacuum was filled. Throughout this period a few military leaders made the decisions while the masses went their way unconcerned or sat on the sidelines and waited. Even the army leaders delayed as long as possible before finally making up their minds and acting. Only Arbenz's refusal to consider separating the Communists from his government led the officers to ask for his resignation. Throughout the crucial period the government's actions were too late even when not based upon faulty premises and erroneous assumptions.

THE GROWTH OF THE OPPOSITION

The opponents of the Arbenz government were handicapped by the fact that in the public eye they were branded as enemies of the Revolution of 1944 and of the gains which the Arévalo and Arbenz Governments had brought to the workers and peasants. Unfortunately, while most Guatemalans felt that the issues of the cold war were remote from their day-to-day lives, they were greatly concerned about the preservation of the fruits of the Revolution of 1944, and there was little in the attitudes or actions of the opposition to indicate sincere support for that goal. Anti-Communism had become the single unifying theme of the various opposition groups, but it was relatively meaningless to the Guatemalan masses, who were interested primarily in a fuller and more satisfying life. While Guatemalans in general had enjoyed more freedom during the 1944-1954 period than ever before, the working class had particular reason to feel loyal to the revolutionary regime. For the first time in Guatemalan history labor enjoyed the rights to organize freely, bargain collectively, and strike. Never before had they felt free to speak out openly and voice their feelings without restraint, much less be confident of gaining a sympathetic hearing from the government. The lower classes enjoyed the novelty of living in a new atmosphere, officially fostered, in which they were treated with a measure of respect and dignity. The fear that the victory of the opposition would mean an end to all this and a return to *Ubiquismo* was enough to keep many persons loyal to the Arbenz government long beyond the time their enthusiasm for it had begun to wane.

The Arbenz government came into office with few active opponents. Many of the groups which had opposed the Arévalo government were disposed to be tolerant and openminded concerning Arbenz, at least until they saw the direction in which he would move. As the Communists came to play a larger and more important role in the councils of the government, many moderates who were wedded to the goals of the Revolution of 1944 began to waver in their support for the Arbenz regime, but their change of attitude did little if anything to weaken it. Their attempt to show that opposition to Communism did not necessarily signify opposition to a genuine social revolution was overwhelmed by the propaganda of the Communists and their allies. The effort to rescue nationalism from Communist exploitation and return the revolution to a purely Guatemalan course was doomed as another case of too little too late. When it became apparent that the only way to rid Guatemala of the growing Communist influence was to overturn the Arbenz government, many resolved their ambivalent feelings by shutting their eyes to the extent of Communist influence and continuing to support the regime. Others withdrew to the margin of the political arena after their efforts to create a third force collapsed. Only a relatively small group of supporters of the Revolution of 1944 chose the road of active opposition to the government.

Composed as it was of a heterogenous collection of groups ranging from these disillusioned backers of the revolution against Ubico through supporters of the murdered Arana to neo-Ubico reactionaries, the anti-Communist camp was plagued by disunity. As late as the January 1953 congressional elections, the opposition was so divided that its 105,000 votes brought it only three seats while the 130,000 ballots cast for the government coalition elected 29 deputies. The five opposition members in the new Congress represented four different parties. Outside the country the exiles were almost equally divided. Not until the beginning of 1954 was this disunity overcome to the extent that the various opposition groups could cooperate effectively.

Although the Arbenz government came into office with only the extreme conservatives of the Unified Anti-Communist Party (*Partido Unificación Anti-comunista*—PUA) in active opposition, an event which occurred less than four months later led to the birth of new opposition groups. In May 1951, Gabriel Alvarado, a Spanish Communist exile and collaborator of Víctor Manuel Gutiérrez, was appointed director of the National Orphanage (*Hospicio Nacional*), which had previously been under Catholic administration. Alvarado tried to replace the nuns who taught there with members of the Communist-dominated teachers' union (STEG). In response to rumors that the nuns and orphans were being mistreated, the militantly anti-Communist market women descended upon the school. The wave of unrest reached such a level that some government officials conveniently entered hospitals for "checkups" while Fortuny himself spent the night of July 11 in the Colombian Embassy. The following day a demonstration in front of the National Palace caused Arbenz to promise that Alvarado would be replaced. When Caribbean Legionnaire and presidential bodyguard Miguel Enrique Viteri Batres attempted to drive his car through the mob, he was beaten and his car burned. Fearing the demonstration would get out of hand, the police fired on the crowd, killing more than a dozen and wounding many times that number.

Partially as a reaction to this incident, the National Civic Committee (CCN) was formed on August 23 and the Committee of Anti-Communist University Students (CEUA) founded two weeks later. A network of local anti-Communist committees were organized in the last months of 1951 and a national convention held on November 26. In March of the following year these organizations sponsored demonstrations in Guatemala City and other major towns. In the latter part of 1952 the main focus of opposition activities shifted to the January, 1953 congressional elections. After much bickering and tedious negotiations, the various anti-Communist groups in the capital united behind two candidates who defeated Communist leader Fortuny and his running mate in the election, but in the nation as a whole the disunity of the opposition contributed to a succession of electoral defeats.

Throughout this period opposition strength was concentrated in the capital. There the market women and university students played a particularly active role in the anti-government movement. In February 1953 the students demonstrated in front of the National Palace and burned a copy of the Constitution as a protest against Arbenz's ouster of the Supreme Court Justices. The police fired upon the students, killing one and wounding several others. The municipal government headed by the Mayor, Juan Luis Lizarralde, weathered several crises provoked by the Communist-controlled labor organizations and the obstructionist tactics of the national government.

In 1953 the opposition turned to conspiratorial tactics under increasing harassment by the Arbenz regime. The failure of the March 29 uprising at Salamá was a severe setback to the opposition. Many anti-Communist leaders were jailed, tortured or exiled. Gradually the various organizations came together under the leadership of Lieutenant Colonel Carlos Castillo Armas, a forty-year-old professional army officer who had led the abortive November 5, 1950, coup. His feat of surviving the massacre which followed his revolt and escaping in July 1951 from the prison in the heart of Guatemala City made him almost a legendary figure and enabled him to forge over a dozen diverse organizations into the "Liberation Movement."

Castillo could claim to represent the "true" spirit of the Revolution of 1944 as he had served as Commander of the *Escuela Politécnica,* Guatemala's West Point, under Arévalo until the assassination of Col. Arana in July 1949. Although even Castillo Armas failed to formulate a concrete program or systematic ideology as an alternative to that of the government, his motto of "God, Country and Liberty" raised the movement at least one step above the negative and often sterile anti-Communism which had preceded it.[2]

By the beginning of 1954 the opponents of the Arbenz regime had achieved a fair degree of unity. Outside Guatemala the exiles were organized under the banner of the Anti-Communist Liberating Front (FLA), whose high command was the Anti-Communist Coordinating Committee (CCA) with headquarters in Honduras. Within Guatemala the National Anti-Communist Front (FAN) attempted to coordinate the efforts of some ten opposition groups, but was hampered by the secret police (*Guardia Judicial*). While the organizations within Guatemala were weakened by a wave of arrests in the last week of January

---

[2] The reader who may be interested in the rather unrewarding task of attempting to determine the philosophy of the Liberation Movement should consult *Ideario del Coronel Carlos Castillo Armas,* Guatemala, 1955, and José Calderón Salazar's *Letras de Liberación,* Guatemala, 1955. In addition there is considerable pertinent material in *Así se Gestó la Liberación* cited above.

and the reign of terror during early June, the exiles with their head-quarters in Tegucigalpa, Honduras, were constantly gaining strength and preparing for the day when they would return to Guatemala to spearhead the attack on the Arbenz regime.

SUPPORT FOR THE ARBENZ REGIME

Largely under Communist initiative and direction, a network of organizations was formed during the last months of 1953 and the early part of 1954 to propagandize the intervention issue and to lend their support to the Arbenz regime. These groups were quite successful in the first of these two tasks, although their capabilities in the field of direct action to defend the government proved limited when the showdown came in June 1954. Among the great variety of these organizations were the so-called Defense Committees, Committees for the Struggle Against Foreign Intervention, and Patriotic Committees for the Defense of National Sovereignty. As early as September 1953 the CGTG decided to form such committees among its larger unions and to use them as the nucleus for rallies, demonstrations and campaigns to impress upon the government the "true sentiment of the workers," which in practice meant to endorse the proposals of the Communist leaders.[3]

The culmination of the Communists' efforts to establish themselves as the leading defenders of the Arbenz regime was the founding of Patriotic Committees for the Defense of National Sovereignty in each Department in which the PGT had substantial strength. For example in Chiquimula this was done on June 14, 1954, with Communists José Domingo Samayoa as Secretary General and Hugo Sagastume as Sec-

---

[3] See 8013:156, CGTG Circular of September 11, 1953; 8011:593-5 or Y-X-2:1739-41, Resoluciones de la Asamblea de Secretarios Generales y de Organización, November 30, 1953. For the work of these committees see Document 409, Y-395 or Y-X-1:1660-1, "Guatemala en pie, y con ella todos las amantes de la libertad y la democracia en América y en el mundo entero," January 23, 1954; Document 1578, Y-X-1:1125-7, or Y-X-1:1662-4, "Ha sido revelada al pueblo de Guatemala la conspiración más basta y criminal contra la Patria, dirigida desde el extranjero por un grupo de traidores," February, 1954. For the line of the CGTG on the eve of the Castillo Armas attack see Document 1229: Guión para el Informe sobre la Situación Nacional rendido ante el Comité Ejecutivo ampliado de la CGTG, June 8, 1954; Document 417, Y-X-1:944-7, or Y-X-2:3352-5; Document 1629 or 8027:85.

retary of Propaganda. The next two most important posts, Organization and Mobilization, were in the hands of the pro-Communist PAR leaders, while the PRG got only the minor posts of Finance and Records.[4] In other areas the Communists also took the lead in the formation of similar committees composed of representatives of the four government parties.

All the Communist-front organizations joined in an attempt to organize a mass rally in support of the Arbenz government on June 18. Under the leadership of Communists Ricardo Ramírez and Elsa de Guerra Borges the organizing committee strove to make this the most impressive show of revolutionary unity yet.[5] Its dismal failure was probably indicative of the apathy of the masses and growing "wait-and-see" policy on the part of the less zealous and fanatic backers of the government. At the last moment the rally was cancelled, due probably to the uneasiness caused by the news that Castillo Armas had crossed the Honduran frontier, although rain was the reason given.

The activists of the labor and campesino organizations cooperated with the authorities by reporting on the activities of suspected oppositionists, watching roads, airports and suspicious movements, and guarding bridges and other key installations. In spite of their repeated requests for arms and military instruction, this was never done, since the officer corps raised strenuous objections. However as late as June 26 the Communist leaders and their allies were telling the workers and campesinos that the matter would soon be favorably resolved.[6] Throughout the crucial days of June 1954 the Communists attempted to influence the President's decisions both through face-to-face persuasion and the mobilization of a flood of messages pledging the undying support of the masses, while at the same time endorsing the Communist-favored policies of no concessions and arms for the workers.[7]

---

[4] See Document 617: papers from the files of Víctor Manuel Gutiérrez; and 8052:4597-9, Informe de la Comisión a Chiquimula al Secretarío General de la CNCG, June 14, 1954.

[5] See Document 787: Mensaje a las organizaciones que participan en el Comité Organizador, June 14, 1954.

[6] See 8051:2973, Leonardo Castillo Flores to Fernando Sicaya, June 25, 1954.

[7] For the hundreds of messages pledging support to the government, requesting arms and military instruction, and generally placing themselves at the President's disposal see 8024:627-777; 8026:118-146, 169, 233, 235, and

Before we can show why these Communist efforts to bolster the Arbenz regime failed, it is necessary to examine more closely the developments during the month preceding the outbreak of the civil war.

THE SITUATION IN JUNE 1954

Two factors were of primary importance in the Guatemalan situation as the Arbenz regime entered its final weeks. One was the unequivocal endorsement which Arbenz had given to the Communists in his annual report to Congress on March 1 and his categorical rejection of all suggestions that he curb them or at least drop Communists from the government. The other was the receipt on May 15 of a shipload of arms from a Communist source in Eastern Europe. The first of these caused many individuals who had supported Arbenz in the belief that he was only "using" the Communists to reconsider their position. The second sharpened the contradictions between the Army and the worker elements of the Arbenz regime by precipitating the issue of arming a civilian militia. It also caused great uneasiness among Guatemala's neighbors.

Nevertheless, Communist gains in Guatemala were continuing almost up to the fall of the Arbenz regime. On the national level, in the Meeting of the National Democratic Front (FDN) on May 18 to decide the allocation of candidacies for the November congressional elections the PAR backed the Communist bid to increase their representation by a possible two seats in the new Congress.[8] On the local level, by the beginning of June, Communist leader Jubal Cetino, with the cooperation of Gutiérrez and the Communist-controlled CGTG

251; 8027:1, 2, 34, 35, 52, 60, 61, 69, 90, 96-102, 106-9, 121, 124-40, 150-5, 186, 190, 211, 213-5, 227, 236-8, 242, 243, and 259; 8050:775, 776, 795-8, 1338, and 1565-7; 8051:1926, 1973, 2712, 2867, and 2972; 8052:3550, 4181, 4358, and 4473-4622; 8032:3203-8; 8022:347, 686, 814, and 832; 8008:7281, 7283, 7843, and 7853; Y-X-5:846, 847, and 1145; Y-X-3:4190; Documents 178, 238, 239, 240, 241, 340, 386, 483, 496, 556, 600, 781, 815, 823, 871, 1130, 1169, 1467, 1468, 1469, 1801, 1832-1888, 1907, 2010 and Y-343. Most of these messages are from local Secretaries General who claim to be speaking for the rank and file members. In the final result these functionaries probably could not have mobilized more than a fraction of the membership of their organizations.

[8] See 8022:376-280, "Informe sobre la reunión del Frente Democrático Nacional del día 18 de Mayo de 1954," by Marco Antonio Villamar Contreras of the PRG.

had brought the campesino unions of Chiquimula into the Communist camp.[9] The President apparently approved the Communists' plan to build up para-military units under their control, if not a full-fledged worker's militia. It appeared that the Communist position was secure as long as Arbenz remained in control.

One of the most important moves taken by the Arbenz regime with an eye to strengthening its position and increasing its capacity to resist attack was the controversial purchase of arms from the Soviet bloc. In the end this gamble, along with the related proposal for arming the workers as an auxiliary force, backfired and contributed to the fall of the regime.

For years the Guatemalan government had been vainly seeking to purchase arms, first in the United States, then from other countries in the hemisphere, and still later from West European sources.[10] Finally Arbenz looked behind the Iron Curtain for help. Major Alfonso Martínez, a long-time crony of the President, left Guatemala for Europe early in January 1954. The widespread rumor at the time was that Martínez had left Guatemala because of his inability to cope with Pellecer and the President's failure to give him the necessary backing as Chief of the National Agrarian Department. Behind this smoke screen, Martínez went to Switzerland to negotiate payment for Czech arms which were to be shipped from Stettin, Poland, by a devious route on board a chartered Swedish ship, the *Alfhem*.[11]

The details of this controversial arms shipment are still shrouded in a certain amount of mystery and official secrecy. Whether the arms were intended for uprisings in neighboring countries, or to equip a peoples' militia in Guatemala, or merely to increase the capability of the Guatemalan army to put down the momentarily expected uprising, this shipment played a crucial role in the course of events that led to the overthrow of the Arbenz government. The news of its arrival caused

---

[9] See 8052:3557-8, Jubal Cetino to Leonardo Castillo Flores, September 6, 1953 and 8052:3633-4, Antonio Catalán Torres to Leonardo Castillo Flores, June 9, 1954.

[10] The self-styled "Black Eagle of Harlem," Fauntleroy Julian, acted as Guatemalan agent in several of these attempts as did Sra. de Arbenz's brother, Antonio Vilanova Castro. See Document 1554: Víctor Annicchiarico to Antonio Vilanova Castro, July 8, 1953.

[11] For the details of this shipment see U. S. Department of State, *Penetration of the Political Institutions of Guatemala by the International Communist Movement,* pp. 28-32 and Annex C, pp. 1-7.

a stir throughout the hemisphere. Guatemala's Central American neighbors, already alarmed by the encouragement given by the Arbenz government to subversive groups within their borders and the extracurricular activities of Guatemalan diplomats, were swept by rumors of impending coups supported by Guatemala. Honduras, already in the throes of a strike which threatened to turn into civil strife and believing that the Guatemalan Communists were the prime movers of a proposed insurrection, feared that some of the arms were intended for the Honduran strikers.[12]

Within Guatemala the officer corps of the army feared that the arms would be used in such a way as to undermine its position or even to bring about its physical liquidation. These fears were fanned into flame by the proposals of the labor and campesino leaders for the training and arming of a peoples' militia to support the government in the threatened civil war.

At the beginning of June, the situation in Guatemala became increasingly tense. On June 2, Minister of Interior Augusto Charnaud MacDonald announced the discovery of a well-organized plot to overthrow the government. Orders went out to the police and all the revolutionary parties and mass organizations to report all signs of suspicious activity. On June 8 the government decreed the suspension of constitutional guarantees, the first time it had resorted to this extreme measure since the July 1951 disturbances. Fully aware of the fact that an attack by the Castillo Armas forces was imminent, the government undertook a campaign of mass arrests designed to break the back of the resistance movement within Guatemala.

The war of nerves had begun. While the radios of the so-called "Liberation Army" predicted a revolt within the next week and called upon the Guatemalan people to join in uprisings timed to coincide with the attack by the exiles, the government struck out at all suspected conspirators. Many opposition leaders who had weathered the March 1953 and January 1954 waves of repression now fled Guatemala or sought refuge in the embassies of neighboring countries to avoid arrest, torture and possible death at the hands of the brutal secret police headed by Major Jaime Rosenberg and Colonel Rogelio Cruz Wer.

---

[12] This strike was centered in the area close to the Guatemalan border on the Atlantic side, very near the port in Guatemala where the arms had been landed.

Many others who were less fortunate either disappeared entirely or were found dead on lonely roads or lake shores.[13]

THE CIVIL WAR: JUNE 18-27, 1954

On the morning of June 18, Castillo Armas' forces struck across the Honduran frontier at three different spots. Militarily the "Liberation Army" was not a very impressive force and, after penetrating into Guatemala up to perhaps twenty miles, it was contained by regular army units loyal to the government. While the skirmishing which went on for the next week received extensive coverage in the world press, no more than a few hundred men were activly involved on either side. The total of seventeen killed on both sides in the main clash, the "battle" of Chiquimula on June 24, was only a fraction of those killed by the police in the same period. While the existence of a battlefront and the nuisance attacks on the capital by two World War II fighters which composed the effective air arm of the Castillo Armas forces put intense pressure upon the Arbenz regime, the really crucial developments took place within Army headquarters and the National Palace.

While the war of nerves continued and conditions at the front were stalemated, the Communists were striving to organize the workers into an effective para-military organization.[14] Union members were organized into thirty-man sections and ordered to be ready for immediate mobilization. In addition Committees of Self-defense were established to handle contacts with the regular army. All was ready except for one

---

[13] While it is not possible to determine the exact number of these cases, there remains little doubt that the Arbenz government must bear the responsibility for the brutal murders of several hundred opposition leaders as well as for the hundreds of others who were cruelly tortured in an effort to uncover the plans of the opposition and to strike terror into the hearts of potential conspirators. Among the materials bearing on this subject is microfilm reel 8023, "Documents Pertaining to Tortures Under the Arbenz Regime," a collection of sworn statements. In addition to *Así se Gestó la Liberación* previously cited, *Genocidio sobre Guatemala,* published by the Secretaría de Propaganda y Divulgación de la Presidencia de la República de Guatemala, 1954, is the best of a variety of official publications on this subject. See also José Alfredo Palmieri's pamphlet entitled *Terror en Guatemala.*

[14] See 8027:113, Comité Patriotico de Defensa de la Soberanía Nacional to Carlos Manuel Pellecer, June 22, 1954; Y-X-2:2640-6, Plan de mobilización de la CGTG en defensa de los derechos de los trabajadores, la Democracia y la Soberanía.

thing: the army balked at giving out arms to these worker and campesino organizations. On June 24, the Communist labor leaders brought
Arbenz word that the army had refused their offers of aid and that
his hand-picked commanders at the front were wavering in their
support for the government

This news came as a blow to the President, who had apparently
believed that his hold over the army was secure. According to his later
statements, Arbenz felt that the Castillo Armas invasion had been
completely checked and that effective pressure could be brought to
bear upon Honduras and Nicaragua through the United Nations, thus
depriving the opposition forces of their base. Elsewhere in Guatemala
the government appeared to have the situation fairly well in hand.[15]
On Friday the 25th the President instructed his loyal Chief of the
Armed Forces, Colonel Carlos Enrique Díaz, to furnish arms to the
revolutionary parties and mass organizations. Arbenz felt secure in
the belief that "counting on the armed populace, we would be perfectly
able to fight, not only the invaders, but also against our own treacherous
army." He was shaken to receive a report from Col. Díaz on Saturday
that the other officers would not allow him to fulfill the order to equip
the civilians.

Meanwhile Gutiérrez had summoned all the "brigades" and "com-
mandos" to gather on Sunday.[16] In addition the labor leaders addressed
an urgent message to the President seeking an interview on the immediate use of the workers in the defense of the regime.[17] However it
was already too late. On the morning of June 27, representatives of the
officer corps met with the President and demanded his resignation.
Unnerved by the rapid deterioration of his position and unwilling or
unable to take the final step of opposing the army, Arbenz agreed to
step aside in favor of Col. Díaz. (Apparently Arbenz, who later called
his faith in the loyalty of the army his greatest mistake, felt that Díaz
would be the most apt to adhere to his wishes and continue the fight
against Castillo Armas.)

Arbenz's decision to resign brought consternation to the ranks of the
Communists, who urged him to resist even at the cost of plunging the

[15] This story is taken largely from an interview of Ronaldo Ramírez with
ex-President Arbenz in Prague which was published in *La Prensa Libre* of
San José, Costa Rica, October 25, 1955.
[16] 8024:660, CGTG boletín para la radio, June 26, 1954.
[17] Document 1400: CGTG to Arbenz, June 27, 1954.

nation into open civil war. While the top PGT leaders severely criticized Fortuny for failing to dissuade the President, Pellecer attempted to organize uprisings in the Communist stronghold of Escuintla. At approximately 9:00 o'clock on the evening of Sunday, June 27, Arbenz read his resignation speech to the nation over the government radio. This short address, written for him by Fortuny, stated that his objective was to avoid the needless shedding of Guatemalan blood and that Col. Díaz had promised to continue the fight against the invaders and prevent reprisals against any of Arbenz's backers.

The sudden resignation of the leader whose slogans had been "we will carry the revolution forward, whatever may happen and whatever may be the cost" and "not a single step backwards" paralyzed most of the government's supporters. The officials of the Arbenz regime and leaders of the revolutionary parties turned their attention to looting the treasury and insuring their personal safety. When it became apparent the next day that Díaz would not be able to control the situation, hundreds of the leaders of the Arbenz regime sought asylum in friendly embassies. This headlong flight was led by Arbenz himself who, accompanied by Fortuny and hundreds of leading *Arbencistas*, crowded into the Mexican Embassy. The Arbenz era had come to its inglorious end.[18]

WHY ARBENZ FELL

While the immediate cause of the fall of the Arbenz regime was the sudden withdrawal of the army's support, this in turn was conditioned and made possible by a number of other developments. Although it had been partially masked by the Communist-organized mass demonstrations in support of the regime, enthusiasm for the Arbenz government

---

[18] The ex-President and his supporters were eventually granted safe conduct by the new government and went into exile, chiefly in Mexico and El Salvador. Arbenz and his family went to Europe and soon disappeared behind the Iron Curtain. Nearly three years after his fall he returned to Latin America and set up his headquarters in Montevideo, Uruguay. Díaz governed for little more than a day before being replaced by a junta of officers headed by Col. Elfego Monzón. After several days of tense negotiations in El Salvador, a new junta was formed with Castillo Armas as the leading figure. In September 1954 the other junta members resigned and Castillo Armas became President. The details of the negotiations in the days immediately following the fall of Arbenz can be followed in a volume put out in 1954 by the Secretaría de Información of the Salvadorean government entitled *De la neutralidad vigilante a la mediación con Guatemala*.

had declined critically during the preceding months. The extent of corruption within the regime had been made evident by several scandals in late 1953 and early 1954. Quarrels within and between the revolutionary parties led to outbursts during which much dirty linen was washed in public. Many middle class individuals who had originally looked favorably upon the government became increasingly disillusioned and grew tired of the continued high state of tension and political agitation.

While the country's general economic position was deteriorating as a result of the government's exaggerated economic nationalism, agricultural production dropped in the aftermath of disorders which accompanied Communist efforts to exploit agrarian reform and use it as an instrument for punishing their enemies. As the gap between the government's promises of spectacular economic gains and actual performance became more noticeable, the enthusiasm of the masses waned. Many better informed Guatemalans resented the diplomatic isolation to which the government's policies had led the nation, while persons who had argued that Arbenz was merely using the Communists began to suspect that the reverse might be true. When in the face of the growing threat posed by Castillo Armas, Arbenz was forced to reveal the repressive machinery behind the regime's democratic facade, erstwhile supporters of the government began to have second thoughts.

The end result of these developments was that when the final denouement came, many Guatemalans who might have been expected to support the regime were torn by ambivalent feelings and adopted a wait-and-see policy. Since the bulk of the population had never taken an active part in national affairs, but had preferred to sit on the sidelines and cheer the winner, the balance of power rested with the armed forces.

Although from the October 1944 Revolution until June 1954 the army did not play a decisive role in Guatemalan politics, it remained an important power factor. (See Chapter III, pp. 42-43.) Arbenz came into the presidency with the support of the army, and it appeared that most of the key officers were personally loyal to him. Several developments in the last month of the Arbenz regime gave these officers an opportunity to test whether the President reciprocated this loyalty. In the eyes of many officers, Arbenz, when presented with a choice between the interests of the army and those of the Communists, chose wrongly. When the final showdown came, the consensus of their opinion was that he had forfeited his claim to their support and that the Arbenz regime was not worth immersing the nation in a bloodbath. Communist influence was the most prominent, but not the exclusive root of their discontent.

In explaining and justifying their actions, these military leaders stated that Communism had disrupted the nation and raised "false passions" which led to virtual civil strife long before the attack by the forces of Castillo Armas. In addition to believing that the Arbenz-Communist regime had seriously jeopardized the interests of the Guatemalan people and embroiled the nation in quarrels with all its neighbors, the officers felt that their own position, if not their very lives, was endangered. Their ultimatum came only after Arbenz had said he was ordering 5000 armed workers to the front and the officers saw their functions usurped by the Communist labor leaders.

Strong elements within the officer corps of the army had for some time been uneasy over the increasingly important role of the Communist-controlled labor organizations in national politics. These officers bore in mind the lesson of 1949 and the repeated assertions by the leaders of organized labor that the workers would fight to defend their gains. As the influence of the Communists in the Arbenz regime became increasingly evident, more of these officers became concerned with the difficult international situation which the foreign and domestic policies of the government were placing the nation. Considering the fact that many of the older officers were conservatively inclined, that others saw the traditional privileged position and political influence of the army endangered by the extensive changes which were taking place, that still other officers bore resentment over the assassination of Arana and the army purge that followed, and that there are always dissatisfied officers who feel their position and prospects would be improved by a successful coup, it was not surprising that when the crisis came the army was not willing to stand squarely behind the regime. Many officers were personally loyal to the President and he had bound others to the regime by giving them important governmental and diplomatic posts, and had conferred material benefits upon the officer corps as a whole. In spite of all this, the army leaders were unwilling to plunge Guatemala into the bloodbath of civil war to support a regime which they finally realized was heavily infiltrated by Communists bent upon undermining the power position of the army.

Uneasiness about the future designs of the Arbenz regime for the army was felt by many of its officers. Although the leaders of the government publicly expressed their esteem for the military, many of them (particularly Alfonso Bauer Paíz and other PRG leaders who were still wedded to the doctrine of *civilismo* as one of the original principles of the Revolution of 1944) were known to be extremely hostile toward the army and desirous of eliminating it as a political force. The Communists were believed to have plans for remaking the army into a "democratic" force, plans which had little room for any but the most "progressive" of the current officers. The army and organized labor generally regarded each other with ill-concealed mutual distrust and suspicion. As the year 1954 progressed, the military leaders were deeply concerned over the efforts of the Communist labor leaders to organize and arm a large-scale workers' militia.[19]

When Arbenz, at the beginning of June, placed Leonardo Castillo Flores in charge of the proposed "peoples' militia" with Major Alfonso Martínez of the DAN and Captain Constantino Bernasconi, Director General of Highways, as his assistants, many regular officers felt that the President was betraying their trust. The matter was brought to a head at the time of the Castillo Armas attack by a widespread belief that the chiefs of the peoples' militia were planning the physical elimination of the officer corps. Although Colonel Carlos Enrique Díaz, the Chief of the Armed Forces, ordered the General Staff to cooperate fully with the leaders of the peoples' militia and with Gutiérrez as coordinator of the regime's defense, the army balked at arming or training the militia.

In early June the officer corps raised the question of Communism in three separate interviews with the President, affording in effect a chance for him to clarify his position and for them to ascertain whether his primary loyalty was to the Communists or to the Army. The President had already publicly rejected proposals that he dissociate himself from the Communists. At the first of his meetings with the officer corps Arbenz stated that he could not be a Communist since he was accustomed to the way of life of a substantial property owner and quoted Perón to the effect that "Communism was like strychnine, beneficial in

---

[19] See Document 950: report to the Consejo Superior de la Defensa Nacional by a commission entrusted with the task of drawing up a plan for the "re-establishment of control over the militias of the Republic by the National Army," May 9, 1954.

small doses but highly dangerous in large quantities."[20] When asked whether he was in a position to know when Communism stopped being beneficial and began to be dangerous, Arbenz gave no answer. Instead he put forth the argument that it was better to have the Communists working in the open than underground and that there were Communists in every democratic country. Arbenz justified their inclusion in his government on the ground of their support of his program as contrasted to the lack of support from the opposition sectors. He reportedly defended his personal friendship with Fortuny, Gutiérrez and Pellecer and argued that these Communist leaders had been of great help in resolving many problems.

On June 5, the *Estado Mayor* or General Staff of the army directed a memorial to the President which in effect recommended the curbing of Communism and the adoption of a moderate and conciliatory policy by the government.[21] Arbenz rejected their proposals and stated that he would continue to follow the same policies as long as he remained President.[22] His attitude on this question began to swing the balance of opinion against him and set in motion the developments which culminated in the demand for his resignation on June 27. Apparently Arbenz either misjudged the temper of the army or felt that his labor support was sufficient to keep the army in line. In either case, he paid dearly for his miscalculations.[23]

RETROSPECT AND A WORD OF CAUTION

The events of the last week of the Arbenz regime showed that Communism in Guatemala had not developed into a successful popular movement. Although they exercised great influence through the key

---

[20] Much of this section is based upon a March 1956 release of the Guatemalan Army's public relations section replying to the statements of Arbenz in the interview cited above. Another useful source is del Valle Matheu, *op. cit.*, pp. 141-50.

[21] See Document 1037: Pliego de consultas de la oficialidad del Estado Mayor del Ejército, preparado por sugestión del Señor Presidente de la República, para los efectos de la plática que dictará el propio alto funcionario oportunamente, en este cuerpo, June 5, 1954.

[22] See Document 1034: replies of Arbenz to the memorial cited above.

[23] It may well be the case that Arbenz had lost touch with the General Staff and the field commanders and judged army sentiment by the officers who formed part of his own staff or held political positions in his government. It seems apparent that he overestimated Díaz's control over the army.

positions which they had attained in the country's rather simple political structure, the Communists had not found sufficient time to build a
broad base or to sink their roots deeply. While they controlled the
machinery of organized labor, their hold over the mass of workers and
peasants was effective largely to the extent that they could provide
direct material advantages. To a considerable degree the same conditions which facilitated the Communists' rapid rise to power contributed
to their ineffectiveness in the final crisis. For example, the fact that
only a relatively few workers took an active part in the affairs of the
unions enabled the Communists to take over and dominate the labor
movement; however, when the showdown came in June 1954 only a
proportionately small number of workers were ready or willing to act.
While the ineffectiveness and opportunism of the other revolutionary
politicians allowed the Communists to exert a degree of influence
completely out of proportion to their numbers, it also meant that these
parties were unable to make any positive contribution to the defense
of the regime. Communist propagandists and agitators found it difficult
to make progress against the conservatism and good natured passivity
of the Indians. The low level of political maturity of the bulk of the
ladino population similarly limited the depth to which the Communists
could sink their roots.

With the collapse of the Arbenz regime, the Communists were
confronted with an entirely new and much more difficult situation.
Accustomed to tolerance or even the favor of the government, they
were suddenly faced with the problem of survival under a hostile
regime whose leaders were dedicated to the destruction of the party
and the eradication of all traces of Communist influence. The new
government outlawed the PGT; dissolved the parties, unions, and mass
organizations which were Communist-influenced; and adopted legislation which proscribed a wide variety of Communist activities.

The few leaders who did not take asylum in foreign embassies faced
an uphill battle in rebuilding the party. Led by Secretary General
Bernardo Alvarado Monzón (until his capture in the fall of 1955 and
subsequent expulsion from the country) and stripped to its hard core
of dedicated members, the PGT went underground. While carrying on
some propaganda activities and exploiting unpopular actions of the
Castillo government, the Communists devoted their greatest efforts to

rebuilding the party and reestablishing their influence among their chief target groups, the workers and the students.

During the first part of 1955 the PGT leaders assessed the reasons for the collapse of the Arbenz regime.[24] They felt that the Communists had relied too heavily upon the middle class, which proved unable to withstand "imperialist pressures." Other mistakes which, in their eyes, contributed to the downfall of the regime included: failure to pay sufficient attention to the army or to effectively neutralize it; allowing the opponents of the regime too great freedom; and expectance that the Organization of American States or UN would act to prevent the "aggression" against Guatemala. In addition the party leaders felt that they had placed too much faith in Arbenz's revolutionary determination. The PGT criticized his "typically bourgeois attitude" in underestimating the role which the masses could play and relying too greatly on the army.[25]

By mid-1956 the PGT leaders had devised a new program and tactical line which took into account past mistakes and was designed to serve as the basis for a comeback by the party.[26]

Picturing the Castillo government as "anti-national, anti-patriotic, anti-democratic and unpopular," the PGT opposed economic concessions to U.S. companies, favored measures to defend native Guatemalan industry from "imperialist domination," and endorsed trade with the "countries of the Socialist camp" as a cure for Guatemala's economic problems. They resolved to organize the struggle of the workers for their "essential demands" and the fight of the peasants for land. The Communist leaders professed to see signs of the "decomposition of the forces of reaction" and an "increase in the peoples' resistance, protest, and struggle for democratic rights."

The PGT recognized that there were many groups, both within Guatemala and among the exiles, which opposed the Castillo regime

[24] Comisión Política del Comité Central del Partido Guatemalteco del Trabajo, *La Intervención Norte-americana y el Derrocamiento del Régimen Democrático,* June, 1955.

[25] The major portion of the blame for the party's shortcomings was borne by ex-Secretary General Fortuny, who was stripped of all offices within the PGT.

[26] Comisión Política del Comité Central del Partido Guatemalteco del Trabajo, *La Situación Nacional y Nuestra Táctica,* Guatemala, 27 de Julio de 1956.

and wished a "reconquest of democracy," a return to *Arevalismo*, or the continuance of the October revolution. In the eyes of the Communists one of the chief tasks facing the party was to convince the "Democratic Bourgeoisie" that they should ally with the PGT rather than with discontented or ambitious military groups. The Communists were alarmed by the tendency of these "democratic" groups to seek an accommodation with U.S. interests. The PGT leaders felt that the students, petty bourgeoisie, and peasantry could play a revolutionary role with proper "impetus and guidance by the proletariat."

Rejecting coups, adventurism, and provocation as "harmful to the advancement of the democratic forces," the PGT emphasized the "steady daily struggle of organizing and activating the masses" as the proper strategy leading toward the "overthrow of the reactionary dictatorship and the establishment of a government of national liberation." Particular attention was to be devoted to the forging of a worker-peasant alliance as the first step towards a united front of the "democratic and progressive classes" in which the proletariat would play the directing role.

Realizing that this would be a long and difficult task, the Communists stressed the need for flexibility in their tactics. Reaffirming their belief that "the triumph over the reactionary dictatorship will be accomplished by the route of revolution," the PGT adopted the view that this must be a mass revolution. Until such time as conditions would guarantee the success of a "peoples' insurrection," the party would concentrate upon organizing the masses and carrying on the struggle for their demands through all legal channels. While stopping short of provocation and avoiding offering the government an excuse for repression, the Communists would support all popular demands and participate in all possible legal organizations. The Communists would seek out points of coincidence with all other "democratic" groups. Although not denying the transitory usefulness of agreements with leaders of other forces, the PGT placed greater stress upon the work of promoting unity from below and developing closer links with the masses.

Although the PGT had made steady progress in rebuilding from its low point at the end of 1954, the party leaders admitted that its propaganda work had been relatively ineffective and that its adjustment to clandestine methods was still incomplete. Nevertheless they were hopeful that they could soon go over to the offensive and the work of the "anti-imperialist and anti-feudal" revolution could be resumed.

Success depends on the heightened consciousness and fighting spirit of the working class, on its alliance with the peasants, and on the unity of all the democratic forces. Organization, unity, and the daily mass struggle are the sure road to see our country free of imperialists and traitors and to win democratic freedoms, the people's welfare, and national independence.

Since the assassination of President Castillo on July 26, 1957, the Communists have had an opportunity to improve their position in Guatemala.[27] During the period of protracted political instability which followed the abortive October 20, 1957, attempt to choose a successor to Castillo, many Communist and *Arbencista* exiles returned to Guatemala and enforcement of anti-Communist legislation was ineffective.[28] Although a Conservative, General Miguel Ydígoras Fuentes, was elected President on January 19, 1958, the leftists showed remarkable strength and the middle of the road party founded by Castillo suffered a humiliating defeat. As the new government came into office, Guatemala stood once again at a crossroads.

Thus the fall of the Arbenz regime, although a severe blow to the immediate aims and aspirations of the Guatemalan Communists, did not spell the end of Communist activity in that country or even the permanent removal of a Communist threat. During the nearly four years which have elapsed since the party was outlawed, its leaders in exile have been able to devote their efforts to study and have increased their theoretical capabilities. Several top leaders have been free for the first time to travel to the U.S.S.R. for advanced training and indoc-

---

[27] The assassin, a member of the Presidential Guard, was apparently a pro-Communist fanatic. However, the investigation of the crime is continuing and many Guatemalans now feel that he was the tool of disgruntled members of the administration. Lt. Col. Enrique T. Oliva, a member of the 1954 junta and head of the National Security Agency at the time of Castillo's death, has formally been accused of implication in the crime and is awaiting trial.

[28] This election was won by the candidate of the official party of the Castillo administration, the National Democratic Movement (MDN). However, popular resentment over widespread electoral fraud and resentment of the left over the interim government's refusal to legalize their party led to rioting in Guatemala City. As a result, the elections were annulled and a new provisional president installed. New and much freer elections were held on January 19, 1958.

trination. Within Guatemala a new secondary level of leaders have developed their talents in the underground movement.

The Communists have carefully studied their failures and worked assiduously to correct their shortcomings. If the non-Communist politicians who are competing for leadership in Guatemala today do not show an equal ability to profit from the lessons of the Arbenz era, Communism may some day regain a position of influence in that troubled Republic.

BIBLIOGRAPHY

PRIMARY SOURCES

The documents upon which this study is based were gathered in July 1954 by the Guatemalan National Committee for Defense against Communism (Comité Nacional de Defensa contra el Comunismo). This organization was established after the fall of the Arbenz regime and given the task of collecting all available information on Communist operations in Guatemala during the preceding decade. Entrusted with wide powers, this committee seized the files of all Communist-infiltrated organizations and leading figures of the Arbenz regime. From the mass of material gathered by the Committee more than 50,000 documents were reproduced and brought to this country for careful analysis. (The original documents remain in Guatemala in the custody of the General Sub-Direction of National Security [Sub-dirección General de Seguridad Nacional].) Upon completion of this study, the microfilms and prints have been donated by the Foreign Policy Research Institute of the University of Pennsylvania to the Library of Congress where they are now available to other scholars.

In addition to material from the files of the Guatemalan Communist Party and its leaders, the collection contains the records and correspondence of the other leading political parties and figures, as well as that of the Communist-dominated labor and peasant organizations.

The major portion of the collection is composed of 50 reels of microfilm which total over 50,000 frames. White on black prints have been made of much of the microfilm material. For ease in identification, the number of the reel and the number of the frame have been included in the citation of this material in the footnotes. For example, 8016:117 would be reel 8016, frame 117.

Reel	*Contents*	*No. of Frames*
8000	Carnets of the PGT	213
8001-8002	Archives of Correspondence of the CGTG, 1952	2,849
8003-8008	Correspondence of the CGTG, Jan. 1953-March 1954	10,169
8009-8010	Archives of the FSM and CTAL	2,035
8011	STEG Correspondence	798
8012	"Actas" of the National Teachers' Association	102
8013	CGTG Miscellaneous Correspondence	1,201
8014	CGTG Correspondence of the Sec. of Organization	1,708
8015	FSM and CTAL Correspondence	404
8016-8017	CGTG and CTG Correspondence	2,300
8018	CGTG Correspondence of the National Textile Federation, 1954	402
8019	Personal Papers of Víctor M. Gutiérrez	433
8020	Documents Showing the Relationship of the PAR, PRG and CNCG	208
8021	Papers of Fortuny, Alvarado Fuentes and the PAR	319
8022	Miscellaneous Correspondence of the PRG	1,013
8023	Documents Pertaining to Tortures Perpetrated by the Arbenz Regime	497
8024	Correspondence of the CGTG and SAMF	1,522
8025	Documents of Various Labor Organizations	647
8026	CTG and CGTG Documents and Correspondence	435
8027	Correspondence of the PRG and PGT	292

In addition to the microfilms and the prints from them, the collection contains several other types of material. There are prints of important documents, letters and receipts (numbered from 1 through 2094, Y-1 through Y-432, and X-1 through X-157); printed material (reports, speeches, handbills, constitutions, laws, etc.); and a miscellaneous collection of reproduced documents, pamphlets and notebooks.

Finally, the collection includes a complete file of the Communist Party newspapers, *Octubre* (weekly from June 21, 1950, through August 14, 1953) and *Tribuna Popular* (daily from August 15, 1953, through June 29, 1954).

INTERVIEWS

Avila Ayala, Manuel María, Guatemala City, June 8, 1957.
Balcárcel, José Luis, Mexico City, June 22, 1957.
Barrera, Armando, Guatemala City, June 11, 1957.
Bauer Paíz, Alfonso, Mexico City, June 25, 1957.
Blanco, Ramón, Guatemala City, May 31, 1957.
Cardoza y Aragón, Luis, Mexico City, June 24, 1957.
Contreras Vélez, Alvaro, Guatemala City, June 4, 1957.
Figueroa, Gerardo, Guatemala City, June 6, 1957.
Galán Paloma, Mario, Guatemala City, June 17, 1957.
Galich, Luis, Mexico City, June 25, 1957.
García, Jorge Mario, Mexico City, June 25, 1957.
García Bauer, Carlos, Guatemala City, June 3 and 5, 1957.
García Granados, Jorge, Guatemala City, June 9, 1957.
Gómez Padilla, Julio, Mexico City, June 25, 1957.
Gutiérrez, Víctor Manuel, Mexico City, June 26, 1957.
Hurtado, Carlos, Guatemala City, May 31, 1957.
Mencos, Mario Enrique, Guatemala City, May 30, 1957.
Monteforte Toledo, Mario, Mexico City, June 24, 1957.
Palmieri, José Alfredo, Guatemala City, May 31, 1957.
Rivas Montes, Mario, Guatemala City, June 1, 1957.
Rosenhouse, Robert, Guatemala City, June 4, 1957.
Simons, Carlos, Guatemala City, June 11, 1957.
Soto, Manuel, Guatemala City, June 10, 1957.
Toriello, Guillermo, Mexico City, June 25, 1957.
Vielman, Julio, Guatemala City, June 4, 1957.
Villagrán Kramer, Francisco, Guatemala City, June 9 and 19, 1957.

BOOKS AND ARTICLES

Aceves, Mario, "Verdugos Rojos de Guatemala," *Mañana* (Mexico), Año 57, Número 575 (4 de Septiembre de 1954), pp. 22-23.
Adams, Richard N., *Encuesta Sobre la Cultura de los Ladinos en*

Guatemala, publicación No. 2 del Seminario de Integración Social Guatemalteca, Guatemala, Editorial del Ministerio de Educación Pública, 1956.

———, (ed.), *Political Changes in Guatemalan Indian Communities: A Symposium,* Publication No. 24 of the Middle American Research Institute, Tulane University, 1957.

Adler, John H., Eugene R. Schlesinger and Ernest C. Olson, *Public Finance and Economic Development in Guatemala,* Stanford University Press, 1952.

Aguilar P., J. Humberto, *Vida y muerte de una dictadura: el drama político de Guatemala,* Mexico, Linotipográfica Nieto, 1944.

Alba, Víctor, *Historia del Comunismo en América Latina,* Mexico, Ediciones Occidentales, 1954.

Alexander, Robert J., *Communism in Latin America,* Rutgers University Press, 1957.

———, "Guatemalan Communists," *Canadian Forum,* Vol. XXXIV, No. 402 (July, 1954), pp. 81-83.

———, "The Guatemalan Revolution and Communism," *Foreign Policy Bulletin,* Vol. XXXIII, No. 14 (April 1, 1954), pp. 4-7.

Almond, Gabriel A., *The Appeals of Communism,* Princeton University Press, 1954.

Alvarez Elizondo, Pedro, *El presidente Arévalo y el retorno a Bolívar,* Mexico, Ediciones Rex, 1947.

Arévalo, Juan José, *Discursos en la Presidencia, (1945-1947),* Guatemala, Tipografía Nacional, 1948.

———, *Escritos Políticos,* Guatemala, Tipografía Nacional, 1945.

———, *Fábula del Tiburón y las Sardinas, América Latina Estrangulada,* Santiago de Chile, Ediciones América Libre, 1956.

———, *Guatemala, La Democracia y el Imperio,* Santiago de Chile, Ediciones Libertas, 1954.

Bauer Paíz, Alfonso, *Cómo opera el capital Yanqui en Centroamérica (El caso de Guatemala),* Mexico, Editora Ibero-Mexicana, 1956.

——— and Julio Valladares Castillo, *La Frutera Ante la Ley,* Publicación No. 1 del Ministerio de Economía y Trabajo, Guatemala, Tipografía Nacional, 1949.

Behrendt, Richard F., "The Uprooted: A Guatemalan Sketch," *New Mexico Quarterly Review,* Vol. XIX, No. 1 (Spring, 1949), pp. 25-31.

Bishop, Edwin, "The Development of Unionism in Guatemala," MS., August, 1956.

Bogardus, Emory S., "Social History of Guatemala," *Sociology and Social Research,* Vol. XXXVIII, No. 5 (May, 1954), pp. 323-28.

Britnell, George E., "Factors in the Economic Development of Guatemala," *American Economic Review,* Vol. XLIII, No. 2 (May, 1953), pp. 104-14.

——, "Problems of Economic and Social Change in Guatemala," *Canadian Journal of Economics,* Vol. XVII, No. 4 (November, 1951), pp. 468-81.

Bush, Archer C., *Organized Labor in Guatemala, 1944-1949: A Case Study of an Adolescent Labor Movement in an Underdeveloped Country,* Hamilton, New York, Colgate University Bookstore, 1950.

Calderón Salazar, José, *Letras de Liberación,* Guatemala, Tipografía Nacional, 1955.

Caplow, Theodore, "Social Ecology of Guatemala City," *Social Forces,* Vol. XXVIII, No. 2 (December, 1949), pp. 113-33.

Cardoza y Aragón, Luis, *Guatemala, las líneas de su mano,* Mexico, Fondo de Cultura Económica, 1955.

——, *La Revolución Guatemalteca,* Mexico, Ediciones Cuadernos Americanos, 1955.

Castellanos, J. Humberto R., "Caída del Comunismo en Guatemala," *Estudios Centro Americanos* (El Salvador), October, 1954, pp. 519-25.

Congreso contra la Intervención Soviética en América Latina, 1st, Mexico, 1954, Comisión Permanente, *El libro negro del Comunismo en Guatemala,* Mexico, S. Turanzas del Valle, 1954.

Cumberland, Charles C., "Guatemala: Labor and the Communists," *Current History,* Vol. XXIV, No. 139 (March, 1953), pp. 143-48.

Dion, Marie-Berthe, "The Social and Political Ideas of Juan José Arévalo and Their Relationship to Contemporary Trends of Latin American Thought," Unpublished Master's thesis, The American University, Washington, D.C., 1956.

Draper, Theodore, "The Minutemen of Guatemala," *The Reporter,* Vol. III, No. 9 (October 24, 1950), pp. 32-35.

Evans, F. Bowen (ed.), *World-wide Communist Propaganda Activities,* New York, The Macmillan Co., 1955.

Ewald, Robert H., *Bibliografía Comentada Sobre Antropología Social Guatemalteca, 1900-1955,* Publicación del Seminario de Integración Social Guatemalteca, Guatemala, Tipografía Nacional, 1956.

Fenwick, Charles G., "Jurisdictional Questions Involved in the Guatemalan Revolution," *American Journal of International Law,* Vol. XLVIII, No. 4 (October, 1954), pp. 597-602.

Galich, Manuel, *Del Pánico al Ataque,* Guatemala, Tipografía Nacional, 1949.

——, *Por Qué Lucha Guatemala: Arévalo y Arbenz: dos hombres contra un imperio,* Buenos Aires, Elmer Editor, 1956.

García Bauer, Carlos, *En el Amanecer de una Nueva Era,* Guatemala, Tipografía Nacional, 1951.

García Bauer, José, *Nuestra Revolución Legislativa,* Guatemala, Tipografía Nacional, 1948.

García L., Graciela, *Las luchas revolucionarias de la Nueva Guatemala,* Mexico, 1952.

Geiger, Theodore, *Communism Versus Progress in Guatemala,* National Planning Association, Planning Pamphlet No. 85, 1953.

Gillin, John, *The Culture of Security in San Carlos,* Publication No. 16 of the Middle American Research Institute, Tulane University, 1951.

—— and Kalman H. Silvert, "Ambiguities in Guatemala," *Foreign Affairs,* Vol. XXXIV, No. 3 (April, 1956), pp. 469-82.

Gorkin, Julian, "La Experiencia de Guatemala: Por una Política de la Libertad en Latinoamérica," *Cuadernos* (France), No. 9 (Noviembre-Diciembre, 1954), pp. 88-93.

Grant, Donald, "Guatemala and United States Foreign Policy," *Journal of International Affairs,* Vol. IX, No. 1 (1955), pp. 64-72.

Great Britain, Foreign Office, *Report on Events Leading up to and Arising out of the Change of Regime in Guatemala,* London, His Majesty's Stationery Office, 1954.

Guatemala, República de, Asamblea Constituyente, *Diario de sesiones de la Asamblea Constituyente de 1945,* Guatemala, Tipografía Nacional, 1951.

——, Consejo de Economía, *La Empresa Eléctrica de Guatemala, S.A.: un problema nacional,* publicación No. 5 del Ministerio de Economía y Trabajo, Guatemala, Editorial del Ministerio de Educación Pública, 1950.

——, Departamento de Publicidad de la Presidencia, *Los Pueblos de la República Contra la Conspiración No. 27*, Guatemala, Tipografía Nacional, 1950.

——, ——, *Una democracia a prueba de fuego*, Guatemala, Tipografía Nacional, 1949.

——, Dirección General de Estadística, *Primer censo industrial*, 1946, Guatemala, 1951.

——, ——, *Oficina Permanente del Censo, April 18, 1950*, Guatemala, Imprenta Universitaria, 1953.

——, Ministerio de Gobernación, *Constitución de la República de Guatemala Decretada por la Asamblea Constituyente el 11 de Marzo de 1945*, Guatemala, Tipografía Nacional, 1950.

——, Presidencia, Publicaciones del Departamento Agrario Nacional, *Decreto Número 900, Ley de Reforma Agraria*, Guatemala, Tipografía Nacional, 1952.

——, Secretaría de Divulgación, Cultura y Turismo de la Presidencia, *Así se Gestó la Liberación*, Guatemala, Tipografía Nacional, 1956.

——, ——, *Democracia, la mejor arma contra el comunismo*, Guatemala, Imprenta Iberia, 1957.

——, ——, *Documentos: reporte gráfico*, Guatemala, n.d.

——, ——, *La Intriga Roja en Guatemala*, Guatemala, n.d.

——, ——, *Liberación: reporte gráfico*, Guatemala, n.d.

——, Secretaría General de la Presidencia, *Proyecto de Ley de Reforma Agraria presentada al Congreso Nacional por la Presidencia de la República para su consideración*, Guatemala, Tipografía Nacional, 1952.

——, Secretaría de Propaganda y Divulgación de la Presidencia, *Genocidio sobre Guatemala*, Guatemala, Tipografía Nacional, 1954.

——, ——, *El Quinto Jinete de Apocalypsis*, Guatemala, n.d.

Hernández de León, F., *Viajes presidenciales*, Guatemala, Tipografía Nacional, 1940.

Holleran, Mary P., *Church and State in Guatemala*, New York, Columbia University Press, 1949.

Hunt, R.N. Carew, *The Theory and Practice of Communism: An Introduction*, 5th Revised Edition, London and New York, The Macmillan Company, 1957.

Ichaso, Francisco, "La Tragedia de Guatemala," *América* (Cuba), Vol. XLIV, No. 2 (Agosto de 1954), pp. 65-66.

Inman, Samuel Guy, *A New Day in Guatemala: A Study of the Present Social Revolution,* Wilton, Conn., Worldover Press, 1951.

International Bank for Reconstruction and Development, *The Economic Development of Guatemala: Report of a Mission,* Washton, D.C., 1951.

James, Daniel, *Red Design for the Americas: Guatemalan Prelude,* New York, The John Day Co., 1954.

Jensen, Amy Elizabeth, *Guatemala: A Historical Survey,* New York, Exposition Press, 1955.

Jones, Chester Lloyd, *Guatemala: Past and Present,* The University of Minnesota Press, 1940.

Kepner, Charles D. Jr., *Social Aspects of the Banana Industry,* Columbia University Studies in History, Economics and Public Law No. 414, Columbia University Press, 1936.

—— and Jay H. Soothill, *El imperio del banano,* Mexico, Ediciones del Caribe, 1949.

King-Hall, Stephen, *The Communist Conspiracy,* London, Constable and Co., 1953.

Kirkpatrick, Evron M., *Target the World: Communist Propaganda Activities in 1955,* New York, The Macmillan Company, 1956.

——, *Year of Crisis: Communist Propaganda Activities in 1956,* New York, The Macmillan Company, 1957.

Krehm, William, *Democracia y Tiranías en el Caribe,* Mexico, Unión Democrática Centroamericana, 1949.

——, "Victory for the West in Guatemala?", *International Journal,* Vol. IX, No. 4 (Autumn, 1954), pp. 295-302.

de León Aragón, Oscar, *Los contratos de la United Fruit Company y las Compañías Muelleras en Guatemala,* publicación No. 4 del Ministerio de Economía y Trabajo, Guatemala, Editorial del Ministerio de Educación Pública, 1950.

Leonard, Olen E., and Charles P. Loomis (eds.), *Readings in Latin American Social Organizations and Institutions,* Michigan State College Press, 1953.

López Villatoro, Mario, *Por los Fueros de la Verdad Histórica,* Guatemala, n.d.

Martz, J. D., *Communist Infiltration in Guatemala*, New York, Vantage Press, 1956.

Mejía, Medardo, *Juan José Arévalo o el Humanismo en la Presidencia*, Guatemala, Tipografía Nacional, 1951.

——, *El Movimiento Obrero en la Revolución de Octubre*, Guatemala, Tipografía Nacional, 1949.

Monroe, Keith, "Guatemala: What the Reds Left Behind," *Harper's Magazine*, Vol. CCXI, No. 1262 (July, 1955), pp. 60-65.

Morris, Bernard S., "Communist International Front Organizations: Their Nature and Function," *World Politics*, Vol. IX, No. 1 (October, 1956), pp. 76-87

Muñoz Meany, Enrique, *El Hombre y la Encrucijada*, Guatemala, Tipografía Nacional, 1950.

Najera Farfán, Mario Efraín, *Los Estafadores de la Democracia*, Buenos Aires, Editorial GLEM, 1956.

Newbold, Stokes (pseud.), *A Study of Receptivity to Communism in Rural Guatemala*, Washington, D.C., Department of State External Research Paper No. 116, 1954.

——, "Receptivity to Communist Fomented Agitation in Rural Guatemala," *Economic Development and Cultural Change*, Vol. V, No. 4 (July, 1957), pp. 338-61.

Ordóñez Argüello, Alberto (ed.), *Arévalo Visto por América*, Guatemala, Editorial del Ministerio de Educación Pública, 1951.

Osegueda, Raúl, *Operación Guatemala $$ OK $$*, Mexico, Editorial América Nueva, 1955.

Palacios, J. A., *Ingreso Nacional de Guatemala*, Guatemala, Banco de Guatemala Departamento de Estudios Económicos, 1951.

Palmieri, José Alfredo, *Terror en Guatemala*, Guatemala, n.d.

Page, Charles A., "Communism and the Labor Movements of Latin America," *Virginia Quarterly Review*, Vol. XXXI, No. 3 (Summer, 1955), pp. 373-82.

Partido Guatemalteco del Trabajo, Comisión Política, *La Intervención Norteamericana y el Derrocamiento del Régimen Democrático*, Guatemala, 1955.

Pike, Fredrick B., "Guatemala, The United States, and Communism in the Americas," *The Review of Politics*, Vol. XVII, No. 2 (April, 1955), pp. 232-61.

Pye, Lucian W., *Guerrilla Communism in Malaya,* Princeton University Press, 1956.

Reynolds, Frank, "La Infiltración Comunista en las Escuelas Públicas de Guatemala," *Todo* (Mexico), No. 1103 (October 23, 1954), pp. 36-38, No. 1104 (November 4, 1954), pp. 27-28, No. 1105 (November 11, 1954), pp. 20-22.

de los Ríos, Efraín, *Ombres contra Hombres: Drama de la vida real,* Mexico, El libro perfecto, S.A., 1945.

Ruiz Franco, Arcadio, *Hambre y Miseria,* Guatemala, Tipografía Nacional, 1950.

El Salvador, República de, Secretaría de Información, *De la Neutralidad Vigilante a la Mediación con Guatemala,* San Salvador, Imprenta Nacional, 1954.

Samayoa Chinchilla, Carlos, *El Dictador y Yo,* Guatemala, Editorial Iberia, 1950.

———, *El Quetzal no es Rojo,* Guatemala, 1956.

Schlesinger, Alfredo, *El Imperialismo Ruso,* Guatemala, Talleres Gutenberg, 1956.

Scully, M., "Inside Story of the Kremlin's Plot in Guatemala," *Readers' Digest,* Vol. LXVI, No. 394 (February, 1955), pp. 73-78.

Seminario de Integración Social Guatemalteca, publicación No. 1, *Cultura Indígena de Guatemala: Ensayos de Antropología Social,* Guatemala, Editorial del Ministerio de Educación Pública, 1956.

———, publicación No. 3, *Integración Social en Guatemala,* Guatemala, Editorial del Ministerio de Educación Pública, 1956.

Seton-Watson, Hugh, *From Lenin to Malenkov: The History of World Communism,* New York, Frederick A. Praeger, 1954.

Silvert, Kalman H., *A Study in Government: Guatemala, Part I, National and Local Government since 1944,* Publication No. 21 of the Middle American Research Institute, Tulane University, 1954.

Simons, Carlos E., "El Comunismo en Guatemala," *Estudios Sobre el Comunismo* (Chile), Año II, No. 5 (Septiembre, 1954), pp. 96-102.

Suslow, Leo A., *Aspects of Social Reforms in Guatemala, 1944-1949: Problems of Planned Social Change in an Underdeveloped Country,* Hamilton, New York, Colgate University Bookstore, 1949.

——, "Social Security in Guatemala: A Case Study in Bureaucracy and Social Welfare Planning," Unpublished Ph.D. dissertation, University of Connecticut, 1954.

Tax, Sol, *Penny Capitalism: A Guatemalan Indian Economy,* Smithsonian Institution, Institute of Social Anthropology, Publication No. 16, Washington, D.C., 1953.

——, and others, *Heritage of Conquest: The Ethnology of Middle America,* Glencoe, Illinois, The Free Press, 1952.

Taylor, Philip B. Jr., "The Guatemalan Affair: A Critique of United States Foreign Policy," *American Political Science Review,* Vol. L, No. 3 (September, 1956), pp. 787-806.

Thorning, Joseph F., "The Soviet Formula for Central America," *World Affairs,* Vol. CXIX, No. 1 (Spring, 1956), pp. 11-12.

Toriello, Guillermo, *La Batalla de Guatemala,* Mexico, Ediciones Cuadernos Americanos, 1955.

Travis, Helen Simon and A. B. Magil, *The Truth About Guatemala,* New York, New Century Publishers, 1954.

Tumin, Melvin, *Caste and Class in a Peasant Society,* Princeton University Press, 1952.

U.S. House of Representatives, Subcommittee on Latin America of the Select Committee on Communist Aggression, *Ninth Interim Report of Hearings,* 83rd Congress, Second Session, Washington, D.C., Government Printing Office, 1954.

U.S. Department of State, *A Case History of Communist Penetration: Guatemala,* Department of State Publication 6465, Inter-American Series 52, Washington, D.C., Government Printing Office, 1957.

——, *Intervention of International Communism in Guatemala,* Department of State Publication 5556, Inter-American Series 48, Washington, D.C., Government Printing Office, 1954.

——, *Penetration of the Political Institutions of Guatemala by the International Communist Movement,* Washington, D.C., Government Printing Office, 1954.

Urrutia Aparicio, Carlos, "Guatemalan Withdrawal from the Organization of Central American States," *American Journal of International Law,* Vol. XLVIII, No. 1 (January, 1954), pp. 145-48.

del Valle Matheu, Jorge, *Guía Sociogeográfica de Guatemala,* Guatemala, Tipografía Nacional, 1956.

——, *Un pueblo que se redime,* Guatemala, Tipografía Nacional, 1954.

——, *La Verdad Sobre "El Caso de Guatemala,"* Guatemala, 1956.

Wagley, Charles, *Santiago Chimaltenango: Estudio Antropológico-Social de una Comunidad Indígena de Huehuetenango,* publicación No. 4 del Seminario de Integración Social Guatemalteca, Guatemala, Editorial del Ministerio de Educación Pública, 1957.

Whetten, Nathan L., "Land Reform in a Modern World," *Rural Sociology,* Vol. XIX, No. 4 (December, 1954), pp. 329-34.

Whitaker, Arthur P., "Guatemala, OAS and U.S.," *Foreign Policy Bulletin,* Vol. XXXIII, No. 24 (September 1, 1954), pp. 4-7.

de Wiche, Josefina, "El Comunismo en Guatemala," *Estudios Sobre el Comunismo* (Chile), Año I, No. 1 (Julio-Septiembre, 1953), pp. 93-96.

NEWSPAPERS

The New York Times, 1949-1954.

Guatemala *El Imparcial,* 1946-1954.

On certain important events in the June 1952 to July 1954 period the author also consulted the following Guatemalan papers: *Prensa Libre, La Hora, Diario de Centro América, Nuestro Diario, Impacto, El Espectador* and *Diario del Pueblo.* A series of six articles by A. B. Magil in the *New York Daily Worker* from March 29 through April 9, 1954, gives the view of a U.S. Communist who visited Guatemala in the fall of 1951 and the spring of 1954. Also useful is a series of fourteen articles by Manuel María Avila Ayala in *Diario de Centro América* from May 7 through May 25, 1957, under the title "De cómo fué lo de los 4 tiros desesperados."

INDEX